Arms Control and Security

Other Titles of Interest

Securing the Seas: The Soviet Naval Challenge and Western Alliance Options, Paul H. Nitze, Leonard Sullivan, Jr., and The Atlantic Council Working Group on Securing the Seas

New Technology and Military Power, Seymour J. Deitchman

Limited War Revisited, Robert E. Osgood

Words and Arms: A Dictionary of Security and Defense Terms: With Supplementary Data, edited by Wolfram F. Hanrieder and Larry Buel

The Myth of Victory: What is Victory in War?, Richard W. Hobbs

Congress and Arms Control, edited by Alan Platt and Lawrence D. Weiler

The U.S. Senate and Strategic Arms Policy, 1969-1977, Alan Platt

World Power Assessment 1977: A Calculus of Strategic Drift, Ray S. Cline

Arms Transfers to the Third World: The Military Buildup in Less Industrial Countries, edited by Uri Ra'anan, Robert Platzgraff, Jr., and Geoffrey Kemp

Analyzing Soviet Strategic Arms Decisions, Karl F. Spielmann

U.S. Intelligence and the Soviet Strategic Threat, Lawrence Freedman

About the Book and Editor

Arms Control and Security:
Current Issues
edited by Wolfram F. Hanrieder

This anthology on current issues in arms control and security begins with an overview of the U.S.-Soviet balance of power since the beginning of the Cold War and of the changing meaning of power and security. Other topics include the SALT talks; the implications of arms control for the Atlantic alliance and NATO; arms proliferation and control; technology and the military balance; and the difficulties of developing equitable and truly balanced arms control agreements.

Wolfram F. Hanrieder is professor in the Department of Political Science, University of California at Santa Barbara. Dr. Hanrieder is currently visiting professor at the Johns Hopkins University School of Advanced International Studies in Bologna, Italy.

Arms and Control and Security: Current Issues

edited by Wolfram F. Hanrieder

Westview Press / Boulder, Colorado

Copyright © 1979 by Westview Press, Inc.

Published in 1979 in the United States of America by
   Westview Press, Inc.
   5500 Central Avenue
   Boulder, Colorado 80301
   Frederick A. Praeger, Publisher

Library of Congress Cataloging in Publication Data
Main entry under title:
Arms control and security.
1. Arms control—Addresses, essays, lectures. 2. Security, International—Addresses, essays, lectures. 3. Nuclear nonproliferation—Addresses, essays, lectures. 4. Détente—Addresses, essays, lectures. I. Hanrieder, Wolfram F.
JX1974.A7689   327'.174   79-4540
ISBN 0-89158-382-3
ISBN 0-89158-385-8 pbk.

Printed and bound in the United States of America

FOR MICHAEL

Contents

About the Contributors

Roger W. Barnett is a commander, U.S. Navy.

Lincoln P. Bloomfield is professor of political science, Massachusetts Institute of Technology. He was formerly State Department planner on U.N. affairs.

The late **Bernard Brodie** was professor-emeritus of political science at the University of California, Los Angeles.

Thomas A. Brown is director of the Rand Corporation's Strategic Assessment Program. Dr. Brown served previously as chief of the Pan Heuristics Division, Science Applications, Inc.

Richard Burt currently covers defense and foreign policy matters for the Washington, D.C. bureau of the *New York Times*. He was assistant director of the International Institute for Strategic Studies, in London, in 1975-1977.

Leslie H. Gelb is a diplomatic correspondent for the *New York Times*.

Colin S. Gray is a member of the professional staff of the Hudson Institute and was formerly assistant director of the International Institute for Strategic Studies, in London.

Helga Haftendorn is professor of political science, *Hochschule der Bunderswehr,* Hamburg.

Wolfram F. Hanrieder is professor of political science at the University of California, Santa Barbara.

Richard G. Head, colonel, U.S. Air Force, is a military assistant to the under secretary of defense for policy. He was formerly a military fellow at the Council on Foreign Relations.

Paul H. Nitze is chairman of the Advisory Council, Johns Hopkins School of Advanced International Studies. He was a member of the U.S. SALT Delegation, 1969-1974; deputy secretary of defense, 1967-1969; secretary of the navy, 1963-1967.

Wiegand Pabsch is head of NATO's Disarmament and Arms Control Section.

Dennis Ross is a member of the Defense Department's Office of Program Analysis and Evaluation.

Lothar Ruehl is special correspondent in Brussels of German Television (ZDF) for international, military, and security affairs.

Stanley Sienkiewicz, an analyst in the Office of the Secretary of Defense, was an international affairs fellow of the Council on Foreign Relations and a research fellow of Harvard's Program for Science and International Affairs.

Henry Trofimenko, a historian, heads the Foreign Policy Department of the Institute of the U.S.A. and Canada, Academy of the Sciences of the U.S.S.R.

Adam B. Ulam is professor of government, Harvard University.

William R. Van Cleave is professor and director, Defense and Strategic Studies, School of International Relations, University of Southern California.

Manfred Wörner is the chairman of the Defense Committee in the *Bundestag* of the Federal Republic of Germany and speaker on defense matters in the parliamentary delegation of the Christian Democratic Union and its Bavarian sister party, the Christian Social Union. He has served in the *Bundestag* since 1965 as a representative of a district in Baden-Württemberg. He is a lieutenant colonel and jet pilot in the West German Luftwaffe Reserve.

Arms Control and Security

1
Introduction

Wolfram F. Hanrieder

Security and power are closely related: the more power, the more security; the less security, the less power. Security is that manifestation of power upon which all other manifestations of power rest. This, in any case, is the conventional wisdom—and it may be true as well. But if security and power define one another, then a change in the meaning of one produces a change in the meaning of the other. Shifts in the balance of power lead to shifts in the balance of security; redefinitions of security entail redefinitions of power.

The dialectic of security and power is complex because its elements are tangible as well as immeasurable, constant as well as changing, physical as well as psychological, crude as well as subtle, glaring as well as hidden. It is a dialectic that is based on both perception and reality. The meaning of security and power is not the same for everyone and does not remain the same for anyone. It depends on a particular configuration of circumstances, on the prevailing perception of these circumstances, and on the kind of values held to be central. Security and power are functions of their historical context. They are relative and contingent, not absolute and unconditional.

The Changing Meaning of Power and Security

The essays collected in this volume deal with one of the most perplexing issues in contemporary international politics and American foreign policy: how to sustain national security and stabilize the arms race in an international environment in which the meaning of security has changed along with the meaning of power.

At the end of the Second World War and at the beginning of the Cold War, the United States wielded unchallengeable economic power, controlled the international monetary system it had created, stood at the peak of international prestige and political influence, and possessed an invulnerable nuclear force that guaranteed America's security and that of its allies. Three decades later, the United States is sharing its predominant economic position with Western Europe and Japan, a weak American dollar is shunned in international monetary markets, American prestige and influence have declined because of mismanagement of foreign and domestic affairs, and the United States appears ready to acknowledge in the Strategic Arms Limitations Talks that the Soviet Union is its equal in nuclear military capabilities.

Given the relative decline of American power, it would appear that the security of the United States and the Western alliance is much more precarious in the late 1970s than it was in the late 1940s. But the meaning of security also changed during those intervening decades. Most fundamentally, traditional security concerns—understood as the preservation of territorial integrity against outside intrusion—have diminished relative to economic issues. Although security can turn into a question of national survival in the nuclear age—and in that sense is unsurpassed in importance—a noticeable shift of emphasis has taken place in world politics, away from the primacy of military-strategic elements of power toward the primacy of economic elements. The likelihood of invasions and direct military aggression has receded, especially in areas of the world where existing borders are uncontested and unambiguous. For a variety of reasons highly industrialized countries are not attractive objects for physical aggression and territorial occupation; and, except in parts of the nonindustrialized world and the Middle East, demands for territorial revisions are not pressing issues in contemporary international politics. A certain old-fashioned, outmoded quality is attached to territorial disputes that contrasts sharply with the bulk of the economic, monetary, and political issues that preoccupy the modern nation-state.

The elements of international power and its overall configuration have changed. Along with the diminishing salience of territorial issues, of importance are the restraints imposed by the nuclear balance, the day-to-day realities of economic interdependence, the loosening of the Cold War alliances, the precarious economic and political development of the Third World, and the increased political leverage of countries that control essential energy and raw materials supplies. Access rather than acquisition, presence rather than rule, penetration rather than possession, control rather than coercion have become the ligaments of power. One of the consequences of the growing economic and monetary interdependence among members of the international community is that such measures of power as military capacity are becoming less relevant. Given appropriate circumstances, economic power is a much more supple instrument of diplomacy than military power. Negotiations over such technical questions as arms control, trade agreements, monetary reform, and technology transfers are not only attempts at problem solving but also reexaminations of the meaning and the sources of power in the last third of this century. Many military-strategic and economic issues are, at bottom, political issues couched in technical terms.

This is not to suggest that force and the threat of using it are no longer arbiters in a political system that continues to lack a central political authority. Nor have the processes of economic interdependence, many of which bypass governmental channels, diminished the role of the nation-state. There exists an extensive residual of traditional international politics, and the international system has remained an interstate system in many of its essential features. Security and welfare continue to be the major preoccupations of the state. But welfare concerns have become preeminent: no matter what a country's institutional arrangements, stages of economic growth, or ideological preferences may be, remedies for the economic and social problems of the individual are sought in public policy and collective action. The modern state is powerful in what it can give, take, or withhold. At the same time, the power of the nation-state, although growing in its domestic context because of the state's responsibilities for mass social and economic welfare, appears compromised in rather novel ways in its international context. It is compromised in part because of the restraints imposed by the nuclear balance of power and in part because the domestic power of the state can be sustained only through international economic cooperation and political accommodation. In order to meet domestic demands for social welfare, the modern state is compelled to interact with other states in ways that, although not lacking in conflict and competition, demand cooperation, acceptance of the logic of interdependence, and a willingness to condone restraints on state behavior and sovereign prerogatives. Internal state power is sustained by external cooperation.

Changes in international politics during the last three decades have also changed the perception of security. The world is no longer as bipolar as it was in the 1950s. The alliance partners of the United States and the Soviet Union have gained a measure of independence and diplomatic flexibility—this is especially true with respect to the North Atlantic Treaty Organization. Also as the relations between the Soviet Union and the People's Republic of China have deteriorated, those between China and the United States have improved. This multipolar trend is underlined as more nations obtain their own nuclear capabilities, and as the North-South conflict is superimposed on the East-West conflict. The global system of the 1970s is infinitely more complex than that of the 1940s and 1950s on the military-strategic as well as the political and economic-monetary levels. Many states see their security interests protected more effectively through the political rather than the military elements of the balance of power.

Concurrent with these developments, Western perceptions of the Soviet military threat have begun to change considerably. As we have moved from American nuclear monopoly to U.S.-Soviet nuclear parity, we also have moved from Cold War to détente. In the early years of the Cold War it appeared as if the Soviet Union, in charge of a seemingly monolithic Communist power bloc, was determined to achieve world domination, by military means if necessary. Whether or not that perception was accurate, Washington's containment policy was implemented primarily through military means, leading to the establishment of NATO, the rearmament of Germany, and a worldwide series of bilateral and multilateral security pacts at the periphery of the Soviet bloc. These security pacts extended from Norway to Turkey and also included the Middle East, Southeast Asia, and the Western and Southern Pacific areas. By the middle 1950s, however, following the inclusion of West and East Germany in their respective military alliances, it had become apparent that the Soviet Union was interested more in solidifying and legitimizing the status quo in Central Europe than in overthrowing it. The United States accepted a Soviet sphere of influence in Eastern Europe and acknowledged that sphere by abstaining from intervention in Hungary in 1956 and Czechoslovakia in 1968. But as Cold War competition intensified in non-European areas, the United States continued to oppose Communist movements, no matter what their national origin and socioeconomic context, with attitudes and policies that had been shaped by the American experience of checking the Soviet Union in Europe. Washington's underestimation of the appeal of nationalism and corresponding overestimation of the appeal of Communism aside, the American debacle in Vietnam resulted from applying containment measures that had proved successful in Europe in an area where such measures were inappropriate. In retrospect, American foreign policy overemphasized the importance of military challenges and overreacted with its military responses. The tensions that have developed in Southeast Asia among Vietnam, China, Cambodia, and the Soviet Union in the late 1970s further demonstrate that containment by military means in Southeast Asia was unnecessary, and that the United States could have relied more confidently on the regional balance of power to contain whatever Washington thought required containing.

This is not to say—and it bears repeating—that military might is unimportant, that the Soviet conventional buildup in Eastern Europe should be ignored, or that the growth of the Soviet navy is not worrisome. On the whole, however, the view prevails among Western policymakers that a direct Soviet military attack on the West is unlikely. They believe that the Soviet military posture should be seen more in terms of political and diplomatic impact than in terms of the threat of physical coercion.

The nature of the weights in this new balance of power is still uncertain, and we do not know yet how they should be measured and compared. But in my view, the shift away from military elements of power has seriously handicapped the Soviet Union and the Republic of China. The Soviet Union suffers from chronic economic and monetary weaknesses that require it to trade with the West and pay for Western technology on a barter basis. Soviet interventions in Africa and elsewhere are costly, and it is doubtful if they will, in the long run, increase Soviet influence in these areas. Also, the attraction of Communism as an ideology is severely limited—in part because nationalism has a more powerful appeal, and in part because ideological prescriptions are not very helpful in solving immediate problems of governance. Because of its own economic and monetary shortcomings, the Soviet Union cannot provide Third World countries across the board with extensive capital investments, stable raw materials prices, and effective voices in rearranging the global monetary system. What the Third World needs most, the Soviet Union can least provide.

The frustrations engendered by these handicaps may explain why the Soviet Union seeks to expand its global influence through traditional power politics, tinged with gunboat diplomacy. This may be a way of compensating for Soviet disabilities in the area of economics and ideology. As a world power, the Soviet Union can effectively compete with the West in terms of military power but not in terms of economic power. Although impressive advances in weapons technology and dramatic explorations of space have helped the Soviet Union consolidate and demonstrate its superpower status, these achievements cannot easily or consistently be turned to diplomatic advantage in the day-to-day conduct of foreign policy. Edward Luttwak, much worried by growing Soviet military strength and its apparent expansionist intent, writes that "... Russian imperial strength has already emerged fully formed in the classic mold. ..."[1] This may well be the case. But is the "classic" mold the best way of extending influence in a world system characterized by economic interdependence and the relative decline of usable military power relative to economic power? Most features of the contemporary international system seem to place the Soviet Union at a large disadvantage relative to the economic power of the trilateral industrialized world.

The Strategic Balance and the Western Alliance: A Historical Overview

Since the beginning of the Cold War, America's European NATO partners have relied on the deterrence value of the American nuclear force. In the late 1940s and throughout the 1950s it appeared to many in the West that the only way to deter Soviet aggression, in light of superior Soviet ground forces, was with the threat of rapid nuclear escalation. Such a punishment was a real possibility (given the American nuclear monopoly) and would threaten catastrophic results. Since the Western powers felt that they could not match Soviet ground forces, the threat of nuclear strikes against the Soviet Union seemed to be the only deterrent that would be both plausible and cost-efficient. But even with a nuclear monopoly, the United States arranged the rearmament of Germany and constantly pressed the Europeans to build up conventional force levels. For a variety of political and economic reasons, the conventional force goals envisaged for NATO in the early 1950s were not met, and the Atlantic alliance continued to rely largely on the American nuclear deterrent. When the Eisenhower administration enunciated a U.S. doctrine of "massive and instant retaliation" by means and at places of Washington's choosing, a catchy slogan was simply added to an already accepted deterrence posture.

A very real threat of American nuclear response to conventional provocation, reemphasized in the doctrine of massive retaliation, was highly attractive to Western Europe as long as the threat was sufficiently credible. Massive retaliation stressed deterrence rather than defense and thus held out the promise that Western Europe would not become a battlefield in a conventional war. When the Soviet Union developed nuclear capabilities and the NATO powers failed to establish sufficient conventional forces, the United States decided to deploy tactical "battlefield" nuclear weapons in Europe. These tactical nuclear weapons seemed attractive since they were expected to make up for America's gradual loss of nuclear monopoly by providing an additional "firebreak" between conventional provocation and all-out nuclear war.

It has been convincingly argued that the West should, at that time, have organized a deterrence posture to match the Soviet Union at all force levels, and that establishing sufficient conventional forces was an essential part of a credible strategic nuclear deterrence posture. But because of their exposed position, Western European nations found the prospect of deterring Soviet ground forces with Western ground forces highly distasteful. This reaction was especially true of West Germany because of its vulnerable forward location. It seemed to these nations that the implicit threat of an immediate nuclear response, which was created by denying the likelihood of a conventional response, would deter a Soviet conventional attack. (As long as the United States was invulnerable to Soviet nuclear counterstrike, such a deterrence posture was reasonably credible.) It was also widely believed in Western Europe that preparations for a conventional response would undermine the credibility of massive retaliation thus increasing the likelihood of war and that such preparations would, in fact, encourage American "nuclear disengagement" from Europe. Since even a limited engagement of conventional forces would turn Western Europe (and especially Germany) into a battlefield, from the Europeans' perspective it seemed better not to extend the range of retaliatory options because more options seemed to weaken the "automaticity" of nuclear response.

Extending the range of options, however, was the heart of the Kennedy administration's strategic thinking. Its doctrine of "flexible response" was designed to multiply Washington's strategic and tactical options in order to avoid the dilemma of choosing between either a nuclear strike (with the risk of a Soviet counterstrike) or the politically disastrous consequences of doing nothing at all. In broad terms the new strategy (which became official NATO strategy in 1967) signaled that the United States would not use nuclear weapons at the outset of hostilities except in reply to a nuclear attack. Small-scale attacks would not elicit a nuclear response at all. And even in case of a massive attack, NATO would first use conventional troops to allow time for negotiations with the opponent and for consultations among the Allies about the initial use of nuclear weapons. Central to this new strategy was the concept of "graduated deterrence," which postulated an initial Soviet attack without nuclear weapons and envisaged a series of controlled steps of escalation: the conventional force level, the "selected and limited use" of tactical nuclear weapons, more general use of these weapons, and, ultimately, the threat of a strategic nuclear attack on the Soviet Union. In short, the new doctrine was intended to provide a more considered and effective meshing of military and diplomatic actions.

The doctrine of flexible response required, above all, a substantial increase in NATO's conventional forces. Washington argued that the credibility of the American nuclear deterrent would be enhanced by the buildup of conventional forces. But European NATO capitals were not reassured. The conventional force buildup demanded by Washington was not strong enough for a viable local defense strategy, yet it seemed to make a U.S. nuclear counterstrike less credible. European NATO members agreed with Washington that NATO's deterrence posture should be strengthened. But the most credible response to a conventional attack, a response with conventional forces, held little attraction for Europeans because it meant total, it nonnuclear, war.

The Kennedy administration also tried to strengthen the credibility of the nuclear deterrent by stressing the feasibility of controlling nuclear war and of preventing "spasmic," irrational nuclear exchanges. Again a conflict of interest was created in the alliance because the European powers believed that the most could be gained by stressing the uncontrollable nature of nuclear war.

In addition, the Cuban missile crisis and the Test Ban Treaty strongly pointed to a Soviet-American common interest on nuclear questions. To many Europeans the Test Ban Treaty, following Washington's exclusion of the Allies from deliberations on the Cuban confrontation, indicated that in the case of a major European crisis the two nuclear superpowers might settle the issue bilaterally, and that the United States was adding diplomatic flexibility to its doctrine of strategic flexibility.

After the early 1960s the evident vulnerability of the United States to Soviet nuclear attack forced Washington to qualify the automaticity of its nuclear guarantee to Europe, impaired the credibility of that guarantee, and ultimately brought the strategically distinct positions of America and Europe into clear focus. The Pentagon, interested in establishing a firebreak between limited East-bloc provocations and all-out devastation of American cities, accepted the possibility of a limited war in Europe (from a European perspective, total war). Deployment of tactical nuclear weapons did not really change that possibility. West European governments had to take refuge in the "hostage" value of American forces on the continent, in the nuclear triggering potential of tactical nuclear weapons, and in the British and French national deterrents. Moreover, as the U.S. commitment became more qualified, in some circles the incentive for maintaining European nuclear forces became stronger. This development further exacerbated transatlantic tensions since Washington viewed national European deterrents as disturbing influences on the stability of Soviet-American strategic rapprochement. Throughout the early and middle 1960s, NATO members engaged in intense discussions about how to convincingly demonstrate the continuing American commitment to the security of Europe. However, attempts to bolster the cohesion of NATO—like the abortive proposal for a NATO multilateral nuclear force and the establishment of the Nuclear Planning Group—could not compensate for diminishing American nuclear superiority and were, at best, political palliatives. But by that time the Europeans' fear of the Soviet Union had diminished so that as dramatic an affront to NATO as the 1966 French withdrawal was, its intention and its effect was more political than military-strategic.

Beginning in the late 1960s debates about security issues within NATO abated. Persisting anxieties among European leaders about the willingness of the United States to sustain a forward strategy on NATO's central front generally were not expressed in public—in part because other problems had become more pressing and in part because it was assumed that public airing of these concerns would, in itself, aggravate them. The issue was swept under the rug, and when it reappeared (whenever the Europeans saw or imagined reasons to question American resolve), the rug was simply adjusted to cover up the issue again. But tensions persisted. European NATO members, above all the Federal Republic, still saw their security interests best maintained by the early use of nuclear weapons. The United States continued to want the use of nuclear weapons postponed as long as possible. This issue of the "conventional pause," which dated back to the flexible response doctrine of the early 1960s, was aggravated further by its corrollary, the question of forward defense. Although NATO planners had all along questioned the military feasibility of defending Western Europe along West Germany's border with East Germany and Czechoslovakia, it was politically imperative to assure the Germans that their geographical position would not condemn them to being the first (and perhaps only) victims of a conventional war. Political and symbolic necessities were expressed in military fiction.[2]

The Carter administration has reiterated the principle of forward defense and also has not excluded the use of tactical nuclear weapons as a question of principle. However, the central question of the timing of tactical nuclear response remains as ambiguous as ever. Since many Europeans view tactical nuclear weapons as an essential link in the chain of escalation from conventional response to a strategic nuclear exchange between the Soviet Union and the United States, American ambivalence regarding when (or even if) tactical nuclear weapons would be used, is seen as undermining the totality of NATO's deterrence structure. These anxieties are deepened by the conviction, shared by political and military experts on both sides of the Atlantic, that NATO's conventional capabilities are insufficient either for purposes of deterrence or for purposes of defense should deterrence fail. A NATO strategy based on a time-buying conventional flexible response implies the sacrifice of West German territory for the overall benefit of the alliance.

In sum, the central dilemma of NATO during the last ten years cannot be resolved: the United States, in seeking to limit the arms race and arrive at a stable nuclear balance, is compelled to deal with the Soviet Union on the basis of *parity*, as was reflected in the arrangements of the Strategic Arms Limitation Talks. At the same time, Washington cannot convincingly guarantee the security of Western Europe except on the basis of an implied American nuclear *superiority*. Neither the United States nor the European NATO Allies can be blamed for this dilemma. And it is unlikely that such a dilemma could have been escaped. Developments in weapons technology and Soviet determination to catch up with the United States brought about nuclear parity between the two superpowers. Parity and its implications led to conflicts between the United States (which now needed to take into account the potential nuclear devastation of the United States and therefore sought to delay the use of nuclear weapons) and NATO partners at the forward line of defense who found unacceptable a strategy that implied sustained conventional warfare at the expense of their territory and population.

Strategic Doctrine, Arms Control, and the Western Alliance

Security policy always has two dimensions, that of defense and that of diplomacy. The connection of the two is central to an understanding of arms control negotiations and their underlying political purposes. Security policy consists of words as well as acts; strategic doctrine signals intentions as well as capabilities; arms control agreements, and the negotiations leading to them, reflect political preferences as well as the desire to stabilize levels of armaments.[3]

From the beginning of the Cold War until the 1960s, the United States acted as the spokesman of the Western alliance in expressing political purpose in doctrinal strategic language. The West Europeans' fear of the Soviet Union and their military, economic, and political dependence on the United States did not permit them to deviate substantially from the course charted by the United States or to express political purposes in military-strategic terms. As long as NATO was relatively cohesive, Washington's political and strategic guidelines were generally implemented by the Western alliance.

When the Eisenhower administration enunciated a doctrine of massive retaliation, the aim was to convey political purposes. The tough language of massive nuclear retaliation was intended to signal a more assertive American attitude toward the Soviet Union, to communicate that Washington wished to augment President Truman's containment policy with a more "dynamic" dimension, and to complement such diplomatic concepts as "liberation of Eastern Europe," "roll-back" of the Soviet Union, and "going to the brink." When the Kennedy administration announced a doctrine of flexible response and graduated deterrence, the intent was to signal a more "realistic" and management-oriented diplomatic-military posture, one that would acknowledge the changing nuclear balance and move beyond what the new administration saw as the entrenched Cold War positions of its predecessor. The drastic difference in strategic language seemed justified by changes in the nuclear balance of power: between the announcement of the massive retaliation doctrine in 1954 and the announcement of the flexible response doctrine in 1961 the Soviet Union had gained sufficient nuclear capabilities to make massive U.S. retaliation rather incredible.

But the outgoing Eisenhower administration had been as aware of that fact as the incoming Kennedy administration; both administrations had urged the Europeans to build up their conventional capabilities; and both continued to act on the basis of the containment policy established by the Truman administration. The stark contrast between the strategic rhetoric of the Eisenhower and Kennedy administrations belied an underlying continuity of political assumptions and military planning.

As the immediacy and intensity of the Soviet threat diminished in the eyes of both Europeans and Americans, their governments shifted priorities from strategic-military matters to political and economic ones, and centrifugal pressures were allowed a freer reign within the Western alliance. American planners still saw NATO's primary function as military, but by the middle 1960s they no longer considered a Warsaw Pact assault on Western Europe probable and were devoting most of their attention to Vietnam. Gradually Washington supplemented its Cold War policy of region-by-region, "forward" containment with attempts to reach a bilateral accommodation with the Soviet Union on matters of overriding mutual interest, such as stabilization of the global strategic balance of power. Containment at the periphery of the alliance blocs was augmented by a core of détente, as exemplified in the Strategic Arms Limitation Talks. During the Nixon administration the United States began to rely more consciously on the workings of the political balance of power and welcomed the People's Republic of China to the exclusive five-power arrangement that Henry Kissinger saw linked through cooperation and competition: the United States, Western Europe, Japan, the Soviet Union, and Red China.

West Europeans, with a similarly relaxed view of the Soviet military threat, began to see the primary function of NATO as political—that is, ensuring a continued U.S. commitment to the political and economic future of Europe and thus ultimately guaranteeing the Continent's military security also. As the West Europeans undertook their own political and economic arrangements with the East bloc, intra-European détente and its dynamics for overcoming the East-West division sometimes conflicted with the more static strategic détente between the two superpowers (which merely stabilized the East-West division). The United States had to deal with the Soviet Union on the basis of recognizing the status quo in Europe, but many Europeans on both sides of the dividing line were seeking to overcome it.

These strategic, political, and psychological developments had a profound impact on the meaning of national security and on the purposes and instruments of arms control. As the likelihood of war in Europe diminished, the Western powers could afford to use military terms to express what were at bottom political concerns. Security policies and arms control proposals became saturated with purposes that were essentially political rather than military. The logic of power was being expressed in the language of security and arms control.

One of the most striking examples of how these new opportunities could be exploited was Charles de Gaulle's policy toward NATO. The French decision to build an independent national nuclear force (which predated by several years de Gaulle's return to power in 1958) was primarily political. The "technical" justifications for French national nuclear forces—that such forces might trigger the American nuclear response, or that they would compensate for lack of size and sophistication through the credibility of their use—seemed much less important than the larger political purposes to which they could be put. French policymakers hoped that a French nuclear arsenal would help France escape from the grip of the superpowers (which had paralyzed French foreign policy in the postwar years) and regain flexibility in her dealings with both her allies and her opponents. The links between strategy and diplomacy were not discovered by de Gaulle, of course; his predecessors in the Fourth Republic were fully aware of them. But the "mini-détente" of the middle 1960s allowed France to use its independent strategic posture to full diplomatic effect. For de Gaulle the technical inadequacies of a French national nuclear arsenal were outweighed by the perfect logic with which it fit his global political program. The *force de frappe* was a supremely political instrument.

After de Gaulle's withdrawal of France from NATO's integrated command structure in 1966, his independent security policy culminated, on the doctrinal level, in the formulation of a deterrence strategy publicized by General Charles Ailleret in December 1967. The so-called "all azimuths" (or "all-horizons") deterrence doctrine threatened nuclear retaliation against any target on the globe. Through this rather unlikely contingency plan France was expressing in strategic terms what were essentially political purposes. The strategy was intended to complement de Gaulle's political-diplomatic program: the Ailleret doctrine was a symbol that France intended to stand apart from the United States as well as from the Soviet Union, and that French interests were global and could not be advanced adequately within the confines of the Western alliance. In 1968 when the Soviet-bloc invasion of Czechoslovakia dashed French hopes for the dissolution of the Warsaw Pact and rekindled, however briefly, the European's fear of the Soviet Union, the grandiose notions of the Ailleret doctrine were quickly replaced by the much more mundane military and fiscal realities of the Fourquet Plan.

French attitudes on European arms control schemes were similarly governed by what were fundamentally political purposes. The Western détente efforts of the middle 1960s, expressed in arms control terms, were focused on two distinct approaches: a "direct" road to European security, which aimed at the *control* and *management* of conflicts by scaling down and stabilizing the military arrangements of Central Europe; and an "indirect" road, aimed at the *resolution* of conflicts in the context of a slowly developing new European order. De Gaulle strongly favored the latter and opposed the former, primarily because the direct approach would have culminated in agreements between the existing military alliances, thus reinforcing the predominant influence of the superpowers that de Gaulle sought to reduce. Essentially the same considerations later led the French to boycott the discussions over conventional force reductions in the context of the Multilateral Balanced Force Reductions (MBFR).

The political uses of strategic language and arms control proposals, and the general shift from military elements of power toward economic ones, were especially important to West Germany, for several reasons. First, because of its geography and history, from the beginning the Federal Republic was a NATO member with special inhibitions, obligations, anxieties, and opportunities. Whatever problems plagued NATO because of waning American nuclear superiority always were felt more keenly in Bonn than in other West European capitals—so much so that by the 1960s conflicts of security interests could be discerned not only between the United States and Western Europe but also between Western Europe and Germany. The security interests of the United States, Western Europe, and West Germany were not congruous— especially not on "lower" levels of provocation, the levels most likely to involve West Germany because of its forward position and its unresolved political issues with the East. The important question of whether the defense of the Western alliance was indivisible was coupled with the equally important question, for Germany, of whether the defense of Western Europe was indivisible. These two questions of defense alone would have made it difficult for the Germans to express political purposes in military-strategic language. But there were other inhibitions as well. Because of Germany's past, had the West Germans followed de Gaulle's example of couching political aspirations in terms of arms, they would have been accused of being unreconstructed militarists. Especially sensitive was the question of any kind of German association with nuclear weapons—the German finger on the nuclear trigger. Whenever German policy touched upon nuclear matters—talks about a Franco-German nuclear consortium in the early 1960s, German's participation in the proposed multilateral nuclear NATO force, Bonn's footdragging in the nonproliferation treaty—anxiety levels rose in the West as well as in the East. The Germans had to speak softly indeed.

The case of West Germany is highly instructive for a second

reason: West Germany was one of the main political beneficiaries of the shift from military elements of power to economic-monetary elements. Aside from the fact that Germany's political and diplomatic leverage increased as its economic and monetary strength grew, economic and monetary "language" provided the Germans with an excellent opportunity to translate political demands—which might still have been suspect because of Germany's past—into respectable economic demands. Although the Germans grumbled a good deal about the fact that they were always called upon to pay "subsidies" of one sort or another to one country or another, the shift from military to economic elements of power was highly advantageous to them. The transformation of economic power into political power, and the translation of political demands into economic demands, compensated for the Germans' handicap of not being able to translate political demands into military-strategic language.

A third factor distinguished Germany from other European NATO members and strongly shaped German attitudes on arms control proposals: West Germany's relations with its eastern neighbors were burdened by large unresolved political issues. These issues stemmed from the refusal of successive Bonn governments to recognize the East German state and to accept as permanent, under international law, the Oder-Neisse borderline between Poland and East Germany. Throughout the first two decades of its existence the Federal Republic was the only European power to question the territorial status quo in Europe. As long as the Cold War was intense, West Germany's hard line toward the East, although castigated as "revanchist" by the Soviet Union and its client states, had the diplomatic support of Bonn's Western allies. Since the prospects for German unity were dim in any case, Bonn's allies had nothing to lose by lending nominal support to West German aspirations for reunification. However, by the middle 1960s, Bonn's refusal to legitimize the European territorial status quo became a stumbling block to détente and was criticized in the West as well as in the East.

Arms control proposals played an important role in East-West diplomacy on the German question, which explains in large part why the West Germans responded to such proposals with caution, suspicion, hesitation, and procrastination. In the middle 1950s, the Germans felt that the proposals for arms control and disengagement, then put forth by the Eastern bloc governments and influential public figures in the West, would reinforce the division of Europe and Germany. These proposals (of which the Rapacki Plan was the most publicized) invariably provided that the status quo—the division of Germany and Europe—would serve as the basis for an agreement between the superpowers on arms control and called for the participation of West Germany and East Germany as equal partners. Thus, acceptance of the proposals would have led to a de facto recognition of the East German regime and to a weakening of the West's military presence at the periphery of the Soviet bloc. Accepting the proposals would have solidified the *political* line of division in Central Europe (reflecting the Soviet interest in legitimizing the territorial status quo) and, at the same time, blurred the East-West *military* boundary running through Germany (reflecting the Soviet interest in denying the West the military and industrial power of West Germany). Disengagement would have ended plans for a Western European Community and, by prying Germany from the Western alliance, would have undermined NATO's "forward strategy," a strategy which the United States was seeking to strengthen for its symbolic effect and in order to make nuclear deterrence appear more credible.

In the middle 1960s, both Western and Eastern Europe showed renewed interest in institutionalized European security arrangements. The proposals, which resembled those of the 1950s, ranged from suggestions for mutual troop reductions to calls for the dissolution of NATO and the Warsaw Pact. Several of these proposals went beyond suggestions for the control and management of conflict situations and sought ways for the final resolution of conflict. In other words, military security arrangements, augmented by increased East-West contacts and cooperative economic and diplomatic endeavors, were expected to assist in solving the political problems of Europe, such as the division of Germany and the unsettled frontier questions.

Since the 1950s these two distinct aspects and purposes of European arms control—the military aspect of conflict control, and the political aspect of conflict resolution—had posed a dilemma for Bonn. Although conflict control and crisis management were even more important to Germany than to its allies, the Bonn government always felt obliged to reject proposals for European arms control because such proposals seemed to lead not to a genuine resolution of conflicts but to the legitimization of the status quo in Central Europe, including the division of Germany. This attitude toward arms control proposals placed Bonn in an awkward position. West Germany's allies, except perhaps France, felt that conflict control and military stabilization were much more pressing than conflict resolution since Bonn's allies had no major political demands to make on the Soviet Union, Eastern Europe, and East Germany. This long-standing difference between the interests of West Germany and those of her allies was reemphasized by the 1968 Soviet invasion of Czechoslovakia, which had a much more damaging effect on the prospects of conflict resolution than on the prospects of conflict control.

Another arms control issue which strained West Germany's relations with her allies and with her opponents was the nonproliferation treaty.

In the middle 1960s, after the Germans had committed themselves to participate in the proposed multilaterial NATO nuclear force, the Soviet Union emphasized that any German association with nuclear weapons (except some consultative arrangement) would stand in the way of the nonproliferation treaty—in effect compelling the Johnson administration to scrap the NATO proposal. The Germans, in turn, were highly suspicious of the treaty, seeing in it far-reaching repercussions for German foreign policy and feeling that they had been insufficiently consulted. Although German co-ownership of nuclear weapons was unlikely, the Germans thought they could use the treaty to force some progress on the reunification question. They had reservations about a nonproliferation agreement, not so much because they wanted to own nuclear weapons, but because they did not want to be deprived of the threat of acquiring them. Considering the widespread apprehension about a German finger on the nuclear trigger, the value of such a threat was doubtful, but the Germans were reluctant to forego an opportunity to extract concessions on the reunification issue. They had had so little leverage on that issue in the past, and it seemed that the Russians' main purpose in negotiating the nonproliferation treaty was to deny West Germany nuclear arms. But many Western leaders viewed Bonn's foot-dragging on the treaty with impatience, seeing in it an obstacle to East-West accommodation.

The long-standing tensions between West Germany's security policy and its policy toward the East were not resolved until Chancellor Willy Brandt completed his *Ostpolitik* through which the Federal Republic formally recognized the status quo in Central and Eastern Europe, legitimized it through international treaties, and attested to it in the wider institutional context of the Conference for European Security and Cooperation. By recognizing the territorial and political realities stemming from the Second World War the Germans meshed their security policy and their Eastern policy, developed a more constructive attitude toward arms control, and fully attuned West German foreign policy to the dynamics of East-West détente—the most pressing item on the foreign policy agenda for both the Warsaw Pact and the Atlantic alliance.

*   *   *

During the last three decades there are discernible three distinct phases of the use of strategic language and of arms control arrangements for political purposes. In the first phase, from the beginning of the Cold War until the middle 1950s, the United States acted as the spokesman for the Western alliance, spelling out the policy of containment, the requisites for NATO's deterrence posture, and the political and economic meaning of the transatlantic compact. At the height of the Cold War, when both camps engaged in an intense arms race, arms control was not at issue in the dealings between the opposing alliances. Arms control was a matter of intra-alliance politics, as when the United States refused to aid France in developing her national nuclear arsenal or when special institutional safeguards were created to supervise the rearmament of Germany within the confines of NATO and the Western European Union. In the second phase, extending from the middle 1950s to the late 1960s, the global and regional patterns of the postwar balance of power changed considerably, allowing alliance members more diplomatic flexibility inside as well as outside of their alliances. Along with the diminution of the Soviet threat, these changes enlarged the possibilities of using arms control proposals for political purposes. In the third phase, from the late 1960s through the present, arms control of strategic nuclear weapons remained an important agenda item for the United States and the Soviet Union, as reflected in the hesitant progress of the Strategic Arms Limitation Talks. The lack of progress in the area of conventional arms control negotiations, however, serves as a constant reminder that arms control arrangements cannot be expected to come about until they are linked to, and reflect, progress on underlying political issues. On the whole, compared to the second phase, during this last phase there has been less of a tendency to express political purposes in arms control terms. This has been true in part because issues of trade, money, raw material, and energy supplies have become more urgent, and in part because such fundamental security concerns as stabilizing the European status quo have been dealt with more directly in political contexts, such as Bonn's *Ostpolitik* and the Conference on Security and Cooperation in Europe. The very name of the Conference reflected this shift—although fundamentally concerned with security, the major impact of the Conference was not in the area of arms but in the area of politics.

The features of the last phase provide the immediate context for the problems dealt with in this book. This context, as I have tried to demonstrate, is large—chronologically, geographically, and politically—and many of the problems are technical, intricate, and intractable. They are technical because the technology of opposing weapons systems is complex and not amenable to clear-cut, one-to-one comparisons: a balanced view of East-West capabilities requires both quantitative and qualitative considerations. The problems are intricate because the asymmetry of weapons is compounded by asymmetries of purpose, geography, historical experience, political will, moral restraint, use of strategic doctrine, and many others. Finally, many of the problems appear intractable because the limits which define mutually acceptable arms control arrangements are the same limits that define political accommodation. When these limits are insufficiently flexible, neither political purpose nor arms control can be realized.

Notes

1. Edward N. Luttwak, "Defense Reconsidered," *Commentary*, March 1977, p. 58.

2. The West German defense issue was revived in the summer of 1977 when Rowland Evans and Robert Novak wrote in the *Washington Post* that they had gained access to the so-called Presidential Review Memorandum 10 in which, among other options, it was suggested to President Carter that Western Europe should not be defended along the West-East German border but along the rivers Weser and Lech in West Germany. The implication was that about one-third of West Germany would be sacrificed in the early phase of an attack from the East. In addition, there was the implication that even after the Weser-Lech perimeter had been breached, the use of tactical nuclear weapons was by no means assured. (Of course, the battlefield use of tactical nuclear weapons at that stage would, in any case, involve the West German population and for that reason alone would be problematic.)

3. The connection between intentions and capabilities is clearly exemplified in the concept of deterrence. In order for A to deter B from taking a certain course of action, three conditions must be met. One, B must assume that A can inflict costs that are for B incommensurate with anticipated benefits. Two, B must consider it likely that A will inflict these costs. Three, A must communicate the first two factors to B. The third factor is as critical as the first two. If B is not aware that A can inflict costs and that A is prepared to do so, B cannot be deterred. Communicative and declaratory aspects are as indispensable to deterrence as are physical capabilities.

This does not mean that strategic doctrine can always adequately articulate political purposes. It is as imperfect as other modes of expression in translating purposes into demands. History is replete with examples of mismatching of political purpose, military planning, and strategic rhetoric. There can be tensions between declaratory policy and physical capability, contradictions between military planning and strategic doctrine (as when force deployment optimizes defense and enunciated doctrine emphasized deterrence), incompatibilities between a dynamic diplomacy and a static military posture, and a variety of other incongruities between words and actions.

2

The Development of Nuclear Strategy

Bernard Brodie

That concept was put forward almost at once at the beginning of the nuclear age that is still the dominant concept of nuclear strategy—deterrence. It fell to me—few other civilians at the time were interested in military strategy—to publish the first analytical paper on the military implications of nuclear weapons. Entitled "The Atomic Bomb and American Security," it appeard in the autumn of 1945 as No. 18 of the occasional papers of what was then the Yale Institute for International Studies. In expanded form it was included as two chapters in a book published in the following year under the title *The Absolute Weapon*, which contained also essays on political implications by four of my Yale colleagues.[1]

I should like to cite one brief paragraph from that 1946 book, partly because it has recently been quoted by a number of other writers, usually with approval but in one conspicuous instance with strong disapproval:

> Thus, the first and most vital step in any American security program for
> the age of atomic bombs is to take measures to guarantee to ourselves in
> case of attack the possibility of retaliation in kind. The writer in making
> that statement is not for the moment concerned about who will *win* the
> next war in which atomic bombs are used. Thus far the chief purpose of
> our military establishment has been to win wars. From now on its chief
> purpose must be to avert them. It can have almost no other useful
> purpose.[2]

It was obvious that this description of deterrence applied mostly to a war with the only other superpower, the Soviet Union, who did not yet

Reprinted by permission of the author and *International Security*, Spring 1978. Copyright 1978 by the President and Fellows of Harvard College. An earlier version of this paper was published by the Center for Arms Control and International Security, University of California, Los Angeles, February 1978, as ACIS Working Paper No. 11.

have nuclear weapons but was confidently predicted in the same book to be able "to produce them in quantity within a period of five to ten years."[3]

Let me mention a few more points in that 1946 essay in order to indicate what any reflective observer of the time would have found more or less self-evident. It stated that among the requirements for deterrence were extraordinary measures of protection for the retaliatory force so that it might survive a surprise attack; that margins of superiority in nuclear weapons or the means of delivering them might count for little or nothing in a crisis so long as each side had reason to fear the huge devastation of its peoples and territories by the other; that while it was possible that the world might see another major war in which the nuclear bomb is not used, the shadow of that bomb would nevertheless "so govern the strategic and tactical dispositions of either side as to create a wholly novel form of war";[4] and that this latter fact had particular implications for the uses of sea power, the classic functions of which depended on an intact home base and the passage of considerable time. It was also observed that while the idea of deterrence *per se* was certainly nothing new, being as old as the use of physical force, what was distinctively new was the degree to which it was intolerable that it should fail. On the other hand, one could add that *"in no case is the fear of the consequences of atomic bomb attack likely to be low,"*[5] which made it radically different from a past in which governments could, often correctly, anticipate wars that would bring them considerable political benefits while exacting very little in the way of costs.

Since 1946 there has been much useful rumination and writing on nuclear strategy and especially on the nature of deterrence, but the national debates on the subject have revolved mostly around three questions, all relating directly to the issue of expenditures. These three questions are: 1) What are the changing physical requirements for the continuing success of deterrence? 2) Just what kinds of wars does nuclear deterrence really deter? and 3) What is the role, if any, for tactical nuclear weapons? Far down the course in terms of the public attention accorded it is a fourth question: If deterrence fails, how do we fight a nuclear war and for what objectives? The latter question has been almost totally neglected by civilian scholars, though lately some old ideas have been revived having to do with what are called limited nuclear options. Otherwise most questions about the actual use of nuclear weapons in war, whether strategic or tactical, have been largely left to the military, who had to shoulder responsibility for picking specific targets, especially in the strategic category, and who were expected to give guidance about the kinds and numbers of nuclear weapons required.

In that connection, one must stress a point which certain young historians who are new to the field have found it difficult to grasp. Virtually all the basic ideas and philosophies about nuclear weapons and their use have been generated by civilians working quite independently of the military, even though some resided in institutions like Rand which were largely supported by one or another of the services. In these matters the military have been, with no significant exceptions, strictly consumers, naturally showing preference for some ideas over others but hardly otherwise affecting the flow of those ideas. Whatever the reasons, they must include prominently the fact that to the military man deterrence comes as the by-product, not the central theme, of his strategic structure. Any philosophy which puts it at the heart of the matter must be uncongenial to him. One military writer significantly speaks of the deterrence-oriented "modernist" as dwelling "in the realm of achieving non-events in a condition where the flow of events is guided, not by his initiatives, but by other minds." And further: "The obvious difficulty with deterrent theory . . . is the yielding of the initiative to the adversary." In the preceding sentence initiative has already been called the *sine qua non* of success.[6]

The Requirements for Deterrence

How does one preserve against surprise attack enough of one's retaliatory force so that the opponent, in anticipation thereof, is deterred? Obviously there is a political dimension to this question, because the need for precautionary measures does vary according to whether or not we think the opponent is straining at the leash to destroy us. There used to be current a notion that if the opponent saw his way clear to destroy us without suffering too much damage in return, that fact alone must impel him to do it. But whether or not that view was ever correct, which I doubt, it is not likely ever to be a feasible option for him. Still, to prepare against *all* possible crises in the future, it is desirable to minimize that proportion of our retaliatory forces which the opponent can have *high confidence* of destroying by a surprise blow and to help keep alive in his mind full awareness of the penalties for miscalculation.

At the beginning, the United States had a period of grace when it did not have to worry about enemy nuclear attack. However, conditions changed with the passing years, but the first sharp public reminder that we had an important vulnerability problem came only with the publication early in 1959 of Albert Wohlstetter's well-known article, "The Delicate Balance of Terror."[7] What is not generally known is that this article was precipitated by Wohlstetter's frustration with the Air Force. He had been leading for over a year a large research project at Rand which had been trying to find the best means of protecting our bomber aircraft against surprise attack. After considering various alternatives, including the "airborne alert" favored by the Air Force (which was itself second choice for them to the Douhetian idea of striking at the enemy before he gets off the ground), the project group decided that the most cost-effective defense of bombers against surprise attack was a slightly below-ground concrete shelter for each aircraft. This solution the Air Force vehemently rejected, invoking slogans which identified concrete with the Maginot Line and with excessive defense-mindedness. Wohlstetter's article was thus an appeal to the public, which by its response showed itself both surprised and alarmed at the situation he depicted—the more so as his elegant use of the facts and figures at his fingertips lent persuasiveness to his message.

However, that problem, too, passed without ever being resolved, because the article appeared on the eve of the coming of the ICBM, which lent itself to being put underground without controversy, and not far behind was the Polaris submarine. Wohlstetter had been concerned with defending bombers, mostly against bomber attack. We still have bombers as one of the legs of our so-called triad, and now these have to fear enemy missile attack. The Air Force still has no shelters for these bombers and does not contemplate any. Obviously, it still relies on their being in the air when the enemy attack arrives. In fact, on the often-mentioned grounds that they can be sent off early because they are recallable, our bombers are frequently projected as virtually a non-vulnerable retaliatory force. Well, perhaps they are, if one knows just how to read and respond to various types of ambiguous warning. The problem is not only not to send them off so late but also not to send them off too early.

However, I do support fully the belief implicit in the Air Force position that some kind of political warning will always be available. Attack out of the blue, which is to say without a condition of crisis, is one of those worst-case fantasies that we have to cope with as a starting point for our security planning, but there are very good reasons why it has never happened historically, at least in modern times, and for comparable reasons I regard it so improbable for a nuclear age as to approach virtual certainty that it will not happen, which is to say it is not a possibility worth spending much money on.

For similar reasons, I must add before leaving the Wohlstetter article that I could never accept the implications of his title—that the balance of terror between the Soviet Union and the United States ever has been or ever could be "delicate." My reasons have to do mostly with human inhibitions against taking monumental risks or doing things which are universally detested, except under motivations far more compelling than those suggested by Wohlstetter in his article. This point is more relevant today than ever before because of the numbers and variety of the American forces that an enemy would need to have a high certitude of destroying in one fell swoop.

The numbers of those forces, incidentally, grew during the nineteen sixties like the British Empire was said to have grown—in a series of fits of absentmindedness. There are reasons why the number 1000 was chosen rather than a lesser number for our Minuteman missiles, in addition to our 54 Titans, and also why we chose to build 41 Polaris-Poseidon submarines capable of firing 16 missiles each, in addition to the 400-plus B-52s we had at the time, not to mention the quick reaction alert forces we have long had in Europe. But whatever those reasons were, they were not a response to Soviet figures. They in fact gave us, or rather continued, an overwhelming superiority, later increased by the application of the MIRV system to over half our Minuteman missiles and three-quarters of our submarines. We are still, today, far superior in numbers of strategic warheads, and we also have a marked advantage in the important factor of accuracy.

In the mid-sixties the United States defense community could look with satisfaction on our immense superiority in retaliatory forces which appeared also utterly secure by virtue of being, for the most part, either underground or underwater. However, our restless research efforts were already tending to undermine that stable and comfortable situation by pushing to fruition the most incredible advances in ballistic missile accuracy, even without terminal guidance. Those advances resulted partly from developments in micro-electronics circuitry, which made it feasible to put complex computers aboard missiles and to integrate them with hypersensitive inertial-guidance gyros. Reliable unclassified estimates put the Circular Error Probabilities of today's American ICBMs at well under 300 yards, which is utterly fantastic for an object being hurled some 4000 miles. When that kind of accuracy is combined with MIRV, the silo-emplaced ICBM begins to be at risk. To be sure, the United States has continued to lead in these developments by a wide margin, and *our* accuracy does not imperil *our* silos, but the long lead times that some systems require make it appear provident, usually, to anticipate the opponent's canceling out of some specific technological advantage of ours.

Meanwhile, new discoveries on the effects of X-rays above the atmosphere had rekindled interest in the development of an ABM system. Progress was proceeding towards the system originally called "Sentinel," which President Nixon was to rename "Safeguard," when the developments in missile accuracy seemed suddenly to give it an important purpose. Up to then it had been a system in search of a mission. Inasmuch as most of its advocates admitted that the ABM could not reliably defend cities, interest focused on its use in defending hard-point targets, which is to say missile silos. Then there arose the great ABM controversy, an amazing chapter in our story because of the intense passions engendered among the adversaries. Moreover, unlike certain other controversies, it was not a debate between the informed and the ignorant. There was plenty of technological sophistication on both sides.

My objectivity in this article will not, I hope, be utterly compromised if I admit that I could never fully understand the pro-AMB position. It always seemed to me that in the expensive and fixed "Safeguard" mode readied for adoption—and later actually deployed at one site in North Dakota—the AMB could in principle be defeated in a number of ways that were already on the horizon, including hardening the reentry vehicle against the X-rays of the Spartan missile warhead; cheaply multiplying the number of reentry vehicles as is done with MIRV; adopting terminal avoidance maneuvering in the RV; or even, if all else failed, abandoning the long-range ballistic in favor of the cruise missile, against which the radar of "Safeguard" would be ineffective.

Now, in retrospect, we can add that it is most questionable whether American ICBMs needed any such protection at the time that "Safeguard" with its complex but fixed technology was being readied for deployment, or whether they will need it for a long time to come, if ever. Only about 23 percent of U.S. strategic nuclear warheads are carried in ICBMs as compared with about two-thirds for the Soviet Union. Our silos have already been super-hardened. An attack on our ICBMs would involve enormous timing problems for the Soviet Union, especially with most of their ICBMs being still of the liquid-fuel variety. No one yet knows what kinds of fratricidal problems will arise among RVs detonating near each other within a short space of time. It would be an optimistic Soviet planner who did not count on some 200 or 300 of our ICBMs surviving even a well-concerted attack from much more accurate Soviet missiles than they have today, and that says nothing about the 7000 to 8000 warheads in the other two legs of our triad. Surely no sensible opponent would try to eliminate our ICBMs in an initial attack unless he believed that he could at the same time with high confidence eliminate by far the major portions of our other retaliatory forces. One important meaning of the triad, in other words, is that each of the legs helps protect the other two. Besides, how would the Russians know that we would not launch our ICBMs on tactical warning or at least *during* an attack which could hardly be simultaneous? In short, the utility of the ABM over the long term was at best dubious, but surely it was desirable to avoid deploying a technologically fixed system well before it was really needed.

Anyway, our Safeguard ABM was effectively canceled by the agreements of SALT I, incidentally demonstrating that the greater utility of arms control agreements lies not in enhancing our security, which is usually beyond their power, but in helping to save both sides from wasteful expenditures.

That brings us to where we are now. The B-1 bomber has effectively been dispatched, but looming over the horizon is the monumentally costly MX missile. Each would be well over twice the weight of the Minuteman III and would carry up to 14 large nuclear warheads. The cost per missile in a 200- to 250-missile program would be some $100 million. It seems reasonable that so costly a missile in which so much power is concentrated be put into a mobile configuration, though that nearly doubles the cost of the system. Whether we need it in addition to Trident, which expands the operating area of our strategic submarines from about 2.5 million square miles to about 40 million square miles, and in addition also to the cruise missile, is not going to be determined on any realistic consideration of vulnerability. Protagonists and opponents will take their positions, rather, on political grounds—that is, depending on whether they harbor such views as incline them towards the Committee on the Present Danger or whether they live on lower levels of anxiety.

How Much Power Is Enough To Deter?

This question has always been with us in one form or another, but it is amazing to find it raised anew with intensified vigor just now when the number of strategic nuclear warheads in the American arsenal must be on the order of at least 9,000 to 10,000. Nevertheless, we have anguished statements like that of Richard Pipes. Mr. Pipes, Professor of Russian History at Harvard University, compels our attention because he was the chairman of that Team B selected at the prodding of Major General George Keegan to straighten out the relevant groups at the CIA, whose interpretation of Soviet intentions had apparently been too relaxed for some tastes. His recent *Commentary* article, which bears the title "Why the Soviet Union Thinks It Could Fight and Win a Nuclear War,"[8] was circulated in reprint form by the Committee on the Present Danger, of which Professor Pipes is a charter member, and also by the like-minded National Strategy Information Center.

The "why" in the title of Mr. Pipes' article preempts the prior question *whether* some entity called the Soviet Union thinks as he says it does. The appropriate question is: *who* in the Soviet Union thinks they can fight and win a nuclear war? The article tells us that it is some Soviet generals who think so, not a single political leader being mentioned. One could, at this point, dismiss the issue by remarking that there are also plenty of U.S. generals who think that the United States could fight and win a nuclear war and are even willing to give a definition for the word "win," though few of us would be comfortable with that definition. Still, it is interesting to notice what kind of evidence Mr. Pipes adduces for his thesis.

A prime piece of evidence for him is that Russian generals believe that "the basic function of warfare, as defined by Clausewitz, remains permanently valid," and he quotes the late Marshal Sokolovskii to that effect, with his own added emphasis: "It is well known that the essential nature of *war as a continuation of politics does not change with changing technology and armament.*"[9]

It is obvious that Professor Pipes reads into that famous dictum of Clausewitz he is alluding to a meaning quite different from that which Clausewitz intended. That might leave open the question what Marshal Sokolovskii intended, except that we know from other portions of his work that Sokolovskii did study Clausewitz, perhaps even with some care. Clausewitz's meaning, which is in fact basic to everything that one thinks about nuclear deterrence, is developed at length in books I and VIII of *On War.* In essence it amounts to the idea that war would be only senseless destruction if it were not in pursuit of some valid political objective. It is precisely the fact that one finds it difficult, if not impossible, to find a valid political objective that would justify the destruction inevitable in a strategic nuclear exchange that makes the whole concept of nuclear deterrence credible. In short, far from finding Marshal Sokolovskii's quoted statement ominous, we should all be able to agree with it with a fervent "amen."

Mr. Pipes takes exception to my thirty-year-old statement on the importance of deterring nuclear wars rather than winning them. He does so on the grounds that it has had a generally bad effect on American strategic thinking. I wonder how he would change it? Pipes and his many like-minded associates imply, or some may even state, that the Soviet Union has interests conflicting with ours which its leaders are so unwilling to inhibit or moderate that they are capable of coldly contemplating waging aggressive war against us. However, they fall short of telling us what those inexorable interests might be, usually falling back on the old standby, "miscalculation." Miscalculation in a crisis is indeed something to be concerned about, but surely not for the sake of circumventing deterrence but for making it work.

General Keegan appears to think that the Soviet leaders simply want to eliminate the United States as a superpower rival, and he has some absurd notions about how their allegedly heroic efforts in civil defense have reduced to a remarkably low level the human casualties they would suffer, though it is still reckoned in millions. However, even he has to admit they would sacrifice virtually all their capital investment above ground, not to mention the amount of fallout they would have to cope with in the environment. Others, including Mr. Pipes, point to the 20 to 30 million Russian lives lost during World War II, as though that had been a matter of choice among the Soviet leaders at the time—a sacrifice willingly offered up as a maneuver to entice the Nazis to their destruction.

Mr. Paul Nitze, another charter member of the Committee on the Present Danger, offers us a scenario in which the Soviet Union delivers a surprise attack which does not, to be sure, eliminate more than a portion of our retaliatory forces but which leaves us so inferior that the President, whoever he is at the time, elects to quit the fight before making any reply in kind.[10] Thus, the Soviet Union succeeds in making that otherwise elusive first-strike-with-impunity! An interesting thought, but it would take an exceedingly venturesome and also foolish Soviet leader to *bank* on the President's not retaliating. Even Mr. Nitze is not really sure; he says only that he *believes* the President would not.

But one must ask: even if all their evaluations were correct, what would these people have us *do*? Start a preventive war? Of course not. In the few instances where an attempt at an answer is offered, it seems to run as follows: abandon deterrence strategies in favor of war-winning strategies. But what does that mean? So long as we would not intiate or welcome the outbreak of a war, our basic peacetime strategy would still be that of deterrence. However, a difference is intended. The military have long been fond of saying that the best deterrence force is a war-winning force. Such a statement has certainly not been without meaning in the past, and even in the nuclear age it has some meaning in terms of tactical or theater forces. But when we speak of strategic nuclear exchanges, it is virtually impossible to find a reasonable meaning except in negative terms. That is, we can say what a war-winning force is not, or, to be more precise, what the people who use these phrases seem to mean by them. They mean a force which is definitely not inferior *in any one* of the several meaningful, or allegedly meaningful, attributes by which rival forces are usually compared.

The United States has about two-thirds the number of ICBMs deployed by the Soviet Union and is substantially inferior in terms of throw-weight. Actually, since 1970 the United States has built and deployed more ICBMs than the Soviet Union (550 versus 330), the difference being that our newer ones replaced older types which were retired, while the Soviet Union has kept active nearly all the ICBMs it has ever built—which incidentally tells us something about the difference in quality between the two forces. And so far as concerns throw-weight, about which so much is heard in some quarters, let us remember that it was a deliberate choice on the part of the U.S. military some two decades ago to go for smaller ICBMs than the Soviets fancied, for at least three good reasons: first, our people favored the increased readiness that would go with a solid-fuel propellant; second, we knew that our accuracy was much superior to that of the Russians, and likely to remain so for some time; and third, our smaller warheads were really not so very small. We keep forgetting that it was only a 14 KT weapon that devastated Hiroshima.

Whether against hard-point targets or any other kind, our retaliatory force with its far greater number of warheads and its much better accuracy and readiness remains today a clearly superior force to that of the Soviet Union—a "war-winning force" if one insists upon it. And if it remains that today, how about the recent past? Where the Committee on the Present Danger in one of its brochures speaks of "the brutal momentum of the massive Soviet strategic arms build-up—a build-up without precedent in history,"[11] it is speaking of something which no student of the American strategic arms build-up in the sixties could possibly consider unprecedented. Since we are looking so hard for the reasons for the Soviet build-up, one possibility that ought to be considered is that it was simply triggered by ours, and that it continues to be stimulated by a desire to catch up.

Against What Do Nuclear Weapons Deter?

This question hardly arose at all in the early years of the nuclear age. The dogma of the time was that every modern war is total war, and the only war one seriously thought about was that between the United States and the Soviet Union. This view survived into the first part of the Korean War, which was regarded by the Pentagon as a Soviet ruse to draw us into the western Pacific while they prepared to launch an attack on Europe. Then came the thermonuclear weapon, which caused some people to think about the necessity of separating general war from limited or theater war, and following that came the Eisenhower Administration with its somewhat atavistic commitment to massive retaliation. The famous Dulles speech of January 1954 caused a strong reaction, which finally came into full bloom at the advent of the Kennedy Administration in 1961 with its remarkable Secretary of Defense, Robert S. McNamara.

The idea developed that strategic nuclear power deterred only the use of strategic nuclear power and hardly any other form of violence. On the contrary, some argued that the existence of strategic nuclear weapons made lesser wars without nuclear weapons more, rather than less, likely, as though the pressure for war was more or less constant and the blockage of it in one direction made it only more insistent to break out in another. Then we began to hear of nuclear weapons being "decoupled" from diplomacy, for obviously they were not going to be used anyway. The next step was to argue that nuclear weapons must not be used in theater warfare even in Europe, and that the way to avoid their use was to build up our conventional forces—together with our allies—so that the threshold for use of tactical nuclear weapons would be raised too high to be breached. Such strong conventional forces, proponents held, made a far better theater deterrence than could any reliance upon tactical nuclear weapons. These ideas were fervently adopted by President Kennedy and Secretary McNamara and, after some hesitation, by the armed forces, especially the Army and Navy. After all, large conventional forces meant more of everything, and they also meant the kind of war that the military leaders felt they knew how to fight.

Thus, what some sixteen years ago was a novel and even radical idea has long since become the conventional wisdom, especially in the United States. And, whether a good idea or not, it has cost this country a great deal of money. The massive retaliation idea was, after all, justified by its advocates mostly on grounds of economy, and the more we departed from it the higher the costs were likely to go.

Because the alleged advantages of the conventional build-up policy have had a good press and are well known, I shall confine myself to expressing a few opposing arguments.

The Role for Tactical Nuclear Weapons

First, one of the strongest reasons consistently advanced by people like Alain Enthoven for doing away with tactical nuclear weapons is their alleged escalatory effect.[12] According to this view, to use one nuclear weapon in the field, however small, is simply to pull the plug on the use of any and all nuclear weapons. One use thus leads quickly and directly to holocaust. It is interesting that our European partners favor the deployment of tactical nuclear weapons because they entertain the same belief, which means they favor it for the same reason that so many of our people oppose it. In my opinion, both are wrong. There was no problem in distinguishing between tactical and strategic bombing in World War II, and in avoiding the latter where it seemed politically desirable to do so. It is hardly self-evident that the distinction would be more difficult where nuclear weapons are involved, especially if we shift to much smaller tactical nuclear weapons than many that presently exist—which we should want to do anyway.

Second, the strategic nuclear forces of each of the superpowers *do* inhibit the other from *any* kind of warlike action against it. This was proved abundantly during the Cuban missile crisis, where our side we know, and the other side we have good reason to guess, each thought it was looking down the barrel of a strategic nuclear war. It is also noteworthy that our people seemed to derive little comfort from the knowledge of having an overwhelming superiority in nuclear arms.[13] It is indeed the fear that escalation is possible, some think probable, that causes the ultimate sanction to have this general deterrent effect, at least between the two superpowers. Granted that we need some military power in the theater so that the opponent knows he could not make a truly aggressive move there without provoking a war, it is nevertheless an area where we can afford to be interested in economies.

Actually, our allies have left us no choice in the matter, and it was predictable that they would not. They simply do not see the Soviet Union as threatening to attack. They have therefore firmly and consistently refused, despite long and continued prodding by our government, to build up to anything like the levels demanded by the conventional war thesis. Thus, we do not presently have and are not likely to get a real conventional capability in Europe, that is, one capable of dealing with a deliberate conventional Soviet attack against the West. For that matter, neither do we have a good tactical nuclear capability, but the latter is much more easily attainable. It would mean mostly changes in doctrine, in training, and in types of weapons, but not large net increases in men or equipment.

Third and most important, we should recognize that inasmuch as all our war plans are predicated upon an act of major Soviet aggression, the choice would not be really ours to make. The Soviets are hardly likely to enter a duel where they leave so critical a choice of weapons up to us. At any rate, we could not assume in advance that they would leave the choice to us. We are presently committed to using tactical nuclear weapons if the Russians use them first *or if we find ourselves losing without them.* The Russians, if they were making a deliberate attack, would refrain from using them, if they refrained at all, only if they were confident they could quickly overwhelm us without them. It is folly to think we could wait to see. Major adjustments in posture and tactics during a fast moving battle are not so easily made, especially if one is in the process of being overwhelmed. Finally, there is virtually nothing in the voluminous open Soviet tactical doctrine to support the notion that they make the sharp and important distinctions we do between use and non-use of tactical nuclear weapons. Far from embracing our favored doctrines, they have quite explicitly rejected them.

The Russians do not appear to be straining at the leash to pounce upon us in Europe. Quite the contrary. It is therefore an area where our investment need be only relatively modest; yet if we have any substantial force at all, it ought to be one that is truly effective as a fighting force and certainly as a deterrent. It is nonsense to hold that a force trained and equipped to fight conventionally—even though it has some essentially unusable nuclear weapons behind it—makes a better deterrent than one of comparable size trained and equipped to fight from the beginning with nuclear weapons designed exclusively for tactical use. By the latter I mean something like the enhanced radiation bomb (the so-called neutron bomb), which should have been presented to the public for what it is—a means of making bombs smaller while retaining optimum effectiveness—and which makes an ideal anti-tank weapon.

The Wartime Use of Strategic Nuclear Weapons

I shall confine myself to commenting briefly on the special views identified with James R. Schlesinger as former Secretary of Defense, though they are more accurately described as a revival of some old ideas.[14] In the form offered by Schlesinger, they have been best described and advanced by an enthusiastic advocate, Benjamin Lambeth.[15] The general idea is to find some options outside what is regarded as the straight-jacketed posture of deterrence, which is viewed as waiting supinely to be struck and then attempting to expend our whole nuclear stockpile as rapidly as possible. The alternative suggested by the Schlesinger school is that we should be prepared during a crisis to initiate the use of strategic nuclear weapons, but only a few at a time, perhaps only one or two, the purpose usually mentioned being to show our "determination" or "resolve." In somewhat more hushed tones, another purpose is sometimes whispered, one that immediately calls up references to the "surgical scalpel," that is, to get the enemy's top command and control apparatus before the few persons who are the key to it have a chance to go underground.

Various people have long questioned the wisdom or even the purpose of planning to deliver all our nuclear weapons as rapidly as possible in replying to an attack, for many targets are not time-urgent and most of our own weapons are not directly threatened. The main war goal upon the beginning of a strategic nuclear exchange should surely be to terminate it as quickly as possible and with the least amount of damage possible—on both sides. The U.S. military have indeed told us that they take a different view. According to General George Brown, Chairman of the Joint Chiefs of Staff, "What we are doing now is targeting a war recovery capability."[16] Their object, in plainer words, is to see to it that in a strategic nuclear exchange the Soviet Union will suffer so much greater damage to its industrial plants and population than we do, that its recovery is much more prolonged. Whatever else may be said about this idea, one would have to go back almost to the fate of Carthage to find an historical precedent. In more recent times the United States has usually put itself to considerable effort and expense to help a defeated enemy recover, normally with the expectation that a vastly changed government in the defeated power will make it adopt an attitude towards the world that is much more congenial with ours. It is incidentally curious, and totally opposed to all the Clausewitzian canons, that so far-reaching a military decision should escape any political input, a situation which no doubts reflects the very low priority which our top political leaders automatically put on war-fighting as opposed to deterrence concerns. Nevertheless, one has to acknowledge that targeting "recovery capability" may put some premium on rapid expenditure of one's stockpile.

However, the proposal of the Schlesinger-Lambeth school is not concerned really with the issue of possibly excessive or excessively speedy *retaliation* to an attack upon us. Its central concern is with getting out of the retaliatory bind, with opening American considera-tions to the possibility of striking first in the hope of winning advantages hitherto disregarded or at least insufficiently considered. The idea of keeping to a low level the number of weapons used does sometimes seem like a mere palliative to the central notion that we should be prepared to initiate the exchange, though of course the idea that weapons be used for mere warning does require that their numbers be kept low. Otherwise the opponent is sure to do what he is all too likely to do anyway, which is to misapprehend our moderately benign intentions.

The Schlesinger-Lambeth school makes much of the advantage of expanding the options of any president during a crisis, a theme which had an especially high rating with Mr. McNamara when he was Secretary of Defense. The notion that it is incontestably good to expand the chief executive's options is rather peculiar. For one thing, it runs directly counter to the basic tenets of constitutional government. The long conflict between the Congress and President Nixon during the Vietnam War concerning what seemed to be the limitations laid down by the Constitution upon presidential prerogatives and war-making powers is a case in point. From both the legal and the pragmatic view, it was not then and it certainly is not now clear that the national interest lay in expanding the President's options. More recently we saw President Ford denied by Congress the right to send a large quantity of munitions to an obviously collapsing South Vietnamese government, and later denied the option of intervening in Angola with munitions if not with troops. In both instances President Ford and his Secretary of State complained most bitterly and offered up dire warnings of the evils that would befall American interests from such unseemly opposition to their wills. In both instances enough time has passed to suggest that the fears conjured up in those warnings were exaggerated, if not wholly imaginary. In short, the President does not always know best.

The above examples refer to legal limitations upon the power of the executive. However they may affect the national interest in any specific instance, the idea that such limitations should exist is considered absolutely basic to democracy as opposed to dictatorship. Of another character, however, are limitations imposed by the lack of specific physical capabilities such as might have been provided in good time if a different outlook had prevailed. In recent times it has generally been taken for granted that the wider the President's range of options in physical means, the better. But why this should be so is also not altogether clear.

Actually, one notices that the thesis has usually been defended in terms of extending the range of options *downward,* as in the arguments referred to above that to increase conventional forces is to reduce or remove the pressure upon the President in particular circumstances to use the nuclear option. Unfortunately, when President Kennedy did expand the conventional ground forces for that reason, his successor found himself with the means early in 1965 of sending combat forces to Vietnam without calling up the reserves! His options had been expanded in a way that particularly suited his own nature and outlook, but it is not obvious that the national interest benefited from the result. Naturally, one should not hinge too much on single cases. President Johnson's conduct does not make a case against having a sufficiency of ground forces. It should, however, be enough to cast doubt on the notion that expanding the President's military options is always a good thing. It may be a good thing if we can always be sure of having wise presidents, but it also throws a heavier burden upon that wisdom, so that any lack of it becomes the more telling. It is an old story that one way of keeping people out of trouble is to deny them the means for getting into it. We have put in the President's hands a huge military power because we believe that the country's security demands that we do so, and we are obliged to trust that he will use it wisely. But to expand that power simply for the sake of expanding his options is to push hard that obligatory trust.

Anyway, if the President did not already have the power to make the kinds of first strikes envisioned in the Schlesinger proposals, which inevitably he does, it would seem a very dubious proposition indeed that we should bestir ourselves to provide it. Certain kinds of weapons, like the cruise missile, may because of their extreme accuracy lend themselves particularly well to the kind of "surgical strikes" which in some people's fantasies bring victory without cost or even danger, but there had better be other reasons for calling for them than the desire to free the President for conducting such experiments.

In fact, the overwhelming odds are that when and if the crisis comes, the man occupying the seat of power in the United States will exercise at least the caution of a John F. Kennedy during the Cuban missile crisis, who by his brother's intimate account was appalled by the possibility that any precipitous use of physical power by the United States might unleash the nuclear holocaust.[17] He had firmly determined upon a confrontation and had made his requirements plain to the adversary. There is no reason to suppose that President Kennedy was anything but well above the mean level of courage we might expect in any president finding himself in a comparable situation. Yet we know from his conduct that the last thing he was interested in experimenting with during the crisis was some violent means of proving his resolve.

There may indeed be worse crises than that of October 1962, but during such crises the man who must make the ultimate decisions for the United States will likely be searching desperately for the resolve he is supposed to show, and may well be the wiser man for having difficulties in finding it. In short, the notion that in an extremely tense crisis, which may include an ongoing theater war, any useful purpose is likely to be served by firing off strategic nuclear weapons, however limited in number, seems vastly to underestimate both the risks to the nation in such a course and the burden upon the person who must make the decision. Divorced from consideration of how human beings actually behave in a crisis, it fits Raymond Aron's definition of "strategic fiction," analogous to "science fiction."[18]

Where Lambeth argues that the Schlesinger proposals introduce flexibility into an area of thinking hitherto marked by extreme rigidity and that they introduce also *strategy* (in the form of choice) where no possibility of strategy existed before, he is simply playing with words. The rigidity lies in the situation, not in the thinking. The difference between war and no war is great enough, but that between strategic thermonuclear war and war as we have known it in the past is certain to be greater still. Any rigidity which keeps us from entering the new horrors or from nibbling at them in the hopes that a nibble will clearly be seen as such by the other side, is a salutary rigidity. And we need not worry whether the choices the President is obliged to make during extremely tense situations fill out anyone's definition of strategy. The important thing is that they be wise choices under the circumstances.

It is especially curious that the notions discussed above should be advanced by many who continue to oppose the use of tactical nuclear weapons because of their alleged escalatory danger! That danger must be by orders of magnitude greater when the weapon or weapons detonated are by type and by choice of target clearly of the strategic variety. Though it would indeed be desirable to condition the people who control our own retaliatory forces not to regard the arrival of one or a few enemy warheads as necessarily the onset of an all-out attack, that kind of conditioning would hardly be dependable even for our own side, and we should certainly not seek to depend upon its existing with suitable firmness on the other.

Finally, a word about what one puts on the line for such proposals. The defense community of the United States is inhabited by peoples of a wide range of skills and sometimes of considerable imagination. All sorts of notions and propositions are churned out, and often presented for consideration with the prefatory words: "It is conceivable that. . . ." Such words establish their own truth, for the fact that someone has conceived of whatever proposition follows is enough to establish that it is conceivable. Whether it is worth a second thought, however, is another matter. It should undergo a good deal of thought before one begins to spend much money on it. In defense matters sums spent on particular proposals can easily become huge.

Schlesinger's original proposal for "limited nuclear options" seems to have been loosely connected to the then new cruise missile, which fortunately has other factors to recommend it. Last year, however, Mr. Colin S. Gray, in a "Letter to the Editor" of the *New York Times*,[19] opined that inasmuch as it is now established that the United States will initiate the coming strategic nuclear exchange, concerning which he seems to have no doubt, we should proceed at once to buy the MX missile system. Fortunately, Mr. Gray is not a senior official in the Defense Department or the military establishment, but his considerable writings have brought him attention within the defense community. Just why he considers the MX especially suited for initiating strikes is not clear—the cruise missile has at least the advantage of extreme accuracy—but his readiness to spend billions of dollars to cover a contingency that most of his peers would regard as extremely dubious is a little breath-taking. Surely the chances of his prediction being realized, even if more than infinitesimal, are not so great that we could not make do, if and when the time came, with vehicles already deployed for retaliatory purposes.

In these matters, to be sure, we are dealing fundamentally with conflicting intuitions. There is no doubt that some people's intuitions are better than others, but the superiority of the former, though sometimes definable and explicable, may be difficult to prove. Still, the thinking up of ingenious new possibilities is deceptively cheap and easy, and the burden of proof must be on those who urge the payment of huge additional premiums for putting their particular notions into practice.

Notes

1. Bernard Brodie, ed., *The Absolute Weapon* (New York: Harcourt, Brace, 1946). Co-authors were Frederick S. Dunn, Arnold Wolfers, Percy E. Corbett, and William T. R. Fox.

2. Ibid., p. 76. The Brodie chapters comprise pp. 21-110 incl.

3. Ibid., pp. 63-69.

4. Ibid., p. 83.

5. Ibid., p. 80.

6. Col. Richard L. Curl, "Strategic Doctrine in the Nuclear Age," *Strategic Review* (U.S. Strategic Institute, Washington, D.C.), Winter 1975, p. 48.

7. Albert Wohlstetter, "The Delicate Balance of Terror," *Foreign Affairs*, Vol, 37, No. 2, January 1959, pp. 211-256.

8. Richard Pipes, "Why the Soviet Union Thinks It Could Fight and Win a Nuclear War," *Commentary*, Vol. 64, No. 1, July 1977, pp. 21-34. See also the several "letters to the editor" provoked by this article in the second issue following: *Commentary*, Vol. 64, No. 3, Sept. 1977, pp. 4-26.

9. Pipes, "Soviet Union Thinks it Could Fight and Win," p. 30.

10. Paul H. Nitze, "Deterring our Deterrent," *Foreign Policy*, No. 25, Winter 1976-77, pp. 195-210.

11. Committee on the Present Danger, "Where We Stand on Salt," July 6, 1977, p. 5.

12. Alain C. Enthoven has for some fifteen years been the outstanding spokesman for this school of thought, which has, however, included such prominent thinkers as Albert Wohlstetter and Thomas C. Schelling. One of Enthoven's most recent articles on the subject was his "U.S. Forces in Europe: How Many? Doing What?," *Foreign Affairs*, April 1975, pp. 512-532.

13. See especially Robert F. Kennedy, *Thirteen Days: A Memoir of the Cuban Missile Crisis* (New York: W. W. Norton, 1969). It is interesting that at no time in his gripping narrative does Kennedy bring up or mention anyone else's bringing up the very clear American superiority in nuclear arms, from which they might have been expected to derive additional hope of deterring Soviet resort to war. That, of course, does not mean that nobody thought about it.

14. An earlier exposition of similar ideas is found in Klaus Knorr and Thornton Read (eds.), *Limited Strategic War* (New York: Praeger, 1962).

15. Benjamin S. Lambeth, *Selective Nuclear Options in American and Soviet Strategic Policy*, RAND Report R-2034-DDRE, December 1976. Despite my criticisms in the text, I should point out here that Lambeth explicitly disavows belief that circumstances of the future are ever likely to favor American limited first use. He simply wants it adopted as a "standing contingency capability,"

though his argument endorsing the capability does wax exceedingly enthusiastic. His report incidentally also includes a brilliant analysis of recent Soviet tactical and strategic thinking.

16. Quoted in *The Defense Monitor* (Center for Defense Information, Washington, D.C.), Vol. 6, No. 6, August 1977, p. 2.

17. See above, *Thirteen Days.*

18. Raymond Aron, "The Evolution of Strategic Thought," included in Alastair Buchan (ed.) *Problems of Modern Strategy* (London: Chatto & Windus, 1970), p. 30.

19. *New York Times,* October 19, 1977.

3
Assuring Strategic Stability in an Era of Détente

Paul H. Nitze

Even though the translation of the Vladivostok Accord on strategic arms into a SALT II treaty has not yet been resolved, I believe it is now timely to take stock of the strategic arms balance toward which the United States and the Soviet Union would be headed under the terms of such a treaty. To that end it is necessary to raise certain basic questions about the maintenance of strategic stability—in terms of minimizing both the possibility of nuclear war and the possibility that nuclear arms may be used by either side as a means of decisive pressure in key areas of the world.

It appears to be the general belief that while such strategic stability may not be assured by the SALT agreements, it is not and will not be substantially endangered—that on the contrary it has been furthered by the SALT negotiations and agreements since 1969—and that in any event the best hope of stability lies in further pursuit of negotiations with the aim of reducing the level of strategic weapons and delivery systems on both sides. Unfortunately—and to the profound regret of one who has participated both in the SALT negotiations and in a series of earlier U.S. decisions designed to stabilize the nuclear balance—I believe that each of these conclusions is today without adequate foundation.

On the contrary, there is every prospect that under the terms of the SALT agreements the Soviet Union will continue to pursue a nuclear superiority that is not merely quantitative but designed to produce a theoretical war-winning capability. Further, there is a major risk that, if such a condition were achieved, the Soviet Union would adjust its policies and actions in ways that would undermine the present détente situation, with results that could only resurrect the danger of nuclear confrontation or, alternatively, increase the prospect of Soviet

Reprinted by permission of the author and *Foreign Affairs*, January 1976. Copyright 1975 by Council on Foreign Relations, Inc.

expansion through other means of pressure.

While this highly distrubing prospect does not mean that strategic arms limitation should for a moment be abandoned as a U.S. (and world) goal, the practical fact we now face is that a SALT II treaty based on the Vladivostok Accord would *not* provide a sound foundation for follow-on negotiations under present trends. If, and only if, the United States now takes action to redress the impending strategic imbalance, can the Soviet Union be persuaded to abandon its quest for superiority and to resume the path of meaningful limitations and reductions through negotiation.

Finally, I believe that such corrective action *can* be taken: (a) within the framework of the Vladivostok Accord; (b) with costs that would increase the strategic arms budget marginally above present levels (themselves less than half the strategic arms budget we supported from 1956 through 1962, if the dollar values are made comparable); (c) with results that would encourage the diversion of the Soviet effort from its present thrust and in directions compatible with long-range strategic stability. At the close of this article I shall outline the key elements in such a corrective program.

II

Let us start with a brief review of the overall state of Soviet-American relations. The use of the word "détente," in its current sense, began in 1971. U.S. efforts to improve its relations with the Soviet Union go back to 1933. They dominated the War and the immediate postwar period, and the early years of the Eisenhower Administration. They formed an important strand of U.S. foreign policy in both the Kennedy and Johnson administrations. The word "détente" as currently used implies something different from these efforts; it implies that their goal has now been achieved and that all that remains to be done is to make détente "irreversible."

The chain of events leading to the present situation goes back to the Sino-Soviet split and the great buildup of Soviet forces facing China. There were about 15 Soviet divisions facing China in the mid-1960s; between 1968 and 1972 the number grew to at least 45 divisions. This caused the Chinese Communists to be deeply concerned about the danger of an attack by the Soviet Union on China. The Chinese turned to the one power that could help deter such an attack; they opened the ping-pong diplomacy that resulted in the so-called normalization of U.S. relations with China.

Mr. Nixon was, I think, correct in taking the position that he wished good relations with both China and the U.S.S.R. and did not want an alliance with either. Moscow, however, wanted to be sure that the new relationship between China and ourselves did not deepen into something closer to an alliance and thus impede Soviet policy toward China. For this and other reasons the Russians began to go out of their way to be friendly to Mr. Nixon and Mr. Kissinger. They opened up a vista of relaxation of tensions and of a growing collaboration between the United States and the Soviet Union. In 1972 not only were the SALT I agreements—the Anti-Ballistic Missile (ABM) Treaty and the Interim Agreement—entered into, but also there was signed at Moscow a document called Basic Principles of Relations Between the United States and the Soviet Union. Together with a subsequent agreement signed in Washington in 1973, this laid out what appeared to be a good basis for continuing relations between the U.S.S.R. and ourselves. Among other things, these agreements called for collaboration to see to it that crisis situations in other parts of the world did not build up into confrontations which could increase the risk of war between the two countries. It was understood that this collaboration was to have special reference to Southeast Asia and to the Middle East. These bilateral agreements were accompanied by the Paris Agreements with respect to Vietnam, and the Soviet Union was among those guaranteeing that the Paris Agreements would be implemented and abided by.

These understandings, however, produced no positive Soviet actions. With respect to the final North Vietnamese takeover in Southeast Asia, the Soviets actually took actions to help the North Vietnamese violate the agreements. With respect to the Middle East, it is hard to sustain the argument that is often made that the Soviets exercised restraint in the October 1973 crisis. There appears to have been little that they refrained from doing to encourage and make possible the attack by Egypt and Syria on Israel and the OPEC action on oil prices and the embargo. The Soviets not only trained and equipped the Egyptians and the Syrians for their surprise attack, but also failed to warn us when they knew that an attack was imminent. When the battle turned against the attackers, they threatened to intervene with their forces.

These two experiences in Southeast Asia and in the Middle East are bound to make us skeptical that the Soviet leaders are in fact moving toward any lasting reduction in tensions, or any abandonment of expansionist aims. A further ground for skepticism comes from what Soviet leaders are saying to their own people, and especially what they are saying in authoritative pronouncements aimed at leadership circles. Here readings from 1975 are all too clear. To take but one example, there were published in January 1975 companion articles, one by Boris Ponomarev, a deputy member of the Politburo, the other by Aleksandr Sobolev, a leading theoretician, each arguing that the evolution of the correlation of forces—in which they include not only military but economic and social forces—has moved very favorably from the standpoint of the Soviet Union over recent years.[1] Hence, they say, it is now possible to shift the target of communist action from the formerly colonial world to the developed world—particularly Europe. This shift in target is made possible by two things: one of them is "détente" and the other is "nuclear parity" (as they interpret the term, in a way we shall examine shortly).

In the sum total there are strong grounds for concluding that in Soviet eyes "détente" is not that different from what we used to call the "cold war." When we talked about the "cold war," we were in part emphasizing the fact that despite the deep hostility of the U.S.S.R. to the West in general and to the United States in particular, it would be a terrible thing if there were to be a "hot war" with the Soviet Union. When the Soviets use the word "détente" in their internal writings, they make it clear that they intend "détente" to mean the same thing as "peaceful coexistence." Peaceful coexistence, they make it clear, implies no change in their basic objectives, while they expect that current tactics will weaken the West and strengthen the socialist states.[2]

III

However one reads these broader signs of present Soviet behavior, a prime touchstone of the reality of détente—not only now but for the future—must lie in the area of strategic arms. If the Soviets are acting (and negotiating) in a way that gives promise of a stable nuclear balance (with meaningful reduction in due course), then the future of détente is clearly much brighter. If they are not, however, then the disturbing signs must be taken more seriously, and the long-term dangers are great indeed.

Let us begin by discussing the similarities and contrasts between Soviet and American views on certain strategic questions.

"Is the avoidance of war—particularly a nuclear war—between the two countries desirable?" On this question I think both sides are in agreement. However, there is a certain difference of approach. Clausewitz once said that the aggressor never wants war; he would prefer to achieve his objectives without having to fight for them. The Soviets take seriously their doctrine that the eventual worldwide triumph of socialism is inevitable; that they are duty bound to assist this process; and that, as the process progresses, the potential losers may stand at some point and feel impelled to fight back. On the U.S. side some say that there is no alternative to peace and therefore to détente. This attitude misses two points. The first is that capitulation is too high a price for free men. The second is that high-quality deterrence, not unilateral restraint to the point of eroding deterrence, is the surest way of avoiding a nuclear war.

This thus leads to a second pair of questions: "Is nuclear war unthinkable? Would it mean the end of civilization as we know it?" We in the United States tend to think that it is, and this view prevailed (except for a small group of believers in preventive war, who never had strong policy influence) even in the periods when the United States enjoyed a nuclear monopoly and, at a later time, a clear theoretical war-winning capability.[3] When the effort was made in the late 1950s and early 1960s to create a significant civil defense capability, public resistance soon aborted the effort, so that today the United States has only the most minute preparations in this area. Rather, Americans have thought throughout the last 30 years in terms of deterring nuclear war, with the debate centering on how much effort is necessary to maintain deterrence, to keep nuclear war unthinkable.

In the Soviet Union, the view has been quite different. Perhaps initially because of the U.S. monopoly, Soviet leaders from the outset discounted the impact of nuclear weapons to their people. But as the Soviet nuclear capability grew, the Soviet leaders still declined to depict nuclear war as unthinkable or the end of civilization. On the contrary, they directed, and still direct, a massive and meticulously planned civil defense effort, with expenditures that run at approximately a billion dollars a year (compared to U.S. civil defense expenditures of approximately $80 million a year).[4] The average Soviet citizen is necessarily drawn into this effort, and the thinking it represents appears to permeate the Soviet leadership. In the Soviet Civil Defense Manual issued in large numbers beginning in 1969 and 1970, the estimate is made that implementation of the prescribed evacuation and civil defense procedures would limit the civilian casualties to 5 to 8 percent of urban population or 3 to 4 percent of the total population—even after a direct U.S. attack on Soviet cities. The Soviets may well overestimate the effectiveness of their civil defense program, but what is plain is that they have made, for 20 years or more, an approach to the problem of nuclear war that does assume, to a degree incomprehensible to Americans (or other Westerners), that nuclear war could happen and that the Soviet Union could survive.

These differences in approach and attitude appear to be basic and deeply rooted. In essence, Americans think in terms of deterring nuclear war almost exclusively. The Soviet leaders think much more of what might happen in such a war. To the extent that humanitarian and moral objections to the use of nuclear weapons exist in the Soviet Union—as of course they do—such objections are subordinated for practical planning purposes to what Soviet leaders believe to be a realistic view.

It may be argued that these differences are more apparent than real, and that with the passage of time and the emergence of near-equality in the respective nuclear capabilities the differences are today less significant. Unfortunately, as the civil defense picture suggests, the trend in comparative nuclear weapons capabilities has if anything accentuated them.

That this is so can be seen in the more concrete realm of nuclear strategic concepts, and the postures that result from them. Often overrefined or expressed in terms hard for the layman to grasp, the range of strategic nuclear concepts available to any nuclear-weapons nation in fact boils down roughly to five:

1. *Minimum Deterrence.* This means a capacity to destroy a few key cities with little, if any, counterforce capacity to attack a hostile nation's military forces. In essence, it relies on the threat alone to deter. As between the Soviet Union and the United States, in the event deterrence failed, this level of American capacity would concede to the Soviet Union the potential for a military and political victory. The Soviets would risk U.S. retaliation against a portion of their industry and population if our action policy in the event deterrence failed turned out to be the same as our declaratory policy before deterrence failed. To reduce this risk of retaliation, the Soviets could limit their attack to U.S. forces and continue to hold the U.S. population as hostage. In sum, the effect of this level of deterrence would be to provide limited deterrence of a full-scale attack on the U.S. population. It would have less strength in deterring a Soviet attack on U.S. forces or on allies whose security is essential to our own.

2. *Massive Urban/Industrial Retaliation.* As the name implies, this posture is designed to destroy many cities, many millions of people, and much productive capacity, and to do so on an assured second-strike basis. This level of deterrence, sometimes called "Assured Destruction," would concede to the Soviet Union the potential for a military victory if deterrence failed, but (it would be anticipated) would make any such victory worthless in political terms. This form of deterrence differs from minimum deterrence largely in the degree of damage to Soviet industry and population it would threaten.

3. *Flexible Response.* In this form of deterrence the United States would have the capability to react to a Soviet counterforce attack without going immediately to a counter-city attack. It would thus increase the credibility of deterrence. The question of military or political victory if deterrence fails would depend upon the net surviving destructive capacity of the two sides after the initial counterforce exchanges. If the net surviving capacity after such a flexible response were grossly to favor the Soviet Union or if each limited exchange placed

the United States in a progressively weaker relative position, we are back to the minimum deterrence or massive urban/industrial retaliation situation, depending on the amount of surviving effective nuclear capability on the U.S. side.

4. *Denial of a Nuclear-War-Winning Capability to the Other Side.* This means a nuclear posture such that, even if the other side attacked first and sought to destroy one's own strategic striking power, the result of such a counterforce exchange would be sufficiently even and inconclusive that the duel would be extremely unattractive to the other side. This level of deterrence, in addition to deterring an attack on U.S. population centers, should also deter a Soviet attack on U.S. forces or those of its allies. In practice, against any major nuclear nation, the posture would also include a capacity for effective massive urban/industrial retaliation if such a strategy were called for.

5. *A Nuclear-War-Winning Capability.* This would be a position so superior that, whatever the initial forms of nuclear exchange, one's own surviving capacity would be enough to destroy the war-making ability of the other nation without comparable return damage. Such a U.S. posture would deter any Soviet attack on the United States and could also limit other serious Soviet military initiatives contrary to U.S. and allied interests. However, Soviet weapons technology and program momentum are such that the United States probably could not obtain this capability.

A review of the choices made by the United States and the Soviet Union among these five concepts goes, I believe, further than any other form of analysis in explaining and clarifying the changes in the strategic balance since 1945. Until roughly 1954, the United States retained nuclear superiority without extraordinary effort. By the late 1950s, the vulnerability of American bomber bases (bombers then being the only effective delivery method) emerged as a serious weakness in the American posture.[5] This weakness, and the rapid advances in missile technology of the period, led the United States between 1956 and 1962 to place great emphasis on ensuring the survivability of its nuclear striking power; average strategic obligational authority during these years was about $18 billion a year in 1974 dollars.[6] As a result the feared intercontinental ballistic missile (ICBM) "gap" of the 1960 presidential campaign never in fact became reality, but on the contrary the United States re-established a clearly superior nuclear capability by 1961-62. This was the situation at the time of the only true nuclear confrontation of the postwar period, the Cuban missile crisis of the fall of 1962.

Up to that point something approaching a war-winning capability seemed to most Americans the best possible form of deterrence, and thus desirable. However, as it became clear that the Soviet Union, too, was developing massive and survivable missile delivery capabilities, this view changed to the belief that even though a nuclear war might be won in a purely military sense, it could not be won in a political sense. That led to the further view that mutual deterrence through mutually assured destruction was the best feasible objective.

I have explained elsewhere at greater length the decisions of the early 1960s, in which I was one of those who participated with Robert McNamara, then Secretary of Defense.[7] In essence, the United States opted at that point to stress technological improvement rather than expanded force levels. While numerical comparisons were not ignored, the basic aim was an underlying condition of what may be called "crisis stability," a situation where neither side could gain from a first strike, and of "mutual assured destruction," where each side would have a fully adequate second-strike capability to deter the other. In such a condition it was believed that neither could realistically threaten the other in the area of strategic weapons, and that the result would be much greater stability and higher chances of the peaceful resolution of crises if they did occur. While nuclear weapons would always be a major deterrent, the conventional arms balance at any point of confrontation would remain important (as it had been in the Berlin crisis of 1958-62 and also in the Cuban missile crisis itself). In short, the aim was to downgrade nuclear weapons as an element in U.S.-Soviet competition and to prepare the way for systematic reductions in nuclear arms. If both sides were to adopt such a concept, it should be possible, over time, to move from what might be called a "high deterrent" posture to a "low deterrent" posture, with the deterrent remaining essentially equivalent on both sides but at successively lower levels.

As the United States thus adjusted its posture, the invitation for the Soviet Union likewise to seek a similar posture—and stop there—was patent both from statements of American policy and from the always-visible American actions. Unfortunately, however, the Soviet Union chose to pursue a course that was ambiguous: it could be interpreted as being aimed at overtaking the United States but then stopping at parity; it could, however, be interpreted as being aimed at establishing superiority in numbers of launchers and in throw-weight[8] and, perhaps ultimately, in a nuclear-war-winning capability on the Soviet side.

It is important to consider the reasons that may have entered into this choice. In part, the Soviet leaders may have been motivated by technological factors—that they had already moved to heavy rockets but were behind in other areas, such as solid propellant technology, accuracy, and MIRVing (the development of multiple, independently targetable reentry vehicles). In part, there may have been an element of traditional Soviet emphasis on mass and size. But it is hard to avoid the conclusion that an important factor was the reading the Soviet leaders gave to the Cuban missile crisis and, to a lesser extent, the Berlin crisis. In the latter case, Khrushchev had briefly sought to exploit the first Soviet rocket firings of 1957—by a series of threats to Berlin beginning in late 1958—but then found that the West stood firm and that the United States quickly moved to reestablish its strategic superiority beyond doubt. And in the Cuban missile case, the very introduction of the missiles into Cuba in the fall of 1962 must have reflected a desire to redress the balance by quick and drastic action, while the actual outcome of the crisis seemed to the Soviet leaders to spell out that nuclear superiority in a crunch would be an important factor in determining who prevailed.

Harking back to the Soviet penchant for actually visualizing what would happen in the event of nuclear war, it seems highly likely that the Soviet leaders, in those hectic October days of 1962, did something that U.S. leaders, as I know from my participation, did only in more general terms—that is, ask their military just how a nuclear exchange would come out. They must have been told that the United States would be able to achieve what they construed as victory, that the U.S. nuclear posture was such as to be able to destroy a major portion of Soviet striking power and still itself survive in a greatly superior condition for further strikes if needed. And they must have concluded that such a superior capability provided a unique and vital tool for pressure in a confrontation situation. It was a reading markedly different from the American internal one, which laid much less stress on American nuclear superiority and much more on the fact that the United States controlled the sea lanes to Cuba and could also have expected to prevail in any con-flict over Cuba waged with conventional arms.[9]

One cannot prove that this was the Soviet reasoning. But the programs they set under way about 1962—above all the new family of weapons systems embodying not only numbers and size but also greatly advanced technology, the development and deployment of which began to be evident beginning in 1971 but which must have been decided upon some years earlier—seem to reflect a fundamental state of mind on the Soviet side that contains no doubt as to the desirability of a war-winning capability, *if feasible.* Believing that evacuation, civil defense, and recuperation measures can minimize the amount of damage sustained in a war, they conclude that they should be prepared, if necessary, to accept the unavoidable casualties. On the other hand, the loss of a war would be irretrievable. Therefore, the best deterrent is a war-winning capability, if that is attainable.

There have been, and I believe still are, divisions of opinion on the Soviet side as to whether such a capability *is* feasible. There are those who have argued that the United States is a tough opponent with great technical expertise and that the United States can be expected to do whatever is necessary to deny such a war-winning capability to the Soviet side. Others have taken the view that the developing correlation of forces—social, economic, and political as well as military and what they call the deepening crisis of capitalism—may prevent the United States and its allies from taking the necessary countermeasures and that the target of a war-winning capability, therefore, is both desirable and feasible. Again, this is not to say that Soviet leaders would desire to initiate a nuclear war even if they had a war-winning capability. They would, however, consider themselves duty bound by Soviet doctrine to exploit fully that strategic advantage through political or limited military means.

IV

The SALT negotiations got under way in late 1969. As a participant in those talks from then until mid-1974, I have described elsewhere some of the difficulties that attended the U.S. side.[10] What was most fundamental was that the U.S. delegation sought at every level and through every form of contact to bring home to the Soviet delegation, and the leaders behind it, the desirability of limitations which would assure "crisis stability" and "essential equivalence"—and that the Soviet side stoutly resisted these efforts.

Indeed, the negotiations very early revealed other major stumbling blocks. One, in particular, revolved around the Soviet conception of "strategic parity." In the SALT negotiations the U.S. delegation consistently argued for the acceptance by both sides of the concept of "essential equivalence." By that we meant that both sides did not have to be exactly equal in each component of their nuclear capabilities but that overall the nuclear strategic capability of each side should be essentially equal to that of the other and at a level, one could hope, lower than that programmed by the United States. The Soviets have never accepted this concept, but have argued instead for the concept of "equal security taking into account geographic and other considerations." In explaining what they meant by "geographic and other considerations," they said that, "The U.S. is surrounded by friendly countries. You have friends all around the oceans. We, the U.S.S.R., are surrounded by enemies. China is an enemy and Europe is a potential enemy. What we are asking for is that our security be equal to yours taking into account these considerations." They never went so far as to say that this really amounts to a requirement for Soviet superiority in capabilities over the United States, the U.K., France, and China simultaneously, but watching the way they added things up and how they justified their position, this is what it boiled down to.

Yet the two sides were able to reach agreement in May of 1972 on stringent limitations on the development of ABM interceptor missiles, ABM launchers, and ABM radars and on an Interim Agreement temporary freezing new offensive missile-launcher starts.

After the May 1972 signing of the ABM Treaty and the Interim Agreement, it turned out that the two sides had quite different views as to how the negotiating situation had been left. On the U.S. side, we told the Congress that the Interim Agreement was intended to be merely a short-term freeze on new missile-launcher starts, and that this, together with the ABM Treaty, should create favorable conditions for the prompt negotiation of a more complete and balanced long-term agreement on offensive strategic arms to replace the Interim Agreement and be a complement to the ABM Treaty. Both sides had agreed promptly to negotiate a more complete agreement to replace the Interim Agreement. And the Interim Agreement specifically provided that its provisions were not to prejudice the scope or terms of such a replacement agreement. We thought such a replacement agreement should be based, as was the ABM Treaty, on the principles of equality in capabilities, greater stability in the nuclear relationship between the two sides, and a mutual desire to reduce the resources committed to strategic arms.

However, the Soviet Union had a quite different view. Its negotiators held that in accepting the Interim Agreement we had conceded that the Soviet Union was entitled to an advantage for an indefinite time of some 40 percent in the number of missile launchers and something better than double the average effective size, or throw-weight, of their missiles over ours. In working out a more complete and longer term agreement, in their view, all that was necessary was to add strict and equal limits on bombers and their armaments, provide for the withdrawal of our nuclear forces deployed in support of our allies capable of striking Soviet territory, and halt our B-1 and Trident programs but not the "modernization" of their systems. The difference of position between the two sides was such that it was difficult to see how agreement could be reached.

In the Vladivostok Accord of December 1974 the Soviets did make concessions from their past extremely one-sided negotiating demands. Those concessions were greater than many in the U.S. executive branch expected. However, does the Accord promise to result in achieving the objectives which the United States has for many years thought should be achieved by a long-term agreement on offensive forces? Those objectives were parity, or essential equivalence, between the offensive capabilities on the two sides, the maintenance of high-quality mutual deterrence, and a basis for reducing strategic arms expenditures. I believe it does not.

The Vladivostok Accord, in essence, limits the total number of strategic launchers—ICBMs, submarine-launched ballistic missiles (SLBMs), and heavy strategic bombers—to 2,400 on both sides, and the number of MIRVed missile launchers to 1,320 on both sides. It limits the Soviet Union to the number of modern large ballistic launchers (MLBMs) that they now have, while prohibiting the United States from deploying any modern launchers in this category.[11] The Accord calls for air-to-surface missiles with a range greater than 600 kilometers, carried by heavy bombers, to be counted against the 2,400 ceiling. The treaty would allow freedom to mix between the various systems subject to these limitations.

There still remain some things to be cleared up: Secretary Kissinger has said that there was a misunderstanding concerning air-to-surface missiles (ASMs), that our understanding was that only *ballistic* air-to-surface missiles of greater than 600-kilometer range are to be included in the 2,400 launcher limit, not *cruise* missiles.[12] That is being argued between the two sides at the present time. There is also a question about mobile missiles, particularly land-mobile missiles: Should they be banned or should they be permitted and counted against the 1,320 and 2,400 ceilings? And there is the open question of what constitutes a "heavy bomber." The Soviets are building a plane called the "Backfire" whose gross take-off weight is three-quarters that of the B-1 and which is two and a half times as big as our FB-111. It is a very competent plane, more competent than some of the planes they now agree should be defined as heavy bombers. The Soviets say the Backfire should not be included in the category of heavy bombers because "we don't intend to use it in that role." However, it can in fact carry, even without refueling (and it is equipped to be refueled), a significant payload to intercontinental distances if the aircraft is recovered in a third country. The way the Vladivostok Accord reads, air-to-surface missiles in excess of 600 kilometers in range, if not carried on a heavy bomber, are not required to be counted at all. So Backfires and FB-111s with long-range missiles would not count in any way against anything. These problems must be resolved in order to have a meaningful agreement.

Then there are the problems of verification. Messrs. Kissinger and Gromyko have been trying to work out a compromise on the verification issue. I personally take the verification issue less seriously than most because the limits are so high that what could be gained by cheating against them would not appear to be strategically significant.[13] However, we should be careful not to establish a precedent which would cause trouble if more meaningful limitations were agreed upon.

A notable feature of the Vladivostok Accord is that it does not deal with throw-weight. The agreement would not effectively check the deployment of the new Soviet family of large, technically improved, and MIRVed offensive missiles. While both sides are permitted equal numbers of MIRVed missiles, the new Soviet SS-19s have three times the throw-weight of the U.S. Minuteman III, and the new SS-18s, seven times. What this comes down to is that under the Accord the Soviets can be expected to have a total of about 15 million pounds of missile throw-weight and bomber throw-weight equivalent. If the Congress goes forward with the B-1 and the Trident system but the United States does not add further strategic programs, the Soviets can be expected to end up with an advantage of at least three-to-one in missile throw-weight and of at least two-to-one in overall throw-weight, including a generous allowance for the throw-weight equivalent of heavy bombers, and two-to-one or three-to-one in MIRVed missile throw-weight. This disparity leaves out of consideration the Backfire, the FB-111, and the highly asymmetrical advantage in air defenses that the Soviet Union enjoys.[14]

Thus, the Vladivostok Accord, while a considerable improvement upon the prior negotiating positions presented by the Soviet Union, continues to codify a potentially unstable situation caused by the large disparity in throw-weight, now being exploited by Soviet technological improvements.

V

The prospects for SALT III center on reductions in the strategic forces on both sides, an aim of the SALT talks since their inception. My personal view is that meaningful reductions are highly desirable, and that the aim of reductions should be to increase strategic stability. But this aim is not served by reducing numbers of launchers, unless throw-weight is also reduced and made more equal.[15]

The agreed reduction of the throw-weight of large, land-based MIRVed missiles, however, would increase stability. I see no reason why the Soviet Union needs to replace its SS-9s with SS-18s, nor why it needs to replace a large number of its SS-11s with SS-19s. Although it is perfectly feasible and permissible under the Vladivostok Accord for us to develop missiles of equally large or even greater throw-weight than the SS-19s and fit them in Minuteman III silos, would not be far better for both sides if there were sub-limits of, say, 50 on the number of SS-18s the Soviets were permitted to deploy and 500 or less on the number of SS-19 and SS-17 class ICBMs that either side was permitted to deploy? Even in a context of no other changes in the postures of the two countries, the reduction in missiles to these numbers would change the missile throw-weight asymmetry to one-and-a-half to one.

It might then be more feasible to work out subsequent reductions in numbers of vehicles which would include the Soviet older un-MIRVed missiles, such as the SS-9, along with our Minuteman II and Titan. But in the absence of throw-weight limitations of some sort, reduction per se will not improve stability.

However, the Russians are opposed to considering throw-weight limitations and have also taken the position that a future negotiation for reductions has to take into account all forward-based systems—all the systems we have in Europe and in East Asia and on aircraft carriers. Thus, it is hard to see how we can have high hopes of getting anything in SALT III that will provide relief for the anticipated strain on the U.S. strategic posture as the Soviet deployments proceed and as their accuracy improves.

VI

The country as a whole has looked at strategic nuclear problems during the last six years in the context of SALT, hoping to make the maintenance of our national security easier through negotiations. It now appears, however, for the reasons outlined above, that we are not likely to get relief from our nuclear strategic problems through this route. Therefore, we have to look at our strategic nuclear posture in much the way we used to look at it before the SALT negotiations began and determine what is needed in the way of a nuclear strategy for the United States and what kind of posture is needed to support it. A fundamental aim of nuclear strategy and the military posture to back it up must be deterrence: the failure to deter would be of enormous cost to the United States and to the world.

Once again, two important distinctions should be borne in mind: the distinction between the concept of "deterrence" and the concept of "military strategy," and the accompanying distinction between "declaratory policy" and "action policy." Deterrence is a political concept; it deals with attempts by indications of capability and will to dissuade the potential enemy from taking certain actions. Military strategy deals with the military actions one would, in fact, take if deterrence fails. A responsible objective of military strategy in this event would be to bring the war to an end in circumstances least damaging to the future of our society.

From the U.S. standpoint, just to level a number of Soviet cities with the anticipation that most of our cities would then be destroyed would not necessarily be the implementation of a rational military strategy. Deterrence through the threat of such destruction thus rests on the belief that in that kind of crisis the United States would act irrationally and in revenge. Yet serious dangers can arise if there is such a disparity between declaratory deterrence policy and the actual military strategy a nation's leaders would adopt if deterrence fails—*or* if there is a belief by the other side that such a disparity would be likely. I think former Secretary James Schlesinger's flexible response program was, in effect, an attempt to get our declaratory policy closer to a credible action policy and thus improve deterrence.

Ultimately, the quality of that deterrence depends importantly on the character and strength of the U.S. nuclear posture versus that of the Soviet Union. In assessing its adequacy, one may start by considering our ability to hold Soviet population and industry as hostages, in the face of Soviet measures to deter or hedge against U.S. retaliation directed at such targets.

In 1970 and 1971—when the focus was almost exclusively on "mutual assured destruction"—the congressional debates on whether or not to deploy a U.S. anti-ballistic missile system recognized clearly the importance to deterrence of hostage populations. Critics of the ABM argued—and with decisive impact on the outcome of the debate—that an effective ABM defense of urban/industrial centers could be destabilizing to the nuclear balance: if side *A* (whether the United States or the U.S.S.R.) deployed an ABM defense of its cities, side *B* could no longer hold side *A's* population as a hostage to deter an attack by *A* on *B*. And in 1972 the same argument carried weight in the negotiation and ratification of the ABM limits in the SALT I agreements.

Yet today the Soviet Union has adopted programs that have much the same effect on the situation as an ABM program would have. And as the Soviet civil defense program becomes more effective, it tends to destabilize the deterrent relationship for the same reason: the United States can then no longer hold as significant a proportion of the Soviet population as a hostage to deter a Soviet attack. Concurrently, Soviet industrial vulnerability has been reduced by deliberate policies, apparently adopted largely for military reasons, of locating three-quarters of new Soviet industry in small- and medium-sized towns. The civil defense program also provides for evacuation of some industry and materials in time of crisis.

In sum, the ability of U.S. nuclear power to destroy without question the bulk of Soviet industry and a large proportion of the Soviet population is by no means as clear as it once was, even if one assumes most of U.S. striking power to be available and directed to this end.

A more crucial test, however, is to consider the possible results of a large-scale nuclear exchange in which one side sought to destroy as much of the other side's striking power as possible, in order to leave itself in the strongest possible position after the exchange. As already noted,

Table 1

Soviet – U.S. Throw–Weight Ratios

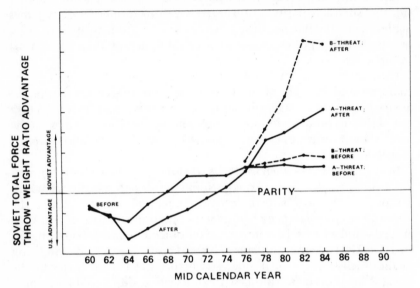

MID CALENDAR YEAR

such a counterforce strategy appears to fit with Soviet ways of thinking and planning; it is a strategy we must take into account.

Tables 1 and 2 apply this test over a period of years running from 1960 to (as it happens) 1984. For past periods, fairly assured estimates are available for both sides. For future years, a median estimate of U.S. programs, based on published data, has been used, while on the Soviet side there are two alternative projections—an "A-threat" based on a representative estimate of Soviet force deployments and accuracy capabilities, and a "B-threat" reflecting the possibility of increased Soviet emphasis on accuracy and other strategic force factors. Both forces are assessed in terms of total available throw-weight, measuring this directly for assumed missile inventories and making full allowance for the bomber equivalent of missile throw-weight for both sides.[16]

The tables assume an exchange in which the Soviet Union has attacked U.S. forces and the United States has retaliated by trying to reduce Soviet strategic throw-weight to the greatest extent possible. To assess the opposing forces *before* attack in terms of their relative throw-weight is of course only a partial measure of their comparative original capability. In working out what would actually happen in the assumed exchange, full account has been taken of all relevant factors—in particular the number, yield, accuracy, and reliability of the reentry

Table 2

Soviet – U.S. Throw–Weight Differentials

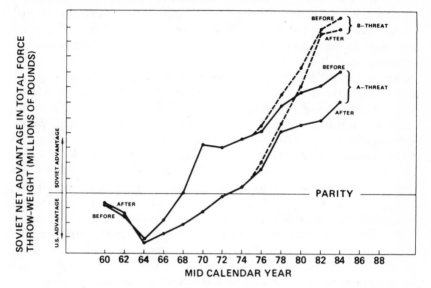

vehicles associated with that throw-weight, and the hardness of the targets against which they are assumed to have been targeted.

It is the situation *after* attack, of course, that is most important. And here, since the targets remaining after the exchange would almost all be soft ones, missile accuracy and other refinements in the original postures no longer have the same significance. Surviving throw-weight thus becomes an appropriate *total* measure of the residual capability on both sides.

As worked out by Mr. T. K. Jones, who served as my senior technical advisor when I was a member of the U.S. SALT delegation, the results of such an assessment are shown in Table 1, expressed in terms of the ratios, and Table 2, expressed in terms of the absolute units of weight—by which one side exceeds the other before and after attack in the various periods and alternative cases examined.[17]

Based on this method of assessment, the United States in 1960 held a slight but increasing advantage over the Soviet Union, and this advantage became greatest in about mid-1964. Thereafter, however, Soviet programs—greatly accelerated, as earlier noted, after the Cuban missile crisis—started to reverse the trend, so that by mid-1968 the total deployed throw-weights on both sides, before a hypothetical nuclear exchange, were roughly equal. However, as the "after" curve shows, the

U.S. operational military advantage persisted for some time thereafter, offsetting the Soviet superiority in deployed throw-weight. For example, if in 1970 the Soviets had attacked U.S. forces, their entire prewar advantage would have been eliminated, leaving the United States with substantial superiority at the end of the exchange. However, this situation began to be reversed in 1973, with the Soviets gaining the military capability to end an exchange with an advantage in their favor. Moreover, in 1976 the "before" and "after" curves of Table 1 cross, signifying that the Soviets could, by initiating such an exchange, increase the ratio of advantage they held at the start of the exchange. By 1977, after a Soviet-initiated counterforce strike against the United States to which the United States responded with a counterforce strike, the Soviet Union would have remaining forces sufficient to destroy Chinese and European NATO nuclear capability, attack U.S. population and conventional military targets, and still have a remaining force throw-weight in excess of that of the United States. And after 1977 the Soviet advantage after the assumed attack mounts rapidly.

In addition to the ratios and absolute differences that apply to the remaining throw-weights of the two sides, there is a third factor which should be borne in mind. That factor is the absolute level of the forces remaining to the weaker side. If that absolute level is high, continues under effective command and control, and is comprised of a number of reentry vehicles (RVs) adequate to threaten a major portion of the other side's military and urban/industrial targets, this will be conducive to continued effective deterrence even if the ratios are unfavorable. These considerations reinforce the desirability of survivable systems and methods of deployment.

VII

In sum, the trends in relative military strength are such that, unless we move promptly to reverse them, the United States is moving toward a posture of minimum deterrence in which we would be conceding to the Soviet Union the potential for a military and political victory if deterrence failed. While it is probably not possible and may not be politically desirable for the United States to strive for a nuclear-war-winning capability, there are courses of action available to the United States whereby we could deny to the Soviets such a capability and remove the one-sided instability caused by their throw-weight advantage and by their civil defense program.

To restore stability and the effectiveness of the U.S. deterrent: (1) the survivability and capability of the U.S. strategic forces must be such that the Soviet Union could not foresee a military advantage in attacking our forces, and (2) we must eliminate or compensate for the one-sided instability caused by the Soviet civil defense program. Specifically, we must remove the possibility that the Soviet Union could profitably attack U.S. forces with a fraction of their forces and still maintain reserves adequate for other contingencies.

As to the civil-defense aspect, the absence of a U.S. capability to protect its own population gives the Soviet Union an asymmetrical possibility of holding the U.S. population as hostage to deter retaliation following a Soviet attack on U.S. forces. Although the most economical and rapidly implementable approach to removing this one-sided instability would be for the United States to pursue a more active civil defense program of its own, such a program does not appear to be politically possible at this time. Its future political acceptability will be a function of the emerging threat and its appreciation by U.S. leadership and by the public.

Two more practicable avenues of action suggest themselves. First, all of the options which would be effective in diminishing the one-sided Soviet advantage involve some improvement in the *accuracy* of U.S. missiles. Differential accuracy improvements can, at least temporarily, compensate for throw-weight inequality.

This is a controversial issue which has been studied extensively. The results of one such study by a member of Congress are shown in the *Congressional Record* of May 20, 1975. According to that study the United States presently holds a 4:1 superiority in the hard-target kill capability of missile forces. The Congressman notes in his opposition to a U.S. high-accuracy maneuvering reentry vehicle (MaRV) program that MaRV would by the late 1980s improve U.S. accuracy to .02 n.m. (120 feet), incorrectly estimating that this would increase the U.S. advantage to 7:1 over the U.S.S.R.—assuming the latter was unable to develop MaRV by that time. However, the Congressman's data also predict that the hard-target kill capability of the Soviet missile force will by the 1980s have increased 100-fold, so that if the United States took no action to improve the accuracy of its missiles, the Soviet Union would have an advantage of 25:1. While it is unnecessary to equip more than a portion of U.S. missiles with high-accuracy RVs, it is clear that substantial accuracy improvements are essential to avoid major Soviet superiority in a critical respect.

Others argue that improvements in U.S. missile accuracy would be "destabilizing." More specifically, such programs "could spur Soviet countermeasures such as new programs to increase their second-strike capabilities by going to (1) more sea-launched strategic missiles, (2) air- and sea-launched cruise missiles, (3) expanded strategic bomber forces, and (4) mobile ICBMs."[18] These arguments ignore the central fact that deterrence is already being seriously undermined by unilateral actions of the Soviet Union. Hence, further self-restraint by the United States cannot but worsen this condition.

Moreover, the Soviet programs cited as consequences of U.S. accuracy improvement are in fact stabilizing rather than destabilizing. Under the SALT agreements on force ceilings, such reactions would compel offsetting reductions in the Soviet silo-based ICBM force, thereby reducing their total force throw-weight. Moreover, the replacement ICBM systems are not likely to achieve accuracy equal to that of the silo-based ICBMs, while throw-weight moved to bombers and cruise missiles, because of the long flight time to targets, cannot be effectively used in a first-strike counterforce role.

In sum, even on the information furnished by those generally opposing improved accuracy of U.S. missiles, improvement *is* necessary to avoid a major Soviet advantage, and the logical Soviet counter to such improvements would move the Soviets in a direction which would stabilize the strategic relationship and reduce the Soviet throw-weight advantage.

Second, the prospective Soviet advantage could be offset by measures to decrease the *vulnerability* of U.S. strategic nuclear forces. Here there are several ongoing programs already under way, notably the development of the Trident submarine and the B-1 bomber; both these delivery systems will be inherently less vulnerable to a counterforce attack than fixed ICBM installations, the submarine by reason of its mobility at sea and the B-1 by virtue of its mobility and escape speed as well as the potential capacity to maintain a portion of the B-1 force airborne in time of crisis. In addition, programs to increase the pre-launch survivability of U.S. bomber forces generally, as well as programs to increase air defense capability through the so-called AWACS system, operate to reduce vulnerability of the total U.S. force. To a considerable extent, however, these programs are already taken into account in the calculations shown on Tables 1 and 2—if they were to be delayed, the effect would be negative, and the contrary if they were to be stepped up and accelerated.

I believe, however, that these measures do not go far enough. The most vulnerable U.S. delivery system today is that of our fixed and hardened ICBM installations, including Minuteman silos. Under present trends, it is only a question of time until a combination of the large throw-weight available to the Soviets and improved accuracy will threaten the destruction of a high percentage of these installations—so that today there is considerable talk in some quarters of actually phasing out U.S. ICBM installations.

I believe such action would be unwise, and that it is entirely feasible, at not excessive cost, to adopt a new system of deployment that would not only permit the retention of our ICBMs—which contribute heavily to the total U.S. throw-weight—but would actually make these a more critical and effective component of the U.S. striking force. The system that would accomplish these ends would be a proliferation of low-cost shelters for what is called a multiple launch-point system. The essence of such a system would be to construct a large number of shelter installations, so that the smaller number of actual missile launchers could be readily moved and deployed among these installations on a random pattern deliberately varied at adequate intervals of time.

The ingredients for such a system are, I believe, already in existence, notably through the availability of sufficiently large areas of western desert land now owned by the Department of Defense. On this land there could be created a large number of hardened shelters, or alternatively the missiles themselves could be encased in hardened capsules redeployable among a large number of "soft" shelters. Preliminary study indicates that the research, development, and procurement costs of a system along these lines would average approximately $1.5 billion a year in 1975 dollars over the next eight to ten years. Inasmuch as the current level of obligational authority for strategic weapons systems is on the order of $7 billion per year—much less, as already noted, than the comparable amounts obligated annually in 1956-62—I believe this is a cost we should be prepared to accept.

The objective of creating such a new system of deployment would be to greatly increase the throw-weight costs to the Soviets of destroying a substantial portion of our deterrent forces. This is achieved with a multiple launch-point system, since in order to destroy the system virtually all of the relevant shelter installations would need to be destroyed. There would be many more hardened shelters or encapsulated missiles than the present number of fixed installations, so that the Soviets would be required to commit a larger portion of their throw-weight to this task than they would to the task of attacking fixed installations—the trade-off of U.S. throw-weight destroyed to Soviet throw-weight used would greatly favor the United States. Thus the Soviet advantage in a counterforce exchange would be drastically reduced or eliminated.

Furthermore, I believe that such a U.S. move would be likely to lead to Soviet countermoves that would have a constructive impact on the overall balance. The logical answer to such a U.S. move would be for the Soviet side to substitute either multiple launch-point missiles or SLBMs for a portion of their large fixed ICBMs. They would thereby increase the survivability of their systems, but at the cost of substantially reducing their throw-weight advantage. Such moves by both sides would greatly improve crisis stability and thus significantly reduce the risk of a nuclear war.

In essence, the multiple launch-point idea is a method of preserving and increasing the effectiveness of land-based systems by making them partially mobile. It is, however, necessary to take account of the usual argument advanced for banning land-based mobile missile systems. This argument is that it is more difficult to verify with confidence the number of mobile and thus redeployable launchers deployed by either side than it is to verify the number of fixed silos. The merit of this argument fades in a situation where up to 10 or 12 million pounds of MIRVed throw-weight can be expected to be available to the Soviet side under the limits contemplated by the Vladivostok Accord. With improved accuracy, less than 4 million pounds of MIRVed throw-weight could threaten the destruction of a high percentage of the fixed silos on the U.S. side. No practicable addition through unverified mobile launchers to the 10 to 12 million pounds of throw-weight permitted the Soviet side would compensate strategically for the additional throw-weight requirement that a U.S. multiple launch-point system would impose. A significant portion of a U.S. multiple launch-point system should survive even if the Soviet Union were to devote to the task of attacking it double the 4 million pounds of MIRVed throw-weight it would have to allocate to the destruction of our Minuteman silos.[19]

Undoubtedly, there are other programs which would also be necessary. In particular, it would seem to be essential, if the Soviet Union is to be permitted an unlimited number of Backfires, that we not grant them a free ride for their bomber forces. This would require a reversal of congressional action limiting support for the AWACS program. But taking everything into consideration, the magnitude of the U.S. effort required would be far less than that which we undertook in the 1957-1962 period in response to Sputnik and the then-threatened vulnerability of our bomber force.

VIII

Some of my friends argue that those knowledgeable about such matters should bear in mind the horrors of a nuclear war and should call for U.S. restraint in the hope the U.S.S.R. will follow our lead. Having been in charge of the U.S. Strategic Bombing Survey team of 500 physicists and engineers who measured the detailed effects of the two nuclear weapons used at Nagasaki and Hiroshima, the only two such weapons ever used in anger, and having been associated with many of the subsequent studies of the probable effects of the more modern weapons, I am fully sensitive to the first point. But to minimize the risks of nuclear war, it would seem to me wise to assure that no enemy could believe he could profit from such a war.

As to the second point, Helmut Sonnenfeldt, Counselor for the State Department, recently described the preconditions for the U.S. détente policy in the following terms:

> The course on which we embarked requires toughness of mind and steadfastness of purpose. It demands a sober view not only of Soviet strengths but of our own. It is an attempt to evolve a balance of incentives for positive behavior and penalties for belligerence; the objective being to instill in the minds of our potential adversaries an appreciation of the benefits of cooperation rather than conflict and thus lessen the threat of war. . . . Interests will be respected only if it is clear that they can be defended. Restraint will prevail only if its absence is known to carry heavy risks.[20]

Unfortunately, I believe the record shows that neither negotiations nor unilateral restraint have operated to dissuade Soviet leaders from seeking a nuclear-war-winning capability—or from the view that with such a capability they could effectively use pressure tactics to get their way in crisis situations.

Hence it is urgent that the United States take positive steps to maintain strategic stability and high-quality deterrence. If the trends in Soviet thinking continue to evolve in the manner indicated by the internal statements of Soviet leaders and if the trends in relative military capability continue to evolve in the fashion suggested by the prior analysis, the foundations for hope in the evolution of a true relaxation of tensions between the U.S.S.R. and much of the rest of the world will be seriously in doubt.

Notes

1. B. N. Ponomarev, "The Role of Socialism in Modern World Development," *Problemy Mira i Sotsializma* (Problems of Peace and Socialism), January 1975, pp. 4-13; A. I. Sobolev, "Questions of the Strategy and Tactics of the Class Struggle at the Present Stage of the General Crisis of Capitalism," *Rabochiy Klass i Sovremennyy Mir* (The Working Class and the Contemporary World), January 1975, pp. 3-20.

2. See comments by Aleksey Rumiantsev, at a conference sponsored by *Problemy Mira i Sotsializma*, Summer 1975.

3. To see how top officials veiwed American nuclear power even in the period of American monopoly, one can now consult the recently declassified text of the NSC 68 policy paper dated in the spring of 1950. Even though Soviet

nuclear capacity (after the first Soviet test of August 1949) was assessed as small for some years to come, that paper rejected any idea of reliance on American nuclear power for the defense of key areas. To be sure, in the 1950s under John Foster Dulles, the United States had a declaratory policy of "massive retaliation." But in the actual confrontations of that period, this declaratory policy was not in fact followed; instead, conventional force was used, for example in the Lebanon crisis of 1958 and, less direclty, in the Offshore Islands crisis of the same year. After 1961 massive retaliation was abandoned.

4. Eugene Wigner, "The Atom and the Bomb," *Christian Science Monitor*, November 13, 1974, p. 4.

5. See Albert Wohlstetter, "The Delicate Balance of Terror," *Foreign Affairs*, January 1959, pp. 221-234.

6. It should be noted that this figure refers to the amounts obligated annually for equipment, matériel, and personnel that can be directly attributed to the program mission, including all support costs that follow directly from the number of combat units. It does not include allocable costs of such related activities as communications, general support, and intelligence.

7. See Paul H. Nitze, "The Vladivostok Accord and SALT II," *The Review of Politics* (University of Notre Dame), April 1975, pp. 147-160, especially pp. 149-150.

8. "Throw-weight" is a measure of the weight of effective payload that can be delivered to an intended distance. In the case of intercontinental ballistic missiles (ICBMs) and submarine-launched ballistic missiles (SLBMs), the throw-weight is a direct measure of such a payload in terms of the potential power of the missiles' boosters. In view of the more variable loads carried by heavy bombers, a formula for equivalence is needed to take account of all factors including explosive power. This point is addressed in note 16.

9. See Maxwell D. Taylor, "The Legitimate Claims of National Security," *Foreign Affairs*, April 1974, p. 582.

10. Paul H. Nitze, "The Strategic Balance Between Hope and Skepticism," *Foreign Policy*, Winter 1974-75, pp. 136-156.

11. There has been no agreed definition of a heavy ballistic missile. However, both sides acknowledge that the SS-9 and the SS-18 are MLBMs and that the U.S. Titan missile, while it is considered heavy, does not fall within the definition of "modern." The U.S. has no launchers for MLBMs and is prohibited from converting any of its silos to such launchers. The Soviets are estimated to have had 308 launchers for MLBMs and are permitted to convert the SS-9 launchers into launchers for the even larger and much more capable SS-18s.

12. There are several relevant points on the 600-km. range and cruise versus ballistic ASM questions. The inclusion of cruise missiles as well as ballistic missiles in the aggregate would offer a distinct advantage to the U.S.S.R. In the first place, cruise missiles with a range greater than 600 km. would significantly contribute to U.S. bomber penetration in the face of the strong Soviet antiaircraft

defenses. Furthermore, the United States needs longer range cruise missiles to reach meaningful targets within the opponent's interior than does the Soviet Union. Secondly, the Soviets now have cruise missiles of large size with large conventional warheads having a range close to 600 km. With smaller nuclear warheads their range could be more than doubled. It is not possible to verify the substitution of nuclear warheads for conventional ones or to tell armed cruise missiles from unarmed ones. In any case, a single cruise missile cannot be equated with a Soviet ICBM carrying 50 times as much warhead weight.

13. The significance of verifiability is a function not only of the confidence one can have in verifying a particular number but of the strategic significance of the number being verified. Fixed ICBM silos are large and the number deployed is therefore readily verifiable; however, the throw-weight of the missiles which can be launched from such silos can vary by a factor of ten.

The provision in the SALT I Interim Agreement that the interior dimensions of silos not be increased by more than 15 percent was an attempt to get at this problem. However, the volume of a missile which can be launched from a silo of given interior dimensions can still vary by a factor of two or three, and the throw-weight of a missile with a given volume can vary by a factor of two. Even if the probable error in directly verifying a throw-weight limitation were 20 percent, such a limitation would be strategically far more significant than any of the preceding limitations.

In addition to throw-weight, there are other significant strategic factors, such as the survivability of the launcher through mobility or hardening, and the accuracy, reliability, and number of RVs (reentry vehicles) carried by a MIRVed missile. None of these other factors is limited under the Vladivostok Accord and, in any case, they are inherently difficult to verify.

14. In mid-1973 the United States had 602 fighter interceptors and 481 surface-to-air missiles, compared to the Soviet Union's 3,000 fighter interceptors and 10,000 surface-to-air missiles. Edward Luttwak, *The U.S.-U.S.S.R. Nuclear Weapons Balance*, The Washington Papers, Beverly Hills: Sage Publications, 1974.

15. Indeed, if total throw-weight is not reduced while the number of launchers is, the fewer launchers become more vulnerable and critical to each side and crisis stability is actually lessened. See Lt. Gen. (then Col.) Glenn A. Kent, "On the Interaction of Opposing Forces under Possible Arms Agreements," Occasional Papers in International Affairs, No. 5, Center for International Affairs, Harvard University, March 1963.

16. A B-52 has been assigned an equivalent throw-weight of 10,000 pounds and a B-1 about 19,000 pounds. The SRAM air-to-surface missile has a yield about equal to that of a Minuteman III warhead; hence, for every three SRAMs carried by a bomber, that bomber is given a throw-weight equivalent equal to the throw-weight of one Minuteman III. Laydown bombs are assumed to have roughly the yield of Minuteman II; hence, for each laydown bomb carried by a

bomber it is given a throw-weight equivalent equal to the throw-weight of a Minuteman II. The alert bomber force is assumed to be 40 percent of the B-52 inventory and 60 percent of the B-1 inventory, degraded to incorporate penetration factors.

17. I regret that, even if space permitted, the full assumptions used in Mr. Jones' study cannot be spelled out here. Security considerations necessarily enter in for some of the underlying data. I have myself gone over Mr. Jones' data and assumptions with care and believe that they represent a careful and objective analysis of the relevant factors. Above all, since his methods are self-consistent from one period to the next, they show a valid trend-line and pace of change— which I believe the more expert readers of this article will find conform to their more general judgments.

18. For additional views of Representative Schroeder see, "Alternative Defense Posture Statement," *Report 94-199 of House Armed Services Committee,* May 10, 1975, p. 130.

19. Under the Vladivostok Accord, both sides are permitted 1,320 MIRVed missile launchers. The maximum MIRVed throw-weight the Soviets could obtain within this limit with the missiles they are currently testing and beginning to deploy is:

> 4,500,000 pounds on 308 SS-18s (about 15,000 pounds each)
> 7,100,000 pounds on 1,012 SS-19s (about 7,000 pounds each)

for a total MIRVed throw-weight of 11.6 million pounds. However, it is unlikely that the Soviets will reach this maximum, as they are currently deploying some SS-17s, which will have a throw-weight of about 5,000 pounds, and they may choose not to MIRV all of their SS-18s. A more likely figure is less than 10 million pounds of MIRVed throw-weight.

A reliable megaton-range RV with a CEP (circular error probable, a measure of accuracy) of 0.125 nautical miles has a probability of damage of 85 percent against a silo of 1,500 psi (pounds per square inch) hardness. The targeting of two such RVs on the silo would give a probability of damage of about 92 percent taking into account both reliability and accuracy. An SS-18 missile may have up to eight megaton-range RVs (International Institute for Strategic Studies, *The Military Balance, 1974-75);* thus a megaton-range RV may require around 2,000 pounds of throw-weight. The net throw-weight required, then, to threaten 92 percent destruction of 1,000 hard silos would be approximately 4 million pounds, assuming the Soviets achieve CEPs averaging an eighth of a mile.

A multiple launch-point ICBM system with 600-psi hard shelters or encapsulated missiles in soft shelters would require considerably more throw-weight for its destruction. To barrage attack such a mobile system deployed on 6,000 square nautical miles of land as an area target would require about 19,000 megaton-range RVs to achieve a 92 percent damage level. The throw-weight required for this force would be considerably above the Soviet available force. Even as low a damage level as 20 percent would require almost 4,000 megaton-range RVs, a throw-weight of at least 8 million pounds.

Assuming the same factors for accuracy and reliability as used above in calculating the potential results of an attack on silo-based ICBMs, an equal probability of damage (85 percent for a single reliable RV) can be achieved against a 600-psi shelter with a 290-kt weapon. Since a Minuteman III, with a total of three RVs of less than 200-kt yield, has a throw-weight of about 2,000 pounds, an RV of 290-kt yield might require about 800 pounds of throw-weight. Thus a U.S. deployment of some 10,000 shelters would require 8 million pounds of Soviet MIRVed throw-weight to threaten destruction of 72 percent of the multiple launch-point system. The entire 10 million pound force would raise the level of destruction to only 77 percent. The cost of adding RVs to the Soviet attack force should be substantially greater than the cost to the United States of adding shelters. In any case, it would appear technologically infeasible to reduce the throw-weight required per RV to less than 300 pounds, even if accuracies were eventually to approach zero CEP.

20. Helmut Sonnenfeldt, "The Meaning of Détente," *Naval War College Review*, July-August 1975, pp. 3-8.

4

The Scope and Limits of SALT

Richard Burt

After almost five years of breakthroughs, setbacks, and mostly stalemate, the Soviet Union and the United States succeeded last September in agreeing on the outlines and some of the details of a new strategic arms limitation accord. Since then, several other details of the proposed SALT agreement have been ironed out. Although it is unclear whether the two sides will be able to complete a new agreement this year, the terms of the proposed accord have already triggered a wide-ranging debate in the United States and among allied states in Western Europe over whether its contents serve American security interests and those of the West as a whole.

It is a complex debate, because the understanding itself is complicated and because it deals with the arcane problem of measuring the superpower strategic balance. It is an enormously important debate, because its outcome will have major consequences for the future evolution of that balance, the character of Soviet-American relations in general, the tenor of Alliance politics, and the ability of the Carter Administration (and perhaps succeeding ones) to conduct foreign affairs. Finally, it is an intense debate, because positions adopted by supporters and opponents of the proposed agreement reflect deeply felt beliefs concerning the character of the strategic balance and the political and military utility of nuclear weapons.

The centrality of the SALT process to American national security policy makes it impossible here to address all the implications of the proposed agreement. But because a central theme in this essay is that both advocates and critics of the Carter Administration's approach to SALT have tended to exaggerate what the talks can and should accomplish, the attempt will be made to judge the emerging terms of the

Reprinted by permission of the author and *Foreign Affairs*, July 1978. Copyright 1978 by Council on Foreign Relations, Inc.

superpower understanding in terms of the dynamics of continuing Soviet-American strategic competition. For if one lesson has already emerged from the mounting debate over SALT, it is that regardless of whether a new agreement is both signed and approved by the U.S. Senate, the United States will not be spared some difficult strategic deployment decisions in the immediate years ahead.

II

To appreciate the present debate, it is necessary to trace the genealogy of the proposed accord back to 1973, when Soviet and American negotiators began talks on a new and more permanent arrangement to replace the 1972 five-year Interim Agreement limiting offensive strategic arms. The Interim Agreement which placed separate ceilings on land-based intercontinental ballistic missiles (ICBMs) and submarine-launched ballistic missiles (SLBMs), provided the Soviet Union with a potential 40 percent advantage in launcher totals: under the terms of the accord, the Soviet Union could have 2,358 missile launchers compared with 1,710 for the United States. Although this disparity was justified in terms of overall American technological superiority (particularly in multiple warheads and missile accuracy), the Nixon Administration, with the prodding of Senator Henry Jackson's amendment calling for numerical equality in future agreements, vowed to replace the Interim Agreement with a long-term treaty establishing parity between the two sides. An additional incentive for institutionalizing numerical equivalence in a new agreement was provided in the summer of 1973, when the Soviet Union began the deployment of a new family of high-payload ICBMs, the SS-17, -18 and -19, all of which had been tested with multiple, independently targetable reentry vehicles (MIRVs). This development not only carried with it the potential for massively increasing the destructiveness of the Soviet Union's 1,600 or so silo-housed missiles, but it also erased the MIRV headstart that many believed was the single most important technological advantage enjoyed by the United States.

The Nixon Administration's effort in 1973 and early 1974 to get the Soviet Union to agree to limit the total payload (or throw-weight) its missile force could deliver resulted in failure. Thus, the new Ford Administration, at Vladivostok in November 1974, returned to the simpler and less controversial principle of only limiting launcher numbers in a new treaty lasting until 1985. Thus, in a tentative accord, the two sides agreed for the first time to place equal ceilings of 2,400 on strategic launchers and of 1,320 on MIRV-equipped missiles. Significantly, the Vladivostok aide mémoire was silent on the subject of halting weapons modernization, and (upon the insistence of American negotiators) both sides were thus free to move ahead with the deployment of land-mobile ICBMs.

The adoption of equal ceilings in numbers of strategic launchers was possible essentially because, unlike the Interim Agreement, the Vladivostok accord included "heavy" bombers, in which the United States had a substantial edge. Moreover, the ceilings did not force the Soviet Union to undertake any reductions in its growing arsenal. Thus, while the tentative accord was criticized in the United States for doing little to hamper the growth of Soviet ICBM capabilities, the Ford Administration defended it on the grounds that it would not impair any American effort to respond to the Soviet buildup, such as deploying a larger proportion of forces at sea or replacing the Minuteman ICBM force with a new mobile missile, such as the Air Force's proposed MX.

Over the next 18 months the two sides failed in their efforts to work out the details of the proposed agreement. In part, this difficulty can be traced to problems in the wider American-Soviet relationship: the Nixon Administration's détente policy was badly undermined by Soviet behavior prior to and during the 1973 Middle East War; domestic skepticism grew during 1974 and was reinforced in 1975-76 by Soviet involvement in the Angolan civil war. However, the major factor blocking a new agreement was integral to the talks themselves: the two sides were simply unable to agree on what weapons were to be limited under the proposed 2,400 ceiling. The Vladivostok aide mémoire said that air-launched missiles with ranges that exceeded 600 kilometers were to be limited in the accord—shortly after the summit, Secretary of State Henry Kissinger told reporters that this referred to air-launched *ballistic* missiles and not to the new generation of precision-guided, long-range cruise missiles that the United States had under development. Despite this, Soviet negotiators insisted that cruise missiles, including sea- and ground-launched variants, had to be constrained in any new agreement, a position that their American couterparts resisted on the grounds that these weapons were peripheral to the central strategic balance and were of primary importance as potential theater systems, armed with nuclear or conventional warheads. In similar fashion, Soviet negotiators resisted American demands to include a new Soviet bomber, known by its NATO code name Backfire, under the 2,400 ceiling on overall launchers, maintaining that Backfire was an intermediate-range system, deployed primarily for use against targets in Western Europe and East Asia—an argument that paralleled, in some respects, American claims over the cruise missile.

In an attempt to break the cruise missile–Backfire deadlock, Henry Kissinger in January 1976 traveled to Moscow and offered a compromise proposal. While the mission did not produce a completed agreement, it is worth noting because of its resemblance to important facets of the approach finally settled upon by the Carter Administration. In Moscow, Kissinger proposed that air-launched cruise missiles (ALCMs) be limited to a range of 2,500 km. and that aircraft deploying them be counted under the 1,320 ceiling for MIRV-equipped delivery vehicles. In return, he offered to keep the Backfire out of the 2,400 ceiling, so long as Moscow agreed to limit its production rate (to two-and-a-half units per month), to place certain restrictions on where the bomber was based, and to lower the overall ceiling on launchers by 10 percent (to 2,160).

Although the Soviet leaders showed interest, by the spring of 1976 the Ford Administration appeared to have backed away from these ideas— which were apparently opposed within the Ford Cabinet. Instead, in its last attempt to achieve an accord, the Administration proposed that the two sides enter into the arrangement outlined at Vladivostok and defer the cruise missile and Backfire issues to a later round of negotiations. Clearly wanting to curb cruise missiles before they were actually deployed, Moscow refused.

III

Announcing in his inaugural address the hope that "nuclear weapons could be rid from the face of the earth," Jimmy Carter and his chief advisers quickly moved to distance themselves from the arms control strategy formulated during the Nixon-Ford years. The new Administration viewed SALT more as an arms control process and less as a political enterprise: the talks, it was said, could be separated somewhat from the wider Soviet-American political relationship, and arms control approached on its own technical merits. This had two important consequences for the Carter Administration's early strategy for negotiations.

First, it suggested that the central purpose of the exercise was not, as in years previous, to provide greater momentum to superpower détente. Viewing Soviet-American relations, as outlined in Presidential Review Memorandum 10, as embodying strands of both competition and cooperation, the predominant view in the first months of the Administration was that progress (or the lack of it) at SALT need not interfere with other Administration policies toward Moscow, such as human rights. SALT, in other words, was not to become a hostage to "linkage diplomacy."

Second, the primary purpose of the negotiations should be to secure a more stable strategic relationship, not simply to codify, as the Vladivostok understanding was accused of doing, a continued Soviet-

American quantitative and qualitative arms race. This meant that overall equality in numbers of strategic launchers was an insufficient objective at the talks. New agreements, it was argued, could not cope with emerging strategic problems, particularly the vulnerability of American land-based missiles, by merely allowing each side to deploy new systems such as mobile missiles. Instead, "real" arms control was supposed to solve the vulnerability problem, making the deployment of new strategic weapons unneccessary.

Thus, the Carter Administration quickly moved to incorporate a much more ambitious range of objectives into the negotiations. The problem that had stalled the talks for two years—the place of "peripheral systems" in the Vladivostok totals—was set aside and attention was focused on new goals: reducing launcher numbers from the 2,400 ceiling, limiting the testing of new missiles, installing a new set of sub-limits on especially threatening systems such as Soviet "heavy" ICBMs, and banning certain new systems.

The result of this reappraisal was the so-called comprehensive proposal that Secretary of State Cyrus Vance laid before Soviet negotiators in March 1977. The proposal consisted of five important parts. First, it would have reduced the Vladivostok ceilings for overall strategic launchers to between 1,800 and 2,000. Second, it would have cut the number of launchers equipped with MIRVs from the Vladivostok total of 1,320 to between 1,100 and 1,200. Third, it would have placed two new sub-ceilings on land-based missiles: a ceiling of 550 on MIRV-equipped ICBMs and of 150 on "heavy" missiles. Fourth, it would have limited ICBM and SLBM tests to six a year and banned the deployment of follow-on systems. Finally, while it sought a 2,500-km. range ceiling for bomber-launched ALCMs (in anticipation, it seems, of President Carter's decision to cancel the B-1 penetrating bomber in July), it proposed a 600-km. limit for sea- and ground-launched cruise missiles.

In what seemed to be an effort to "sweeten" the comprehensive offer, the Administration in March 1977 also resurrected, as an alternative, the last proposal offered by President Ford: both sides could enter into the Vladivostok arrangement and defer the cruise missile and Backfire issues until a later phase of the talks. Neither proposal, however, met with Russian approval and in an extraordinary statement, Soviet Foreign Minister Andrei Gromyko particularly criticized the comprehensive proposal, accusing the Carter Administration of trying to achieve "unilateral advantages" in the talks.

In some respects, Mr. Gromyko's remarks deserve to be taken seriously. The Administration's proposals did reflect a growing concern over both the political and the military implications of Soviet missile modernization. The comprehensive proposal was not just designed to bring about a general reduction in strategic forces—a mostly cosmetic objective—but it also sought to single out a special category of weapons for reduction and qualitative restraint—MIRVed land-based missiles. Under the Vladivostok formula, there would be nothing to stop the Soviet Union from deploying over 1,000 new MIRV-equipped ICBMs (including over 300 "heavy" SS-18s), which, with further testing and improvements in accuracy, seemed certain to pose a threat to the Minuteman force in the 1980s. For the Carter Administration, then, the Soviet MIRVed ICBM, and not the Backfire, had become the central stumbling block to securing a new agreement. What the Carter Administration viewed as the most serious threat to strategic stability— the increasingly accurate, high-payload, MIRVed ICBM—the Soviet leadership undoubtedly viewed as the cornerstone of its strategic power.

The compromise arrangement formulated by the Administration following the March 1977 debacle—which forms the basis of the agreement now in the final stages of completion—is probably best viewed as an amalgam of the comprehensive and the deferral proposals. First submitted to the Soviets in May, the arrangement envisaged three different agreements: a *treaty* lasting until 1985, a *protocol* lasting for three years, and a *statement of principles* to guide negotiators during the next phase of negotiations. Although the Soviet Union accepted the idea of the "three-tier" agreement in May 1977, it was not until Gromyko's visit to Washington in September that the two sides actually agreed on the substance of much of the new accord. Since the September breakthrough, the two sides have gradually narrowed their differences on details of the proposed agreement. While some differences still remain, the proposed agreement can now be described in some detail.

The *treaty*, lasting until 1985, will consist of 13 major components:

1. A ceiling of 2,250 is to be placed on the aggregate number of launcher vehicles possessed by each side. This is slightly higher than the figure proposed by the Administration in September (2,160), but it was apparently accepted in return for Soviet acquiescence to the sub-ceiling placed on total numbers of land- and sea-based MIRVed missiles (see below). The ceiling will require the Soviet Union to undertake a small reduction in its existing arsenal (some 250 launchers), but whether this cut is to be completed by December 1980 (the American preference) or somewhat later remains unresolved.

2. Within the 2,250 aggregate, a sub-ceiling of 1,320 will be placed on the total number of land- and sea-based MIRVed missiles as well as heavy bombers equipped with ALCMs. No limit has been placed on the number of ALCMs each existing heavy bomber can carry. A ceiling,

however, may be placed on the number of ALCMs permitted aboard a new generation of wide-bodied aircraft carrying cruise missiles.

3. A sub-ceiling of 1,200 is to be placed on total numbers of land- and sea-based MIRVed missiles.

4. A further sub-ceiling of 820 is to be placed on numbers of MIRVed ICBMs. This represents the first time that this separate class of systems has been restricted. However, within this ceiling, the Soviet Union will be permitted to MIRV its entire force of SS-19 "heavy" systems, some 313 missiles.

5. While permitted to MIRV its existing heavy missile force, the Soviet Union will not be permitted to build additional ones. Nor will it be allowed to deploy new systems with useful payloads exceeding those of the new Soviet SS-18 "heavy" ICBM. In addition, new missiles with payloads exceeding the Soviet SS-19 "medium" missile will be counted as "heavy" ICBMs. The United States, which presently does not possess any "heavy" missiles, will not be permitted to deploy them during the period of the treaty.

6. In order to aid in the verification of sub-ceilings placed on MIRVed launchers, the two sides have agreed that any missile of a type tested with a MIRV is to be counted as a MIRVed launcher when deployed. This means that while the Soviet Union has deployed single-warhead versions of the SS-19 and the SS-18, all these missiles will be considered as MIRVed for purposes of the agreement.

7. The testing and deployment of long-range ALCMs are to be restricted to heavy bombers: American B-52s and Soviet Bear and Bison aircraft. (Whether this will apply only to nuclear-armed ALCMs or to conventionally armed versions, too, is unclear.) In order to keep open the option of deploying ALCMs aboard a new generation of cruise missile carriers during the 1980s, the United States is also willing to take steps to differentiate such carriers (probably modified 747s) from civilian transports, in order to aid Soviet verification efforts.

8. A limit of 2,500 km. is to be placed on the range of ALCMs deployed aboard heavy bombers, but this has been defined to allow these missiles additional range to follow a zigzag course toward their targets.

9. To prohibit the rapid reloading of ICBM silos, the storage of excess missiles at launching sites is to be prohibited.

10. Although the deployment of mobile ICBMs is not banned in the draft treaty, the Soviet Union is prohibited from deploying the SS-16 ICBM in a mobile mode because of its similarity to the now-deployed SS-20 intermediate-range missile, which is not limited in the accord.

11. Both sides have agreed not to circumvent the agreement, including not taking actions through other states that could weaken the provisions of the accord. This would appear to rule out the transfer of

weapons limited in the treaty to allied governments in Western Europe.

12. Both sides are to provide each other prior notification of missile testing and information on the size and performance of their respective arsenals, and both would agree to refrain from interfering with national technical means of verification, such as reconnaissance satellites.

13. Last, the Backfire bombers will not be counted under the ceilings set by the treaty. However, the production rate of the bomber will be frozen, with the possibility that restrictions will also be placed on the basing, refueling, and modernization of the aircraft. What form an agreement covering the Backfire would take—an exchange of letters or a formal accord requiring Senate approval—is still unclear.

The *protocol*, on the other hand, is a temporary agreement, primarily designed to codify some of the restrictions on weapons modernization sought by the Administration in its earlier comprehensive proposal and to meet Soviet concerns over the American sea- and ground-launched cruise missiles. The Administration proposes that it run until December 1980; the Soviet Union, however, has argued that the protocol should expire three years after it enters into force, which could run into 1981 and conceivably beyond. The most important provisions contained in the protocol are:

1. A ban would be placed on the testing and deployment of "new types" of missiles, with certain exceptions. The Soviet Union desires to be allowed to deploy a new single-warhead ICBM as well as a new SLBM, the Typhoon. (This would be in addition to being able to deploy two other SLBMs—the SS-NX-17 and the SS-NX-18—which have been tested and are thus deemed eligible for deployment.) The United States is also proposing that each side should be allowed to deploy a new ICBM, but that each side be allowed to choose whether it would be MIRVed or unMIRVed. The Administration is also proposing that if the Soviet Union is allowed to deploy the Typhoon, the United States be permitted also to deploy a new longer-range SLBM, Trident II. There are indications that, as the two sides narrow their differences on what new systems would be exempted from the "new types" ban, they may move this provision from the protocol into the longer-term treaty.

2. The significant improvement of existing systems will be restricted, with substantial upgrading of boosters, post-boost vehicles and guidance systems ruled out. The deployment of new MIRVs that increase the number of warheads aboard existing post-boost vehicles may alo be prohibited. Electronic improvements to existing guidance units—to achieve higher accuracies—would not be restricted because they could not be verified.

3. The testing and deployment of mobile ICBMs would be banned, but the testing of ICBMs (from fixed launchers) actually intended for

deployment aboard mobile launchers after the expiration of the protocol will apparently be permitted.

4. The testing and deployment of armed (nuclear or conventional) cruise missiles with ranges exceeding 2,500 km. would be barred. Deployment of cruise missiles (land-, air-, or sea-launched) with ranges exceeding 600 km. on platforms other than heavy bombers would be banned, but these systems could be developed and tested at ranges up to 2,500 km.

The third component of the proposed SALT package, the *statement of principles*, is intended to provide a framework for future negotiations, meant to begin shortly after the conclusion of SALT II. The United States is asking that the negotiations focus more heavily on reductions in forces and on the new qualitative limits (testing and research and development), while the Soviet Union, apparently less enthusiastic about the whole concept of a statement to guide a SALT III dialogue, is pushing for recognition of the concept that American nuclear-capable aircraft in Western Europe (so-called forward-based systems, or FBS) and allied strategic nuclear forces (the British and French SLBM forces) be subject to limitation in a future agreement.

IV

Not unexpectedly, much of the controversy that has surrounded this complex package has focused on two interrelated issues: (1) the possible asymmetries in the overall strategic balance that could emerge during the course of the treaty, and (2) the dampening effect that the three-year protocol could have on American technological initiative.

In making its case for the treaty, the Administration argues that it provides, for the first time, overall equality in strategic launchers and that, in particular, it places a ceiling on the expansion of the most dangerous element of Soviet strategic power—land-based MIRVed missiles. Critics, however, contend that overall equality in strategic launchers is a poor measure of parity and that the proposed ceiling of 820 on MIRVed ICBMs is unlikely to put any real dent in Soviet military capabilities, especially against hardened military targets such as missile silos.

The problem of measuring the strategic balance is a familiar one, and comparative figures may provide little real indication of actual military capabilities under the proposed treaty. However, within the constraints laid down by the treaty, the Soviet Union is likely to increase its overall edge in deliverable megatons (a measure of destructive potential against area targets) as well as throw-weight (a measure of how payloads can be exploited). The Soviet edge in these measures will become particularly pronounced for ICBMs: by 1985 the Soviet Union is likely to enjoy a seven-to-one lead in deliverable megatons and a five-to-one advantage in throw-weight. These Soviet advantages in overall capabilities are offset somewhat by the American edge in total warheads, but this edge is likely to decline somewhat after 1982. However, even then, with American deployment of ALCMs aboard bombers and the new MIRVed Trident I missile, the United States will maintain a substantial lead in bomber and SLBM warheads.

In overall terms, it is difficult to escape the conclusion that, during the treaty, a shift in the strategic nuclear balance will in fact occur. It is important to note, however, that this shift has little to do with the ceilings and sub-ceilings laid down in the treaty and is really the result of a continuing and unprecedented buildup in Soviet capabilities. Since the 1972 SALT agreements, the Soviet Union had deployed four new ICBMs, two new SLBMs (with two more under development), and a new bomber. For its part, the United States has tested and cancelled a new bomber, finished the deployment of a new SLBM, and begun the testing of another. What the shift represented in these crude indices reflects, then, is not necessarily an inequitable agreement but unequal momentum in Soviet-American strategic arms competition.

Whether the various asymmetries that could arise under the treaty are significant is a difficult question to answer. In the case of many, they are symbolic—reflecting the fact that Soviet strategic power in overall terms *is* growing faster than that of the United States. While this may have little immediate impact on real Soviet military options, it is much more difficult to argue that a shift in the perceived balance will not affect Soviet behavior in other areas, as well as the confidence of allied governments in the West, and possibly the confidence of American leaders.

A much more difficult problem, however, is posed by the prospect that, between now and 1985, the treaty will permit the Soviet Union to develop a new military option—the ability to threaten the destruction of most, if not all, of the Minuteman ICBM force in a disarming first strike. Whether the Soviet Union is likely to achieve the technical capacity to actually undertake what Secretary of Defense Harold Brown has called a "cosmic roll of the dice" is still very much in dispute. But with over 5,000 separately targeted warheads and a force of 820 SS-18 and SS-19 ICBMs possessing accuracies below 0.2 nautical miles the Soviet Union will pose a strategic threat in the mid-1980s that American planners will be hard-pressed to ignore, despite the many uncertainties attached to any first-strike scenario against the Minuteman.

The emergence of a real probability of Minuteman vulnerability during the course of the treaty must be immediately troubling for

President Carter, for as we have seen, a central Administration aim has been to use SALT to establish a more stable strategic relationship. Under the comprehensive American proposal of March 1977, the low limit proposed for MIRVed ICBMs (550) and, more importantly, the limit on missile tests (six per year) would have gone a long way to reduce the emergence of Minuteman vulnerability. However, as Administration officials have come to acknowledge, the limits on Soviet ICBMs (or the lack of them) laid out in the present accord are likely to do little to forestall the Soviet achievement, at least on paper, of a credible first-strike capability against the most flexible and responsive component of the American triad. As the Administration as well as many critics of the treaty recognize, this means that the United States will probably be forced to take some unilateral step, during the coming decade, such as moving ahead with a land-mobile ICBM, to cope with the silo-vulnerability problem. More immediately, however, it means that the Administration, by failing to solve the problem at SALT, has been unable to achieve what was earlier a primary objective in the negotiations.

V

While the debate over the treaty will surely focus on strategic trends, the controversy over the protocol is likely to concern whether or not it can be kept temporary in character. Although the protocol's terms place a broad range of restrictions on options for weapons modernization, it has been primarily designed to limit cruise missiles in a manner acceptable to both parties. As the experience following the Vladivostok Tentative Accord demonstrated, the Soviet Union is unwilling to enter into an agreement that does not place some type of restrictions on long-range cruise missiles, particularly land- and sea-based versions that could proliferate in the thousands in and around Western Europe, posing threats not only to Soviet capabilities in Eastern Europe but to the Soviet homeland as well. At the same time, the United States remains similarly unwilling to foreclose any options for the cruise missile, despite the fact that American planners are unsure how the new technology can best be exploited. The solution to this impasse has been to place a three-year ban on cruise missile deployment (but not development)—which could set a precedent for limiting these systems in SALT III but which does not in itself rule out their possible deployment at a later date.

In purely legal terms, the Administration is on firm ground in arguing that limits on sea- and ground-launched cruise missiles will have no impact on existing American deployment plans, which do not envisage deployment until 1981 at the earliest. But while the United States will remain free, under the protocol, to continue to develop long-range versions of these systems and, if judged necessary, to deploy cruise missiles after the protocol ends, there will be powerful forces working on any Administration not to do so. For a start, with cruise missiles limited by a SALT agreement (whatever its label), any effort to move ahead with their deployment in the 1980s will be viewed by many—in and out of government—as a retrogressive step in arms control. Thus, once controls are placed on the technology at SALT, it may be politically difficult, as many critics of the protocol argue, for the United States to simply plunge ahead with cruise missile deployment. This would be particularly true if, as seems likely, the protocol expired in the midst of negotiations on a follow-on SALT III agreement; in such circumstances a U.S. cruise missile deployment would be viewed and portrayed by Moscow (as well as by many arms control supporters in the United States) as severely damaging the chances of achieving a follow-on agreement.

In fact, Soviet statements on the protocol make it very clear that Moscow views it as only the first step toward achieving a more comprehensive set of constraints on the cruise missile. Placing temporary limits on the cruise missile within the protocol does appear to have enabled the two sides to surmount a central negotiating obstacle that has hindered agreement since 1974. The protocol, however, is not a solution to the cruise missile problem; it only defers the issue to a later stage of negotiations, and it does so in a way that the United States could regret.

The possibility that, despite its temporary character, the protocol could emerge as a much more permanent fixture also has implications for the problem of Minuteman vulnerability, discussed above. Although the treaty would not prohibit the United States from responding to the threat by developing a land-mobile ICBM in the 1980s, the protocol (on present indications) would ban for its duration the testing and deployment of a system such as the MX, being proposed by the U.S. Air Force.

Again this prohibition, in theory, would have no real impact on American options because the MX is at an early development stage and the United States has no plans to deploy, or even to test, a mobile ICBM over the next three years. But, as with sea- and ground-launched cruise missiles, the dynamics of future SALT negotiations could create pressures to place longer-term limits on mobile ICBM deployment. For example, because the protocol would also limit the Soviet development of a new family of follow-on ICBMs, it will probably be argued that an American decision to allow it to expire would open the floodgates to a new generation of far more threatening Soviet systems. Although this might be true, extending the protocol would deny the United States the means of coping with the problems created even by existing Soviet ICBMs. When viewed together, then, the implications of the treaty and the protocol appear indeed troubling: while the treaty is likely to do little to forestall the emergence of Minuteman vulnerability during the 1980s, it is possible that the protocol could work to limit American options for responding to the problem.

VI

Although the key issues posed by the proposed agreements concern the effect of the treaty on superpower strategic stability and the possible impact of the protocol on American options, three other potential problems arising out of SALT also merit discussion.

The first concerns the possible impact of the new agreements on the cohesion of the Atlantic Alliance. So far, the problems that a new SALT accord could create for the Alliance have been understood to revolve around the issue of technology transfer. Would a new agreement restrict the ability of the United States to continue existing programs for nuclear weapons collaboration with its NATO allies or to undertake new ones? As with many other parts of the accord, the answer, at this stage, is unclear. As outlined above, the two sides have agreed not to take steps through "other parties" that could weaken the proposed accord. While this noncircumvention provision, as the Administration is quick to point out, does not specifically rule out the American transfer of weapons, their components, or their blueprints to allied partners (what the Soviet Union originally sought to achieve in the accord), it also fails to outline specifically what types of Alliance cooperation would be permitted under the accord. Clearly, the United States, along with its allies, will attempt to define the provision in a way that would minimize any possibility for disrupting existing practices, such as the American sale of Polaris A-3 missiles to Britain or any future assistance that might be offered, say, in the development of a European cruise missile force. The Soviet Union, on the other hand, can be expected to take a more restrictive approach to the provision and might capitalize on its vagueness to challenge a wide range of European-American programs for cooperation. Despite this, it seems unlikely that the differences of interpretation that could flow out of the accord's noncircumvention language will pose serious problems either for superpower relations or for NATO. This is simply because, for the foreseeable future, NATO allies are unlikely to seek large-scale American help in expanding European strategic forces and, if they did, it is doubtful that the United

States would respond with massive assistance.

A much more serious threat to Alliance unity, and one that has been neglected in recent discussions, is the possible impact that the accord could have on efforts to improve American capabilities in and around Western Europe. During the first round of SALT, one of the sensitive issues within the Alliance was the possibility that, in an agreement, the Nixon Administration might sacrifice its freedom to maintain or improve forces earmarked for the defense of NATO. Attention was particularly focused on nuclear-capable aircraft based in Europe and assigned missions in the European theater, but which, in theory, possess the capability to strike the Soviet homeland. Had the Administration agreed to limit FBS aircraft in the 1972 agreements, European governments would have perceived this as an American decision to pursue superpower arms control at the expense of NATO defense. As it happened, American negotiators successfully resisted Soviet pressures on this score, and strike aircraft were excluded from the ceilings laid down in the Interim Agreement, a precedent that is continued within the new accord.

But while the Carter Administration has been able to sidestep the FBS issue in the new agreement, it has not succeeded in minimizing the potential impact of the new accord on future American contributions to NATO defense. This, of course, is because the Administration has accepted the concept of limiting long-range sea- and ground-launched cruise missiles. While the contribution these systems could make to NATO's theater nuclear (and conventional) capabilities is still under study, there are strong reasons to believe that cruise missiles deployed in the European theater would greatly enhance the survivability and responsiveness of NATO's existing nuclear posture.

However, as we have seen, the limits laid down in the protocol could mean that the United States will be unable to exercise this option over the coming decade. In theory, if a new NATO deployment of these systems is judged necessary in the early 1980s (the earliest point the systems would be available), the three-year protocol could be allowed to lapse. If, on the other hand, the cruise missile option does not appear as interesting in the early 1980s as it does at present, the Administration maintains that it will use the possibility of cruise missile deployment as a significant bargaining chip to achieve Soviet concessions in a future round of SALT.

The crucial question, of course, is how much flexibility the Administration will realistically possess in moving ahead with the deployment of sea- and ground-launched cruise missiles as the protocol nears expiration. At that point, the same political and "image" problems already noted as to other parts of the protocol would arise for this one as well. Thus, the United States could be tampering with its ability to replace existing NATO FBS systems in the future.

The problems posed for NATO by cruise missile constraints are exacerbated by the fact that equivalent Soviet long-range theater nuclear systems, such as the SS-20 missile or the Backfire bomber, are not to be limited in the new SALT agreement. It is possible, then, that as the Soviet Union expands its "Euro-strategic" missile and bomber forces, West European governments will be led to argue that NATO's best instruments for responding to this buildup—American cruise missiles —have been withheld from the Alliance. This impression could be further reinforced by the very structure of the protocol itself. In general terms, it can be argued that the agreement limits American weapons of greatest relevance to the defense of Western Europe (sea- and ground-launched cruise missiles) in return for Soviet restraint in weapons that primarily threaten the United States (a new family of four ICBMs). Thus, over time many Europeans may conclude that the United States— in order to reach a new agreement—has mortgaged systems that are most likely to serve Western, rather than strictly American, interests.

VII

This review has only touched on what are viewed as the most significant issues raised by the proposed SALT agreement. Other problems have already been identified by other authors, and these, too, will receive attention in the coming debates over the new accord. One of these, the question of what limits, if any, will be placed on the Backfire is still an issue in dispute in the talks. However, even if the Soviet Union is willing to agree (through restrictions on where the bomber is deployed and its ability to be refueled) to limit its capability to strike targets in the American homeland, the fact that the bomber is not to be included in the overall ceiling of the treaty is certain to arouse concern in the Senate.

The same is true for procedures in the agreement for verification. The Arms Control and Disarmament Agency has already informed the Senate that it will be able to monitor Soviet compliance with the new accord with confidence, but it has acknowledged that certain provisions—for example, those dealing with cruise missile range and limits on missile modernization—will be difficult to verify. In general, Soviet efforts to take advantage of verification problems posed by the new accord would not result in any decisive strategic advantages in the near term. So the Administration is probably correct in arguing that Moscow would be unlikely to jeopardize the new agreement by seeking marginal advantages through cheating. At the same time there is growing sentiment within the United States, whether it is justified by the Soviet record at SALT I or not, that Moscow will seek to use ambiguities or loopholes in arms control accords to further its strategic interests. Thus, regardless of their strategic significance, apparent opportunities for violating the new agreement are certain to be seized upon in the SALT debate.

There can be little doubt that the new accord will receive rough treatment if and when the Administration presents it to the Senate for approval. In addition to the largely symbolic concerns generated by the Backfire and the problems of verification, the agreement appears to countenance (1) an overall shift in the strategic balance in favor of Moscow, (2) the emergence of Minuteman vulnerability, and (3) the growth of serious strains within the Atlantic Alliance. These are not happy prospects, and it is understandable that supporters of the agreement have begun to argue that while it is not ideal, the United States would be far worse off without a new SALT accord. Representative Les Aspin has suggested, for example, that without a lid of 2,250 on overall launcher numbers, the Soviet Union might be capable of deploying some 3,500 launchers by 1985.

However, this seems a curious way to build public support for SALT. For a start, it suggests that the accord itself is somewhat inadequate and, accordingly, can only be sold by comparing it with a more unpleasant state of affairs. More important, by arguing that without a new agreement the American-Soviet balance would be bound to worsen, the Administration is in danger of appearing unable or unwilling to compete with Moscow over the coming decade. This is hardly the image the Administration wants to convey when it seeks Senate approval for a new accord.

While supporters of SALT may be making a mistake by emphasizing the dire consequences of not achieving a new accord, critics appear to be promoting a reverse fallacy—pretending that it is SALT, and SALT alone, that will be responsible for the emergence of the various strategic problems described above. As we have seen, the shifting overall balance as well as the more specific problem of Minuteman vulnerability are not really the products of arms control negotiations. Instead, they are the results of earlier Soviet and American weapons procurement decisions that have been inevitably reflected in the outcome of negotiations.

In spite of this, the impact of the new agreement will be debated in terms of cause and effect, in part, because of the Carter Administration's earlier hopes for what SALT could accomplish. In seeking substantial reductions and qualitative controls on strategic forces last year, the Administration raised expectations for SALT beyond what the talks are probably capable of accomplishing. Raising expectations is not an unfamiliar characteristic of the Carter Administration's general approach to foreign policy, but the problem, this time, is that many members of the Senate seem inclined to take the White House at its word. Thus, in its haste to practice "real" arms control, the Administration, in a bold initiative last year, sought to solve most of the outstanding strategic problems confronting the United States through the vehicle of SALT. Whether the initiative was hopelessly naïve, as some argue, or merely premature, as the Administration contends, is really unimportant. For the agreement that has finally emerged from the talks accomplishes little the Administration originally set out to do.

This does not mean, however, that the SALT agreement now nearing completion must be judged as a failure. Compared with the Vladivostok guidelines, it appears superior in several respects: it provides for lower overall launcher numbers, it limits Soviet MIRVed ICBMs, and it permits the deployment of American ALCMs aboard bombers. But judged in terms of the Administration's March 1977 proposal, it is likely to be viewed by many as inadequate: it has not placed a really restrictive ceiling on Soviet ICBMs, and in particular, it has not cut into the Soviet advantage in heavy missiles. Even without the legacy of the March proposal, the new agreement would still be controversial. But having asked SALT to do too much, the Carter Administration now runs the risk of having its modest accomplishment characterized as an embarrassing failure. An agreement, in other words, that should be understood as an accommodation to reality is now widely perceived as an accommodation to the Soviet Union.

The Administration's problems, of course, have been compounded by other actions that have added to its image as being naïve both in the talks and in its wider dealings with Moscow. The decision to cancel the B-1, for example, suggested that the Administration was not only insensitive to how such budgetary decisions affect American negotiating leverage at the talks, but that it viewed the negotiations as an end in themselves rather than as an instrument of American security policy. Other actions, such as deferral of the so-called neutron bomb, while not directly related to the talks, have only served to reinforce the image of an Administration uncertain over how to respond to the growth of Soviet military power. Finally, Soviet military involvement in Africa has served to deepen skepticism on Capitol Hill and elsewhere over Moscow's motives and the prospects for a cooperative superpower relationship.

Under the circumstances, arguments that were unheard of during the 1972 SALT debate have begun to surface—the suggestion, for example, that only by defeating a new agreement might the United States be alerted to the changing strategic balance and might the Soviet Union recognize the risks it is undertaking in continuing its massive buildup and becoming involved in foreign adventures far from its shores. As these arguments gain currency, it becomes more difficult for the Administration to argue, as it has already begun to do, that failure to ratify a new agreement will come as a profound shock to Soviet-American relations, which could lead to new superpower tensions and increased defense spending. For many, the emergence of a clear disparity in strategic capabilities over the next decade is a much more troubling vision than the traumatic failure of SALT. At least one-third of the Senate membership, in the final analysis, may decide that no SALT agreement is preferable to what they believe is a bad one.

VIII

There is, of course, little the Administration can do to the agreement itself to make it more acceptable to critics. But in order to achieve Senate approval, the Administration will have to consider committing itself to a variety of measures to build congressional confidence in U.S. security under a new SALT regime. The Senate is sure to request assurances concerning the ability to monitor the agreement. And, on the controversial protocol, the Administration would be wise to promise that any extension would only take place following Senate debate and approval.

More importantly, the price of Senate approval is also likely to include an accelerated program of strategic modernization, including upgrading of the Minuteman III missile, a speedup of Trident submarine and ALCM procurement, and perhaps even a second look at the B-1. Because of the sensitivity of the Minuteman vulnerability issue, the Administration might particularly defuse concerns over a new agreement by making a commitment to a new mobile ICBM. Many of these improvements, ironically, are steps that the Administration earlier hoped that a new agreement would make unnecessary. However, a commitment by the Administration to boost defense spending and accelerate new strategic programs is probably a political necessity to gain approval for the accord. It will force the Administration to recognize the close interconnection between the arms talks and the defense policy process.

A commitment by the Administration to ensure that the strategic balance is not allowed to change dramatically over the coming decade may well provide the margin that the White House will need in winning congressional support for its policies at SALT. But an acceleration of the American defense effort will not solve a different class of problems posed by the new accord, problems that may not figure significantly in the Senate's review of SALT but which could have a profound impact on superpower arms control.

As the cruise missile issue has made abundantly clear, the ability of the two superpowers to continue to discuss their own strategic relationship at SALT without reference to the possible impact that agreements could have on the security of their allies is rapidly declining. New classes of highly flexible weapons—possessing both strategic and tactical attributes—have made it no longer possible for Washington and Moscow to "compartmentalize" their strategic relationship at SALT. Thus, it is no accident that the major stumbling blocks to agreement following the Vladivostok summit were weapons, like the cruise missile or the Soviet Backfire bomber, that did not easily fit into the categories erected by strategic thinkers a decade ago. These were weapons that seemed to affect primarily theater military balances—in Europe or in Asia—but their ability to also perform strategic missions placed a high premium on including them in SALT.

The Carter Administration has finessed the cruise missile problem by constructing the three-year protocol. But this is not a solution to the dilemma; it simply puts off the matter while some means is sought to find a formula for reconciling Soviet, American, and West European interests reflected in the cruise missile issue. This will not be an easy task.

A more permanent arms control solution to the cruise missile problem will require both superpowers to begin addressing not only the strategic balance, but the wider NATO-Warsaw pact nuclear balance. Whether cruise missiles, the Backfire, the new Soviet SS-20, and the British and French nuclear forces should be introduced into SALT or made the subject of yet another arms control forum is a question that has only begun to be asked. But an answer will be necessary before the end of the decade. Thus, both the Administration and critics of the proposed agreement should ensure that the coming debate does not merely focus on its details and possible military impact. If the SALT process itself is not put under scrutiny, superpower arms control may not survive beyond the protocol.

5
Détente under Soviet Eyes

Adam B. Ulam

"What is the answer. . . . What is the question?" It would be well if these immortal words of Gertrude Stein were pondered by every politican, editorial writer, and public-minded citizen who turns his mind to the excruciating dilemmas of U.S. foreign policy in this election year. In fact, much of the trouble we have had in dealing with the Soviet Union during the last 30 years has resulted from our propensity, and here I speak of our statesmen as well as public opinion, to explode with answers before formulating the question.

What precisely has been the nature of the Soviet, or, as it is sometimes put, Communist challenge, to counter which we have constructed a network of worldwide alliances, spent billions upon billions of dollars, and expended thousands of American lives in areas far away from the Soviet Union as well as the United States? Some of the answers—policies we adopted—turned out to be highly beneficial, e.g., the Marshall Plan; some, like the massive intervention in Vietnam, disastrous. But in both cases we failed to ask the real question: How would the given policy offset the challenge posed by the Soviet Union and/or Communism? What passed for analysis was, most often, rhetoric: Communism, declared President Truman in enunciating the doctrine which bears his name, spreads in "the evil soil of poverty and strife." The Russians, it was asserted in the 1950s, respected only strength. In the 1960s we set out to demonstrate that "wars of liberations" don't pay. At times we rushed into conclusions about the Soviets' intentions and capacities which not only expert knowledge but sheer common sense should have pronounced as unreasonable. In the late 1940s and early 1950s it was widely believed that it was only the American monopoly and

Reprinted by permission from *Foreign Policy*, Fall 1976. Copyright 1976 by National Affairs, Inc. Edited by the author for this edition.

overwhelming superiority in nuclear weapons that kept the Red Army from racing to the English Channel. Hardly anyone asked whether the Soviet Union, which had lost 20 million people in World War II and which was trying to rebuild its shattered economy, could have even considered the possibility of an armed conflict with the power which produced close to half of the industrial production of the world. And, paradoxically, in the late 1960s and early 1970s, many in the West became firmly convinced that the now infinitely stronger Soviet Union was now no longer a threat. Burgeoning Soviet "consumerism" and "troubles with China" were bound to make the Kremlin behave, even with the United States torn by the reverberations of Vietnam and Western Europe still disunited.

And so with détente. Without trying to understand what it has actually meant in terms of Soviet policies, some in this country have already condemned it as a euphemism for appeasement, while others cling to it as "the only alternative" to a cold, if not indeed hot, war. In the rhetoric of the primaries, détente has been blamed for the Cuban intervention in Angola and that country's subsequent fate. The Soviets' unpleasant practices with their dissidents and Jews violate the spirit of détente and of corollaries such as the famous "third basket" of the Helsinki accords. Contrariwise, many who are by no means pro-Soviet protest that our policies fail to adhere to the new spirit of U.S.-Soviet relations.

Such claims on behalf of and against détente must arouse a great deal of amusement, but also a certain impatience, within the Kremlin. Détente, Brezhnev and his colleagues must feel, has never been presented by them as implying that the Soviet Union would refrain from extending its influence wherever it was safe and profitable for it to do so, still less that the Soviet internal system should be changed to reflect the wishes of the editorial board of the *New York Times,* the AFL-CIO, or various senators.

Détente in the Soviet view has meant a new type of *relationship* with the United States, but this relationship does not *automatically* put the Soviet Union under an obligation to pursue policies Americans would approve. Détente was never assumed by Moscow to mean a specific agreement or a series of agreements, not to mention an alliance. It was meant to provide a framework within which the two powers could seek agreement, an atmosphere conducive to political bargaining free from threats of war enabling both sides (the Russians obviously hoped primarily themselves) to gauge more accurately each other's interests and intentions. But the mere existence of détente does not, the Russians feel, put any restraints on their policies, even though they are pleased when the State Department feels it does put restraints on America's.

But that is precisely what he has suspected, an irate American critic of détente would exclaim. At best, this wretched French word stands for a meaningless charade of state visits and summit meetings, at worst it is a cover-up, allowing the Russians to go on doing what they damn well please, while we, fearful of damaging that precious détente, let ourselves be bamboozled. But a brief look at the postwar history of U.S.-Soviet relations will suggest that détente does not have to be a one-way street, and if it continues to be so, we will have no one but ourselves to blame.

The Dark Age of the Cold War

The dark age of the cold war is explained by the revisionist historians as being caused by America's imperialist strivings which led the Kremlin to become justifiably apprehensive and, not quite so justifiably, repressive in Eastern Europe and at home. What might be called the orthodox school sees the source of the Soviet policies of that period in Stalin's admittedly unpleasant and overly suspicious personality. But while the first thesis is absurd, the second is based on an oversimplification. Whoever ruled the Soviet Union in those days would have had to feel, as Stalin did, that America's vast strength and Russia's relative weakness made it imperative for the latter to assume the posture of ominous isolation. A more affable Soviet Union would have been pressured and conceivably compelled by the United States to modify its policies in Germany and Eastern Europe. In contrast, Moscow's harsh rhetoric and its uncompromising attitudes on practically all issues of international life persuaded the West's leaders that any attempt to tamper with the Soviet Union's sphere of interest risked war. In fact, they breathed with relief when the Soviet blockade of West Berlin was not extended to its air approaches and when American intervention in the Korean conflict did not lead to a Soviet countermove. It was widely (and falsely) believed that the Soviet army had hardly been reduced from its wartime strength, and that since the Russians apparently did not realize the vast destructiveness of the atom bomb—witness Stalin's nonchalant attitude on the subject—it might not be a deterrent to their unleashing millions of soldiers westward.

The cold war, then, represented a virtual cessation of diplomatic intercourse between the two superpowers. Nor would Stalin's basic premises allow any other form of close relationship with the West. How could the Soviet Union have afforded the kind of contacts which would have been necessitated by her association in the Marshall Plan? Even today in Brezhnev's Russia, much more powerful and prosperous and much less repressive than Stalin's, such contacts are still a major source of worry for the regime.

Granting the essential soundness of Stalin's basic premises, his technique of dealing with the United States still was, his successors were to feel, unduly risky and, in certain cases, counterproductive. They lacked his self-assurance and skill in brinkmanship that for several years masked Russia's real debility and persuaded the Western powers that they were much weaker vis-à-vis the Soviet Union than, in fact, they were. In addition, the menacing appearance of the Soviet Union prior to 1953 occasionally frightened the West into the kind of policies Moscow had hoped to prevent, such as the creation of NATO and the series of moves which culminated, after Stalin's death, in the decision to rearm the German Federal Republic. Also, the virtual absence of meaningful negotiations between 1946 and 1953, on occasion, cost the Soviet Union very dearly. It did not require much imagination for Stalin's heirs to realize that Communist China was bound to become their number one problem. And it is just conceivable that had the United States and the Soviet Union agreed prior to 1948 that Mao's realm should be confined to Northeast China, the Chinese Communists would have had to adhere to that decision and would today be docile allies of the Soviets.

With the sorcerer gone, his disciples would try for the next 20 years to dismantle or to domesticate the monstrous apparitions he had conjured, but that they no longer were confident they could control. They would proceed to reduce the intolerable level of tension with the West, attempt first to appease Mao's China and then to prevent her from becoming a nuclear power, and offer concessions and greater autonomy to their satellites in Eastern Europe.

The Soviet Search for Détente

The Soviet search for détente may be said to have begun with the August 8, 1953, speech of Malenkov. Along with other declarations designed to lessen world tensions, the Soviet premier abandoned the tone of bristly hostility which had so often characterized Stalin's and Molotov's references to the United States. Instead he said, "We stand, as we have always stood, for the peaceful coexistence of the two systems." And Malenkov amazed as well as heartened public opinion throughout the world by allowing that a nuclear conflict would result in *universal* destruction, rather than, as the Communist spokesman had hitherto insisted (even when their own stock of nuclear weapons had been puny when compared with that of the United States—as in fact it still was), in the doom of capitalism alone. In fact, the relief felt in the West because of this admission of the Soviet leader must have been judged to be excessive by his colleagues. Future Soviet statements would return to the old refrain that terrible as a new war would be, it would signal the end of capitalism and the worldwide triumph of Communism.

This story neatly illustrates the difficulty the Soviets have had in reversing the Stalinist pattern of diplomacy and entering upon meaningful negotiations with the West. The image of the Soviet Union as ruled by people who, unaware of or underestimating the power of the new weapons, might plunge the world into the unthinkable calamity of a nuclear war was still, in the Kremlin's view, an important psychological asset in dealing with the West. The tragicomedy of West-East relations between 1953 and the late 1960s lay in the fact that while seeking an understanding with the West, the Soviets did not wish to have their fears and aspirations understood too well by their antagonists. Unlike the situation before 1953, the Soviet Union now sought negotiations and a dialogue with the United States; in fact, Krushchev's penchant for summitry verged on an obsession. At the same time, once in a conference room, the Soviet negotiators were almost invariably incapable of formulating concrete proposals, since to do so would have meant to reveal their fears and hence the weakness of their position.

One of the main goals of Soviet foreign policy during the Khrushchev era was to prevent both Bonn and Peking from developing and possessing nuclear weapons. It is quite conceivable that had this objective been stated plainly, the United States and the Soviet Union could have reached a nonproliferation agreement sometime in the 1950s, with Washington undertaking to exact nuclear self-denial from Bonn and Moscow promising to the same thing vis-à-vis Peking. (How effective the Soviets would have been in extracting such a pledge from the Chinese is another matter, but as late as 1959 Chou En-lai still endorsed Khrushchev's slogan of making "The whole Pacific Ocean area . . . a zone free of atomic weapons.") But to spell out such proposals the Soviets believed, would have put them at a fatal disadvantage at the conference table. The United States might feel inclined to bargain the nuclear-free Free Republic against an alteration in the status of East Germany. Any public admission as to the actual condition of the "unshakable unity of the Soviet and Chinese peoples" would have had a dire effect on the Soviet standing throughout the world and would have led to a break with China even more drastic than the one which eventually took place, without necessarily securing an agreement with the United States.

The whole poignancy of the futile charade which characterized U.S.-Soviet relations for so long is well epitomized in the story President Eisenhower related about his talk with the Soviet leader during his visit to Washington in 1959. Khrushchev asked him if he wanted to discuss China. "I answered that I thought there was little use to do so, for the

simple reason that Red China had put herself beyond the pale insofar as
the United States was concerned. He took my refusal in good part.... He
did add . . . that allegations of differences between the Soviets and Red
China . . . were ridiculous by their very nature. He and Mao were good
friends; the two nations would always stand together in any
international dispute."[1]

The fatal flaw of Khrushchev's search for détente was his inability to
tell his American interlocutors what he really wanted and thus to
persuade them that it was in their own interest as well. Instead, he
embarked on a sinuous and dangerous method of accomplishing his
purpose, through threats and *faits accomplis*. It is clear that the Berlin
crisis was but a lever with which he hoped to pry out a Western
agreement to a German peace treaty, with its essential provision being a
ban on nuclear armament for West Germany. And most likely those
Soviet missiles in Cuba were to be used as a bargaining chip. Had the
United States agreed to a German treaty, and perhaps also a nuclear arms
free zone in the Pacific, the missiles would have been withdrawn. But he
was not only oversubtle but unlucky in what his successors were to
characterize as "harebrained schemes." The nuclear test ban agreement
was but a small residue of that many-sided accommodation with the
United States into which Khrushchev had hoped to scare the
Americans.[2]

Washington's Folly

The Brezhnev-Kosygin team did not have to resort to Khrushchev's
dangerous improvisations. Washington's folly handed it a most
valuable bargaining asset: Vietnam. Few now recall this, but the fact is
that the main rationale for our original decision to intervene massively
in Vietnam was to stop the alleged expansionist tendencies of *Chinese*
Communism. The Soviets, some members of the Johnson administration evidently hoped, would see our intervention as directed against
Peking and possibly help us out of any predicament in Southeast Asia.

The Chinese Communists had from the beginning a truer perception
of the role the Vietnamese war played in Moscow's calculations, even if
they formulated it with some exaggeration. The Russians, thundered
the *Peking Review* on November 12, 1965, "in giving a certain amount
of aid to North Vietnam are trying to keep the situation under their
control in order to gain a say on the North Vietnam question and to
strike a bargain with U.S. imperialism. . . ." Of course, it is hard to gauge
how far the Soviet Union could or would have pressured Hanoi to call
off the civil war in the south had "U.S. imperialism" approached the
Soviet Union with some quid pro quo, say a German peace treaty in 1964

or 1965. But afterward it would have been not only indecorous but illogical for the Soviets to help America; the U.S. overcommitment and failure in Southeast Asia was working in their favor, enabling the Soviet Union to realize some of its most cherished postwar policy goals. North Vietnam, from having been a Chinese preserve, now became dependent on the Soviet Union. Some of the things for which the Soviets would have bargained a few years before now fell in their lap, e.g., West Germany's renunciation of nuclear arms through her signing the nonproliferation agreement and the legitimization of Communist rule in East Germany and of Poland's western frontier under Chancellor Brandt's Ostpolitik. America's European allies, largely as a result of Vietnam, now sought an accommodation with the Soviet Union with such, from the Kremlin's viewpoint, profitable by-products as increased trade and credits, as well as the general loosening of their ties with Washington.

But this pleasant state of affairs could not continue indefinitely. By 1971-1972, the Soviets realized that they had already drawn their maximum benefit out of the Vietnamese conflict and America's general discomfiture in world affairs. Not to seek a détente now risked the possibility that the United States would draw much closer to Communist China. The primary cause and purpose of détente (apart, of course, from minimizing the possibility of a nuclear conflict) was for the Kremlin to prevent a too close rapprochement between Washington and Peking. The value and actual meaning of détente oscillates in the Soviet's eyes not only according to what the West can do and is doing for them, but also according to what it might do for Communist China. If, as at present, China is experiencing political turbulence, which judging by the tenor of the speeches at the Twenty-Fifth Party Congress the Soviet leaders consider more serious than we do, they feel much less inhibited about seizing new opportunities, be it in Angola or anywhere else. By the same token, a united leadership in Peking actively seeking American technological and economic help would have a near magical effect in making the Soviet Union observe what is called in the West the "spirit of détente."

The other dimension of Soviet decision making is, of course, their appraisal of the strength, purposefulness, and alertness of the other side. The reasons, as North Vietnam's General Dung has recently spelled out with admirable candor, that were decisive in North Vietnam's decision to launch a drive in the south in 1975 were undoubtedly similar to those which persuaded the politburo to authorize the Cubans' descent on Angola: "The internal contradictions within the U.S. administration and among U.S. political parties had intensified. The Watergate scandal had seriously affected the entire United States. . . . [It] faced economic recession, mounting inflation, serious unemployment, and an oil crisis."[3] It is probably genuinely incomprehensible to Brezhnev and his colleagues that anyone can seriously believe that in 1976 détente places them under the same obligations it did in 1972. Then the Soviets had undoubtedly used their good offices to clear the path to the Paris agreement of 1973. But three years later, as a Philippine Communist indiscreetly blurted out at the Twenty-Fifth Party Congress, "The confrontation of socialism with imperialism in Indochina has demonstrated that with the help of the Soviet Union, one can achieve national liberation without threatening either world peace or détente.

This dialectical view of détente clashes with the usual American interpretation: a series of specific agreements on the one hand, and an undertaking by both superpowers to act responsibly, i.e., not to try to change the balance of power through unilateral action, on the other. But, the balance of power *has* changed to America's disadvantage, and the Russians are not to blame for the vagaries of American domestic politics and the disunity of the West on such issues as the oil crisis and the Third World.

Brezhnev's View

Were Brezhnev to formulate candidly his rationale for détente, it would probably run something like this: "Détente is a process rather than a specific agreement, or sets of agreements. It enables the two superpowers, through increased contacts and more amicable discourse, to avoid the dangers inherent in the previous era when both of them would resort occasionally to drastic measures, without any possibility of gauging whether they would trigger off a violent reaction on the other side, e.g., the Soviet Union sending missiles to Cuba and the United States initiating the bombing of North Vietnam. The actual nature of this process depends entirely on the circumstances. If, as it is likely, the West continues to decline in strength and cohesion, détente will enable the Soviet Union to keep this decline from being accompanied by violent convulsions which might set off a nuclear conflict. If the West recovers from its faltering course and there is a new spirit of realism and resolution in U.S. policies, then under the umbrella of détente we can strike some mutually profitable deals. To resume the old way of dealing with the United States, i.e., to try to outshout and outscare the Americans, would profit no one but Peking."

In reviewing the course of détente to date, the Soviet leaders are unlikely to feel that they have in any sense tricked the Americans. On the contrary, like most politicians, they tend to credit themselves with a great sense of generosity. If at times they've enjoyed an upper hand, this has been due to certain peculiarities of the American political system, and hence Washington's frequent inability to bargain realistically. It is clearly unreasonable, though understandable, that the United States displays so much interest in the treatment of dissidents and Jews (especially) in the Soviet Union. The Kremlin undoubtedly considers that it has catered to this rather childish preoccupation of American policymakers to an extent unimaginable under Khrushchev, not to mention Stalin. But while the whole subject must be quite painful emotionally to the Soviets, with their intense nationalism and their usual lack of introspection, since they feel that they have been subjected to foreign interference in their internal affairs, there is, on the other hand, probably a certain amount of relief. The Americans' preoccupation with this subject keeps them from being more tenacious about things which really matter: armaments, the terms of trade, the games the Soviets play in Africa and elsewhere.

SALT

Strategic arms limitation has been considered by the United States as the very keystone of détente. This in itself made sure, quite apart from the awesome intricacy of the problem, that the negotiations over SALT I and SALT II would be long-drawn, with the Soviets constantly airing new demands and creating new complications. If the other side wants something badly, it is obviously advisable to appear *almost* intractable on this subject, thus increasing the probability that it will seek to mollify you on another, to you perhaps more important, issue. Witness Stalin's obduracy over procedural problems and membership in the United Nations in 1944-1945. Very early in the first SALT talks, the Russians wanted to bring in the problem of China.[4] In fact, since their primary objective—virtual nuclear parity with the United States—has been achieved, the Soviets must feel as eager as anyone else to prevent a further arms race.

Increased trade with the West, and with the United States in particular, probably ranks as high as nuclear arms control on the list of benefits the Soviets hope to derive from détente. This at first may appear surprising, since even with the heavy sale of grain in 1973, imports from the United States constituted but a tiny proportion of the Soviet gross national product, and so they still would if this trade tripled or quadrupled. But the Soviets don't see the problem as a strictly quantitative one. The dream of mastering the most advanced industrial techniques by importing them from the leading capitalist country has been with them since Lenin's time. Perhaps they have an exaggerated estimate of America's economic achievements as compared with those of

West Germany or Japan, but then they are what might be called technological snobs. Unwilling, or unable, to effect major structural changes in their own economy, they believe that even a quantitatively small infusion of technology from the United States would work miracles, especially with consumer goods. The regime, determined to preserve the full rigor of the police state and not to permit even such modest departures as occurred under Khrushchev, feels that it can maintain this policy without undue risk only if it continues to improve the lot of the Soviet consumer.

The secondary reason for the emphasis on trade lies in the Soviet conviction that détente thereby gains an important ally in American businessmen, the class they believe still most influential in determining policies of the republic. And, perhaps, the reaction of American farmers to a recent temporary suspension of grain sales to Russia does demonstrate that "leverage" can work both ways.

Does détente have enemies within the Soviet establishment? We simply have no evidence to answer precisely. Usually we learn about a Soviet leader's dissenting views (and at that not always truthfully) only after he has been fired, and that is why it is unreasonable to assign this or that position to the "military," Suslov, etc. At times, the Soviets privately encouraged such games, saying, in effect, "hurry up and sign with us, or the hard-liners will take over" or sponsoring rumors that Shelest or Shelepin were dismissed because they were enemies of détente.

It is reasonable to assume that various aspects of détente do lead to disputes within the politburo; for example, should the Soviet Union declare *publicly* its readiness to allow a specified number of Jews to migrate? Some will fear that perhaps the Soviet Union still might not get extensive credit, and the next thing the Americans might demand is the establishment of a two-party system. The Soviets have always been fearful of ideological pollution from abroad, somewhat paranoid about contacts and ties with foreigners, and apprehensive about any type of association, whether for themselves or their protégés, with people of a different creed. In fact, this phenomenon goes back to the grand duchy of Moscow. It is thus idle to ask whether they are enthusiastic or fearful about the prospect of the Italian Communists coming to power. They are both. And so it is natural that there should be people in high position who fear that the new relationship which détente implies is full of uncertainties and dangers, that when no longer in a posture of menacing hostility vis-à-vis the West, the Soviet Union will no longer inspire the same fear and respect among its satellites and clients. Some of the latter might attempt to play off one superpower against the other, as occurred with Egypt. Even mere rhetoric, such as the Helsinki declaration about human rights, is likely to have a demoralizing effect on the domestic front. And for all the insistence that détente does not mean the end of class struggle, friendlier relations with the West, even when limited in scale, have always led to the lowering of ideological vigilance and to Soviet society being exposed to some of the ailments of the capitalist world.

But such voices must be in a decided minority. Nothing indicates that the concept of détente as sketched above is a serious bone of contention among the 20 or so people who rule the Soviet Union.

*   *   *

Notes

1. Dwight D. Eisenhower, *Waging Peace, 1956-1961* (New York: Doubleday, 1965), p. 445.

2. This hypothesis is developed in my *Extension and Coexistence*, 2d ed. (New York: Praeger, 1974), pp. 620-621 and pp. 661-667.

3. The *New York Times*, April 26, 1976.

4. "The Soviets, in effect, were proposing no less than a superpower alliance against other nuclear powers." John Newhouse, *Cold Dawn: The Story of SALT* (New York: Holt, Rinehart & Winston, 1973), p. 189.

6
The "Theology" of Strategy*

Henry Trofimenko

It would not be an exaggeration to say that, with the perfection of nuclear weapons and the steady growth in the number of countries and experts involved in elaborating a theory of using those weapons, nuclear strategy, as expounded by many of its Western proponents and mere admirers, is becoming a sort of religious cult. Like any cult, it has acquired its rites and Holy Apostles, not to mention numerous disciples who recite the atomic catechism day and night. But, what is most important, it has developed its own articles of faith, created in large part by Western (above all, American) experts. I mean here dogmas and canons, not realistic concepts and theories, because much in today's "strategic theology," as it is being preached in the West, is based not on facts or experience but on faith.

If one believes in the original immorality of the Russian strategic school and in the high moral pathos of nuclear retaliation, then one is a true follower of the new faith. But if one questions this indisputable proposition, then one is worse than a heretic or apostate, not worthy of ascending even to the porch of the Holy Temple of Strategic Analysis where the initiated perform rites of passage—from the humility of deterrence to the pugnacity of counterforce capability. The occasionally sagging enthusiasm of the congregation is bolstered by the Pentagon's frequent revelations, which steadfastly serve to preserve the dogmas, set once and for all, in their original purity.

Reprinted by permission from *ORBIS*, fall 1977. Copyright 1977 by the Foreign Policy Research Institute.

* I borrowed this expression from James Schlesinger who, during his tenure as secretary of defense, once remarked: "Despite all the nuclear calculations and theology, we cannot forget geopolitics as the world becomes truly interdependent." *(Report of the Secretary of Defense James R. Schlesinger to the Congress on the FY 1976 and Transition Budgets, FY 1977 Authorization Request and FY 1976-1980 Defense Programs, February 5, 1975* [Washington: GPO, 1975], p. 111-116.)

When strategic theology originated in the West some thirty years ago, its primordial tenet was the omnipotence of the atomic bomb, by means of which any military or political problem could be quickly and successfully solved. To realize this solution, one needed only to leapfrog the front lines with aircraft (later, missiles) and to inflict unbearable suffering on the civilian population and leadership of the enemy, which would then inevitably surrender. Tested in Hiroshima and Nagasaki, this became the main tenet of American strategic theology and remained so until it turned out that the "potential adversary" could also leapfrog the ring of American military bases surrounding it, inflicting unacceptable damage on the continental United States.

Thereafter, the precept of "massive retaliation" as a universal method of strategic action was shelved, having failed to meet the national interests of the United States. At the same time, doubts surfaced in regard to the presumption that any solution, any action, is permissible for the United States in the world arena: "We must face the fact that the United States is neither omnipotent nor omniscient" and that "we cannot impose our will on the other ninety-four percent of mankind,"[1] acknowledged President Kennedy. But it took much more time and the lesson of Vietnam for Kennedy's conclusion to begin to be shared by broader segments of the American establishment.

Massive bombing of the enemy population having collapsed as a dogma, some other concept was needed to revive faith in the invincibility of the United States. The required new tenet of strategic theology was found in the notion of the "disarming first-strike" as a method of winning wars. This notion appeared in the early 1960s, when the United States began producing strategic weapons on a tremendous scale: in the five years from 1960 to 1965, the United States inceased the number of its land-based ICBMs forty-six-fold and its submarine-launched ballistic missiles fifteen-fold.[2] According to the new dogma, by delivering a first-strike against the Soviet Union, the United States (owing to its superiority in the number of delivery vehicles) could reduce the potential Soviet counterstrike to such an extent that losses would be acceptable to the United States, which could thereby "win the war."

I will not now discuss whether or not the United States actually intended to strike against the USSR, but it can be said with confidence that the dogma of the disarming first-strike served at least two aims: (1) to compel the Soviet Union to devote serious attention to protecting its strategic offensive systems, i.e., to divert a part of its resources for this purpose, and (2) to create for the United States a psychological "position of strength" that could be used in diplomatic bargaining to impose American solutions.

Two things became clear to American strategists in the early

1970s: (1) Theoretically, the ability to deliver a disarming strike could not be regarded as an American monopoly. (2) The concept of a disarming first-strike was untenable in view of a) the extensive deployment, both by the United States and the Soviet Union, of retaliatory forces—i.e., submarine-launched ballistic missiles—and b) the many uncertainties undermining the strategists' and—even more so—the American political leadership's confidence in such a strike's effectiveness. Moreover, despite current attempts to scare the American public with the "development by the Soviet Union of a disarming first strike capability against the United States," the most authoritative American experts emphasize that neither side can attain such capability, since each possesses a large, virtually invulnerable offensive strategic force.[3]

The collapse of the dogma of a possible disarming first-strike led to the inception of the so-called Schlesinger Doctrine—which postulated the possibility of limited strategic strikes against individual military targets, allegedly causing but minimal losses among the civilian population.[4] Let us parenthetically note that American strategic thinking has come full circle, returning from the concept of war as something waged by the specialized military complex of one side against the population of the other side to the concept of war as a confrontation between the specialized complexes of both sides—that is, counterforce war!

It is this latest revision of the tenets of American strategic theology that was inherited by the Carter administration, which is presently coming forward with further modifications while, at the same time, preserving elements of the Schlesinger approach. To sum up, then, throughout the entire post–World War II period, it is the United States that has tried to impose on the "potential adversary" rules of the game (i.e., rules of conflict behavior) which would maximize the one-sided technical advantage enjoyed by the United States at any given moment and minimize the capabilities of the adversary. That is what the entire American doctrinal progress boils down to.

In response to the objection that my conclusion is far-fetched, I add that the United States could switch from one kind of strategic targeting to another without making it general knowledge because, to this day, only a very small circle of the country's top leaders knows how the American missiles are really targeted. Thus, during McNamara's tenure as secretary of defense, U.S. strategic forces were targeted quite differently from the way McNamara publicly claimed they were. This was admitted by Secretary Schlesinger, who stated: "A targeting doctrine which stresses going only against cities is not an adequate deterrent for most purposes. . . . In fact, this is not the way the [U.S.]

forces were targeted, but the overt public doctrine stressed only going against cities."[5]

From this admission it clearly follows that the so-called U.S. strategies publicly proclaimed in the period since the Second World War were intended primarily to exert psychological pressure on the other side. It follows further that there exists at all times a discrepancy between the officially proclaimed and the genuine strategies of the United States. Finally (and this is of paramount importance), recurrent changes in the rules of the game publicly offered by the Pentagon, in step with changes in the quantitative and qualitative characteristics of American strategic weaponry, confirm beyond all doubt that the United States was the instigator of the strategic arms race. It strove to squeeze a maximum conceptual gain from the lead it enjoyed (in order to maintain a "position of strength" and psychological pressure on the potential adversary) before the other side acquired a corresponding military-technical capability.

In its desire to maintain the "position of strength," the Pentagon often hurried to raise to the category of "strategies"—that is, to conceptualize—not only the new military and technical capabilities already on hand, but also those that were to come with the implementation of various modernization plans (e.g., the drastic increase in ballistic-missile accuracy and, in the late 1960s, the plans for developing a national ABM network). The moment some new technical idea is glimpsed at the Defense Department's Office of Defense Research and Engineering, the "whiz-kids" instantly elevate it to a "doctrine" or a "strategy" and, without any hesitation, start to threaten the other side with a newly acquired American edge.

II

That the United States is the generator of the arms race is also corroborated, paradoxical though it may seem, by the so-called gaps between U.S. and Soviet forces, over which Pentagon spokesmen raise a clamor with nagging regularity. For example, there was much noise in the mid-1950s about the alleged U.S.-Soviet "bomber gap." That campaign enabled the Pentagon to secure a new, accelerated bomber-construction program; soon thereafter, it was admitted that no such gap had ever existed.

A self-serving campaign was likewise whipped up in 1960 over the "missile gap."[6] Later it turned out that the Soviet "missile threat" was exaggerated fifteen- or twenty-fold. As the Americans themselves have revealed, the Soviet Union reached parity with the United States in the sum total of land-based and sea-launched missiles only in 1970,[7] having been compelled, to perserve its own security, to counter the tremendous U.S. missile build-up.

In the late 1960s, yet another "gap" appeared—the so-called ABM gap. A tremendous fuss was raised, and again it turned out to be a Pentagon fabrication, needed to push allocations through Congress for the construction of twenty-five (Project Sentinel) and, later twelve to fourteen (Project Safeguard) ABM complexes. It was only at the signing of the 1972 U.S.-Soviet treaty on the limitation of ABM systems that Pentagon officials finally had to acknowledge to the American public that the USSR possessed only one ABM site and fewer ABM launchers than were allowed by the treaty.

The "throw-weight gap" appeared early in the 1970s. Once again, the Pentagon juggled information on the military balance to fit its own designs and requirements. As is invariably the case, it was "suddenly discovered" (in the style of the Pentagon's propaganda department) that the decisive parameter for comparing offensive strategic forces is not the number of strategic launchers, not the number of individually targetable warheads, but the so-called throw-weight of missiles.

By the Pentagon's interpretation, throw-weight turned out to be an absolutely critical factor; and, in view of the Pentagon and Senator Jackson, it is precisely by this crucial indicator that the United States is losing the race with the Soviet Union. Posing the problem in this way instantly brings forth a multitude of perplexing questions from the objective observer: If throw-weight is so critical, why has it never before figured as the prime characteristic of America's own strategic capability? Why is such a crucial indicator not even mentioned as a term by the U.S. armed forces? For it turns out that this "critically important" indicator is missing from the latest editions of the official *Dictionary of Military and Associated Terms* of the Department of Defense, a dictionary that is annually updated by the U.S. Joint Chiefs of Staff! And if throw-weight is such a supersignificant criterion, to which all the other features of a strategic missile should be subordinated, why did the United States, in 1962-1963, create the Titan II (to this day, the world throw-weight champion)[8] and then deploy only fifty-four of them, switching to Minuteman missiles which carry a much smaller payload?

Could it really be that sabotage explains this strange state of affairs?[9]

Furthermore, even if we admit the possibility of usefully comparing the strategic forces of two countries by their total throw-weight, it is logical to ask why American experts usually compare not the *total* throw-weight of the U.S. and Soviet strategic forces (as defined in the Vladivostok Accord), but only the throw-weight of the U.S. and Soviet *ICBMs.*[10]

Paul Nitze has become quite adept at this sort of comparison in recent months, and he is surely the undisputed heavyweight champion among those who throw misinformation into the pages of the press. When Mr. Nitze starts his calculations by ascribing to the B-1 strategic bomber a throw-weight of 19,000 pounds,[11] while its actual payload is 150,000 pounds,[12] all his other estimates (many of which are based on unverifiable data and must be taken at face value)[13] can only be suspected as similarly distorted.[14] This, then, is how the myth of the throw-weight gap is being created. Its frailty is revealed both by the above-cited data and by the Pentagon's inner-sanctum indifference (as opposed to its excited public posture).

III

Only recently, two more "gaps" have sprung up in the United States—the "military appropriations gap" and the "civil-defense gap."

By now established tradition, the "military appropriations gap" surfaced precisely at the time the U.S. Department of Defense decided to push for drastic increases in military-hardware appropriations. In theory, if one assumes not a political but a purely technical and economic point of view, one can understand why America's Department of Defense presently needs such a drastic increase in the military budget. It stands on the threshold of purchasing a whole series of extremely costly strategic and tactical systems—cruise missiles, Trident submarines, AWACS planes, the neutron bomb, as well as new tactical aircraft, attack submarines, and surface ships. In previous years, these systems were in the RDT&E stage, and allocations for them ran into tens of millions of dollars. Now, however, the price tag is in tens of billions. In the post-Vietnam environment, with a slump in the U.S. economy and a climate of détente, it is no simple task to substantiate the "need" for recarving the federal budget in favor of the military sector. As is well understood by the top Pentagon brass, it is much easier to push the budget through if it can be presented as a response to Soviet military measures, to a "growing Soviet threat."

Hence, although the Soviet military budget has remained stable in the 1970s (about $23 billion by the present rouble exchange rate),[15] and although military allocations as a share of the total Soviet budget and GNP are continually declining, the CIA and the Pentagon's intelligence crew have been instructed to "prove" the steady growth of Soviet military allocations against a background of constantly declining U.S. military expenditures.[16] Cooperation between the CIA and the Defense Intelligence Agency (DIA) resulted in fabricated data showing that the "real" Soviet military budget when estimated in roubles is three times greater than the official sum of 17 billion roubles, while the gap between the military budgets of the USA and the USSR expressed in dollars is even more in favor of the Soviet Union. [17]

As in the estimates made by Paul Nitze, the detailed methodology by which the above-mentioned U.S. agencies arrived at such staggering revelations remains classified, depriving me the opportunity of analyzing, in depth, the substance of the falsification. As for the general approach that enabled the American experts to multiply the Soviet military budget by three to five times, it centered on figuring out how much it would have cost the United States to maintain a military complex similar to that of the Soviet Union's.[18]

Just to show the extent of distortion involved: during hearings before his Subcommittee on Priorities and Economy in Government, Senator William Proxmire drew attention to the fact that the American F-14 fighter is estimated to be sixteen times more expensive than is the MiG-21.[19] Similar distortions exist in regard to other weapon systems.[20] Instead of criticizing the CIA and DIA experts, perhaps I really ought to thank them for ballooning the Soviet military budget by only four times and not by sixteen times: estimating the value of Soviet weapon systems according to American market prices, they could have easily done so. Incidentally, this "methodology" looks doubtful not only to Senator Proxmire but to many others in the U.S. Congress.

More than that, even Lt. Gen. Graham (who surely cannot be suspected of wanting to downgrade Soviet military spending) admitted to Congress in 1975 that "any attempt to measure the efforts of a command economy such as the USSR's in terms of the currency of a free economy such as ours is doomed to produce misleading results. I doubt that the Soviets, with full access to the data denied to us, could produce a valid dollar value of their defense efforts. . . . The absolute value figures remain suspect, and the aggregation of such figures into a total [Soviet military] budget number is highly suspect." He went on: "I think I know enough about the Soviet Union to say you cannot go that dollar route and come up with anything that makes sense."[21] General Wilson, who replaced General Graham as DIA director, turned out to be more pliant in this regard. Even he admits, however, that there are certain inconsistencies in this "methodology."[22]

Dollar estimates of the cost of the Soviet Union's military personnel— again along the lines of "what it would have cost the U.S. Treasury"— play an equally important role in doctoring Soviet military-budget figures.

What do the statisticians from the CIA and the Pentagon do when comparing the cost of American and Soviet military personnel? They calculate the size of the Soviet force by adding 1 million men to the number of American active-duty military personnel in 1974, and multiply the total by the average pay of an American serviceman. In this manner, they get a figure of about $40 billion.[23] This suited them in 1974. But in 1975 it started to look meager, so they resorted to yet another distortion. By increasing the size of the Soviet armed forces by yet another million men,[24] they arrived at the desired figure—double the amount spent by the United States on military pay!

The book *Arms, Men and Military Budgets*, which included a foreword by the tireless Paul Nitze,[25] bears witness to the fact that estimates are actually made in this admirably simple way, without any subtleties. David Mark, former deputy director for research in the Bureau of Intelligence and Research, U.S. Department of State, was even more candid about this phenomenon in 1969, when specialists from the American intelligence community were just beginning to refine their "methodology." He said: "We know that the Soviet soldier gets a very low rate of pay compared to the American GI, but in the cost calculations that go into the $60 billion figure, that is, in translating what the Soviets do into dollar terms, we would calculate the Soviet soldiers' pay at American levels, because that is the comparable figure in the U.S. economy[?!] At that rate, we build up [!] to the $60 billion result [the Soviet military budget as then appraised by the CIA]."[26]

The CIA/DIA figures on the cost of supporting Soviet military manpower are an outright fabrication! For even the average annual pay of a Soviet industrial or office worker in 1975 amounted to the equivalent of only $2,311.[27] Simply because they had to show a drastic increase in the 1975 Soviet military budget from that of the previous year, the CIA and the DIA decided to expand the Soviet armed forces in that one year by nearly 1 million men—although it was clearly stated by the USSR's defense minister, Marshal of the Soviet Union D. F. Ustinov, that "over the past few years neither the Soviet Union nor the other Warsaw Treaty member-states have increased their armed forces, and their numerical strength remained unchanged."[28]

IV

Now for the currently fashionable "civil-defense gap." Some years ago, in 1974, it became evident from U.S. publications that the Pentagon was again giving serious consideration to plans for strengthening U.S. civil defense, including preparations for mass evacuation.[29] Before 1974, toward the end of the sixties, the most zealous advocate of civil defense in the United States, physicist Eugene Wigner, was talking up the idea for the second time around.[30] Professor Wigner suggested almost paranoid plans for a grid system of reinforced-concrete tunnels under the streets of the most important U.S. cities.[31] At present, Wigner is trying to prove (and we in the USSR are reading this) that vigorous civil-defense measures will guarantee, not "assured destruction" but the "assured survival" of 95 per cent of the U.S. population and more than 50 per cent of America's industrial capacity, even if the retaliatory strike should be delivered against American cities and industry rather than against military targets.[32]

This kind of campaigning for improved civil-defense measures is not surprising. Flirting with "counterforce war" (even a limited one)—and that is precisely what the Schlesinger Doctrine is all about—inevitably requires parallel steps to "limit damage" through passive defense measures. This is so axiomatic that it hardly calls for substantiation in the pages of this journal.[33]

It can thus be said that during the past twelve to fifteen years, the U.S campaign for vigorous civil-defense measures has gone through two phases: (1) the well-known campaign of 1961, when President Kennedy urged his compatriots to build their own fallout shelters, and (2) the campaign of 1973-1975, which included accusations that the Soviets were stepping up their civil-defense measures.

I share to a certain extent the view of a number of American experts (Albert Wohlstetter, for example) who insist that the military-development programs of the United States and the USSR cannot by any means be explained entirely in the framework of an action-reaction process. Much relates to original strategic concepts peculiar to each side. Nonetheless, a degree of mutual influence, a mechanism of action-reaction, cannot be ruled out. In the case of civil defense, the Soviet Union's measures are a classic example of reaction to the United States' action.

What, may I ask, was the Soviet Union to do? Early in the 1960s, the USSR was faced with a dual U.S. challenge: the decision to drastically increase the arsenal of strategic offensive weapons—which, given the balance of forces, was tantamount to threatening a disarming first-strike[34]—and the simultaneous determination to advance a large-scale, damage-limiting program of civil defense.[35] This dual challenge was supplemented in 1967 by a third ingredient—Washington's decision to develop a national ABM system!

Naturally, when faced with such momentous challenges to its security (remember, the United States led the Soviet Union in the number of deliverable warheads by five- or four-to-one),[36] the USSR could not but take counteraction. And it is understandable that the main thrust of that counteraction was toward the creation of a retaliatory-strike capability which could not be destroyed by a first-strike.[37] Civil-defense measures had to be put off for the time being. Eventually, however, the wave of American civil-defense measures and propaganda could not be left unanswered, and steps were taken to improve the Soviet Union's civil-defense system.[38] Soviet measures, by the way, related not only to training the population for organized action during the difficult conditions of a military attack, but also to mastering procedures for coping with floods, large-scale fires, and so on. The last-mentioned procedures were necessitated by natural calamities in some parts of the country: e.g., the severe forest fires resulting from the drought of 1972. Soviet civil-defense measures, then, were a belated and very modest reaction to the intensive civil-defense effort and accompanying propaganda campaign of the United States. Yet, they are being painted by such American experts as General Keegan and Vice-President Boileau, of the Boeing Company, as "preparations for a disarming strike" against the United States.[39]

The Soviet Union does not subscribe to the "first-strike doctrine." This fact is well known and has been reaffirmed recently by General Secretary of the CPSU Central Committee L. I. Brezhnev in his important foreign policy speech in Tula on January 18, 1977. Brezhnev described as "absurd and totally unfounded" the allegation that the Soviet Union "strives for superiority in armaments with the aim of delivering a 'first strike'. . . . The Soviet Union has always been and remains a convinced opponent of such concepts."[40]

At to civil defense, this is by no means a secret Russian weapon: its methods and techniques have long been known and in no way provide the key to victory in a nuclear war. Evidently, that is precisely why the American military leadership, despite the improvement of the U.S. civil-defense system, continues to earmark the preponderant portion of its funds for weapon systems such as the M-X mobile ICBM, the strategic cruise missile, or Trident, and not for passive defense. At the same time, one cannot help but note that the Soviet Union, though well aware of the enormous civil-defense programs of the United States, has never declared these measures a threat to peace or to the security of the USSR; nor has it ever tried to portray them as an obstacle to arms limitations.

Thus it turns out that every time the American military wants to accelerate one of its programs, it cries wolf and points an accusing finger at the other side. Although the boy in the well-known story could not make the people believe him the third time, the Pentagon's warning cries continue to find a receptive audience. Today, the "missile-accuracy gap" is shaping up, and it can be predicted that the near future will produce a "deterrence-potential gap."[41] But the fact is that the Pentagon is constantly in the lead in the military-technological race, compelling the Soviet Union to respond with measures aimed at stabilizing its position of parity.

V

Yet, all these myths fostered by the Pentagon—which I have had to dwell on in such detail simply because the American press has lavished so much attention on them—do not constitute the main core of strategic theology. The latter is not restricted to these petty fictions which have been elevated to articles of faith; nor is it restricted to wagging an accusing finger at the other side. The true essence of strategic theology is manifest in the fact that *what American theoreticians are discussing is not the strategy but the tactics of war.*

It so happens that the cliches about "counterforce strategy," about "strategies" of the first- and second-strike, about the nuances of simultaneous launch or arrival of strategic missiles, are somehow divorced from the understanding that strategy—above all, Grand Strategy—is supposed to provide an answer not to the question, How? but to the question, What for? The great theoretician of strategy, von Clausewitz, defined war as "the continuation of political relations with the admixture of other means"—and this is the classical definition. It is shared in principle by any strategic theoretician worthy of the name. What is the political goal of the country confronting another country (or countries)? This is the paramount question to be answered by Grand Strategy. Then, and only then—on the second and third levels of strategic planning—should it be decided (1) whether or not to employ military force for the attainment of that goal,[42] and (2) if military force is to be employed, on what scale and in what way (i.e., tactics).

In many contemporary strategic debates, however, American theorists assume that military force can be rationally used, and all deliberations on "strategy" boil down to the question of how to employ weapons. Meanwhile, careful consideration shows that the feasibility or expediency of employing nuclear military force is by no means as predetermined as American strategists imply.

I will not dwell on the truism that military strength is not nowadays automatically translated into political power; the events relating to the 1973 oil embargo have confirmed the validity of this thesis or, to be more exact, have shown that power entails more than military strength per se. But if one subscribes to the thesis that war is a continuation of politics, then inflicting casualties cannot be an end in itself! To achieve a political goal through the use of armed force (and this is precisely what strategy is all about) is not tantamount to the killing of tens of millions of people on this or that side.

What would be the political purpose of such a war? It seems that those who write scenarios for an atomic blitzkrieg give little thought to the question. What matters to them is that they can prove that it is technically feasible to launch missiles under any circumstances, that those missiles will fly, and that a certain portion of them will break through to the target. That is all there is to their "scenarios." By raising this question, we pass from the sphere of strategic theology (which does not apply itself to such "philosophical" problems but simply postulates that killing a certain number of people, or preserving a certain advantage over the other side in throw-weight or "equivalent weapons" after a nuclear exchange, signifies victory) to the sphere of true strategy—indeed, to the sphere of geopolitics—where one has to think, above all, of the political consequences of a nuclear exchange for each nation in the "multipolar world."

I envisage objections to the effect that American strategists *do* think about this, which is precisely why they are advancing the concept of "limited nuclear war" as an "optimal method of warfare" under modern conditions. But let us, first of all, clarify what "an exchange of limited strategic strikes" may mean in today's world. In various speculative exercises of the Pentagon experts (here, again, we are in the sphere of theology),[43] it is contended that under certain circumstances the Soviet Union might limit itself to strike only against selected military targets in the United States (e.g., only bomber bases). What for?, one feels bound to ask. How can one ascribe to the Soviet Union the belief that it is possible to deliver a nuclear strike against several bases in the United States and get off cheap with only a limited retaliatory strike? Moreover, what would be proved by such a trial of strength, regardless of which side might resort to it? Such hypothetical speculations are sheer mental calisthenics. They are not strategy—given, of course, that military strategy and war are a continuation of policy and not vice versa.

Now for the other version of the strategy (read: tactics) of limited exchange—a strike against all military targets of the other side, destroying them and thereby disarming the enemy and "winning" the war.[44] The Pentagon has estimated that such a disarming strike would require the launch of more than 2,000 warheads against the enemy targets.[45] Tell me, who, with the exception of God himself, in the few minutes available, could determine that this vast number of warheads already in mid-flight is a "limited" counterforce rather than an all-out countervalue attack and, accordingly, give the command for an appropriate limited retaliation? That this is humanly possible is beyond belief. It is quite significant that when Mr. Schlesinger was bluntly confronted with this problem by Senator Muskie, he could not provide a coherent answer.[46]

Once, when it was pointed out to Secretary Schlesinger that the development of a hard-target kill capability in the Trident missile system was having a destabilizing effect, he argued in reply that it was not a destabilizing move since "the Soviets could have a capability to launch their strategic force on warning of an impending attack."[47] But if that is the "alternative" for the USSR or the USA—"launch on warning" when it appears that the other side might be delivering a disarming strike—what good, then, is all the talk about a "painless," virtually bloodless (a *mere* 7 million dead!) limited nuclear exchange? In this context, one cannot but agree with the view of the present U.S. secretary of defense, Harold Brown, who stresses that "limited strategic war is almost impossible. Anyone who contemplates one is fooling himself if he thinks the chances are not overwhelming that it would become an all-out urban and industrial attack."[48]

American theorists, who of late have been making a particularly strong effort to frighten Americans with the "Soviet threat," are still treating the problem of nuclear war too lightly—I would even say irresponsibly. I am inclined to agree with Bernard Brodie, McGeorge Bundy, Henry Kissinger,[49] and other American experts who oppose conjectural mathematical computations being passed off for strategy, since national strategy—"the art and science of developing and using the political, economic, and psychological powers of a nation, together with its armed forces . . . to secure national objectives"[50]—is quite a different thing.

And this is precisely the difference between strategic theology and strategy. No matter how unpleasant this may be to those reared on the idea of the omnipotence of strength, it must be admitted that in our age truly strategic solutions cannot be achieved through military force. That is why those who still cling to military solutions, who insist on the usability of nuclear weapons, and who try to portray nuclear-weapons tactics as strategy shy away from answering genuine strategic questions. Strategists should not be reduced to counting the dead; rather, they must be called upon to solve the problem of ensuring the survival of nations. Long-term strategic decisions in the present-day environment cannot be other than decisions directed at demilitarizing politics. With this approach, the problem of ensuring national security can be solved not by military build-ups, not by threats and saber-rattling, but by way of increasingly comprehensive measures to limit and reduce armaments, including strategic ones!

Notes

1. *New York Times*, November 17, 1961.

2. *The Military Balance, 1969-70* (London: Institute for Strategic Studies, 1969), p. 55.

3. "Neither side, for the foreseeable future, is likely to acquire a disarming first strike capability against the other, even if fixed, hard ICBM forces become more vulnerable in the 1980s." *(Report of the Secretary of Defense James R.*

Schlesinger to the Congress on the FY 1976 and Transition Budgets, FY 1977 Authorization Request and FY 1976-1980 Defense Programs), February 5, 1975 (Washington: GPO, 1975), p. 11-13.

4. The Schlesinger Doctrine would appear to refer not so much to exchanges of limited strategic strikes against the national territories of the Soviet Union and the United States, but rather to the restriction of such strikes to theaters outside those territories. This view is expressly confirmed by the admission of the U.S. secretary of defense that there exist "operational plans for limited use, as necessary, of [American] strategic forces in support of theater conflict." (James R. Schlesinger, *The Theater Nuclear Force Posture in Europe: A Report to the United States Congress in Compliance with Public Law 93-365* [Washington: GPO, 1975], p. 12)

For this reason, the "flexible response" doctrine, rather than encouraging U.S. allies in Western Europe, actually unnerves them. "The idea that a nuclear exchange may be rationally limited to counterforce targets is of little value to the Germans who are sitting on those counterforce target areas," noted an American military writer. (Maj. Donald A. Mahley, USA, "The New 'Nuclear Options' in Military Strategy," *Military Review,* December 1976, p. 6.)

5. U.S. Senate, Committee on Foreign Relations, *U.S.-USSR Strategic Policies,* top secret *Hearing* before the Subcommittee on Arms Control, International Law and Organization, March 4, 1974, 93rd Congress, 2nd Session, p. 8. ("Sanitized" and made public on April 4, 1974.)

6. It has now been established that the "missile gap" story was first put into circulation by the authors of the 1957 Gaither Report. See *Deterrence and Survival in the Nuclear Age: The "Gaither Report" of 1957* (Washington: GPO,1976), pp. 1, 26-27.

7. See *Statement of Secretary of Defense Melvin R. Laird on the FY 1972-76 Defense Program and the 1972 Defense Budget, March 9, 1971* (Washington: GPO, 1971), p. 165. See also *The Military Balance 1973-74* (London: International Institute for Strategic Studies, 1973), p. 71.

8. Reading in the early 1970s the frightening statements by Secretary of Defense Laird, one could not help recalling a statement made by Mr. McNamara while he held that post: "New warheads—for example, a 35-megaton warhead for our Titan II—could be developed and stockpiled with confidence that they would work." *(New York Times,* August 14, 1963.) See W. W. Kaufmann, *The McNamara Strategy* (New York: Harper & Row, 1964), p. 153.

9. It should be noted that, in their attempts to scare the American public with the throw-weight of Soviet ICBMs, the Pentagon alarmists apparently count on the short memory of America's readers and listeners. They think everyone has forgotten about the "megatonnage gap," which some had used in the 1960s to try to whip up panic. Responding to that campaign, Secretary of Defense McNamara explained that President Eisenhower, acting on the unanimous recommendation of the Joint Chiefs of Staff, approved a reduction of the total

megatonnage of the U.S. nuclear stockpile by 40 per cent, preferring lighter and more compact warheads. "President Kennedy carried out that decision," McNamara added. (Interview in *Life*, September 29, 1967.)

Gross megatonnage and throw-weight, it must be said, are practically one and the same thing. Thus, it seems that with the passage of years, the Pentagon's imagination is petering out.

10. As was done, for instance, by James Schlesinger in his much publicized testimony at the top secret hearings on March 4, 1974 (see n. 5, above). From the (declassified) text of those hearings, now gospel for American strategists, one learns that Mr. Schlesinger had compared the optimal gross throw-weight of American ICBMs in 1974 with the maximum possible throw-weight of Soviet ICBMs *in some distant future* ("in the out years").

11. See, for instance, Paul H. Nitze, "Assuring Strategic Stability in an Era of Détente," *Foreign Affairs*, January 1976 [reprinted in this collection] and "Deterring Our Deterrent," *Foreign Policy*, Winter 1976-1977, p. 200.

12. See "The Joint Strategic Bomber Study," *Congressional Record*, May 20, 1976, p. S7709; also, Ray S. Cline, *World Power Assessment: A Calculus of Strategic Drift* (Washington: Georgetown University, Center for Strategic and International Studies, 1975), p. 72. Mr. Nitze, of course, endeavors to explain his figures. He reasons that the B-52 and the B-1 are designed to carry not bombs but SRAM missiles, each having a yield equal to the nuclear charge of a single Minuteman III warhead. Hence, Nitze's tally of the B-1's throw-weight. (Though, if calculated this way, the throw-weight of a B-1 carrying twenty-four SRAM missiles ought to be 16,000 pounds, since the throw-weight of a Minuteman III [with three warheads] equals 2,000 pounds; thus Mr. Nitze, if he so wished, was free to slice off another 3,000 pounds!) Along these lines, Nitze equates throw-weight with the actual payload of the American bombers, even though there is virtually an eight-fold difference between the two figures! The point here is that Mr. Nitze and his colleagues jettison all such subtleties the instant they begin to evaluate the throw-weight of the Soviet strategic systems. Discarding all pretense at thoroughness, they declare the maximum conceivable throw-weight to be the actual combat payload. Now, what is the value of these double-standard calculations?

13. Actually, all the calculations Mr. Nitze cites in his latest articles to demonstrate the "growing Russian threat" were made by his senior technical adviser, T. K. Jones. As Nitze himself puts it, because of "security considerations . . . the full assumptions used in Mr. Jones' study cannot be spelled out"! ("Assuring Strategic Stability . . . ," p. 64, n. 17) Presumably for similar reasons, the tables provided by Nitze in his *Foreign Affairs* and *Foreign Policy* articles (see n. 11, above) lack any uniform reference scale or any numerical denomination of the magnitude of the "gaps" he uses to browbeat his readers.

14. This is not solely my view. It is shared by a large group of distinguished American experts. Here is the opinion given by Sydney Drell, John Wilson

Lewis, Wolfgang K. H. Panofsky, and Lawrence D. Weiler in their commentary on Nitze's January 1976 *Foreign Affairs* article: "It is inconsistent now to choose that one indicator [throw-weight] which we discarded ten years ago and herald it as a measure of U.S. strategic inferiority. Interestingly Nitze participated in that decision." *(Congressional Record,* March 11, 1976, p. S3306.) Jan M. Lodal, no less knowledgeable on the strategic balance and formerly the National Security Council's leading expert on these matters, wrote: "Paul Nitze's calculations assigned our B-52 bombers an equivalent throw-weight of 10,000 pounds and our B-1 bombers 19,000 pounds, although these bombers actually carry significantly more payload than this. Furthermore, he degraded the payload of the US bomber force both for its 'alert rate' and for 'penetration factors'. While I would agree that some adjustment of gross bomber payload might be appropriate, Mr. Nitze's assumptions go too far in favoring the Soviets. If one were to use gross US bomber payload, the Soviet projected throw-weight advantage in 1984 would disappear. While this is going to the other extreme, it illustrates that by picking a different yet still not absurd definition of aggregate throw-weight, one can obtain radically different views of the relative balance." ("Assuring Strategic Stability: An Alternative View," *Foreign Affairs,* April 1976, p. 466n.)

15. See *The USSR Economy in 1975: Statistical Year-Book* (Moscow: Statistika, 1976), p. 742.

16. I will not go into the matter of just how well the contentions about a steady decline in the American military budget correspond to reality. I refer all specialists interested in my opinion on this subject, which differs somewhat from the official Defense Department interpretation, to my book *USA: Politics, War, Ideology* (Moscow: Mysl Publishers, 1976), pp. 311-313. In that book I draw the conclusion that U.S. military budget allocations on weapons procurement grew, in constant dollar, by about 25 per cent from 1965 to 1974.

17. See U.S. Congress, Joint Economic Committee, *Allocations of Resources in the Soviet Union and China—1976, Hearings* before the Subcommittee on Priorities and Economy in Government, May 24, June 15, 1976, 94th Congress, 2nd Session, pt. 2, pp. 81-82. (Hereafter, "1976 Allocations.")

18. Lt. Gen. Samuel V. Wilson, director of the DIA, stressed that "these dollar values *do not purport to represent what the Soviets have spent,* but rather what their forces would cost us to support." ("1976 Allocations," p. 82; emphasis added.) This reservation, however, strangely evaporates when the CIA-DIA estimates, plucked from thin air, appear in public discussions and in the press as "the true military budget of the USSR."

19. *Interavia Air Letter,* April 29, 1972, p. 2.

20. Realizing that they were climbing out too far on the limb by admitting such a huge disproportion in the prices of analogous weapon systems, CIA representatives at subsequent Proxmire hearings began to increase the "dollar value" of Soviet military hardware. (See for example, U.S. Congress, Joint

Economic Committee, *Allocations of Resources in the Soviet Union and China—1975, Hearings* before the Subcommittee on Priorities and Economy in Government, June 18, July 21, 1975, 94th Congress, 1st Session, p. 52.)

21. Ibid., pp. 93, 121.

22. "1976 Allocations," p. 113.

23. Quite naturally, if one adds the number of civilians employed by the armed forces to the number of servicemen, the figure will be greater.

24. *U.S. News & World Report*, February 15, 1975, p. 5.

25. See Francis Hoeber and William Schneider, Jr., eds., *Arms, Men and Military Budgets: Issues for Fiscal Year 1977* (New York: Crane, Russak, 1976), pp. 271-272.

26. U.S. Congress, Joint Economic Committee, *The Military Budget and National Economic Priorities, Hearings* before the Subcommittee on Economy in Government, June 23-24, 1969, 91st Congress, 1st Session, pt. 3, p. 973.

27. *Pravda*, February 1, 1976; *Izvestia*, January 29, 1976.

28. *Kommunist*, February 1977, no. 3, p. 17.

29. See *Report of the Secretary of Defense James R. Schlesinger to the Congress on the FY 1975 Defense Budget and FY 1975-1979 Defense Program*, March 4, 1974 (Washington: GPO, 1974), pp. 78-79. "As the first step in crisis relocation planning," the report read, "we are developing allocations schemes to permit the population from some 250 of our urbanized areas to be assigned to appropriate host areas." (p. 79.)

30. See U.S. Senate, Committee on Foreign Relations, *Strategic and Foreign Policy Implications of ABM Systems, Hearings* before the Subcommittee on International Organization and Disarmament Affairs, May 14, 21, 1969, 91st Congress, 1st Session, pt. 2, pp. 551-587.

31. See F. Bellinger, "Problems of Civil Defense," *Ordnance*, March-April 1967, pp. 509-510.

32. Conrad V. Chester and Eugene P. Wigner, "Population Vulnerability: The Neglected Issue in Arms Limitation and the Strategic Balance," *ORBIS*, Fall 1974, pp. 764-765.

33. "The development of civil defense procedures requiring the massive evacuation and relocation of population during crises has recently been proposed *as necessary adjunct to the new strategy* [retargeting doctrine]," noted Sydney Drell and Frank von Hippel. ("Limited Nuclear War," *Scientific American*, November 1976, p. 33; emphasis added.)

34. See Robert McNamara's speech in Ann Arbor, Michigan, in the *New York Times*, June 17, 1962.

35. See President Kennedy's radio and television speech on July 25, 1961. (*Public Papers of the Presidents: J. F. Kennedy, 1961* [Washington: GPO, 1962], p. 534.)

36. See Robert S. McNamara, *Essence of Security: Reflections in Office* (New York: Harper & Row, 1968), p. 57. See also President Nixon's White House press

conference on April 18, 1969: "At the time [during the Kennedy administration] all of the professional experts agreed that the US superiority was at least 4 to 1, and maybe 5 to 1, over the Soviet Union in terms of overall nuclear capability. Now we don't have that today; that gap has been closed." (*New York Times,* April 19, 1969.)

37. The fact that the Soviet Union succeeded is now admitted by all competent experts in the United States, including McNamara, Schlesinger, and the chairman of the Joint Chiefs of Staff, General George Brown. "I think [that] on the strategic nuclear force level," General Brown said, "we have essential equivalence. We have a general balance. Our best estimate is that the Soviets do not have a first-strike capability against the United States, nor do we, realistically, have a first-strike capability against them." (U.S. Senate, *Fiscal Year 1977 Authorization for Military Procurement, Research and Development, and Active Duty, Selected Reserve, and Civilian Personnel Strengths, Hearings* before the Committee on Armed Services, January 29, 1976, 94th Congress, 2nd Session, pt. 1, p. 497.)

38. Many American authors note that the USSR's civil-defense measures have not included any large-scale training or exercises, which would have been essential in the event of a genuine effort to drill the population in methods of mass evacuation or mass use of shelters. "If there had been any such rehearsals we would have heard about them," wrote Drell and von Hippel. (p. 34.) "They would be very difficult to conceal, and many people who would have participated in them or would have had knowledge of them have now left the USSR and would have called attention to them. Yet no evidence of such exercises has been presented. The editor of the US Government translation of the official Russian civil defense manual for 1974 comments that 'the Soviet Union has not conducted mass shelter living experiments or even simulated ones as *has been done in the US*.' " (Emphasis added.)

Speaking of American fictions about Soviet "mass measures" in the area of civil defense, it is quite to the point to remind the reader of such all too real events as the regular, nationwide civil-defense alerts of the 1950s and 1960s in the United States, during which atomic attacks against the country were simulated. Neither can one overlook the fact that one of the first things President Carter did after his inauguration was to try out (February 11, 1977) his special "doomsday plane," designed to be an airborne command center during nuclear war. As the American press pointed out, Mr. Carter was the first president to fly on such a plane!

39. See the interview with General Keegan in the January 3, 1977, issue of the *New York Times.* One gets the impression that he was simply reciting the extensive recommendations on civil defense in the 1957 "Gaither Report" to the American leadership, and ascribing the fulfillment of all these recommendations to the Soviet Union.

40. *Pravda*, January 19, 1977.

41. I have been somewhat apprehensive that this "deterrence-potential gap" may lead the Pentagon to demand even greater weapons allocations than those called for by the "counterforce" doctrine. Current Pentagon budget requests and recent pronouncements by Pentagon spokesmen on doctrinal matters substantiate my appraisal. Incidentaly, Paul Nitze's assessment (see "Assuring Strategic Stability . . . ," pp. 195-210) of the balance of forces remaining after an attack against the United States, and his proposals for the deployment of M-X missiles, Trident submarines, B-1 bombers, and other strategic systems, confirm once again the existence of such a tendency. This, despite the fact that there is apparently nothing the Pentagon wants that is not being procured: the value of the principal weapon systems now being manufactured on orders placed by the Pentagon exceeds, according to my calculations, $300 billion.

42. That is, whether one should try to achieve the set aim through nonmilitary means, such as economic or psychological pressure.

43. See, for example, *Analyses of Effects of Limited Nuclear Warfare,* prepared for the Subcommittee on Arms Control, International Organization and Security Agreements of the Committee on Foreign Relations, U.S. Senate (Washington: GPO, 1975).

44. The Pentagon, which bases its arguments on extremely dubious estimates, contends that such an exchange would claim no more than 7 million lives in the United States and, consequently, a roughly similar amount in the USSR. (Ibid., p. 148.)

45. The figure actually used in the U.S. Defense Department's published estimates is 2,158 strategic warheads. (Ibid., p. 149.)

46. When pressed, the secretary of defense had to agree with the senator— *Senator Muskie:* "But with respect to the other side, the decision-maker responsible for determining the nature of the response [to a strategic attack], he will not know what the limitations are until the strike is over." Secretary Schlesinger: "Quite right, Mr. Chairman." (Ibid., p. 126.)

47. U.S. House, Committee on International Relations, *The Vladivostok Accord: Implications to U.S. Security, Arms Control and World Peace, Hearings* before the Subcommittee on International Security and Scientific Affairs, June 24-25, July 8, 1975, 94th Congress, 1st Session, p. 26.

48. *Time*, January 3, 1977, p. 34.

49. See Bernard Brodie, *War and Politics* (New York: Macmillan, 1973), esp. chap. 9; McGeorge Bundy, "To Cap the Volcano," *Foreign Affairs,* October 1969; Henry Kissinger, "The Permanent Challenge of Peace: U.S. Policy Toward the Soviet Union," speech before the Commonwealth Club and the World Affairs Council of Northern California, San Francisco, February 3, 1976 (Department of State release). "To be sure," Kissinger noted, "there exist scenarios in planning papers which seek to demonstrate how one side could use

its strategic forces and how in some presumed circumstance it would prevail. But these confuse what a technician can calculate with what a responsible statesman can decide."

50. Definition of "national strategy," in U.S. Joint Chiefs of Staff, *Dictionary of Military and Associated Terms* (Washington: Department of Defense, September 3, 1974), p. 222.

7

SALT and Soviet Nuclear Doctrine

Stanley Sienkiewicz

The euphoria in some quarters of the American strategic community following the SALT I accords was largely based upon the inference that Soviet agreement to a virtual ABM ban signified fundamental agreement on strategic nuclear doctrine. Many concluded that this provided a hopeful basis for further collaboration in strategic nuclear arms control. Subsequent disillusionment has been triggered by the slow pace of SALT II and the continuing Soviet strategic buildup.[1] The result has been a growing pessimism that divergent strategic doctrines preclude significant strategic accommodation. One strain of determined optimism about SALT even argues that reconciliation of nuclear doctrine be placed first on the SALT agenda, as a necessary basis for substantive agreement.[2] There are, however, structural and ideological barriers to any explicit reconciliation of nuclear doctrine. Barring the most thorough-going transformation of the Soviet system, these appear insurmountable.

Until 1953, Soviet military thought, like all other significant aspects of Soviet life, was constrained by a primitive Stalinist orthodoxy. In military thought, this orthodoxy did not extend beyond the assertion of the decisiveness of Stalin's so-called permanently operating factors. These were: the stability of the rear, the morale of the armed forces, the quantity and quality of divisions, the equipment of the fighting forces, and the organizational abilities of the commanders.[3] Coupled with the asserted superiority of the Soviet social order, based upon the Marxist-Leninist science of society, these factors amounted to a theological assertion that the Soviet Union would prevail in any future conflict. This recipe, expounded by the "greatest military genius of modern times," precluded the possibility that other factors, such as nuclear

Reprinted by permission of the author and *International Security*, Spring 1978. Copyright 1978 by the President and Fellows of Harvard College.

weapons or the element of surprise, could affect the outcome of war. Not only was this a prescription for avoiding reassessment of the lessons of the Great Patriotic War (in which the "surprise" had resulted from Stalin's personal obduracy), but it prevented any serious attempt to evaluate the impact of nuclear weapons upon Soviet security.

Despite the homily that armies seem always to be preparing to fight the last war, the military is fundamentally a pragmatic and empirically-based profession, though to call it scientific might be to overstate the point. It is clear, in retrospect, that the Soviet military had chafed under the Stalinist orthodoxy because it was grossly at variance with the post-war world. They had, after all, endured the consequences of surprise in 1941 and could not easily swallow Stalin's assertion that the rapid German advance had been part of a carefully designed strategy to lure the enemy deep into Russia, as Kutuzov had done to Napoleon in 1812.[4] They were also well aware of the effects of thermonuclear weapons. Thus the debates over military doctrine which emerged soon after Stalin's death were inevitable. That they became public is perhaps related to the weakening of control at the top produced by the power-struggle between the Malenkov and Khrushchev factions. Reviewing these debates provides significant insight into the character of Soviet defense thinking in the nuclear age—an insight which has an important bearing on the contemporary U.S.-Soviet strategic dialogue.

In fact, a review of these debates and their outcomes compared to the parallel debates in the United States helps to explain why military doctrines, particularly nuclear doctrines, are unlikely to converge.

The Evolution of Soviet Doctrine

The classic studies of the post-Stalin military debates were produced at The Rand Corporation nearly two decades ago by Herbert S. Dinerstein and Raymond L. Garthoff.[5] The most prominent issues in the debates were the inevitability of war[6] and the potential decisiveness of surprise attack. What can be inferred from the Rand reconstructions is that these issues were associated with two quite separate debates.

The inevitability of war arose as a largely instrumental issue in the leadership struggle between the Malenkov and Khrushchev factions. Soon after Stalin's death, Malenkov and his associates began to argue that war between the capitalists and the Soviet Union was no longer inevitable.[7] This attempt at revising fundamental dogma was probably linked to Malenkov's effort to shift resources from military spending and the supporting heavy industry to consumer goods.[8] However, it also provided Khrushchev with a convenient opportunity to attack Malenkov. Manlenkov's argument was not only revisionist (and therefore dangerous in so pervasively doctrinaire a political system) but also associated with a threat to reduce allocations to the military. Thus, Khrushchev gained a significant bureaucratic ally.

The subsequent history of this struggle is well known. By 1957 Malenkov and his associates were vanquished and Khrushchev was in full control. He then completed the shift toward the Malenkov position which he had already begun at the 20th Party Congress in 1956.[9] By the 21st Party Congress in 1961 he had established Malenkov's proposition that war was no longer "fatalistically inevitable" as a tenet of official Soviet doctrine. It has not been repudiated to this day, though it is hardly mentioned by the Brezhnev regime.

Khrushchev also adopted the policy which Malenkov had associated with his view of the non-inevitability of war. He pressed for reallocation of resources from the defense to the domestic sectors, most prominently to agriculture. He advocated a one-third reduction in the Soviet armed forces,[10] and he reduced naval surface-ship construction.[11] In general, he argued the obsolescence of many elements of traditional military capability and the primacy of nuclear missile forces.[12] More importantly for the argument that follows, Khrushchev premised his view of the Soviet deterrent posture upon a secure capability to retaliate.[13]

The military, who had allied themselves with Khrushchev in opposition to Malenkov, may well have felt betrayed when faced with Khrushchev's attempts to cut defense spending and conventional forces in favor of the domestic sectors. They may even have felt perversely vindicated when the Cuban Missile Crisis demonstrated Soviet strategic and naval weaknesses. One might infer a residue of self-interested concern about the "vulnerability" of senior Soviet political leaders to the American ideas of finite deterrence; this might help explain the continuing intensity of some of the military literature on these subjects. For example:

> The premise of Marxism-Leninism on war as a continuation of policy by military means remains true in an atmosphere of fundamental changes in military matters. The attempt of certain bourgeois ideologists to prove that nuclear missile weapons leave war outside the framework of policy and that *nuclear war moves beyond the control of policy, ceases to be an instrument of policy* and does not constitute its continuation is theoretically incorrect and *politically reactionary.*[14] [Emphases added.]

This is as clear a statement as one is likely to find that the position adopted by Khrushchev (and widely held in the West) is not only wrong but revisionist according to Marxist strictures. That position is based upon the conclusion that nuclear war can escalate to levels of destruction beyond all sensible ends of policy. Thus, one reaches the basis for arguments that once such levels of destructiveness are available in both arsenals, deterrence is assured and there is little need for additional capabilities. In fact, the Soviet military seem to be trying to have it both ways, for it is commonly asserted that even very limited nuclear exchanges will inevitably escalate to all-out levels of destruction. Yet, Soviet doctrine continues to assert that massive strategic nuclear exchanges may be followed by a long and ultimately decisive "conventional" war. This leads directly to requirements not only for substantial strategic nuclear forces, but for large and diverse conventional capabilities to fight a war—a war seemingly unaffected by the exchange of thousands of nuclear weapons. The solution to this paradox may be found in considering the different audiences to which such arguments may be addressed, as well as the different purposes which they may be intended to serve. The view set forth above can be read as intended for internal consumption (perhaps even for remaining strands of "radical or modern"[15] thought within the armed forces themselves). It may be seen as shoring up the barriers against the kind of Malenkovian/Khrushchevian revisionism that has been associated with attempts to cut Soviet defense budgets. The argument on the inevitability of escalation, on the other hand, is more plausibly interpreted as intending to strengthen deterrence by persuading Americans that there is nothing to be gained from limited nuclear strategies.

One should not necessarily conclude, however, that the predominant military motivation is merely pragmatic defense of their budgets. An important component may well be a sincere belief that the political leaders—who in the past have "misunderstood" the requirements of military security—may mistakenly risk that security. Thus the two views are easily able to coexist in the military mind.

This juxtaposition brings us to the debate among the professional military. It was concerned primarily with the potential decisiveness of surprise. By contrast to the debate reflecting the political struggle, this issue was not instrumental, but rather was substantively important in shaping the Soviet defense posture.

The Stalinist assertion of the dominance of the permanently operating factors ruled out the possibility that such a so-called transitory factor as surprise could be decisive in war. Such a view obviously constrained practical efforts to improve the Soviet defense posture against surprise attack. Yet military planners were well acquainted with the destructive effects of nuclear weapons and the prospects for long-range delivery systems. They could easily extrapolate the effects of a large-scale nuclear surprise attack, and no doubt found it difficult to reconcile such calculations with the Stalinist proposition that surprise attack—even with such weapons—remained a relatively insignificant and merely transitory factor.

This debate was short and its resolution conclusive. The potential decisiveness of surprise attack in the nuclear age was clearly established. As then-Marshal of Tank Forces Rotmistrov concluded: "[Surprise attack in the nuclear age could] . . . cause the rapid *collapse of a government whose capacity to resist is low as a consequence of radical faults in its social and economic structure and also as a consequence of an unfavorable geographic position.*" (Emphasis added.)[16] This quotation raises interesting questions in terms of the Aesopian communication that characterizes Soviet public discourse. They are worth pondering from today's perspective. Although the debate was carried on in very general terms, the problem which provoked it was the defense of the Soviet Union in the nuclear age. Thus one wonders what "government" Rotmistrov had in mind: It was the Soviet Union which was ringed by NATO bases deploying nuclear-armed aircraft (though he could also have been referring to small European countries within easy range of the Soviet Union). Certainly the geographic position of the United States remained the least "unfavorable." What were the "radical faults in social and economic structure"? Were they inadequate organization and regimentation of the population in an effective civil defense program,[17] inadequate dispersal of industry, or inadequate allocation of resources to heavy industry and to military preparedness?

The issue of surprise attack, then, was clearly resolved. It *could* decide the outcome of war in the nuclear age. The military were now free to seek "real-world" solutions to the problem. Or were they? The admission that a confident solution might be impossible could pose a serious doctrinal problem for the Soviet Union. It would undermine the Marxian prediction of the inevitable victory of socialism. Thus, if too explicitly argued, it could be construed as a revision of a more fundamental kind. The Soviet political system was imposed and has been maintained by force; it has pursued its social goals by forcibly extracting enormous sacrifice from its people. It has done so on the utopian premise that it was consistent with and supportive of the inevitable course of history. It would therefore carry substantial risk to openly admit that the rationale for this history of suffering had been fundamentally mistaken, that in fact the ultimate victory of socialism could be prevented if Soviet deterrence failed and the capitalist powers mounted a nuclear surprise attack.

From the start, the Soviet search for "real-world" solutions to the security dilemma of the nuclear age was inhibited by this Marxist-Leninist doctrinal context. It is a context which makes very difficult any approach premised upon the admission that no confident defense can be erected, preserving at least the appearance of inevitable Soviet victory.

The Soviet solution, therefore, had to be premised upon the assertion that even were a surprise attack to be mounted, Soviet military forces could still ensure victory. The obvious answer was to assert the capability to strike preemptively and blunt the Imperialist attack. It was in fact the conclusion of many in the West that a preemptive first-strike capability was what the Soviets were after.[18]

The Soviet assertion that in countering a surprise attack, the Soviet armed forces will "repel the attack successfully . . . deal the enemy counterblows, or even preemptive surprise blows of terrible destructive force"[19] has continued to be characteristic of the military literature on nuclear war. This assertion, however, creates difficulty with the other frequent assertion that the Soviet Union will not initiate war—that it will limit itself to preemptive rather than preventive attack.[20]

Defense Management and Military Solutions

Though in important respects pragmatic or empirical, the military profession is also characteristically conservative. This is a characteristic that might provoke deep suspicion of the idea that military security may be found in acknowledging the vulnerability of one's society to the principal adversary, and vice versa. The logical corollary is still worse. It is the idea that military security may be maintained by agreeing to cooperate with the adversary in maintaining that condition. This is not the idea of deterrence, *per se*, for deterrence is a well-established concept in military thought. Historically, however, it has not been distinguished from defense. In the new doctrine emerging in the United States, (with which Khrushchev so dangerously flirted), security was not maintained by automatically seeking military/technical solutions to an adversary's threatening capabilities, but rather by maintaining solely punitive capabilities. In the traditional military view, if the enemy develops a capability to attack one's homeland with long-range forces, there is no doubt about the proper response: it is to devise ways to defend that homeland. Depending upon the nature of the technical problem, there is no principled distinction among active defense, passive defense, and preemptively offensive capabilities. The distinctions are entirely pragmatic. If the problem is difficult and no single measure stands out in its effectiveness, then all are pursued.

It is important to understand the implications of this approach because of the current role of the Soviet military in all areas of national security management, especially as compared with the United States. Both defense establishments may be seen as organizational pyramids, functionally differentiated and performing all the tasks necessary to the management of the national security apparatus. In the Soviet Union, however, all aspects of this activity—from intelligence and analysis to the production and deployment of weapon systems—are almost entirely in the hands of the professional military.[21] Does this mean that major issues of resource allocation among defense and other sectors—or even within the defense establishment—are decided solely by the military? This is unlikely. What it does suggest is that they frame the defense problem and specify the range within which military solutions are to be sought. To argue that security in the nuclear age is to be found in agreeing to a posture of mutual vulnerability, therefore, is not only doctrinally risky, but at radical variance with all of the traditions and professional instincts of the Soviet defense establishment. This is the basis for the central difference between the American and Soviet approaches to the problem of military security in the nuclear age.

But what is the role of ideology in the Soviet military? If the profession of arms is fundamentally a pragmatic business, it is likely to be as resistant to cumbersome Marxist-Leninist ideological impositions as it was to Stalinist dogma. Here lies the crux of the matter.

In a highly arbitrary yet fundamentally ideological political system, perhaps the most dangerous error is the ideological one. The accusation of doctrinal deviation is more powerful than the accusation of stupidity or mistaken judgment. Whether or not one believes literally in relevant tenets of Marxism-Leninism, it is prudent in policy debate to avoid positions which can be attacked as doctrinally wrong. It is this phenomenon which inhibits Soviet public behavior rather than any literal belief in the doctrinal orthodoxy. The inhibiting effect is indirect but hardly inconsiderable.

In the case of military doctrine, however, this effect may be less than in other areas of political life, and not only because of the pragmatic nature of the profession. The military is among the more autonomous of the occupations despite the system of political controls created to ensure their reliability. The military promote their own, probably up to quite senior levels, largely on the basis of traditional military criteria. It is in the military more than in any other pursuit in Soviet society that we find the most reliable, functioning system of promotion and tenure rules. Thus, the explanation for the Soviet solution to the problem of security in the nuclear age derives more from the fact that it is a solution devised by the *military* profession, and not that it was devised by the *Soviet* military profession.

The thoughtful military planner recognizes not only the extreme importance of his task, but also its pervasive uncertainty. No matter how carefully analyzed the problem and how well-designed the armed forces, the imponderables of warfare—morale, leadership, and chance—may determine the outcome of battle. And it is the task of the peacetime military planner to predict the outcome of hypothetical wars. These conditions imply that the professional military cannot be satisfied short of unambiguous superiority over any combination of enemies. The notion of sufficiency or parity, on the other hand, is not merely an *American* invention. It is more importantly a *civilian* invention.

Khrushchev's position on the primacy of strategic forces (thus the possibility of reductions in conventional forces) was not widely shared in the military.[22] The absence of severe resource constraints on military spending since 1964 largely precludes this point of view as a rationale in intra-military resource allocation debates. In fact, it seems likely that a bargain was struck in 1964 between the military and the Brezhnev faction which has permitted, among other things, across-the-board Soviet military growth ever since. It appears to have established both an unprecedented degree of independence for the military in the management of their own affairs and a significantly more prominent voice in the shaping of foreign policy.[23]

In this light, the Soviet military buildup of the Brezhnev period appears natural. It is the fulfillment of the military planner's dream, the opportunity to hedge against virtually any important uncertainty. If it cannot yet confidently be ruled out that the West could successfully mount a surprise attack, then one continues to pursue all plausible measures to preclude it (i.e., civil defense, air defense, vigorous ABM R&D, and hard-target counterforce capabilities—though these latter are probably as much the descendent of technological necessities as of any conscious choice to build big missiles). If there is still insufficient confidence in the state's security, then one must be prepared to fight conventionally after the strategic nuclear exchanges in order to occupy a relatively intact Europe or to defend against an opportunist China. The best overall deterrent, furthermore, is a sufficiently impressive across-the-board military capability to intimidate any possible combination of enemies.

It takes only a small leap of imagination—putting oneself in the shoes of the Soviet military planner—to produce a long list of worrisome contingencies, and thus requirements for military forces. Perhaps the worst case from his perspective is the two-front war against the Chinese hordes to the east and the capitalist industrialist machine to the west. With decisive escalation deemed too risky in either case, recourse to strategic nuclear forces is deterred. Such a scenario may help explain the very large investment in war production capabilities in recent years.

Civilian Strategists and Strategies

The conclusion of the Soviet military debate—that surprise attack could be decisive—was almost, but not quite, the same formulation as that reached in the United States. American strategic thinkers agreed that surprise attack could be decisive in the nuclear age. Thus the task of military policy was to make surprise attack infeasible. American strategists concentrated on a particular kind of surprise attack, the so-called first-strike disarming attack in which the victim's capabilities for a substantial retaliatory strike would be destroyed. This emphasis arose from the fact that American strategists went a logical step further than their Soviet counterparts; this step may have been foreclosed to the Soviets by the strictures of Marxism-Leninism and, perhaps, by the traditions of military problem-solving.

The Americans agreed that surprise attack could be decisive because the great destructiveness of thermonuclear weapons—combined with great numbers and modern, long-range delivery systems—produced a variety of attacks against which defense was at best problematic. The Soviet formulation and military posture has been based upon the opposite premise: that a defense must be erected, no matter what the cost. This was the step which separated the problem of defense from that of deterrence, making it clear that for most kinds of superpower warfare the central issue was one of deterrence. In all likelihood, this step had to be imposed by civilian strategists; it is the point of departure from the traditional military perspective on deterrence and defense. How was deterrence to be created and maintained in an age in which there is no longer a defense? Deterrence would henceforth be based primarily upon large and secure punitive capabilities.

The American formulation of the surprise attack problem was crucially different from the Soviet formulation. For the Soviet military thinkers, surprise attack with nuclear weapons could be decisive because it could destroy the ability of the government to function and of their military forces to *defend* their state. For the American strategists, surprise attack could be decisive if it could eliminate the enemy's punitive capabilities.

American strategic thought thus shifted from preoccupation with "military solutions" (i.e., attempts to counter in a technical-military fashion any capabilities the adversary deployed which could conceivably be seen as threatening) to the unique civilian invention of deterrence as the peacetime manipulation of largely punitive threats. This is almost entirely unconnected to the problem of defending against nuclear attack.

The result of the American approach is obvious. If the problem of surprise attack has to do primarily with a fairly narrow band of capabilities threatening the adversary's second-strike forces, then we have, *prima facie*, a basis for limited superpower cooperation toward enhancing the security of both. They could cooperate, explicitly or tacitly, in managing force postures so as to minimize the threats posed to their respective second-strike capabilities. The United States has of course always adjusted its own forces to prevent the emergence of threats to its punitive capabilities. This is the basis of the American definition of stability, a definition not acknowledged by the Soviets.

The three principles of American doctrine have been: the maintenance of secure second-strike forces; limited war forces, to extend and enhance deterrence;[24] and the avoidance of threats to Soviet second-strike forces. The implications for force postures and defense budgets have been intensely debated, but the principles have generally been accepted. Whereas the American answer to the military security problem has entailed an explicit distinction between deterrence and defense, the Soviet answer has not. The idea of preempting an American surprise attack is inherently a defensive idea predicated upon the traditional military solution. It continues to treat deterrence as a direct function of aggregate military capability.[25]

The implicit scenario for the Soviets requires successful anticipation of an imminent U.S. "surprise attack." Thus, the stragegic forces of the United States, assuming sufficient warning of the impending American attack, would be largely destroyed by a preemptive strike. Those U.S forces which survived Soviet preemption and were actually launched would be met by the massive Soviet air defenses, and greatly degraded. Those, finally, which succeeded in delivering their weapons to their targets would have attacked a population effectively organized and, to the degree feasible, protected by a vigorous civil defense program and an economy and political control structure also organized to cope with such an attack. Combining such across-the-board capabilities with a strong emphasis upon offensive action[26] wherever possible, has been the Soviet solution to the problem of military security in the nuclear age.

Concern that such a posture was in fact feasible was more appropriate in a period when the strategic delivery capabilities resided exclusively in aircraft. There was a real prospect of preemptive capability against soft, slow bomber forces deployed on small numbers of airfields— particularly if they were in Europe or elsewhere on the Soviet periphery. Extensive air defenses could be expected to substantially degrade surviving bomber forces attempting to retaliate, and the still-limited nuclear weapon stockpiles of the 1950s made such a doctrine far more plausible than is possible today.

It is likely that the early Soviet deployment of medium- and intermediate-range ballistic missiles targeted against the NATO bases on which U.S. strategic forces were only recently deployed was the outgrowth of this kind of perspective. Unfortunately, the American strategic forces were in the process of being withdrawn to the continental

United States, as increasing range in follow-on aircraft permitted.[27] This, in turn, helped to stimulate increased Soviet efforts to deploy intercontinental-range ballistic missiles. The deployment of MRBMs and IRBMs proceeded, since NATO bases continued to deploy nuclear capable aircraft.[28]

Conditions are, of course, far different today. Given the dominance of ballistic missile delivery systems of virtually constant readiness (a large proportion of which remain highly survivable aboard ballistic missile submarines), and the absence of effective anti-ballistic missile systems, a large nuclear attack cannot be effectively blunted. The American strategic literature recognized this prospect clearly by the end of the 1950s. Yet Soviet doctrinal literature on nuclear war still does not concede this point, for to do so could create both the ideological problem for Marxism-Leninism referred to above and risk another Khrushchevian attempt to cut the defense budget. It would be similarly difficult to agree in SALT with the American formulation of the surprise attack problem. This would mean implicitly agreeing that there is no defense against strategic nuclear attack, that such an attack could in fact halt or reverse the "inevitable" course of history, and that the only solution lies in the essentially "non-military" approach devised by the Americans— the relationship of mutual assured destruction (MAD). Such a position means that once the security of second-strike forces is assured—and this might be achieved cooperatively—there is a *prima facie* basis for arguing that little, if anything, more is necessary in the way of military forces. This argument supports a policy of "sufficiency"—uniquely a product of civilian defense strategists or political leaders. The Soviet formulation, by contrast, is a prescription for relatively unrestrained defense spending[29] following the traditional military approach to national defense.

It is unnecessary to impute purely budget-protecting motives to those who resist the American deterrence model whether they are Soviet soldiers or American "hawks." Rather, one might impute a belief that such a posture is simply too risky, and cite the consequences of the Cuban Missile Crisis in support. Whatever the mixture of motivations, these views are more likely to be shared in the military—hence the significance of the role of the Soviet military in the management of Soviet defense. By contrast, American nuclear strategic ideas were developed almost exclusively by the "civilian strategists."[30] The power of their ideas came to dominate both the scholarly strategic community and, under Secretary of Defense McNamara, the top levels of the national security establishment in the United States. Civilian dominance has remained and, if anything, grown in American security planning—a crucial difference between the United States and the Soviet Union.

Nuclear Doctrine and the Future of SALT

Two important factors have largely determined the evolution of Soviet nuclear doctrine. One is the sometimes inhibiting effect of the Marxist-Leninist doctrinal context within which all Soviet intellectual activity occurs. The other is the strong influence produced by the exclusive authority of the Soviet military over virtually all military activity below the major Politburo-level choices. The doctrinal inhibition raises obstacles to any strategic concept that would require a logical admission of the "non-inevitability" of the ultimate victory of socialism. This would remain true even were a civilian strategic establishment to arise advocating such a concept. The dominant shaping influence, however, has been the preeminence of the professional military in all spheres of military and strategic thought. Thus, for Soviet nuclear doctrine to become more like that of the United States, requires a class of strategic thinkers substantially freed of both traditional professional military perspectives and Marxist-Leninist constraints, as well as the political influence to impose the change upon a resistant system.

The absence of such conditions has resulted in a fundamental difference between U.S. and Soviet strategic theory. Soviet doctrine does not dismiss deterrence. On the contrary, most of the open military literature seems preoccupied with enhancing it. It is a theory of deterrence, however, which is substantially at variance with the American formulation. As a result of the difference, Soviet doctrine denies the American formulation of stability—the absence of threats to each side's punitive capabilities—but rather defines it, when it does, more generally and self-servingly as the absence of any significant innovation or new deployment above what is described as parity. This is not a sign of inability to comprehend the American strategic analysis. More likely, it is an inability to exit from the corner into which their doctrinal evolution has painted them. The Soviet military almost certainly recognize the dangers posed by American developments which threaten the survivability of Soviet second-strike forces; this is evident in their doctrinal writing and in their deployments. To acknowledge that such developments are especially threatening, however, would be to admit the validity of the American strategic concept, and perhaps more important, to concede an important bargaining advantage in SALT. For it is *Soviet* ICBM forces which pose the earliest threat to the survivability of a major U.S. strategic force component. And it is these ICBM forces which have been the major SALT concern of the United States since the ABM Treaty was signed. It is also the Soviet Union which maintains large investments in other "damage limiting" capabilities, such as air and civil defense programs. The only practical Soviet position, therefore, has been to deny the U.S. formulation of the strategic arms problem, while bargaining in entirely pragmatic terms.

Soviet nuclear doctrine has been the basis for the development of Soviet strategic forces which today appear to pose precisely the threat which their public doctrinal debates of two decades ago made clear they would like to pose. The large throw-weight of Soviet ICBMs lends itself to an early threat to the U.S. Minuteman Force. Yet we must keep in mind that this has been the major Soviet strategic program for two decades. In addition, large ICBMs have turned out to be the vehicle for catching the United States in one of the major measures of strategic competence, multiple independently-targetable re-entry vehicles (MIRVs). To concede the validity of the American theories of deterrence stability thus sacrifices the argument against the central U.S. theme in SALT (i.e., that constraints upon threats to the survivability of each side's retaliatory capabilities ought to be the central focus). This concession would have a major impact upon the most important Soviet strategic modernization programs, and none of consequence upon U.S. programs.

Seeking doctrinal convergence as a formal goal in SALT thus seems impractical at best.[31] But does this fundamental irreconcilability warrant the pessimism in some Western strategic circles about the prospects of any progress in SALT? The answer is a qualified no. First, the Soviets have shown themselves able to reach SALT agreements at variance with their military doctrine. The obvious example is the ABM Treaty. Second, the United States may find arrangements desirable which do not visibly conflict with the prescriptions of Soviet doctrine (though they may conflict with military judgments about what is prudent). Here, a variety of lesser measures may prove marginally useful. High ceilings on weapon numbers would be roughly compatible with Soviet doctrine, as would a variety of constraints ensuring the effectiveness of warning and verification systems. In the longer run and perhaps not so much longer, given the age of the current leadership, the Soviet Union may again have a leader like Khrushchev who is more amenable to American ideas about deterrence and sufficiency, and more interested in shifting resources into non-military investment.

How are we to deal with SALT in the absence of doctrinal convergence? Here the ABM Treaty is instructive. The ban on ABM systems embodied in SALT I is consistent with the American view of the nuclear problem and its solution. Observance of the treaty precludes any hope of effective defense against major ballistic missile attack. In fact, there was some euphoria in the American arms control community when it was signed, as some believed it signaled Soviet acceptance of the

American strategic view. Disillusionment eventually replaced excessive euphoria (although more pragmatic satisfaction with the concrete consequences remains). The alternative explanation for Soviet agreement on ABM is that they were in technological difficulty and could not rule out the possibility that American ABM research might lead to a competent deployed system.[32] The ABM Treaty thus was a straightforward bargain—pay the Americans their price to get them to stop something which might eventually prove worrisome.

This interpretation could testify to a Soviet understanding of—and perhaps even some tacit agreement with—the American formulation, perhaps more convincing than an open Soviet announcement would have been. Why else would they pay any price at all to halt a purely defensive American program if they did not perceive that it might eventually affect their deterrent? Though their deterrent is not formally premised upon a second-strike capability, they have never successfully elaborated a convincing case that preemption might actually work with contemporary forces. In any case, they have worked hard to attain an unquestioned capability for major strategic attack upon the United States, whether preemptively, preventively, or in a de facto second-strike.

This is the key to long-run progress in SALT—pragmatic case-by-case bargaining. It will not be found in some chimeric search for a formal common understanding on strategic principles. The United States is, in any case, more interested in Soviet strategic behavior—in what forces they do or do not deploy in answer to U.S. attempts to influence those choices. We are unlikely to influence Soviet choices by asserting our good intentions or by demonstrating conclusively the flawless logic of American theories. This game is played with sticks and carrots, threats (necessarily subtle and as private as possible), and incentives. For the necessary chips with which to play, we should expect to pay a price, and therefore seek to accumulate and maintain sufficient amounts of the appropriate currency.[33]

Notes

1. The dimensions of the buildup or continuing emphasis—civil defense, air defense, hard-target counterforce capability—lack only one element—ABM—of a comprehensive damage-limiting posture, a posture based upon a different view of deterrence and nuclear strategy than has shaped the U.S. strategic forces in the nuclear age.

2. See, for example, Alton Frye, "Strategic Restraint, Mutual and Assured," *Foreign Policy*, Summer 1977.

3. Cited in Herbert S. Dinerstein, *War and the Soviet Union*, p. 33.

4. Described in Bernard Brodie, *War and Politics* (Macmillan, New York, 1973), pp. 443-445.

5. Herbert S. Dinerstein, op. cit.; Raymond L. Garthoff, *Soviet Strategy in the Nuclear Age* (1958), *The Soviet Image of Future War* (1959).

6. Lenin held that as Capitalism-Imperialism declined, the Capitalists would war against themselves and ultimately against Socialism. This would be the vehicle for the ultimate victory of the Socialist camp. Stalin's formulation remained consistent with this view. (Dinerstein, op. cit., p. 66.)

7. Adam B. Ulam, *The Rivals* (Viking: New York, 1971), p. 219.

8. Ibid., p. 221.

9. ". . . when he amended the Leninist thesis of 'inevitable war.' " Thomas W. Wolfe, *Soviet Strategy at the Crossroads*, p. 2.

10. Arnold L. Horelick, "The Strategic Mind-Set of the Soviet Military," *Problems of Communism*, March-April 1977; Wolfe, op. cit., p. 31.

11. George E. Hudson, "Soviet Naval Doctrine and Soviet Politics, 1953-1975," *World Politics*, October, 1976.

12. Wolfe, op. cit., p. 31; Garthoff, Introduction to V. D. Sokolovsky, *Military Strategy: Soviet Doctrine and Concepts* (U.S. Air Force Translation, Praeger: New York, 1963), pp. viii-ix.

13. Ibid.

14. From *Communist of the Armed Forces*, November 1975, cited by Foy D. Kohler in the Foreword to Leon Gouré, *War Survival in Soviet Strategy*.

15. Garthoff, Introduction to Sokolovsky, op. cit., p. ix.

16. Marshall of Tank Forces P. Rotmistrov, "On the Role of Surprise in Contemporary War," *Voennaia Mysl'*, February 1955, cited in Dinerstein, op. cit., p. 186.

17. It is worth noting that this was also a period of concern and debate over civil defense in the American defense community. See, for example, Klaus Knorr, "Passive Air Defense for the United States," in William W. Kaufmann, ed., *Military Policy and National Security*, 1956; *Deterrence and Survival in the Nuclear Age* (the so-called Gaither Report), 1957, declassified 1973.

18. Dinerstein, op. cit., pp. 200-208.

19. Rotmistrov, op. cit., cited in Dinerstein, p. 187.

20. Bernard Brodie, among others, discussed this issue with great insight. See particularly chapter 7 of *Strategy in the Missile Age*, 1959. The Soviets themselves were not insensitive to the difficulty, as Dinerstein's analysis makes clear; see Dinerstein, op. cit., chapter 6, particularly p. 188.

21. The Western consensus on this point is strong. See for example Horelick, op. cit., p. 81; John Erickson, "Soviet Military Capabilities," *Current History*, October 1976, p. 97; Thomas W. Wolfe, *Military Power and Soviet Policy*, Rand Paper P-5388, March 1975, pp. 15-18; and William R. Van Cleave, "Soviet Doctrine and Strategy," in Lawrence L. Whetton, ed., *The Future of Soviet Military Power*, 1976. This is a consensus supported by remarks at a seminar at

the Massachusetts Institute of Technology, April 15, 1977, by Dr. Mikhail Milstein, (Lt. Gen-retired), of the Institute for the Study of the USA and Canada. Richard Pipes, however, implies some difference of view. "Soviet military planning is carried out under the close supervision of the country's highest political body, the Politburo." If my inference is correct, it would be interesting to see the evidence for this assertion. See Pipes, "Why the Soviet Union Thinks it could Fight and Win a Nuclear War," *Commentary*, July 1977, p. 27.

22. In professional military circles, this issue arose in a debate about whether the next war would be a short, decisive nuclear war or whether it could also be long and conventional. The answer, of course, would shape the force structure and the result was a predictably military compromise. It could be either. Thus a requirement for both kinds of forces. See, for example, Sokolovsky, op. cit., pp. 194-204.

23. At least one scholar discerns a growing visibility to the military establishment in all spheres of Soviet life, though he seems to conclude that rather than a potential problem for the party or the political leadership, this is the result of a choice explicitly made by that political leadership. See William E. Odom, "Who Controls Whom in Moscow," *Foreign Policy*, Summer 1975, and his "Militarization of Society," *Problems of Communism*, Sept.-Oct. 1976. Pipes, op. cit., p. 29 would take Odom's judgment much further.

24. Both sides maintain a variety of limited war forces. It is the difference in rationales which is suggestive. For the Soviets, such forces are obviously needed to fight the possible long war, occupy territory, and defend against similar capabilities possessed by the adversary. For the U.S. the rationale is almost always that such forces *enhance* the *credibility* of an extended deterrent, first, and only secondarily, that they might be needed to fight the Soviets at various limited war levels.

25. Van Cleave, for example, agrees, but seems to prefer the Soviet view on this point. Op. cit., p. 48.

26. One of the lessons the Soviet military appears to have drawn from World War II, and perhaps from Soviet and Russian history more broadly, is the importance, whenever attacked, of going over to the offensive as rapidly and decisively as possible. See, for example, A. A. Sidorenko, *The Offensive*, Moscow 1970. Translated and published under the auspices of the U.S. Air Force, 1974.

27. Another of the architects of American strategic thought in the nuclear age, Albert Wohlstetter, was the central figure in the pathbreaking "Basing Study" which raised the question of the survivability of U.S. retaliatory forces to projected Soviet surprise attack capabilities (Wohlstetter, et al., *Selection and Use of Strategic Air Bases*, Rand Corporation, R-266, Santa Monica, CA: April 1954). His subsequent and seminal *Foreign Affairs* article ("The Delicate Balance of Terror," January 1959) was among the earliest detailed expositions of the logic of deterrence via assured second-strike capabilities.

28. I am indebted for this insight to the anonymous reviewer of an earlier draft of this essay.

29. Thomas W. Wolfe and William R. Van Cleave, among others, share this view. See, for example, the citation from Wolfe in Van Cleave, op. cit., p. 47.

30. A remarkable group of analysts and scholars, whose paths intersected at The Rand Corporation. The principal figures, in my view, are Bernard Brodie, Herman Kahn, William W. Kaufmann, Thomas C. Schelling, and Albert Wohlstetter. On this point see the brief essay by Michael Howard, "The Classical Strategists," in *Problems of Modern Strategy*, Institute for Strategic Studies, 1970.

31. Frye, op. cit.

32. This is my interpretation, but it is consistent with the view of, among others, Raymond L. Garthoff, a long-time and highly regarded observer of Soviet military affairs and a participant in SALT I. See Garthoff, "SALT and the Soviet Military," *Problems of Communism*, January/February 1975. On this point also, Pipes is in fundamental agreement (op. cit., p. 33), though his cryptic comments about the ABM treaty (". . . certain imprecisely defined limitations . . .") and its connection to Soviet air defenses suggest once again a strategic perspective quite at variance with the American consensus described above.

33. My thinking, in pursuing this analysis, was clarified, though perhaps despite himself, by exposure to Dr. (Lt. General-Retired) Mikhail Milstein of the Institute for the Study of the USA and Canada of the Soviet Academy of Sciences, in several seminars at Harvard and M.I.T. during April of 1977.

8
Rethinking Soviet Strategic Policy: Inputs and Implications

Dennis Ross

Over the last few years the American public has been warned with increasing urgency about the emerging Soviet strategic threat. Concern about the danger and purpose of developing Soviet military might and capabilities may have reached its zenith with the leaking of "Team B's" National Intelligence Estimate.[1] Among other things, Team B concluded that the Soviets rejected our stated objective of strategic parity and on the contrary were engaged in a relentless drive toward comprehensive military superiority—a superiority which at the very least was designed to yield political payoffs and at the very most would allow the Soviets to survive a nuclear war.

Given the composition of Team B—Paul Nitze, William Van Cleave, Richard Pipes, et al.—it is hardly surprising that they would draw these kinds of conclusions. Indeed, Nitze and Van Cleave have for some time argued that the Soviets have not shared our strategic attitudes or concepts. Specifically they have argued that the Russians reject the principle of mutual assured destruction and either reject or, more benignly, ignore the concept of deterrence.[2]

Citing Soviet strategic doctrinal calls for superiority, weaponry which can be linked to or explained by this doctrine, and Soviet political objectives which are perceived as unchanging, Nitze and Van Cleave posit that the Soviets continue to "cling to their goal of worldwide domination,"[3] and therefore simply do not approach strategic matters the way we do.

This article orginally appeared as ACIS Working Paper No. 5, published by the Center for Arms Control and International Security, University of California at Los Angeles, June 1977. It is reprinted by permission of the author and the Center. The article was written while the author was a research fellow at the UCLA Center for Arms Control and International Security. The views expressed are his alone and are not necessarily representative of the views of the Defense Department's Office of Program Analysis and Evaluation of which the author is a member.

I would like to thank Alex Alexiev, Bernard Brodie, Robert Jervis, Roman Kolkowicz, Dmitry Ponomareff, Jeffrey Porro, and F. L. Propas for their helpful comments on earlier drafts.

What is clear from this line of argument is that it hinges not on a different set of Soviet attitudes or perceptions but rather on different Soviet goals—i.e., the Soviets reject our strategic concepts because these concepts don't suit their goals and not because they think or approach these problems differently.

But is this really true? Indeed, isn't it possible that for historical, ideological, or systemic reasons the Soviets approach these questions, and conceive of appropriate answers, differently from American strategists? And isn't it possible that by interpreting Soviet strategic behavior according to our logic or preconceptions, and not theirs, we necessarily draw overly negative conclusions—e.g., according to how we would logically or theoretically use them, the Soviet development of big missiles can only be interpreted in an offensive, threatening manner.

Aside from almost mindlessly linking intentions with capabilities, the problem with such an interpretation is that it blithely ignores the possibility that the Soviets may believe big missiles make deterrence more, not less, secure. That the Soviets could have such a different view of successful deterrence highlights our need to come to grips with the attitudes that underpin Soviet strategic policy. In an effort to do so, this paper will characterize the values of those primarily responsible for formulating Soviet strategic thinking and will also show how these values relate to and are reinforced by ideological and historical factors.

In the course of this discussion the central argument of this essay will become clear, viz., that although different subjective inputs yield a Soviet strategic mind-set whose emphases are different from ours, these disparities 1) need not be de-stabilizing if understood, 2) allow Soviet strategic behavior to be explained in terms of deterrence, and 3) indicate that even in the abstract, Soviet capabilities should not be interpreted in a totally offensive, threatening light. By way of additionally proving the latter point and at the same time critiquing the all-too-prevalent notion that Soviet intentions can be derived from their capabilities,[4] we will point out that even where similar types of inputs shape American and Soviet strategic policies, they tend to produce different outputs. That is, although bureaucratic routine, institutional interests, and military balance considerations influence both U.S. and U.S.S.R. strategic arms behavior, these factors nevertheless render different strategic preferences and policy choices because they conform to separate experiences and traditions and are perceived through distinct conceptual prisms.

In order to outline these distinct prisms we will turn presently to an examination of the "subjective" inputs into Soviet strategic policy. By subjective inputs we refer to such factors as the general belief system, military doctrinal perspectives, and systemically determined needs.

These subjective elements constitute what might be called the Soviet strategic conceptual framework or style.

The Soviet Strategic Style

In very general terms, one might say that a unique Soviet strategic style grows out of a peculiarly Russian-Soviet psychology. For example, a traditional emphasis on "bigness" as a symbol of "goodness" or greater effectiveness seemingly has maintained a persistent influence over Soviet approaches to weaponry. Thus as former SALT negotiator Alexis Johnson has observed, even with regard to the most advanced ICBM, the Soviet approach remains the same as it has historically been toward artillery-like weapons: "The bigger, the better."[5] (In this connection, a suggestive relationship exists between the psychological inclination to favor super-sized missilry and the deployment of the SS-9 and SS-18 missiles.)

Similarly, the firmly rooted Russian-Soviet sense of insecurity (the product of invasions, ubiquitously perceived threats and enemies, and the traditional economic, industrial, and general development inferiority when compared to the West, etc.) has very likely bred a natural inclination to overcompensate and overinsure on security matters. The possession of far more numerous, and particularly in the case of missiles, vastly larger weaponry than their chief adversary may reflect concrete examples of overcompensation. (Ideological symbolism also may bear on Soviet attitudes toward the number and size of weaponry; i.e., the belief that the Soviet Union, as the leading socialist state, should have a superior military capability of some kind may find expression in the possession of superior size as well as numbers of arms.[6])

At any rate, psychological and indeed socio-cultural elements may yield Soviet predispositions when it comes to dealing with matters concerning the most efficacious kinds of weapons, their necessary amounts, how much is enough for defense, and the overall relationship of strategic nuclear forces. While psychological factors may thus inspire wide-ranging inclinations,[7] the Soviet strategic conceptual framework or style has been more directly shaped by Soviet military and strategic doctrine—which, of course, also bears the imprint of historical experiences and ideological beliefs and expectations. Here we are using the term doctrine in its generic, not Soviet, sense—a body of principles that underpins a theoretical approach (to the strategic nuclear age).[8]

With regard to Soviet strategic theory, it is important to emphasize that Soviet strategic thinking about the nuclear missile age, unlike our own, generally reflects the basic biases and interests of its military establishment. That this is so is largely explained by the immobilized nature of Soviet strategic thought until Stalin's death, the deeper roots of pre-nuclear Soviet strategy, institutional resistance to any fundamental change in thinking, and, perhaps most significantly, the absence of authoritative specialists capable of redefining basic military roles and purposes. With respect to the latter factor, it is worth noting that as opposed to the experience in the United States where high-powered RAND-type civilians proceeded to educate our military in matters of war and peace in the nuclear age, in the Soviet Union there was no body of experts outside the defense establishment who could provide a fresh approach to the problem.[9] Consequently, the molding of Soviet nuclear strategy has been heavily influenced by the attitudes, actual experiences, basic traditions, and institutional preferences of the Soviet armed forces.

As a result, Soviet strategic doctrine tends to be conceptually grounded in more traditional military concerns and considerations; that is, it focuses on the more classical and standard roles assumed by the military in warfare—e.g., emphasizing the ability to ensure success in warfare and, as an underpinning factor, highlighting the importance of having Soviet military capabilities direct their primary thrust against targets of military value (weapon systems, troop formations, etc.). In this sense, deeply engrained Soviet military traditions—e.g., "combined arms" (success in warfare is contingent on the use of all arms and services), "primacy of the offensive" (emphasis on preemption), etc.—continue to have as much meaning in current Soviet strategic doctrine as they had in the pre-nuclear era.

While more traditional American military principles might also still dominate our strategic theory had civilians not shaped our strategic-nuclear attitudes, the fact that they have has produced a gulf between American and Soviet strategic prescriptions. Thus, whereas it is quite natural for Soviet strategic doctrine to emphasize a war-fighting thrust, it is not surprising, given essentially civilian definitions of nuclear deterrence, that American strategy does not.

The fact that there is a general distinctiveness between Soviet strategic-nuclear doctrine and American deterrence perspective, however, should not be taken to mean that deterrence is not the Soviet military's primary mission. It is. The overwhelming destructiveness of nuclear weaponry leaves little doubt that the military's most important function is deterring a nuclear strike against the Soviet heartland. What this general distinctiveness should be taken to mean is that the Soviets have a different operating definition for *strategic* deterrence; while believing no less in its importance, most Soviet leaders, for military, doctrinal, and related historical and ideological reasons, conceive of strategic deterrence achievement in different terms than their American counterparts.

To be specific, the general Soviet attitude toward successful deterrence is rooted in essentially traditional military maxims which emphasize the war-fighting capacity of weaponry. Consequently, as several observers have noted, "Soviet doctrine and military posture do not distinguish between deterrent and war-fighting nuclear capabilities, but appear to view them as 'fused together' in dialectical unity."[10] In this connection, the Soviet view appears to be that the better their armed forces are prepared to fight and win a nuclear war and the more any adversary knows this to be the case, the more successful is Soviet deterrence.

The underlying premise of this perception apparently is that the best way to guarantee that your enemy will never attack you is to convince him that no military advantage or meaningful success can ever be accrued by launching a first strike. The Soviets apparently strive to operationalize this premise in both verbal and practical-strategic ways; i.e., on the one hand, their claims of socialist victory–imperialist defeat in all-out nuclear war[11] (aside from having internal political-military payoffs*) might well be designed to convince the West that attacks on the U.S.S.R. are at best futile and, more likely, are militarily disadvantageous. On the other hand, the Soviet development of a strategic posture capable of fighting wars and limiting damage to themselves might also be designed to dissuade an adversary from thinking it can gain any objective by striking first. To actually achieve such a strategic posture, a counterforce–damage limiting strategic doctrinal orientation is apparently required.

Significantly enough, such an orientation conforms to the traditional military focus so dominant in Soviet strategic thinking, and, of equal importance, also corresponds closely to the Soviet's declaratory policy; e.g., in an authoritative statement, the late Marshal Grechko characterized the mission of the backbone of the Soviet strategic forces in a predominately counterforce manner:

> The Strategic Missile Forces, which form the basis of the combat might of our Armed Forces are intended for the destruction of the enemy's means of nuclear attack, his large troop formations and military bases, the destruction of the aggressor's defense industry, the disorganization of his state and military command and control and of the operations of his rear and transportation.[12]

Similarly, from a specific damage limitation perspective, although the ABM agreement would seemingly suggest diminished Soviet interest in active missile defense, the military's continuing public obeisance to

---

*Such statements have political-military payoffs—e.g., they help to preserve 1) a sense of innate socialist superiority and 2) high morale in the armed forces.

the concept of defense,[13] together with intensive research and development on a hyper-sonic "Sprint-like" interceptor missile and transportable phased-array ABM radars (e.g., the X-3 radars),[14] leave room for doubt about whether the Soviets have closed the book on the achievement of an active ABM-damage limitation policy. That damage limitation remains a Soviet objective is at least implied by the Soviet passive or civil defense measures. In this regard, while the increasingly extensive Soviet civil defense measures to harden and disperse industrial complexes and populations in conjunction with intensive civil defense public education are ideologically useful as socializing and mobilizing devices—as well as active reminders of the need for vigilance—they apparently have a damage limitation purpose as well. For example, Soviet officials have observed that civil defense measures are designed to enhance the country's "ability to rapidly liquidate the consequences of enemy nuclear strikes, promptly render extensive and diverse aid to casualties, and secure the conditions for the more normal functioning of the facilities of the national economy."[15]

Here again we are reminded of the Soviet vision of deterrence; i.e., the Soviets, in the main, perceive the achievement of deterrence as being predicated on convincing one's adversary that he will be denied victory even should he strike first. In this context, active civil defense measures represent a crucial factor in limiting and, at the same time, coping with damage that might be inflicted by an adversary; the better the civil defensive measures, the better the limiting and coping mechanisms, and the less chance any adversary has (and must know he has) of ever being able to defeat or gain advantage over your country by striking first, or so the Soviet logic goes. That Soviet perceptions of the utility of civil defense correspond to this logic—reflecting its integral role in Soviet deterrence—is suggested by the following Soviet spokesman's statement: "Improvement of Soviet Civil Defense and an increase in its effectiveness constitute one more *major obstacle* in the way of the unleashing of a new world war by the imperialists."[16]

That the Soviets may thus believe that civil defense contributes to their deterrent* lends credence to the claim that the Soviet calculus of deterrence primarily derives from the premise that "if your enemy knows he can't be victorious or gain advantage by attacking you, he won't."

Before applying a particular phraseology to this Soviet conception of deterrence, it is important to point out that the Soviets do understand the logic underpinning retaliatory second-strike capabilities. At a mini-

---

*Another statement by the above Soviet commentator specifically underscores this contention: "Soviet civil defense does not incite, does not promote and does not provide impetus to war." It is clear that this view is in direct contrast to the American premise for stable deterrence, namely, that stable deterrence is based on having cities held hostage.

mum, the Soviets, wanting to be certain that the United States is denied any possible incentive for striking first, appreciate the importance of having essentially invulnerable-survivable weaponry. Hardening of missile sites and the deployment of SLBMs ameliorate the problem of vulnerability and related incentives for attack, and thus were enacted by the Soviet Union.

Moreover, the Soviets have implicitly evidenced an appreciation of the deterring value of a retaliatory capacity—e.g., as Brezhnev observed at the 24th Party Congress, "any possible aggressor knows well that should he attempt a missile attack on our country, he will receive an annihilating retaliatory blow."[17] Further, Admiral Gorshkov has even apparently assigned a second-strike role to the Soviet SLBMs by having noted that missile-carrying submarines represent a threat of inevitable "nuclear retaliation."[18]

Since the foregoing suggests that the Soviets accept the importance and utility of possessing retaliatory second-strike capabilities, we might reasonably conclude that the Soviet conception of deterrence is composed of two tiers of thinking. First, for reasons partly flowing from the Soviet's more traditional military approach to strategic-nuclear questions, their primary tier, or level, of deterrence thinking focuses on conveying to an adversary that he cannot gain anything (and presumably stands to lose) should he contemplate attacking the U.S.S.R. A counterforce–damage limiting posture logically follows from this premise for deterrence. The second or sub-level, which may well be a product of American example or education,[19] supports and reinforces the primary level by further minimizing incentives for attack by guaranteeing retaliation. It might be posited, therefore, that in Soviet eyes the most fully reliable deterrent is provided by having a mix of primarily preemptive and secondarily retaliatory capabilities.

In deterrence terminology, the Soviet philosophical or conceptual position might be classified as representing a deterrence strategy primarily based on denial. While American denial strategies tradition-ally have been placed in only conventional or tactical military contexts,[20] we are suggesting that the Soviets conceive of strategic deterrence on an essentially denial basis.

By "deterrence through denial,"[21] we mean actor A deters actor B by convincing B that he cannot carry out a successful attack; in other words, actor B is deterred by the knowledge that no military gain can be derived by striking first. B can be so convinced by A's visible capacity to disarm B (at least partially) and limit damage to himself. A deterrence through denial strategic posture, therefore, clearly requires some combination of the ability to destroy the other side's military force and at the same time provide additional measures for one's own defense.

As opposed to a Soviet deterrence through denial cognitive approach, one can characterize the traditional nuclear era calculus of Western-U.S. deterrence as being largely based on a "deterrence through punishment" logic; i.e., actor A deters actor B from launching a first strike by being able to guarantee a severely punishing retaliatory attack. Stated simply, actor B is deterred from launching a first strike because he knows that any military advantage or gain that might accrue from such an attack would not be worth the cost or the pain that would result from A's retaliatory blow. Herein lies an important difference between the Soviet and the American* conceptions of deterrence—whereas the American deterrence through punishment approach accepts the fact that whoever strikes first will be militarily better off yet is deterred from doing so by the knowledge that unacceptable and horrendous damage will be wreaked on his population and industrial base in retaliation, the Soviet deterrence through denial approach seeks to deny or minimize any advantage in striking first in the belief that reducing the prospect of military gain is a more certain guarantor of deterrence than is the ability to inflict wide-scale damage on an attacker's society.

What would seem necessary to produce a strategic deterrence through denial mind-set? In addition to having one's strategic-nuclear thought dominated by standard military biases and predilections, it is also logical to expect the existence of 1) a belief that your adversary is unremittingly hostile and out to destroy or defeat you,** and 2) a deep-seated sense of vulnerability to attack. In the Soviet case, the ideological belief system, together with general historical experiences, have almost certainly engendered the existence of both of these outlooks among the Soviet leadership.

After all, from the perspective of ideology, Soviet leaders have been inculcated to believe that the Western "imperialists" are inherently hostile to socialism, that they must continually seek to "reverse the course of history," and that, therefore, the danger of war must persist as long as differing social systems exist. Indeed, in this context, Brezhnev has more than once stated, "History teaches that while imperialism exists, the danger of new aggressive war remains."[22] Not surprisingly, military spokesmen also acknowledge a direct relationship between the existence of imperialism and the continuing threat of war, only they tend to treat the subject with an air of greater certainty about its likelihood: e.g., the well-known military commentator Lt. General Zhilin has stated, "So long as imperialism and armed adventurism exist,

---

*It should be noted that the Schlesinger Doctrine represents a step away from a strategic-nuclear posture based purely on deterrence through punishment.

**This is to say that if your adversary perceives an opportunity to attack you, he will.

they will inevitably, if only by virture of their own momentum, unleash armed actions. . . ."[23]

In addition to the threat of aggressive war that imperialism inherently projects, Soviet leaders are also socialized to believe that the capitalist world understands that the U.S.S.R., as its "deadly enemy," must at some time destroy it, and seeks the opportunity to do so.[24] When this general belief is combined with the conviction that the imperialists will not be constrained from resorting to war by moral or value considerations (and relatedly will become more desperate as socialist successes multiply and the crisis of capitalism deepens), it is not surprising that Soviet leaders might conclude that the threat of wide-scale societal destruction will be insufficient to deter an imperialist attack. That is, Soviet leaders may believe that merely being able to inflict widespread destruction on capitalist population and industry is simply not enough to deter the West if its leaders see an opportunity to destroy/defeat socialism and thereby reverse the tide of history. Indeed, to successfully deter the West, so the Soviet thinking may go, the imperialists must be convinced that there is no hope of achieving their goal through military means.*

In short, the ideological code of Soviet leaders does emphasize the unceasing antagonism of its adversary and, as the foregoing suggests, does relate directly to a deterrence through denial perspective. As noted, coupled with a belief in the persistent hostility and resultant threat posed by one's adversary, the existence of a strong sense of vulnerability fosters a deterrence through denial perspective and is seemingly present in the U.S.S.R.

In the case of a sense of vulnerability, the rather sobering Russian-Soviet historical experience of isolation, encirclement, and repeated invasion must certainly have contributed to a feeling of vulnerability to attack. In addition, the basic conspiratorial framework of the Bolshevik weltanschauung, which has engendered a very deep sense of suspicion and mistrust toward the Russian people and the outside world, also figures to have heightened Soviet feelings of insecurity and vulnerability. Put briefly, the Soviets have a more expectant view of invasion and a sense of vulnerability to such military onslaughts and, consequently, have a natural predisposition to think in terms of "frustrating,""negating," or "preempting" adversary attacks.[25] In sum, Soviet

---

*To any observer of the Soviet media, it is clear that the Soviet literature is replete with references to the absolute importance Soviet military power plays in making imperialists understand that military means cannot solve the historical struggle between the differing social systems.

fears of vulnerability, together with their perception of Western hostility and persistent threat, have produced a natural tendency to conceive of deterrence in denial terms.

Beyond merely fostering a natural denial inclination, their comparatively greater expectation of war must also make the Soviets believe in the higher reliability of a deterrence posture based on denial. That is, because a denial, unlike a punishment, strategic posture is predicated on counterforce or war-fighting capabilities, it promises a "rational" means of defense should deterrence fail. On the one hand, according to Soviet predispositions and perceptions of its adversary, this factor should dissuade an aggressor from attacking—thus producing the most reliable and credible form of deterrence. On the other hand, this consideration and its war-survival implications must also be more reassuring to a leadership that is charged with the responsibility of securing the survival and victory of socialism and yet continues to believe that nuclear war remains highly possible.

In this sense, it is not difficult to see why the Soviets might have little faith in the security provided by an assured destruction posture. Besides simply not believing that an assured destruction posture yields reliable and effective deterrence, the Soviets must also view assured destruction or deterrence through punishment as unacceptable because it fails to provide any recourse or option should deterrence fail.

More than having little faith in assured destruction itself, there is also no small measure of distrust toward this posture when it is applied to a mutual or Soviet-American framework; after all, a mutual assured destruction posture means the acceptance of mutual and assured vulnerability to retaliation. While in any event the Soviets may have intellectual difficulties in directly linking their security to that of their adversary's,[26] it is also quite probable that elements of the Soviet leadership fear that a situation of what Americans refer to as mutual vulnerability will leave the Soviet Union in an inferior, exposed position. In an assured destruction environment, the Soviets do not see themselves having the same kinds of hedges against American breakthroughs in science and technology. Because they have always been concerned about superior American scientific prowess, the Soviets tend to be fearful that technological breakthroughs will yield U.S. strategic advantages and make any military balance premised on mutual vulnerability inherently unstable and threatening. Indeed, a Soviet spokesman rather explicitly argued against the mutual assured destruction concept on the grounds that "new scientific discoveries could lead to the creation of essentially new types of weapons, which could sharply upset the 'balance of fear' [mutual vulnerability] and create a state of general instability."[27]

In addition to believing that mutual assured destruction might actually diminish or endanger Soviet security, there are those within the Soviet leadership who have solid institutional interest reasons for being opposed to a strategic posture based on assured destruction. Here, we are principally referring to the Soviet defense establishment—the military, the defense planners, defense-heavy industries, etc. These groups are not likely to favor an assured destruction (or deterrence through punishment) posture because it is inherently limiting; i.e., once the ability to inflict assured destruction or punishment is guaranteed, further increments of arms become largely unnecessary.

Indeed, we are here reminded that a deterrence through denial or counterforce posture is institutionally self-serving for the defense establishment.* Unlike a deterrence through punishment approach— with its intrinsic limits—a deterrence through denial posture is totally open-ended and without limits. To achieve even partially effective counterforce–damage limitation capabilities, one always needs more—i.e., as one's adversary upgrades his forces, he mitigates the ability of yours to carry out their counterforce mission, and further buildups and/or qualitative improvements inexorably become necessary. Placing this factor in the super-power context, it is apparent that the warning systems and vast and redundant nuclear capabilities on both sides make a significant damage limitation capacity unachievable. To base one's force sizing and planning on an objective that even in minimal terms may not be attainable is, in reality, to provide a built-in dynamic for ever-more weapons procurement and to eschew concepts of defense limits or controls.

Quite naturally, then, the Soviet military establishment has very strong institutional reasons to favor a strategic philosophy which provides a continuing rationale for ever-increasing defense expenditures and developments. Similarly, as mentioned earlier, the Soviet military also psychologically finds a denial rather than a punishment or assured destruction posture consonant with its traditional missions—i.e., directing Soviet military capabilities against the other side's military forces (not his cities), concentrating on the defense of the country, and not allowing Soviet cities to be held hostage.

In sum, the military, for both broad security and institutional budgetary and psychological reasons, is likely to be opposed to mutual assured destruction; additionally, the political leadership, out of security and ideological-philosophical considerations, is also likely to be chary of the stability and deterring value of a mutual vulnerability relationship.

At this point, having outlined the underpinning factors behind

*We will be discussing the role of institutional interests as an input into Soviet strategic deployment in the next section.

general Soviet adherence to a deterrence through denial perceptual framework and, in addition, having noted why a denial or damage limitation strategic posture is generally preferable to a punishment or assured destruction strategy, it is important to point out that there is a minority within the Soviet civilian-political elite which, while not actually advocating mutual vulnerability, seemingly does adhere to a logic of "strategic sufficiency"; i.e., there are some in the non-military elite who *indirectly* argue that strategic superiority is unattainable, that counterforce strikes are at best futile and at worst destabilizing, and that nuclear wars are not winnable.* For example, in general terms while A. Karenin has referred to the "dreams [illusions] of nuclear superiority,"[28] G. A. Trofimenko has questioned the ability to attain meaningful counterforce capabilities, in an era where the invulnerability of the ballistic missile submarine "makes the task of disarming the forces of retaliation insoluble in the observable stages of military technological development."[29] Rather than questioning the feasibility of counterforce capabilities, V. M. Kulish has preferred to highlight the destabilizing logic of a counterforce approach: "Far-reaching international consequences would arise in the event that one side possessed qualitatively new strategic weapons which would serve to neutralize the ability of the opposing side to carry out effective retaliatory action."[30]

The most significant challenge to the predominant deterrence through denial logic has come from Georgi Arbatov. Arbatov has suggested that "prevention of nuclear war equally serves the interests of the U.S. and U.S.S.R. since nuclear war would be suicide for both."[31] Similarly, in explaining why the achievement of political ends by military force has lost all meaning in the nuclear age, Arbatov asserted that "no policy can have the objective of destroying the enemy at the cost of complete self-annihilation. . . ."[32]

This latter statement by Arbatov directly counters the central premise of what we have identified as the general Soviet strategic perceptual attitude toward deterrence; viz., whereas the Soviet "denial" posture is predicated on the belief that the threat of great destruction may not be sufficient to deter the West should it see the chance to defeat socialism, the Arbatov position quite clearly maintains that the specter of its own

---

*Because explicit Soviet political-military doctrine cannot be directly challenged (e.g., legitimacy and need of socialist superiority, definition of military missions in terms of defeating the enemy, etc.), political-military writers must critique these precepts implicitly—e.g., by critiquing American efforts in these areas, the futility of striving for superiority or meaningful counterforce can be highlighted. The arguments used against the prominent U.S. efforts can be applied to comparable Soviet attempts as well. Indeed, the Karenin, Trofimenko, and Kulish quotes which were essentially referring to American capabilities are being treated here as having general, Soviet and American, applicability.

destruction will always be enough to deter an aggressor. The Arbatov position, therefore, seems to reflect a deterrence through punishment logic and at least implies that a minority within the Soviet elite does accept such an approach.

Because a discussion of who constitutes this minority and why their perspective is different is beyond the scope of this essay,* we will restrict ourselves to a cursory explanation of why their views are not likely to predominate in the area of strategic doctrine and attitudes.[33]

Two general reasons account for this. The first might simply be that the formulation of strategic theory/doctrine remains largely within the province of the military. In the area of devising strategic needs, force sizing, force employment, and overall strategic theory/doctrine, there is no effective counter to the Soviet military. Indeed, in this regard, there may only be a smattering of civilians that even have knowledge of the character and composition of Soviet military capabilities—e.g., at the outset of SALT, such a senior non-military official as the chief of the Soviet delegation, Deputy Foreign Minister V. S. Semonov, apparently knew very little about the basic data concerning Soviet strategic forces and weapon systems.[34]

That, outside of some small pools of expertise, there may be no independent civilian source of substantive analytical advice on strategic matters suggests that even while leading political members of the Politburo ostensibly make broad strategic decisions and shape doctrinal approaches in the Defense Council, they do so on the almost exclusive basis of military input and recommendations. As a consequence, given the military's tradition, historical attitudes, institutional preferences, and ideological outlook (and seeming exclusivity of input), one cannot expect there to be any real change in a strategic theoretical approach that emphasizes deterrence based on denial.

---

*Put very briefly, adherents of the "Arbatov deterrence logic" are to be found in what might be termed the foreign affairs apparatus (the Foreign Ministry, relevant institutes in the Academy of Sciences, the International Department of the Central Committee, etc.) and among the economic managers in the state bureaucracy. Institutional functions and resultant interests largely explain the differing perceptions of some in these groups; i.e., on the one hand, the first group's responsibilities range from assessing American and Western statements and behavior to concretely furthering Soviet political objectives through a negotiatory, non-military process. Beyond possibly being influenced by that which they analyze, the members of the foreign affairs apparatus certainly find their general prerogatives and importance enhanced by the pursuit of military-political policies which make negotiations more likely and feasible. Similarly the state economic planners, who are responsible for the growth, development, and modernization of the Soviet economy, are institutionally desirous of policies that hold the promise of providing them with larger budgets and resulting greater influence. In this connection, only under conditions of a relaxation of tensions and a heightened sense of Soviet security can the desired policies of greater Western trade and diversion of defense monies to internal construction be pursued.

While strategic-military thinking or doctrine puts the military on record and certainly influences political leadership attitudes, the fact that it conforms to the leadership's predisposition or inclinations also determines whether there is any impulse to question it. In this context, the second reason why the minority's strategic attitudes won't predominate, at least in the near future, can be highlighted. To begin with, it is important to note that the cardinal difference between the bulk of the Soviet elite and the remainder, who are inclined to favor the "Arbatov position," relates to their differing estimates of whether the West still believes that it can *militarily* defeat socialism. Thus while all within the Soviet elite—given the ideological-historical prism through which they see the world—share the same long-range goals for the U.S.S.R. and perceive the West as hostile and threatening, there is a difference over the perception of Western rationality. On the one hand, the minority (the Arbatov position) accepts the premise that Soviet nuclear and overall military power has already and demonstrably* 1) sobered the American imperialists, 2) impelled them to give up their penchant for dealing with the Soviet Union from a "position of strength," and 3) forced them to recognize the futility of contemplating attack on the U.S.S.R. and militarily trying to "export counterrevolution" to defeat "anti-imperialist" national liberation movements.[35] Thus massive growth in Soviet military capabilities is perceived as unnecessary, of little utility, and, by possibly catalyzing American action, even counterproductive.

On the other hand, the dominant view seems to be that the current realism of Western policies, while being good for world peace and the future, nevertheless may be transitory because, in the face of inevitable Soviet successes, Western-imperialist leaders will be driven to count on, in Brezhnev's words, "achieving military supremacy, undermining the foundations of peace and, at a favorable moment, resolving the international dispute between capitalism and socialism by military means."[36] In this sense, Western "irrationality" may occur at any time. Thus to minimize the extent to which the West may waver in its realism, to continually reduce the prospect that it will think about attempting to resolve its struggle with socialism through military means, and, in the final analysis, to be prepared for sudden Western reversals or threats, policies based not on military sufficiency but rather on upward, open-ended military development will continue to be perceived as necessary. To the majority of the Soviet political elite, then, continual military growth and indeed a deterrence through denial orientation will, for the foreseeable future, be more reassuring than any alternate approach.

In short, the essentially military formulation of strategic needs and

---

*For example, détente, Helsinki, SALT, and the acceptance of failure in Asia.

theory, in conjunction with less sanguine political leadership beliefs about the degree to which the imperialists have become and will stay "sobered" or "rational," largely explains why the Arbatov position is not likely to predominate in the area of strategic doctrine and attitudes.

Before concluding this section, it should be added that even were the Arbatov-type views to become more accepted among the political leadership, one would not necessarily see any significant change in Soviet strategic behavior or deployment policy. The clearest explanation for this relates to the operational character and constraints of the Soviet decision-making system. Without detailing the precise reasons, suffice it to say that the Soviet system has become increasingly oligarchical. As a result of its growing oligarchic character, and largely because of ideological-legitimating factors of Party infallibility, the myth of leadership homogeneity, and relatedly the absence of institutional means for authoritatively resolving disputes, a premium is put on minimizing elite conflict and maintaining the leadership coalition.

In the abstract, coalition maintenance is engendered by the operation of a unanimity principle;[37] in the actual Soviet environment, a consensual decision-making style in the Politburo evidently occurs,[38] approximates a coalition maintenance unanimity characteristic, and carries with it logical policy implications—i.e., the operation of a unanimity principle dictates policies that must win the minimal acceptance of every leading institutional actor. In practical terms, this means the pursuit of lowest common denominator policies or, in effect, the whole Politburo literally "signs-off" or actively consents before high-level political action or policies can be undertaken.

With regard to major allocative decisions—e.g., agreeing to a basic strategic arms thrust or orientation—one can expect essentially consistent policies that change only at the margins. After all, those actors that most support and identify with the current thrust of strategic policy are not likely to easily acquiesce to any major change. Indeed, while the military's ability to say "x is necessary for our security" makes it difficult to imagine any such changes, the exigencies of internal elite politics seem to guarantee that for any modification at all the military and like-minded institutional actors will be able to exact some mollifying price.*[39]

---

*An underlying and implicit theme of this section has been that the Soviet military has a very significant impact on decisions affecting Soviet strategic policy. Beyond the set of values and outlooks the political leadership shares with the military, the military's influence tends to be a function of its monopoly of information and the factional character of Soviet leadership politics. With reference to the latter, the support of the military is important at any time, but is especially important during times of leadership debate or instability.

In the end, even should a change in strategic attitudes occur in the Soviet political leadership, the political realities of the Soviet system suggest that the military establishment, together with its supporters in the political elite, are sufficiently well ensconced in the leading political bodies to prevent any rapid or radical change in Soviet strategic behavior. Thus, we are once again reminded that Soviet strategic policy responds to Soviet, and not American, needs or logic. It therefore should be interpreted according to Soviet, and not American, reality.

In this section, we have dealt at some length with what we have called the subjective input into Soviet arms policies. By subjective factor, we have most particularly referred to the Soviet strategic style or conceptual framework. In this regard, we have pointed out that the combination of a largely military formulation and peculiarly Russian-Soviet ideological and historical outlook has forged a strategic doctrinal framework somewhat different from that held in the United States.

As a result, Soviet attitudes toward strategic deterrence are not symmetrical with American views; however, while not being consonant with the American conception, the Soviets nevertheless do accept and adhere to a principle of deterrence. In this sense, Soviet strategic-nuclear doctrine should be placed in a deterrence-achieving light and not in an exclusively offensive-aggressive context. Indeed, what may appear to us as threatening strategic declaratory statements and weapons deployment may reflect a Soviet strategic doctrinal input that conceives of deterrence on a denial basis. Relating this factor to apparent "counterforce" weaponry and damage limiting software—e.g., SS-9s, SS-18s, and ABM radars—it might be said that such capabilities represent the seeming marriage between capabilities and doctrine. However, it must remain the "seeming" marriage because the doctrinal-conceptual factor represents but one, albeit important, input into Soviet strategic weapons policies.

In saying this we refer to the fact that a variety of other, what might be termed objective, inputs help to shape the contours of Soviet strategic policy. For example, bureaucratic routine, institutional interest, and strategic balance considerations—factors which are likely to impact on the arms decision of any modern industrialized great power—affect the type and number of weapon systems the Soviets deploy. To indicate how these factors affect Soviet strategic deployment and, therein, to show why Soviet strategic intentions should not be directly inferred from their military capabilities, we shall turn to a more detailed discussion of their operation in the Soviet political setting. (Since bureaucratic tradition and institutional interests are closely related, we shall discuss them in tandem.)

Bureaucratic Tradition and Institutional Interest

In the Soviet Union, bureaucratic tradition and routine make the prevailing patterns of weapons acquisition and deployment difficult to alter. In addition to general military style and preferences, these patterns essentially emerge from 1) long-term strategic plans and 2) the technology available during the preliminary stages of weapons development.

With regard to the first, the technological requirements of modern weaponry have necessitated long lead times between the initiation of a preliminary design and the operational deployment of a weapon system. As a result, long-range developmental plans on the order of 10 to 15 years have apparently been formulated to guide Soviet procurement policies. While long-range strategic planning is certainly also found in the United States, Soviet "plans" in general impose more rigid constraints on development. Whereas American planning constitutes more of a fiscal guide with allowance for discretionary authority, Soviet plans, as Matthew Gallagher points out, tend to impose a "specific set of instructions for detailed production targets and precise schedules for fulfillment."[40] When one relates this general factor to the number of competing groups that have a stake in (and must agree to) the composition of the more specific weapons "blueprint,"* it is not hard to see why Soviet long-term strategic plans give rise to basic patterns of weapons development.

As for the second factor, the limits of technology during the initial phase of development provide the impetus for clear-cut weapons design patterns; that is, technological constraints may permit only a certain kind of design during one period and yet because these designs become firmly entrenched, they set the direction for future periods.

These designs become so entrenched because the Soviet weapons deveopment and design sector is an extremely rigid establishment. It has a dominant set of routines and clearly established processes of work and is known for its conservatism with respect to new approaches. Consequently, as one observer has noted there is a built-in tendency to favor the improvement of old designs to the creation of completely new ones.**[41] (The MiG-series fighters, "T"-series tanks, Frog-series battlefield support missiles, etc., seem to bear out this contention.)

---

*Here we refer to the rival services in the military, the General Staff, the defense industries, Military-Industrial Commission, Defense Council, etc.

**Such attitudes and style interact with and reinforce the generally lower rate of Soviet technological progress—i.e., the slower rate of Soviet technological change makes it natural to think in terms of refining old systems rather than creating new ones.

The supportive relationship between a design necessitated by the technology of the time and the design sector's conservative style and routine is evidenced by the Soviet development of their ICBMs. For example, the first Soviet ICBM, the SS-6, had a decidedly large booster which was required by the only technologically available atomic warheads—bulky and low-yield plutonium fission warheads. Even though subsequent breakthroughs in thermonuclear weapons technology allowed the reduction of size and weight of warheads, the SS-6 program, followed-on by similar "heavy" missile SS-7s and SS-8s, fostered a Soviet tradition of powerful boosters.[42]

What understandably makes this and other Soviet weapons traditions difficult to reverse is the fact that the interests of the responsible designers, among others, are enhanced by the continuing operation of these weapons patterns. That is to say, the *institutional interests* of those segments most closely identified with various kinds of armaments are served by the maintenance of the prevailing weapons approaches. In this connection, the institutional interests of designers, producers, and their attendant services and branches in the armed forces require that relevant weapons production continue, that follow-on systems be developed and deployed, and that future generational systems have incorporated into them characteristics commonly associated with the work or function of a specific set of designers, producers, and services.

It is important to add that since the institutional and personal prosperity of these groups is often contingent on the level of activity in their respective spheres, there is, as the memoirs of the famous Soviet weapons designer Alexander Yakovlev indicate, rather fierce competition over the allocation of resources for the various systems.[43] Indeed, Yakovlev, in writing about the possibly damaging consequences of the MiG-15 being chosen over his own Yak-25, indirectly highlighted how the selection of another design group's weapon system could adversely affect the health and morale within one's institutional base: "I was worried about the situation developing in our design bureau. You see behind me stood 100 people who might lose faith in me as the leader of the design collective."[44]

In addition to fierce designer and producer competition, it should be emphasized that all of the various branches of the military are obviously desirous of sustaining deployment of those arms which are defined as either crucial to their respective missions or necessary for their continuing institutional well-being. Thus the leading elements of the Strategic Rocket Forces will seek persistent upgrading and successor generation ICBMs, those in the Navy will press for and justify the utility of capital ships, the PVOs will push for better air defense capabilities, etc.

In short, because the persistence of weapons programs and styles secure the institutional primacy and, in a sense, also reflect the political primacy of the revelant design, producer, and military segments, armaments traditions do not die easily in the Soviet political-military universe. Hence, in critiquing the widespread notion that Soviet capabilities directly inform us about their intentions, it is important to point out that in many circumstances Soviet military capabilities may be far more reflective of dominant bureaucratic traditions and institutional interests than the mere product of any purported intent. For example, with reference to the Soviet rejection of American SALT proposals to equalize throw-weight asymmetries (perhaps the factor most alarming to those concerned about Soviet weapons capabilities), the Soviet unwillingness to retreat on this issue may well be "less the result of a calculated intent to maximize future counterforce" potentials and far more a function of the need to avoid upsetting standard institutional practices, styles, and interests in the Soviet missile design and manufacturing establishment.[45] Indeed, Soviet commentator G. A. Trofimenko has suggested as much by complaining that the United States makes proposals that are "radically at variance with the tradition and principles of the other side's [the Soviet] military-technical policy."[46]

While a strong case for the impact of bureaucratic tradition and institutional interest on the type of Soviet weapons deployments can thus be made, it must nevertheless be remembered that general Soviet deployment decisions do not occur in an external vacuum and hence do not respond only to an internal dynamic. The Soviets must, after all, be aware of threats and opportunities that present themselves within the context of their strategic relationship with their major adversary. Thus, we shall presently turn to the probable role that strategic balance considerations have on broad Soviet weapons policies.

Strategic Military Factors and Balance Considerations

In the abstract, it would appear to be a truism that the Soviet military and political leadership, at the very least, must take into account American military capabilities and the climate of relations between the two powers when weighing the choices for, or the pace of, weapons deployment. In this regard, Soviet leaders cannot afford to ignore, in the most general sense, how their strategic weaponry stacks up against the overall American capacity and threat. Thus questions must be addressed concerning the nature of projected American military threats, related areas of U.S. superiority, appropriate Soviet responses to perceived strategic disadvantages or threats, and the relative ability of the Soviet defense posture to fulfill its political-military missions. The answers to such questions no doubt affect Soviet perceptions of strategic needs.

It should be noted that while these kinds of questions and their answers are of concern to the military, they may have even greater utility when used to justify politically the acquisition of institutionally desirable weaponry. In any event, whether out of believed necessity, political utility, or as a useful rationalizing vehicle to serve the military's interest, one can expect that perceptions of the general strategic balance will have a significant effect upon, and thus rate as a major input into, Soviet strategic weapons deployment.

By way of example, it is useful to take a specific weapon system and portray the way in which strategic-military needs may have underpinned its deployment. In viewing the case of SS-9 deployment (a particularly significant case because it was cited by our then Secretary of Defense as clear evidence of Soviet first-strike intentions[47]), a number of potent strategic needs and concerns were assuaged by its acquisition. First, in a broad strategic sense, the SS-9s were needed to provide the Soviets with a more certain capability to penetrate any prospective (and in reality soon to be deployed) American ABM system. Because the SS-9 carried both vastly improved chaff-decoy penetration aids and the first Soviet developed multiple re-entry vehicles (MRVs), it, unlike other Soviet missiles, seemed to guarantee penetration of an American ABM.

Secondly, in the context of strategic arms balance considerations, the SS-9 helped to overcome certain Soviet deficiencies and thus ensured a rough equality with the United States. Simply stated, deployment of a super-sized missile with a tremendously large warhead yield* largely offset the American technological superiority in guidance and accuracy. Consequently, the Soviets gained a comparable position to the United States in their ability to destroy hard-targets. To place this factor in the strategic context of the mid-to-late 1960s, it might be said that whereas the deployment of large numbers of cheaper and smaller SS-11s allowed the Soviets to catch up with and overcome the American quantitative lead in land-based ICBMs, the SS-9 acquisition enabled the Soviets to equalize, in part, American qualitative-technical advantages.

In the end, strategic-military considerations alone probably were an influence on the decision to deploy the SS-9. However, they did not represent the only input, and this fact again permits us to highlight a central premise of this paper—namely, that Soviet weapon systems are the product of a number of variable inputs. To the degree to which this premise is true, it casts doubt on a cardinal assumption built into the hypothesis that Soviet intentions can be specifically linked to, or derived

---

*The SS-9 carried either a 25-MT warhead or three 5-MT re-entry vehicles.

from, strategic capabilities—i.e., that because a weapon system can do something, it must perforce have been designed for that purpose.

In the case of the SS-9, the supportive confluence of bureaucratic tradition/routine (e.g., the powerful-booster tradition), institutional interests (e.g., the "big-missile" design team[48] and the Strategic Rocket Forces), and a set of strategic-military needs and values (e.g., more secure AMB penetration and minimization of American technological-guidance superiority and related hard-target advantages), probably directed and determined SS-9 deployment far more than any long-range and inchoate "first-strike" design or intent.

It should be added that because these various inputs naturally complemented the doctrinal (e.g., denial) reasons which favored the deployment of the SS-9, their impact was enhanced. In this sense doctrinal or subjective factors, by indirectly consecrating certain bureaucratic traditions or institutional interests, may make them especially hard to challenge. For example, challenging a big-missile tradition, which serves the interests and prerogatives of designers, producers, and elements of the Strategic Rocket Forces, is made far more difficult by the existence of a strategic doctrine which emphasizes the importance of denial capabilities.

However, lest one conclude that subjective or conceptual factors totally determine which institutional traditions or interests will be favored, the character of the Soviet political system must be kept in mind. That is, given a coalition maintenance decision-making process, the existence of powerful leadership segments with institutional and vested interests in the prevailing strategic arms policies presumably allows for only small margins of change in policy. Thus, even should strategic conceptual attitudes be transformed, significant changes in strategic policy cannot be expected. This leads one to conclude that objective factors—bureaucratic tradition, institutional interest, strategic balance considerations—have an impact on strategic weapons deployment independent of subjective or conceptual inputs.*

In the final analysis, a number of inputs ranging from bureaucratic tradition and interest to peculiar Soviet strategic doctrine ultimately direct Soviet strategic arming policy. Two implications are suggested. First, discerning intentions (usually sinister) from Soviet weapons capabilities is at best problematical; after all, the existence of multiple inputs suggests that there is not a direct relationship between the function and purpose of Soviet weapon systems.[49]

---

*Here one sees the nexus between objective and subjective factors. On the one hand, systemic operation emphasizes the importance of institutional weight and interest. On the other, conceptual attitudes can be affected by strategic balance considerations and U.S. strategic actions.

Secondly, the existence of multiple inputs suggests that little change can be expected in the character and pace of Soviet strategic weapons programs. In this regard, the built-in logic and momentum of a number of the inputs, coupled with the lowest-common-denominator nature of the Soviet decision-making process, will likely preclude any substantial transformation of Soviet strategic policies. Consequently, American decision-makers, while not reading into Soviet weapons capabilities negative or overly threatening intentions, nevertheless should be prepared for continual growth in Soviet strategic programs; necessarily, therefore, Soviet superiority in the static indicators of nuclear power (e.g., missile launchers, warheads, throw-weight, etc.) and more pronounced asymmetries in Soviet and American force structures will ensue unless the United States undertakes a range of new strategic programs. How the United States should best respond to the challenge of Soviet strategic arms development and to the related advent of Soviet numerical superiority is an extremely important question and one to which we shall now turn.

The Appropriate American Strategic Response

In determining the most appropriate U.S. response to the logical implications of the ongoing Soviet strategic programs, perhaps the crucial question to be asked is whether superiority in the static indicators of strategic nuclear power has any real meaning. Since a detailed analysis of this question is unnecessary for our purposes, we will limit ourselves to a very brief discussion of the Paul Nitze–James Schlesinger view toward it. They posit that superiority in the number of missile launchers and warheads and in throw-weight does matter. (Although formerly Nitze seemed to emphasize the importance of aggregate throw-weight as a significant power index,[50] he now suggests that available throw-weight after an exchange of nuclear strikes may be the most valid yardstick for comparative strength.[51] On this basis, Nitze is particularly alarmed by the specter of increasing Soviet throw-weight advantages after mutual counterforce strikes. While it is difficult in any case to see how throw-weight advantages serve as a real inducement to strike first,[52] it is important to point out that Nitze's scenarios of post-attack Soviet throw-weight superiority are contingent on the Soviets always striking first.[53] Beyond the difficulty of imagining what political goals or objectives could possibly be worth enough to encourage the Soviets to take a step so laden with risk, it should be noted that the advantages Nitze cites may be more apparent than real. See footnote 57.) Put simply, Nitze and Schlesinger feel that superiority in launchers, warheads, and throw-weight can be translated into diplomatic, political, and military gains.[54] In order to prevent the Soviets from ineluctably achieving these advantages—with their presumed desta-bilizing implications and logic—Nitze and Schlesinger argue that the United States must "batten down the hatches," drastically increase its own throw-weight potential, and deploy an impressive array of new strategic weaponry.[55]

There are, however, solid grounds on which to question the Nitze-Schlesinger argument and conclusions. On the one hand, the vast and redundant strategic forces on both sides make true first-strike capabilities chimerical. On the other hand, there are "residual doubts" about whether *limited* first strikes will, in fact, yield any military advantage and whether, in any event, they are likely to be responded to *only in kind*. (The uncertainty of the advantages of a limited first strike is a product of 1) the possibility of limited launched-on-warning counterstrikes;[56] and 2) the inherent difficulty of executing limited strikes against hardened targets, what with problems of missile and warhead reliability, fratricide, and physical and timing sequential factors. It is worth noting that upon incorporating these variables into a model for attack scenarios, John Steinbruner and Thomas Garwin came to the conclusion that the attacker is seldom likely to be better off after an attack than the victim.[57]) These doubts act to vitiate incentives for initiating limited nuclear strikes or "slow-motion wars-of-attrition." As a result, there is little reason to believe that the mere possession of superiority in the static indicators of nuclear power either undermines mutual deterrence or mitigates crisis stability.

If this is so, then it is reasonable to argue that the kind of strategic superiority that Nitze and Schlesinger fear the Soviets will eventually have is not particularly meaningful. Indeed, because asymmetries in the nuclear balance are not likely to affect the functioning of mutual deterrence, such Soviet superiority should not, unless we psychological-ly allow it, be politically usable.

In this light, two conclusions might be drawn. First, the existence of asymmetrical strategic forces and attitudes should not create an unstable situation; i.e., since the continuing American second-strike capability logically precludes any meaningful Soviet damage limitation abilities or incentives for striking first, an American deterrence through punishment approach can and should stably coexist with a Soviet deterrence through denial strategy. Secondly, the non-utility of asymmetrical capabilities indicates that the United States need not link the sizing and structuring of its strategic forces to the Soviet posture. In this sense, as long as the United States can maintain unmistakable and somewhat flexible deterrent capabilities (and it should be noted that our ability to do so is not all that sensitive to force disparities), there is no particular need to respond to Soviet deployments.[58]

In short, the Schlesinger-Nitze advocated responses to current and foreseeable Soviet strategic deployments may simply be unnecessary. Beyond being unnecessary, however, there are grounds to believe that they are also counterproductive; that is, the pursuit of the Schlesinger-Nitze strategic programs, with their inherently greater counterforce orientation, is likely to reaffirm in Soviet minds the correctness of their strategic approach. After all, given the probability that the Soviet deterrence through denial mind-set grounded on a very high threat perception of its adversary, American actions that pose a heightened military danger or greater war-like threat must reinforce general Soviet strategic attitudes. While it may seem inconceivable to us that the Soviets could genuinely interpret Schlesingerian calls for strategic targeting options (and therein hardpoint kill weaponry) in a first strike, war threatening light, the existence of a very high percentage of their nuclear force in fixed land-based installations,[59] in combination with their perceptions of ultimate American objectives, apparently makes just such an interpretation a reality.*

Thus, the Schlesinger approach by projecting an "offensive" threat to the Soviet Union tends to underscore negative Soviet predispositions about American behavior. As a result, rather than serving as an incentive for Soviet restraint, the Schlesinger doctrine adds further impetus and rationalization to the Soviet strategic weapons buildup.** While an alternative American posture of restraint is not liable to produce any immediate changes in Soviet strategic policies, it might at least serve to erode the credibility of dominant Soviet strategic attitudes. In this regard, the arguments of those in the Soviet elite who adhere to a more

---

*That this is so has been suggested by the "scare" picture of American capabilities that the Soviets presented at the June 1974 Moscow summit and by the fact that Brezhnev, himself, is reported to have attributed the American retargeting plan to a U.S. design to achieve a disarming first-strike capability.

Furthermore, it might be added that the Soviets continually emphasize that the new American retargeting plans make war more likely and reflect an American intent to fight a nuclear war under favorable circumstances. (For a Soviet argument in terms similar to these, see an article by Major General Simonyan in *Krasnaia Zvezda* entitled "The Concept of 'Selective Options,' " September 28, 1976.)

**Herein another fallacy of the Schlesinger approach can be highlighted—namely, that by threatening our own massive buildup, we would provide the Soviets with an incentive for restraint. The problem here is that the Soviets probably focus far more strongly on the danger projected by the American threat, than the gains that might accrue from doing what the U.S. desires. In this sense, the Steinbruner "cybernetic decision-maker" seemingly characterizes Soviet behavior; i.e., the threat exercised against the Soviet decision-maker is likely to become a separate issue in itself and is likely to induce a counter threat. See John Steinbruner, "Beyond Rational Deterrence," *World Politics*, January 1976.

deterrence through punishment logic would have a greater chance of emerging and eventually having an impact.

In any event, since any foreseeable force asymmetries are not likely to be destabilizing nor readily translatable into political assets or liabilities and since the United States has a secure and at least partially flexible deterrent capability, we can afford to practice restraint in our strategic arming policies. What does this mean in practical terms for American defense policy? It means that there is no need to emulate Soviet programs (as Nitze and Schlesinger appear to suggest), and it means that only those programs that make our second-strike capability more certain are justifiable. While we may not militarily need certain follow-on or next generation weapon systems—e.g., Trident, the Cruise missile, or the B-1—they may be unavoidable for political and psychological reasons. In this connection, it would be politically difficult to oppose any or all of those programs while Soviet developments continued unabated. Moreover, at least parts of these programs might prove necessary for psychologically reassuring reasons; i.e., for our own leadership to feel confident that weapons asymmetries did not matter, the further enhancement of our retaliatory capabilities—as reflected in Trident, Cruise, or B-1—might be required.

Additionally, because the stability of the Soviet-American strategic relationship (i.e., stable coexistence of deterrence through denial and deterrence through punishment postures) depends on an unquestioned American second-strike capability, certain hedges against possible future threats to our retaliatory capacity are crucial. Trident, Cruise, and/or B-1 may be necessary in this respect.

It might be noted that the most certain way to provide for hedges against any future unknowns or possible instabilities in the strategic balance is not by means of offensive force deployments but rather by broad-based research and development programs. As John Steinbruner has pointed out, a research and development effort that emphasized 1) long-term developments independent of anticipated procurement, 2) competing technologies at the prototype state, and 3) defensive protection of strategic forces would not be destabilizing and would allow for wide choice and rapid response if a serious threat to the strategic balance developed.[60]

In short, what we are suggesting is a defense posture that tolerates ineluctable force disparities, emphasizes hardware and software improvements in our retaliatory capacity, and focuses on R&D efforts that are less likely to produce pressure for certain deployments and yet do provide hedges against the uncertainties of the future.

It should be added that this posture would include the enhancement of command-control facilities and the upgrading of retargeting capabilities—as embodied in the Command Data Buffer System—in order to enable the United States to respond selectively in the event of an accident, miscalculation, or other than total nuclear warfare. At the same time, this defense posture would specifically rule out deployment of bigger throw-weight missiles, "pinpoint" accuracy weapons, or arms that are inherently difficult to monitor or verify. In this general context, the M-X would be excluded; cruise missiles would only be deployed if acceptable methods and formulas of verification could be derived; MARVs on the Trident or land-based missiles would not be deployed unless it became clear that potential Soviet ABMs endangered our second-strike capability otherwise.[61]

Lastly, there would be little retrenchment of conventional capabilities in this posture. To the extent that national images might be affected by military wherewithal, a strong American conventional posture, in conjunction with an assured deterrent ability, would assuage any allied or Soviet doubts about the American willingness to vigorously pursue its broad foreign policy objectives.

In conclusion, we have suggested that as a result of the combination of certain subjective and objective inputs, Soviet strategic deployment policies cannot be expected to change in the near future. Although inevitable Soviet superiority in static measures will ensue, we have argued that the United States need not "batten down the hatches" and can afford to practice a kind of restraint. We have done so on the grounds that "superiority" or asymmetries in the nuclear balance are neither militarily destabilizing nor politically detrimental.

On the contrary, we have posited that American security, foreign policy objectives, and overall nuclear stability can be guaranteed by U.S. actions that relate primarily to consolidating "defensive" second-strike capabilities. In the final analysis, it it possible that such an American response to the continuing massive Soviet arms efforts can, in time, alter Soviet perceptions and convince a larger portion of their leadership that security, among other objectives, can be bought for a lot less. If it fails, only the Soviets will be the losers.

Notes

1. For a good discussion of why "Team B" was formed, who was on it, and what their conclusions were, see David Binder, "New CIA Estimate Finds the Soviets Seek Superiority in Arms," *New York Times*, December 26, 1976, pp. 1, 14.

2. See for example Paul Nitze, "Assuring Strategic Stability," *Foreign Affairs*, vol. 54, no. 2 (January 1976) [reprinted in this collection], and William

Van Cleave, "Soviet Doctrine and Strategy: A Developing American View," in *The Future of Soviet Military Power*, edited by L. Whetten (New York: Crane Russak, Inc., 1976).

3. This is a quote taken from Nitze's statement in announcing the formation of the *Committee on the Present Danger;* while Nitze is a director and one of those responsible for the formation of the committee, Van Cleave, at the very least, shares the values which underpin the committee.

4. Nitze, for one, appears to operate on the assumption that intentions can be inferred from capabilities. On at least one occasion he implied that attention to Soviet capabilities or publicly stated objectives really does inform us about Soviet intent. See Paul Nitze's letter to Adlai Stevenson, reprinted in the *Congressional Hearings on Civil Preparedness and Limited Nuclear Warfare*, The Joint Committee on Defense Production, issued April 28, 1976, p. 111.

5. Alexis Johnson said this in a lecture at the Stanford Arms Control Center in August of 1976.

6. David Holloway, "Strategic Concepts and Soviet Polity," *Survival*, November 1971, p. 366.

7. Shawn Johnston and I have been working on a more socio-psychological approach to this whole problem. Johnston, as a social psychologist, is introducing a number of interesting theoretical and methodological innovations into this field of study—e.g., "attribution theory" and "information processing."

8. Matthew Gallagher and Karl Spielmann, *Soviet Decision-Making for Defense: A Critique of U.S. Perspectives on the Arms Race* (New York: Praeger Press, 1975), p. 36.

9. In Soviet terms, military doctrine is viewed as a "higher formularized set of theses about the nature of a future war that reflect the broad guidelines adopted by the soviet political and military leaderships for the development of the armed forces." See Matthew Gallagher, "The Military Role in Soviet Decision-Making," in *Soviet Naval Policy: Objectives and Constraints*, edited by M. MccGwire, K. Booth, and J. McDonnell (New York: Praeger Press, 1975), pp. 55-56.

10. Leon Gouré, Foy Kohler, and Mose Harvey, *The Role of Nuclear Forces in Current Soviet Strategy* (University of Miami Press, 1974), p. 8.

11. With regard to the outcome of all-out nuclear war the late Defense Minister Grechko said, "We are firmly convinced that victory in this war would go to us—to the socialist system" (*Krasnaia Zvezda*, March 28, 1973). On another occasion, Grechko focused more directly on the theme that an imperialist attack would end only in an imperialist defeat—e.g., "If the imperialist aggressor risks encroaching on our country, he will be beaten everywhere—on the ground, in the air, on the water, and underwater" (*Krasnaia Zvezda*, March 14, 1974).

12. A. A. Grechko, *Na Strazhe Mira i Stroitel'stva Kommunizma* (On Guard Over Peace and the Building of Communism) (Moscow: Voeizdat, 1971), p. 41.

13. Gouré, Kohler, and Harvey, op. cit., pp. 116-117.

14. See Clarence Robinson, "Soviet Grasping Strategic Lead," *Aviation Week and Space Technology*, August 30, 1976.

15. Quoted in Gouré, Kohler, and Harvey, op. cit., p. 120—from N. V. Karabanov, et al., *Filosofskoye Naslediye V. I. Lenina i Problemy Sovremennia Voiny* (The Philosophical Legacy of V. I. Lenin and Problems of Contemporary War), Translations on U.S.S.R. Military Affairs, no. 930, July 29, 1973, p. 96.

16. Ibid.

17. *Pravda*, March 31, 1971.

18. Quoted in Gouré, Kohler, and Harvey, op. cit., p. 115.

19. Soviet appreciation of invulnerable-retaliatory capabilities followed American deployment of such forces and open discussion of the importance of such capacities. See Benjamin Lambeth, "The Sources of Soviet Military Doctrine," in *Comparative Defense Policy*, edited by F. B. Horton, A. C. Rogerson, and E. L. Warner (Baltimore: Johns Hopkins University Press, 1975), p. 207.

20. The distinction between deterrence through denial and deterrence through punishment comes from Glenn Snyder, *Deterrence and Defense* (Princeton University Press, 1961), pp. 14-16. Snyder and also Steven Canby (*The Alliance and Europe Part IV: Military Technology and Doctrine*, Adelphi Paper no. 109, pp. 2-3) apply denial strategies to essentially conventional or tactical military contexts. (Snyder, however, implies that they can have a more strategic utility.)

21. Yair Evron, who spent the summer of 1976 at the UCLA Arms Control Center, used this phraseology to describe Israeli deterrence attitudes—he at least partially inspired my own research.

22. See *Pravda*, June 28, 1972; March 28, 1973; January 31, 1974.

23. Lt. General P. Zhilin, "Military Aspects of Detente," *International Affairs* (Moscow), December 1973, p. 25.

24. See Gouré, Kohler, and Harvey, op. cit., p. 48—taken from Professor F. Ryzhenko, "Peaceful Coexistence and the Class Struggle," *Pravda*, August 22, 1973.

25. See Gouré, Kohler, and Harvey, op. cit., pp. 1-8.

26. The point here is that the Soviets have a long-standing habit of relying only upon themselves for their security. To seemingly be dependent on an adversary runs very much against the grain.

27. Iu. Kostko, "Military Configuration and the Problem of Security in Europe," *Mirovaia Ekonomika i Mezhdunarodnyye Otnosheniia*, no. 9 (September 1972), pp. 19-20.

28. A. Karenin in Thomas Wolfe, *The SALT Experience: Its Impact on U.S. and Soviet Strategic Policy*, Rand report R-1686-PR (September 1975), p. 190.

29. G. A. Trofimenko, "Some Aspects of American Political-Military Strategy," *SShA*, October 1971, p. 26. See also Chapter 6, this book, for

Trofimenko's views.

30. V. M. Kulish, *Military Power and International Relations* (translated by JPRS), May 8, 1973, p. 174.

31. Quoted in Gouré, Kohler, and Harvey, op. cit., p. 59.

32. Ibid.—see *World Marxist Review*, no. 2 (February 1974), p. 56.

33. Marshall Shulman argues that, in fact, this different attitude has already been accepted by the current political leadership; as proof he cites the Soviets' acceptance of the ABM treaty and their public calls for equal security. However, two factors argue against this interpretation. First, the Soviets may have adhered to the ABM treaty not because they have accepted the principles behind it, but rather because they sought to prevent the United States from deploying a technologically superior system. In this regard, while people like myself may not have believed that the Safeguard was technologically viable, it is quite possible that the Soviets believed that our superior system put them at a disadvantage— therefore it was important to preempt its deployment. Secondly, Soviet calls for equal security have been punctuated by declarations calling for Soviet advantages in the nuclear balance to offset asymmetries (e.g., geographic and technological) favoring the United States. Hence Soviet definitions of equal security may not be consonant with ours. See Marshall Shulman, "SALT And the Soviet Union," in *SALT: The Moscow Agreements and Beyond,* edited by Mason Willrich and John Rhinelander (New York: Free Press, 1974).

34. Ibid., p. 115.

35. Quoted in Gouré, Kohler, and Harvey, op. cit., p. 69.

36. *Krasnaia Zvezda*, March 28, 1973.

37. See John Schwarz, "Maintaining Coalitions: An Analysis of the EEC with Supporting Evidence from the Austrian Grand Coalition," *The Study of Coalition Behavior,* edited by Sven Groennings, E. W. Kelley, and M. Leiserson (San Francisto: Hold, Rinehart and Winston, 1970), pp. 235-249.

38. See Brezhnev's comments on the Politburo operation made to Western correspondents in June 1973. Theodore Shabad, "Brezhnev Who Ought to Know, Explains the Politburo," *New York Times,* June 15, 1973. Thomas Wolfe cites this and provides a good discussion of the consensual nature of Soviet decision-making. As Wolfe notes, Vladmir Petrov, "Formation of Soviet Policy," ORBIS, Fall 1973 and Gallagher and Spielmann, op. cit., pp. 28-33, are also quite useful.

39. An example of a mollifying price may be seen in the context of SALT; i.e., in return for acquiescing in SALT, one can argue that the Soviet military has had weapons desires met—e.g., the weapons systems that are emerging now had lead times that coincided with the timing of Soviet decisions to enter into SALT I agreements. If there is, in fact, a correlation here, it may be that the seeds of SALT's ultimate destruction are planted by the internal tradeoffs necessitated to arrive at the preliminary SALT agreements.

40. Gallagher, op. cit., p. 52.

41. Arthur Alexander, "Weapon Acquisition in the Soviet Union, United States, and France," in Horton, Rogerson, and Warner, op. cit., p. 429.

42. Edward Warner, "Soviet Strategic Force Posture: Some Alternate Explanations," in Horton, Rogerson, and Warner, op. cit., p. 313.

43. Alexander Yakovlev, *Tsel'znizni: zapikski aviakonstrukotora* (The goal of life: notes of an aviation designer), 2nd ed. (Moscow: Izdatel'stvo Politicheskoi Lieteratury, 1968).

44. Ibid., p. 491. Also quoted in Warner, "The Bureaucratic Politics of Weapons Procurement," in MccGwire, Booth, and McDonnell, op. cit., p. 76.

45. Thomas Wolfe, op. cit., p. 190.

46. Quoted in ibid., p. 152. See also G. A. Trofimenko, *SShA*, September 1974, p. 18.

47. Then Secretary Laird said that the SS-9 proved "they are going for our missiles and they are going for a 1st strike capability. There is *no question* about that."

48. Warner, "Soviet Strategic Force Posture", op. cit., p. 313.

49. Our characterization of Soviet strategic doctrine in deterrence framework suggests that even were doctrine to be the only input, we would not be justified in interpreting Soviet intentions in exclusively aggressive terms.

50. See Nitze, "The Strategic Balance Between Hope and Skepticism," *Foreign Policy*, no. 17 (Winter 1974-75). His example or scenario on pp. 148-149 clearly does place great importance on aggregate throw-weight as a crucial indicator of military power.

51. See Nitze, "Deterring Our Deterrent," *Foreign Policy*, no. 25 (Winter 1976-77).

52. Throw-weight represents but one index of nuclear power—it is probably less important than accuracy and taken alone sheds little light on incentives for striking first.

53. In "Deterring Our Deterrent" Nitze essentially says that the best U.S. deterrent is one based on our always maintaining a military advantage even after a Soviet first strike. This seems to suggest an attitude toward deterrence increasingly like the Soviet attitude. Indeed, whereas we formerly "taught" the Soviets about nuclear strategy, perhaps the Soviets are unknowingly teaching American strategists like Paul Nitze.

54. Paul Nitze, "Nitze Calls for 'Essential Equivalence,' " *Avaiation Week and Space Technology*, Special SALT Issue, pp. 31-33; James Schlesinger, *Department of Defense Posture Statement, Annual Report for FY 1976 and FY 1975*, I-13 to I-17 and II-1 to II-18.

55. See Nitze, "Assuring Strategic Stability"; and the Schlesinger Posture Statement.

56. Given the American ability to track and monitor all missiles from the U.S.S.R., the Soviets (notwithstanding American protestations to the contrary) cannot be assured that the United States would not launch a limited launched-

on-warning counterstrike in the face of an actual attack.

57. As an example, Steinbruner and Garwin observed that under a combined degradation of reliability, accuracy, and plan mistiming with an attack of 4000 warheads, 694 American land-based missiles would survive and the Soviets would only have a residual force of 333-467. See John Steinbruner and Thomas Garwin, "Strategic Vulnerability and the Balance Between Prudence and Paranoia," *International Security* (Summer 1976), p. 171.

58. In this regard, Maxwell Taylor has suggested that because of superpower incompatibility of missile numbers, accuracy, reliability, megatonnage and indestructibility, direct comparisons between Soviet and American strategic forces can have only limited meaning. Hence, he argues that "the only rational way to measure the adequacy of our strategic forces is by their ability to destroy all Soviet targets and/or systems which they may be ordered to attack, regardless of the circumstances. This measurement, then, is not primarily dependent upon the size of the Soviet forces." See Maxwell Taylor, "The United States—A Military Power Second to None?" *International Security* (Summer 1976), p. 51.

59. Estimates range from 60-85 percent of the Soviet strategic fire power being in fixed land-based installations. See Wolfe, op. cit., p. 196.

60. John Steinbruner, "Beyond Rational Deterrence," *World Politics*, vol. 29, no. 2 (January 1976), pp. 242-243.

61. Despite claims to the contrary, there is not reason to believe that American MIRVs are not more than merely sufficient to overwhelm and saturate any Soviet ABM system. For claims that the Soviets are on the verge of being able to deploy a viable city ABM (therefore necessitating our MARV deployment), see Clarence Robinson, op. cit. Not surprisingly, the arguments about Soviet ABM capabilities that were used to justify U.S. MIRV deployment in the late 1960s have been resurrected to mobilize support for MARV deployment.

9
Strategic Adaptability
William R. Van Cleave
Roger W. Barnett

The advent of nuclear weapons and long-range delivery systems altered and bifurcated the concept of war. Superimposed upon the traditional image was one of a long-range nuclear duel between "superpowers," which came to dominate modern discussions of strategy. In *this* image, when the possibility of massive civilian destruction was considered, the notion of "winning" seemed to become obsolescent: victors and vanquished would be indistinguishable; there could be no winners, only losers.

Deterrence of war between nuclear powers thus came to be considered the only appropriate objective. As if to make this image of war a self-fulfilling prophecy, a "strategy" of deterrence developed that had as its aim, not winning, but assuring that all would be losers. No longer could a chief of armed forces approach his political leadership and proclaim palindromically, "Now, Sir, a war is won!"

If it is allowed, on the other hand, that "winning" may mean "not losing," or alternatively "securing an objective," pursuing relative advantage, or improving the outcome of a war, the term does not seem intrinsically evil or necessarily obsolescent—assuming that one cares who wins. "Winning" in this sense lies at the core of strategic policymaking and planning for national defense.

Participation in a strategic nuclear exchange, the "success" of which is measured in devasted cities and tens of millions of deaths, must be excluded entirely from all definitions of "winning." Preventing such an exchange must also unequivocally be classified as "not losing," or winning. But ensuring that nuclear war takes the form of such an exchange does not qualify as strategy; strategy does not seek to guarantee that both sides lose, that there will be no winners.

Reprinted by permission from *ORBIS*, Fall 1974. Copyright 1975 by the Foreign Policy Research Institute.

The opinions and assertions contained herein are those of the authors. They are not to be construed as official or as reflecting the views of the Navy Department.

Deterrence of a strategic nuclear attack on the United States must certainly comprise the cornerstone of U.S. strategic policy. On this untarnished principle there is no debate. But the matter clearly does not end there. Deterrence is not static, either in what must be deterred or in the way deterrence is to be accomplished. Nor is deterrence alone the sum total of strategy. In brief, the key to strategy is *adaptability,* and adaptability is the key to recent changes in U.S. strategic nuclear doctrine.

Strategic adaptability presumes, in agreement with Professor Donald Zoll, that "strategy reduces itself to the arts of war designed to achieve objectives short of the vital interests of states—for whose protection, presumably, the full national power of the state must be unleashed— coupled with those plans necessary to deal with the contingency of a nuclear strike of irrevocable dimensions."[1] This hearkens back to the dual nature of winning—that if one wants to win, more is required than the ability simply to assure massive destruction in the name of forestalling a catastrophic nuclear exchange.

A New Debate?

A new great debate over strategy, expected from Defense Secretary Schlesinger's espousal of what we are here calling strategic adaptability and from Secretary of State Kissinger's later appeal for a national debate on strategy, has yet to bloom despite a smattering of journalistic articles largely denouncing or decrying the "Schlesinger strategy," and a lesser number of more scholarly treatments.[2] The principal reason for this is that there appears to be little latitude for such a dramatic debate if the issues and alternatives are accurately defined; and when the issues are dramatically but erroneously posed and strawman alternatives are drawn, only a false and futile debate can result. Yet even if no great debate takes place, one notes intellectual ferment and a rethinking of established strategic and arms control precepts, a new, skeptical look at what has been for a long time orthodox wisdom, accompanied by substantial—though hardly mass—apostasy. As two scholars writing on this renaissance of thought correctly pointed out, a "widespread and deep-seated dissatisfaction today with many of the fundamental premises underlying American strategic weapons policy" has been brought about by disillusionment with SALT and Soviet intransigence therein, by the vigor of Soviet strategic weapons programs, and by other manifestations of Soviet strategic doctrine and policy that have combined to produce a "general skepticism of Russian intentions."[3]

It is ironic that counterforce was eshewed as a major U.S. objective in order to exercise a self-restraint that, it was assumed, would induce similar self-restraint on the part of the Soviets; but it must now be seriously reconsidered because the lack of Kremlin restraint has produced a Soviet strategic capability rendering "assured destruction"—or any massive strike option—questionable as a planned response. In other words, the reconsideration has been necessitated not so much by our own volition or acumen as by the determination of our major adversary. The doctrine of assured destruction and the concept of "mutual assured destruction" might have remained the dual cynosure of U.S. strategic and arms control thought had not steady growth of Soviet strategic offensive capabilities and steadfast Soviet rejection of those notions forced a rethinking of our doctrine and concepts.

There still remain more or less ritual recitations of mutual assured destruction dogma, and the statements of the Secretary of Defense earlier this year were met with the usual rhetorical overkill of that school of thought. Increasingly, however, a new thoughtfulness is evident, even where disagreement remains. It is this thoughtfulness that should be encouraged in any national debate, where too often (as in the Safeguard case) the objective is to win points rather than to clarify and promote judicious choice.

A debate on matters of national strategy, subject to strong emotions in such areas as strategic force planning and targeting, may by its very nature muddle issues rather than clarify them. Alternatives become dramatically, if not apocalyptically, cast in spurious either-or terms, which themselves are seldom descriptive or analytic but polemic. Carrying normative or pejorative connotations, these often imprecise terms are employed as missile words to be launched against one's opponents: arms control, stability, arms race, overkill, first strike.

In actuality the choices—and the modifications represented by Schlesinger's announcements—are matters of degree, not of either-or. In many cases they merely involve clearer thinking and tuning declaratory policy more closely to actual policies for acquisition, deployment, and employment of forces. Some would have the choices defined sharply as being between "counterforce" and "assured destruction," between "war-fighting capability" and "deterrence," even though these can never be contrasted, have never been either-or choices, and never will be. Any modern strategic force has *some* inherent counterforce capability, whether against soft, hard, or hardest military targets.[4] Any plan for the use of such forces will necessarily include some military targets: for example, defenses may have to be suppressed before other attacks take place. Any force, to deter, must be capable of being used. Does anyone seriously suggest that a military force have *no* war-fighting capability?

Whether U.S. strategic offensive forces have had and have now the ability to attack enemy military targets—even hardened ICBM silos—is no real issue. They have had and do have *some* such capability. The question is whether that capability is sufficient. Our present capability, even if improved to a great extent by major force programs not now planned, would not provide a first-strike disarming capability against Soviet land-based strategic forces, much less a preclusive disarming capability, as the Secretary of Defense has explained.[5] Thus, there is no real issue concerning possibly unsettling effects of a first-strike capability.

Indeed, it is difficult to make an issue of "flexibility," per se. As Schlesinger observed, "when you get down to the hard rock of selectivity and flexibility in targeting plans, there really is very little criticism of that."[6] (However, as Professor Wohlstetter points out, there is a strong tendency among those who accept flexibility in principle to argue that "fortuitously, we have just the right amount of flexibility that we need and, it seems by good luck, exactly the right degree of accuracy.")[7]

Hence, the issues are not either-or as frequently suggested, but more or less: more or less enhanced flexibility; more or less selectivity; more or fewer options; more or less emphasis in planning on limited strikes, on restraint, on precision, on military targets.

The questions related to those issues are simple ones that need not be confounded by resort to polemical jargon or dramatic descriptions of alternatives and consequences. Will the adjustments proposed mean that we will be more or less able to deter various threats and to negate the effectiveness of threats to the United States and its allies? Are the adjustments more likely to increase or decrease our chances for controlling escalation in the event of war? Does deterrence, if it fails initially, also have to fail totally? Do we wish to be more or less able to discriminate between military targets and civilian ones, to attack militarily relevant targets selectively without the necessity of widespread urban and population destruction? To what extent do we want that capability? Do we wish to improve it principally by changes in targeting plans, or to improve it still further by changes in the physical capabilities of our forces?

Answers to such questions, because they signify decisions on strategies and on force programs, must be derived on balance since considerations on both sides must be weighed. But the choices are unlikely to be as stark as they are editorially presented. The issues are more a matter of the general direction to take in strategic policy—the direction that will guide research and development, force acquisition and deployment, the planning of options for employment, and, finally, declaratory policy, since it is clearly a purpose of the Defense Secretary to have declaratory policy somewhat more consistent with actual policies than it may have been in the past.

Even in the matter of direction, however, there has been some confusion. Many accounts, in the guise of arguing against a putative movement away from assured destruction toward counterforce, actually would have U.S. planning move toward a more rigid and pure adherence to urban assured destruction. An inflexible Catonic strategy of city destruction, which would in all likelihood be mutual, would be substituted for continuing force improvements and plans enhancing the ability to use forces selectively in a manner that might induce restraint in an adversary—i.e., to hit and to confine damage essentially to point targets other than population concentrations.

It is always necessary to ask first what we want our strategic forces to *do*. Some would answer simply, to deter. But to deter what? How? Until those answers are determined, the capabilities we wish our forces to have and the strategies to be followed cannot be established. The tendency has been to try to isolate "deterrence" from usefulness of nuclear forces, from flexibility, "war-fighting," denial of an adversary's objectives, and damage limitation. Concurrently, deterrence, undifferentiated by considerations of varied threats and tailored ways of countering those threats, has been seen by many as exclusively associated with the infliction of retaliatory punishment. In this view, the greater or more "assured" the destructiveness, the surer the deterrent; the more "usable" the forces, the more likely they were to be used, thereby presumably weakening deterrence. Destructive capability was emphasized over credibility. In the nuclear sphere at least, this was a direct reversal of the criticisms of "massive retaliation" that grew and became widely accepted in the late 1950s.

Presumably, in such thinking the overriding objective is not deterrence, per se, much less defense, but avoidance at all costs of the use of nuclear weapons: our use to be deterred as much as enemy use. But if that is one's primary value, one should be candid about it and not disguise it under the rubric of deterrence. Such a posture evokes questions: Should deterrence be based upon *unusable* weapons? Can it be?

Inherently high levels of destructiveness do not constitute an optimum deterrent or even a satisfactory policy against some kinds of threats—at the tactical nuclear weapons level, for example, and where deterrence might best be accomplished by the credible ability to defend or to respond with restraint rather than to threaten mass destruction reflexively. Now, for military or political coercion, there are varieties of strategic nuclear threat possible, against which assured destruction or massive retaliation is not as credible as *measured* retaliation. Since deterrence is some product of capability and credibility, the capability to use nuclear forces in a rational and nonapocalyptic fashion, when compared with the credibility of massive strikes in response to nonmassive attacks, and when the adversary has his own massive capabilities in reserve, may become a better—and infinitely safer— deterrent. Contrary to what many seem to believe, increasing the credibility of use does not promote a breakdown of deterrence and the ultimate use of nuclear weapons. The objective is deterrence, and if both capability and credibility of the use of strategic weapons are sufficient, deterrence will be strengthened.

But deterrence may fail in any case, and the weapons may have to be used. The ability to conduct selective and limited nuclear strikes for express and restricted purposes while holding major retaliatory forces in reserve (where they are of more value for coercion than if used for urban-industrial destruction) provides an important hedge against the inability to predict deterrence thresholds for a range of situations, promotes the possibility of escalation control, and increases opportunities for war termination without major urban damage. Flexibility in the application of strategic weapons thus supports the requirement of adaptability in strategic policy.

Hence, while it is true that strategic flexibility has been considered and debated in the past, it is timely to consider it again. Despite the similarity of some points in Secretary McNamara's June 1962 Ann Arbor speech and Schlesinger's current proposals, there are issues and considerations about limited strategic options and flexibility that are unique to the 1970s: for example, both technology and the strategic balance have changed in ways that prompt a re-examination of the utility of flexibile and limited options.

Genesis of Assured Destruction

Through the 1960s "assured destruction" grew from an analytical tool to the principal criterion for gauging U.S. retaliatory force sufficiency, to the dominant strategic concept among the intellectual defense community and even among official planners, to a philosophy for arms control and mutual deterrence. After early flirtations with strategic flexibility, counterforce, and damage limitation, "assured destruction" became the "badly needed" theory of requirements, the "conceptual framework for measuring the need and adequacy of our strategic forces."[8]

Strategically, assured destruction came to be measured in terms of destroying arbitrarily determined percentages of population and civil industry: (a) because of a lingering association of "strategic" bombing with city bombing; (b) because during the formative years of the concept the combination of yield and inaccuracy then characteristic of strategic forces failed to lend itself to discriminate attacks avoiding major collateral damage, at least on targets in or near urban areas; (c) because many regarded, and continue to regard, such destruction as inevitable (Panofsky asserts it to be "a physical fact" insensitive to policy) or at least easily accomplished, so that—if both sides designed their strategic forces on this premise—costs of strategic forces could be decreased, mutual deterrence would increase, and arms limitation agreements could be brought about; and (d) because population fatalities and gross urban-industrial destruction, given a few assumptions, seemed readily calculable and thus a fine accounting or measuring device.

However, the linkage of strategic bombing to city bombing need not be so rigid. Accuracies have been achieved that allow discriminate attacks without the accompaniment of widespread civilian collateral damage. There is nothing inevitable in massive population destruction or escalation. Likewise, there is a significant distinction among numbers killed, even at high levels. Strategic forces, even in the heyday of assured destruction, have been designed for capabilities and missions other than city busting.[9] Furthermore, there is ample evidence that the Soviets reject the concept outright. It has neither reduced arms competition nor produced meaningful arms control; to the contrary, it may have contributed to Soviet incentives for a strategic buildup to the extent that it provided them first with an opportunity to gain strategic parity, and then with an opportunity for measurable superiority.

The term assured destruction connotes a misleading simplicity and certainty: it reduces strategic calculations to the easily grasped tenets of a Catonic strategy and implies that this destruction is not only calculable but easy. Neither is the case. Nothing is "assured"; certainly not that the United States would so respond, not even that the planned or assumed destruction would take place if the United States did so respond.[10] In a situation where such use of U.S. forces would in all probability bring about condign destruction of U.S. cities—and thus amount to an act of self-destruction—it is hardly "assured" that U.S. forces would be put to that use.

In view of the rhetoric of assured destruction, the dominant role the concept has assumed in stratetgic intellectualizing, and its importance in guiding strategic force decisions and evaluating strategic arms limitation packages, it is essential to keep repeating that it is basically an analytical test, and not necessarily strategy. At least, if it is the "cornerstone of U.S. deterrence strategy," it exist in variations other than deliberate and methodical destruction of urban population. Ultimate reliance on assured destruction, however defined, does not preclude other options or prohibit all other strategies of employment. Even so primary an advocate as Alain Enthoven acknowledged: "The assured-destruction test did not, of course, indicate how these forces would actually be used in a nuclear war."[11]

For the most part, the arms control community in the United States has been the driving force for converting what was originally one analytical tool to aid evaluation of strategic retaliatory sufficiency into unidimensional strategic policy. The success of that endeavor has been largely in the realm of academic theorizing and declaratory policy (and even that has usually been hedged to include other possibilities)—although assured destruction calculations *did* become the predominant test of strategic forces and of various arms limitation packages considered for SALT from 1968 to 1972.[12] The staggering notion that the United States would actually wage a war, should that become necessary, according to criteria the analysts found useful and the academics beguiling—however monstrous in execution—was allowed to grow and harden into conviction without adequate objection. Pursuit of "stable deterrence" and arms control could not be interrupted by distinctions regarding what was to be deterred, or by questions about what should happen if deterrence failed. Stripped of its trimmings, the response was simply: It *won't* fail.

Even an argument that large-scale destruction is a by-product of large strategic attacks[13] is much different from judging the adequacy of strategic forces by population destruction, and the latter is a far cry from basing force employment strategy on deliberate attempts to achieve such results. As Albert Wohlstetter wrote:

> a policy of unrestrained, indiscriminate attack on Russian civilians, executed without reserve, with no attempt to induce restraint in the Soviet leadership, can serve no purpose of state under any circumstances. If "Mutual Assured Destruction" means a policy of using strategic force only as a reflex to kill population, it calls for a course of action under every circumstance of attack that makes sense in none.[14]

Thus, we are conscious of persistent questions: Is threatening massive urban and population destruction necessary to deter Soviet attacks on the United States? Is it an effective deterrent against limited threats? Even against the most extreme threats to the United States, is it a better deterrent than the threat of large-scale attacks on the enemy's military capability, natural resources, or basic industries?

Exodus of Assured Destruction

Strategic doctrine in the interim between the McNamara era and the present was officially based on assured destruction, but the so-called sufficiency principle neither expressed the assured destruction criterion explicitly in terms of population fatalities nor made assured destruction equivalent to sufficiency. Resulting from an interagency study in 1969, the four criteria for strategic sufficiency insofar as a direct threat to the United States was concerned were:

Maintaining an adequate second-strike capability to deter an all-out surprise attack on our strategic forces.

Providing no incentive for the Soviet Union to strike the United States first in a crisis.

Preventing the Soviet Union from gaining the ability to cause considerably greater urban/industrial destruction than the United States could inflict on the Soviets in a nuclear war.

Defending against damage from small attacks or accidental launches.[15]

Overall, these criteria—which have not been repealed publicly— clearly announced that assured destruction is not enough and that "how much is enough?" in strategic forces must be judged by additional considerations. However, certain changes in wording in the current (FY 75) Department of Defense Report seem to imply a new set of sufficiency criteria.

In March 1974 the Secretary of Defense described the "principal features that we propose to maintain and improve in our strategic posture" as, *inter alia*:

. . . a capability sufficiently large, diversified, and survivable so that it will provide us at all times with high confidence of riding out even a massive surprise attack and of penetrating enemy defenses, and *with the ability to withhold an assured destruction* reserve for an extended period of time.

. . . command-control capabilities required by our National Command Authorities to direct the employment of the strategic forces in a *controlled, selective, and restrained* fashion.

. . . the forces to execute a *wide range of options* in response to potential actions by an enemy, including a *capability for precise attacks on both soft and hard targets, while at the same time minimizing collateral damage.*

. . . an offensive capability of such size and composition that all will perceive it as in overall balance with the strategic forces of any potential opponent.[16]

This formula calls for:

(1) Not only an assured destruction capability, but the ability to withhold it in reserve for an extended period of time. The assured destruction force becomes a last-ditch deterrent threat, its primary value resting in its influence on an enemy's restraint while it is not used, rather than in the principal employment option.

(2) A wide range of employment options enabling controlled, selective, restrained, and precise attacks against both urban and

nonurban targets, soft and hard, in a manner to limit collateral damage.

(3) "Essential equivalence" with the strategic forces of any enemy, both actually and perceptually. This equivalence refers not only to observables such as the relative size of strategic forces, but also to counterforce capabilities. It does not, however, require force symmetry or the matching of all opponent capabilities. Rather, it requires "overall balance" wherein enemy advantages may be canceled by U.S. advantages in other areas.

The problem then is not so much assured destruction. As an analytical tool, it may be useful if not overdone. As a force capability, it is necessary—but insufficient. Nor is the change proposed a move entirely away from it. There are two differences: (1) Instead of relying on assured destruction as our primary response capability and allowing it to dominate all other options, we now want more planned limited-strike options, some of which would be quite discriminate, while the assured destruction capability would be held in reserve with the objective of dampening escalation. Such a reserve would serve to make even clearer the limited nature of the other options. (2) In view of President Nixon's charge that measuring population fatalities is inconsistent with American values, and similar comments by Secretary Schlesinger, we may now prefer to judge the adequacy of the assured destruction capability with regard not so much to population fatalities and urban destruction as to objectives of greater political-military relevance to a war and its aftermath—such as (a) reduction of the enemy's military capability, both to prosecute the war and to exert postwar power beyond his borders (or, for that matter, to maintain domestic control and protect his own borders), (b) destruction of elements critical to his postattack recovery capability, and (c) disruption of political control mechanisms.

To conduct a reasonable discussion of what changes are suggested for U.S. strategic doctrine and what are not, and of the reasons for the changes, it is best to understand exactly what the Secretary of Defense has said.

Adaptability: Measured Deterrence

On January 10, 1974, Secretary Schlesinger first announced that there has taken place "a change in the strategies of the United States with regard to the hypothetical employment of central strategic forces. A change in targeting strategy as it were." (He did not say it was a thorough change.) He went on:

> To a large extent the American doctrinal position has been wrapped around something called "assured destruction" which implies a tendency to target Soviet cities initially and massively and that this is the principal

option that the President would have. It is our intention that this not be the only option and possibly not the principal option.

Because of the growth of Soviet force capabilities, "the range of circumstances in which an all-out strike against an opponent's cities can be contemplated has narrowed considerably and one wishes to have alternatives for the employment of strategic forces other than what would be a suicidal strike against the cities of the other side."[17]

That a broadening of the options available in U.S. targeting plans (the SIOP—Single Integrated Operational Plan) was in the wind should have come as no surprise. Concern had been expressed about overly restricted options and changes had been suggested in each of President Nixon's four previous annual messages on U.S. foreign policy.

In a news conference on January 24, Schlesinger explained his earlier remarks. In the first place, he said, the key to understanding the modifications—rather than focusing on counterforce versus assured destruction—is to recognize that the "emphasis is upon selectivity and flexibility; that does not necessarily involve what is referred to as major counterforce capabilities. . . . The emphasis is on the selection of targets." Nor does this selectivity necessarily require new force programs. More important, the Secretary emphasized, is a change in attitude and planning. "In order to have a strategy of selectivity and flexibility one must consciously adopt that and adjust plans to doctrine. That is a considerable change."[18]

In his annual report to Congress in March, Schlesinger elaborated on the changes and the reasons for them.[19] U.S. thinking about strategic deterrence, he said, has not kept pace with the evolution of the threat. "The scope of the Soviet program as it has now emerged is far more comprehensive than estimated even a year ago . . . a truly massive effort." It has developed "ahead of rather than in reaction to what the United States has done," and it will pose a much broader range of real threats to the United States and its allies than in the past.

To counter the more extreme views of assured destruction advocates, the Secretary reiterated that the United States has had targeting options in the past:

> Although several targeting options, including military only and military plus urban/industrial variations, have been part of U.S. strategic doctrine for quite some time, the concept that has dominated our rhetoric for most of the era since World War II has been massive retaliation against cities, or what is called assured destruction.[20]

Concurrently he explained to the Muskie Subcommittee of the Senate Committee on Foreign Relations:

Of course, all our delivery vehicles are targeted against specific targets. The point that is different about the targeting doctrine that I have outlined to you is the emphasis on selectivity and flexibility. In the past we have had massive preplanned strikes in which one would be dumping literally thousands of weapons on the Soviet Union. Some of those strikes could to some extent be withheld from going directly against cities, but that was limited even then.

With massive strikes of that sort, it would be impossible to ascertain whether the purpose of a strategic strike was limited or not. It was virtually indistinguishable from an attack on cities.[21]

We have, then, had options. However, they have (a) required the release of a very large number of weapons and therefore involved high levels of destruction; (b) been too few in number and insufficiently selective or limited to suit future requirements—we have made no real effort to develop adequate limited options either in planning or in force capabilities;[22] and (c) not been precise enough against military targets or, as Schlesinger later testified, particularly efficient against harder military targets.

We still plan to have an assured destruction capability, but today that is neither sufficient nor reassuring:

> Such reassurances may bring solace to those who enjoy the simple but arcane calculations of assured destruction. But they are of no great comfort to policymakers who must face the actual decisions about the design and possible use of the strategic nuclear forces. Not only must those in power consider the morality of threatening such terrible retribution on the Soviet people for some ill-defined transgression by their leaders; in the most practical terms, they must also question the prudence and plausibility of such a response when the enemy is able, even after some sort of first strike, to maintain the capability of destroying our cities.
>
> Since we ourselves find it difficult to believe that we would actually implement the threat of assured destruction in response to a limited attack on military targets that caused relatively few civilian casualties, there can be no certainty that, in a crisis, prospective opponents would be deterred from testing our resolve.
>
> Today, such a massive retaliation against cities, in response to anything less than an all-out attack on the U.S. and its cities, appears less and less credible.[23]

Yet, deterrence may fail in many ways; the problem, therefore, is a lack of sufficient options between no response and large-scale responses. The requirement stipulated is for a series of measured responses as more credible deterrents to a range of threats, and more rational responses to limited failures in deterrence, responses that bear some relation to the provocation, have prospects of terminating hostilities before general nuclear war breaks out, and leave some possibility for restoring deterrence.

Flexibility of response is also essential because, despite our best efforts, we cannot guarantee that deterrence will never fail; nor can we forecast the situations that would cause it to fail.... To the extent that we have selected response options—smaller and more precisely focused than in the past— we should be able to deter such challenges. But if deterrence fails, we may be able to bring all but the largest nuclear conflicts to a more rapid conclusion before cities are struck. Damage may thus be limited and further escalation avoided.[24]

It is important to note that, in contrast to ideas of damage limiting that would seek to deprive the enemy of his strategic capabilities through major counterforce operations and active defenses, the emphasis here is on *targeting restraint.* Restraint is characteristic of limiting and terminating conflict once deterrence has failed.

In discussing limited-strike options, Schlesinger indicated that

targets for nuclear weapons may include not only cities and silos, but also airfields, many other types of military installations, and a variety of other important assets that are not necessarily collocated with urban populations. We already have a long list of such possible targets; now we are grouping them into operation plans. . . . To the extent necessary, we are retargeting our forces accordingly.

The choice of options would depend on the nature of an enemy's attack and his objectives. In addition, he acknowledged that "we may also want a more efficient hard-target-kill capability than we now possess" in order to enhance deterrence. "The real issue is how much hard-target-kill capability we need."[25] The latter must be determined not only by our own assessment of the requirements of flexibility and selectivity, but also in light of the continued development of Soviet strategic force capabilities.

The Secretary stated candidly that we want to improve our counterforce capability somewhat, particularly through better accuracies. Although he requested research and development funding for a follow-on Minuteman warhead with larger yield, as well as improved accuracy, it is clear that the fundamental vehicle will be the removal of past restrictions on accuracy and other improvements to make selective targeting and retargeting possible. These improvements do not constitute expensive or major programs. In the Senate hearings in March, he pointed out that "retargeting . . . does not require any change in our force structure," and that "the long-term costs of improvements which can be related to the new targeting doctrine are about $300 million, including $186.7 million which has already been obligated. The FY 1975 Defense budget includes $33 million to complete development and to continue procurement of the Command Data Buffer," which has been an approved and ongoing effort, and $65 million for development (not procurement), mostly of data acquisition, processing, and communication capability.[26]

In separating targeting changes and new programs, the Secretary went even further:

> The change in targeting doctrine does not require new capabilities. There are some aspects for which we are asking the Congress this year for additional funding, but the change in doctrine is not dependent upon the additional funding. We are asking money in this budget for improved command and control, and for some improvement in accuracy, but the change in targeting doctrine does not depend for its efficacy upon our getting this money.[27]

While the door may be left open for future requests for program funding, these will be determined in view of developments in SALT and in the Soviet Union, as well as from continued assessments of our own requirements. In any case, that issue would be one of more-or-less, over which—including requests for funding—Congress and the public will have a say.

Essential Equivalence

There are, of course, new program requirements established for other reasons; e.g., to replace aging systems, to maintain necessary survivability and penetrability, and to prevent the United States from slipping into a position of actual or perceptible strategic inferiority to the Soviet Union. The last has been referred to as the requirement for "essential equivalence," which should be considered separately from the targeting issue, although it is somewhat related. Retargeting and improvement of strategic flexibility are desirable goals regardless of the size and throw-weight of our strategic missile forces and their comparison with those of the USSR. A policy of strategic adaptability requires enhanced flexibility in whatever strategic force we have. Whether this force may be reduced or must be increased depends upon SALT, Soviet activities, and the principle of essential equivalence, which insists that our forces not be significantly inferior to the strategic forces of the Soviet Union in numbers, throw-weight, or counterforce capability.

Since equivalence includes counterforce capability as well as size, improved targeting flexibility is related to it to the extent that it also involves counterforce improvements. In fact, if essential equivalence is to guide U.S. force decisions it will demand greater hard-target counterforce capability than will the more flexible targeting, simply because of the enormous hard-target counterforce potential inherent in the Soviet ICBM force now being developed.

Essential equivalence thus has to do with the sizing of forces and depends upon Soviet force developments;[28] targeting improvement has to do with neither. Similarly, improving targeting flexibility has nothing to do with SALT or with any attempt to coerce or influence the Soviet Union. Essential equivalence is directly related to SALT—we hope to establish it by agreement to hold forces down equally—and may also be an attempt to gain leverage in the negotiations and to induce the Soviets to exercise greater restraint in their programs.

To be realistic, however, it must be acknowledged that essential equivalence may go the way of many other labeled policies and become little more than flummery. While it is an admirable goal, it is not an exact one and may become more elastic over time, as it grows clearer that equivalence in the three properties so far defined will be most difficult to attain if limited to those central strategic offensive forces contained in strategic arms limitation agreements. Taken literally, the term looks a bit strange when juxtaposed with projections of ten to twelve million pounds of ICBM throw-weight and 7,000 to 15,000 ICBM MIRVs for the Soviet Union, against two million pounds' throw-weight and 2,000 to 3,000 MIRVs, respectively, for the United States.[29] Even if applied to the launcher limits established by the SALT I agreement, equivalence requires that we go up or they come down.

To attain essential equivalence, the forces to be included may have to be so defined as to render the concept sterile: by including more U.S. systems (bombers, noncentral systems) while excluding comparable Soviet systems, by comparing noncomparables such as bomber payload (carefully restricted to "heavy bomber" payload) and missile throw-weight, and by weighing (exaggerating?) alleged advantages in U.S. technology and in nonlimited systems.[30]

The conclusion is ineluctable that we can achieve improved targeting flexibility, selectivity, and discrimination more easily than essential equivalence (in any meaningful sense of the term) and without any necessary association of the two. Enhanced flexibility of U.S. strategic forces may promote equivalence in targeting capability, but it does not depend upon "essential equivalence," however defined. It is an objective in and of itself, unrelated to the sizing of forces.

This is important to understand in view of expressed concerns that increasing our ability to plan more flexible and selective attacks and to strike targets more discriminately will somehow provoke a Soviet reaction, thereby fueling an "arms race" and/or destabilizing the strategic balance.

But how could this be? As the Secretary of Defense has pointed out, critics of options cannot have it both ways:

> If the nuclear balance is no longer delicate and if substantial force asymmetries are quite tolerable, then the kinds of changes I have been discussing here will neither perturb the balance nor stimulate an arms race. If, on the other hand, asymmetries do matter (despite the existence of some highly survivable forces), then the critics themselves should consider seriously what responses we should make to the major programs that the Soviets currently have underway to exploit their advantages in numbers of missiles and payload.[31]

There has been a tendency on the part of many advocates of mutual assured destruction and critics of counterforce, limited strategic options, and arms modernization, to argue at the same time that strategic deterrence is inherently stable (because of the impossibility of disarming first strikes and the inevitability of great civil devastation from even a small number of strikes in retaliation), but that improvements in counterforce, damage limiting, or flexibility would be destabilizing and increase the risk of nuclear war. They also argue that the inevitability of great population destruction—essentially, assured destruction—is insensitive to policy (Panofsky), but that a change in policy away from reliance on that principal option toward more limited and selective options would, again, be destabilizing. If deterrence is so stable and population devastation so certain, if counterforce and damage-limiting measures are so meaningless, how can qualitative improvements in weaponry and adjustments of targeting policy be so destabilizing?

On the one hand, it seems, we have reached a plateau from which there is no escape; on the other hand, the merest hint of escape is bad. Man has devised a situation where, in the event of strategic nuclear warfare, excessively high levels of destruction are unavoidable; yet any attempt to relieve or to escape from this inflexible situation is both bad and a priori doomed to failure. We are eternal captives of what we ourselves have devised, according to the advocates of the inflexible mutual hostage strategy. (One might ask: Why, if such a condition is inevitable, is it necessary to advocate it?) Yet, they fear that changes will be upsetting. Of what?

At the same time it is argued that the proposed changes will be destabilizing in another sense: they will provoke major Soviet reactions and produce, or propel, an arms race. This concern seems to trouble even some who reject the mutual hostage theory or the notion that deterrence will be destabilized by the proposed changes, and who may on balance favor the changes. But (leaving aside for the moment that an "arms race"—or more accurately some increased arms competition—may be preferable to continuation of the existing situation and of recent trends in strategic arms relations) this reservation, as remarked by the Secretary of Defense, in reality is as baseless as the first concern, for the reasons cited in the next section.

Arms Pacing

In the first place, it is not proposed that the United States increase its forces, but that the flexibility and capability of the forces we have be improved; and for the most part the changes necessary do not now seem to involve major programs. Ensuring viable and adequately survivable forces in the future probably *will* involve major programs, and the test of essential equivalence *may* do so, but these requirements depend upon what the Soviets do. In the second place, while the Soviets have been arms racing, the United States has been arms walking or crawling;[32] with SALT's failure to meet our expectations, the problem is now one of pacing, and the less pacing we do immediately, the sooner we will be placed in the position of having to catch up.

Moreover, war winning and counterforce capability have been consistent keynotes of Soviet strategic doctrine and strategic force development for some time, and it is abundantly clear that American pedagogy and restraint have not succeeded in steering Moscow away from such objectives. As two writers recently observed, "the Soviet Union has or will have great targeting flexibility and counterforce capability in its own strategic forces. . . . Soviet writers have consistently advocated a capability to engage in and to win a strategic nuclear war."[33] That the brightness of MAD truths must surely penetrate even the murkiness of primitive Soviet military thought to close the intellectual gap between the strategic doctrines of the two countries can no longer appear convincing even to the most credulous.[34]

Critics of increased flexibility, which they interpret to signify increased counterforce capability on the part of the United States, include among their arguments the assertion that the USSR would be seriously concerned about any indication of increased hard-target-kill capability in U.S. strategic forces. At the same time they assert that the United States, by dint of its triad of mutually supporting strategic forces, need not fear a Soviet disarming first strike, since attack timing problems, the fratricide factor, and the assured survival of a large number of U.S. weapons would deter it. In view of the prevailing strategic balance (the significantly larger numbers of Soviet ICBMs and SLBMs and the potentially great number of RVs), the mix of strategic forces on both sides, and the natures of the two different political systems involved, this alleged concern over U.S. intentions and Soviet reactions becomes "curiouser and curiouser."

Even if improvements in U.S. targeting capability were to mean substantial improvements in counterforce capability, one must ask: What more can the Soviets do to develop *their* counterforce capability? It is most difficult to see what they could do beyond what they are already doing. And if there is a reaction, *to the extent that* the Soviets become concerned with U.S. hard-target counterforce capability, their reaction must be in the direction of improving the survivability of their own forces. Is that bad for the United States? Efforts and resources the Soviets must put into survivability measures are efforts and resources unavailable for a quest for strategic superiority, for their own menacing counterforce capabilities, or for other purposes more detrimental to U.S. interests.

Down the Up Escalator

In conclusion, this article expresses the conviction that the enhanced targeting flexibility proposed by Secretary of Defense Schlesinger is a step in the right strategic direction. By promoting strategic adaptability and credibility with restraint, it will strengthen deterrence and promote U.S. interests in the event of war without increasing the risk of long-term detriments about which many are concerned. It is not a proper goal of strategy to increase war's destructiveness, particularly so meaninglessly; the object is, rather, to avoid losing, to preserve and to pursue U.S. interests, to control escalation, and to promote a more satisfactory war termination than that implied by assured destruction. An attempt to limit war damage, while maintaining or improving prewar and intrawar deterrence, is laudable and an essential objective of both national military strategy and arms control. To insist that deterrence depends upon maximizing—or inflicting very high levels of—civil destruction as a necessary consequence of retaliation is execrable.

The programs suggested to improve current targeting capabilities are not costly and hardly constitute a "first-strike" threat. The degree of further improvement through future programs will be a matter of congressional (and thereby public) approval. No increase in force levels is contemplated; but that, too, is an option for future consideration, depending upon the need to adapt to Soviet capabilities and upon the outcome of SALT.

In essence, advocates of strategic adaptability merely call for a return to more traditional, sensible, time-tested, and proven strategic thinking—a return from a bizarre detour to a path with origins as far back as Sun Tzu:

What is of supreme importance in war is to attack the enemy's strategy....

Next best is to disrupt his alliances. . . .

The next best is to attack his army. . . .

The worst policy is to attack cities. Attack cities only when there is no alternative.[35]

Notes

1. Donald A. Zoll, "New Aspects of Strategy," *Strategic Review*, Fall 1973, p. 43.

2. Examples of the latter include Colin S. Gray, "Rethinking Nuclear Strategy," *ORBIS*, Winter 1974, and the relevant parts of Albert Wohlstetter's article in the same issue, "Threats and Promises of Peace: Europe and America in the New Era." Also, Colin S. Gray, "The Urge to Compete: Rationales for Arms Racing," *World Politics*, January 1974; Ted Greenwood and Michael L. Nacht, "The New Nuclear Debate: Sense or Nonsense?," *Foreign Affairs*, July 1974; and Bruce M. Russett, "Short of Nuclear Madness," *Worldview*, April 1973.

3. Greenwood and Nacht, op. cit. For a description of these factors, see the testimony of Defense Secretary Schlesinger, *U.S.-U.S.S.R. Strategic Policies, Hearing* before the Subcommittee on Arms Control, International Law and Organization of the Committee on Foreign Relations, U.S. Senate, 93rd Congress, 2nd Session, March 4, 1974, made public on April 4, 1974.

4. It may be useful to emphasize here that counterforce is not synonymous with hard-target kill. Some counterforce targets have been hardened to nuclear and blast effects, some have not, and some cannot be. To use counterforce to describe only missile silo destruction is an impoverishment of the term; using it solely in that sense is a distortion. Counterforce targets may be soft, hard, harder, and hardest, from an ability to withstand only a few pounds per square inch additional overpressure to perhaps 1,000 psi, with only silos and some command facilities in the last category. Moreover, even for hard-target capability, its significance resides in the degree to which it exists. Statistically, there is some hard-target counterforce capability in all ICBM forces. The measurement of accuracy (CEP) is a statistical expression of where we may expect 50 per cent of the weapons to detonate relative to the target, and hard-target kill probability is a function of the number of weapons one is willing to dedicate to a single target, as well as of the accuracy and yields of those weapons. If one is willing to dedicate a

large number to a single target, high or significant kill probabilities may be achieved; but this may not be an efficient use of that number of weapons, it may not result in anything close to a favorable exchange ratio, and it may be far from a first-strike capability.

The differences in the hard-target potentials of different warheads, or MIRVs, must also be understood. Here accuracy is the most important single factor. An improvement in accuracy by a factor of two has the same effect against a hardened target as increasing yield by a factor of eight; or, 100 KT at .25 nautical miles (nm) gives about the same psi overpressure and single-shot kill probability as 800 KT at .5 nm. (Neither is very good against hard targets: about .10 probability against a 1,000 psi target and about .16 against a 500 psi target, which demonstrates the difficulty of attaining even high single-shot kill probabilities against such targets.) However, yield, too, is important, particularly where there are large differences. The following chart gives some examples of variable combinations of accuracy, yield, and numbers of (reliably arriving) RV's in terms of kill probability against a target hardened to 500 psi, and also demonstrates clearly the differences in hard-target counterforce capability between U.S.-type MIRVs and Soviet-type MIRVs:

Yield	.04 MT		.15 MT		2 MT	
No. of RV's:	1	3	1	3	1	3
.4 nm	.04	.11	.09	.25	.42	.8
.3 nm	.07	.20	.15	.39	.62	.95
.2 nm	.15	.38	.32	.68	.89	.999

First-strike or significant hard targeting of even fixed land-based forces is much more complicated than this simplified chart would suggest, since there are major problems of timing and coordination, degradations to be expected in accuracy and system performance, and possibly detrimental effects of the nuclear detonations of some warheads on other arriving warheads (i.e., "fratricide").

5. *U.S.-U.S.S.R. Strategic Policies*, op. cit., and *Report of Secretary of Defense James R. Schlesinger to the Congress on the FY 1975 Defense Budget and FY 1975-1979 Defense Program*, 93rd Congress, 2nd Session, March 4, 1974. (See page citations from the latter below, referred to as *FY 75 DOD Report*.)

6. *U.S.-U.S.S.R. Strategic Policies*, op. cit., p. 10.

7. Wohlstetter, op. cit., p. 1135. Greenwood and Nacht, op. cit., take essentially this approach, as does Wolfgang Panofsky in "The Mutual-Hostage Relationship between America and Russia," *Foreign Affairs*, October 1973, though Panfosky seems to reverse himself, from first arguing that high levels of population destruction are inherent in any strategic strike to suggesting that we have sufficient flexibility and options other than civilian destruction.

8. Alain C. Enthoven and K. Wayne Smith, *How Much Is Enough?* (New York: Harper & Row, 1971), p. 170. This process is described in Chapters 5 and 6.

9. "United States strategic offensive forces have been designed with the additional system characteristics . . . needed to perform missions other than assured destruction, such as limited and controlled retaliation." Ibid., p. 195.

10. See the article by Conrad V. Chester and Eugene P. Wigner, "Population Vulnerability," *ORBIS*, Fall 1974, pp. 763-769.

11. Enthoven and Smith, op. cit., p. 195.

12. As one of the present authors has pointed out in congressional testimony, assured destruction calculations were almost exclusively the test of various SALT limitations packages. Statement of William R. Van Cleave, *Military Implications of the Treaty on the Limitations of Anti-Ballistic Missile Systems and the Interim Agreement on Limitation of Strategic Offensive Arms, Hearing* before the Committee on Armed Services, U.S. Senate, 92nd Congress, 2nd Session, July 1972, pp. 569-592.

13. Panofsky's "physical fact" levels are much lower than those used by McNamara for hypothetical city targeting, and limited strikes—depending on the limitations and civil defense effectiveness—may reduce casualties further yet. Improvements in accuracy and Soviet civil defense plans combine to make possible discriminate attacks not accompanied by the high levels of population fatalities commonly postulated.

14. Wohlstetter, op. cit., p. 1133.

15. *Statement of Secretary of Defense Melvin R. Laird before the House Armed Services Committee on the FY 1972-1976 Defense Program and the FY 1972 Defense Budget,* 92nd Congress, 1st Sesstion, March 9, 1971.

16. *FY 75 DOD Report,* pp. 44-45. (Emphasis added.)

17. Remarks by Secretary of Defense James R. Schlesinger, Overseas Writers Association Luncheon, International Club, Washington, D.C., January 10, 1974. Mimeo. transcript, Office of the Assistant Secretary of Defense for Public Affairs (OASD/PA).

18. News Conference by Secretary of Defense James R. Schlesinger at the Pentagon, January 24, 1974. Mimeo. transcript, OASD/PA.

19. *FY 75 DOD Report,* especially pp. 32-45.

20. Ibid., p. 33.

21. *U.S.-U.S.S.R. Strategic Policies,* op. cit., p. 9.

22. Whatever has been said about options before, "nobody at the political level from 1961 to 1971 has put the energy behind developing the doctrine and the plans. . . . Now we are consciously basing our deterrent strategy upon the achievement of flexibility and selectivity." Ibid., p. 26.

23. *FY 75 DOD Report,* pp. 35, 37-38.

24. Ibid., p. 38.

25. Ibid., pp. 39-41.

26. *U.S.-U.S.S.R. Strategic Policies,* op. cit., pp. 7, 29.

27. Ibid., p. 8.

28. This does not mean to imply that essential equivalence is not promoted

through advanced capabilities and the quality of technology, which is obvious in its counterforce criterion. Nor is it to suggest that technological advantages may not make up in important respects for quantitative disadvantages. Technological advance is probably the most fruitful route for the United States to take *if* it is pushed vigorously enough to offset Soviet quantitative advantages.

29. *U.S.-U.S.S.R. Strategic Policies*, op. cit., pp. 5-7.

30. One is reminded here of Dr. Edward Teller's comment, in congressional testimony eleven years ago, on intelligence concerning capabilities easily seen and those not so easily assessed. "I am disturbed by the fact that in the region which is easily observed, we admit the Russians are ahead. Whereas in those regions where observation is more difficult we still claim superiority." *Nuclear Test Ban Treaty, Hearings* before the Committee on Foreign Relations, U.S. Senate, 88th Congress, 1st Session, August 1963.

31. *FY 75 DOD Report*, p. 39.

32. See the two-part article by Albert Wohlstetter, "Is There a Strategic Arms Race?," *Foreign Policy*, Spring and Fall 1974; also Gray, "The Urge to Compete . . . ," op. cit.

33. Greenwood and Nacht, op. cit.

34. An exception is John Newhouse, *Cold Dawn: The Story of SALT* (New York: Holt, Rinehart and Winston, 1973).

35. Sun Tzu, *The Art of War*, translated and with an Introduction by Samuel B. Griffith (Oxford, England: Oxford University Press Paperback, 1971), pp. 77-78.

10
The Strategic Forces Triad: End of the Road?

Colin S. Gray

By the early to mid-1980s, the United States will be unable to repose confidence in the ability of all save a small fraction of its silo-housed missile force to ride out a Soviet first nuclear strike. The possible implications of this early predictable development, and the policy choices that it poses for the U.S. government, are the subjects of this article.

For nearly 20 years the United States has maintained a triad of strategic forces, comprising silo-housed intercontinental ballistic missiles (ICBMs), submarine-launched ballistic missiles (SLBMs), and manned penetrating bombers. An entire leg of this triad is approaching mass obsolescence—as currently deployed in fixed hardened sites. Although the growing debate over the meaning of silo vulnerability is focused heavily upon the issue of whether or not a follow-on ICBM, called MX (missile experimental), should be developed and procured— and if so, how it should be deployed—the MX debate is operating as a catalyst to open, or reopen, discussion of a wide-ranging set of strategic and political issues. At stake in, and closely related to, the MX/ICBM debate are matters of far deeper significance than might immediately be discerned. At one level, it is the technical merits of a particular weapon system, in all aspects, that are being debated—but behind the technical issues lurk such questions as the following: What will the United States ask of its strategic forces in the 1980s and 1990s (i.e., what quantity and quality of strategic posture will be appropriately supportive of American foreign policy)? How do we deter the Soviet Union in plausible (or not implausible) crises and conflicts in the 1980s and 1990s? How do the strategic forces contribute to that deterrence?

To a major degree, technical answers must be driven by broad political-military choice. Our foreign policy goals, be they more or less expansive than in the past, should point to a prudent strategic doctrine for the United States—and such a prudent strategic doctrine, in turn,

Reprinted by permission of the author and *Foreign Affairs,* July 1978. Copyright 1978 by Council on Foreign Relations, Inc.

should indicate greater or lesser interest in particular kinds of strategic capability.

Moreover, the principal (at least potential) adversary cannot sensibly be ignored while Americans debate what *they* would like to do vis-à-vis their strategic nuclear posture. To some highly debatable degree, any U.S. strategic posture has to be relevant to Soviet anxieties, defined, as best we can determine, by Soviet officials and analysts. It should never be forgotten that American strategic forces are about the business of posing not-incredible negative sanctions in Soviet minds and, if need be, of imposing such sanctions in action. The current Director of the U.S. Arms Control and Disarmament Agency, Paul C. Warnke, has argued that the United States should not invest in strategic capabilities that mirror Soviet programs, if such capabilities are held *by us* to be undesirable.[1] While there is some sense in this argument, it would be foolish, and could prove fatal, for the United States to neglect the development of the kind of programs that have high leverage in Soviet estimation.

II

Many people, not excluding some of those knowledgeable about military affairs in general, have great difficulty comprehending what strategic nuclear forces are all about. Their analysis is viewed as an arcane exercise almost totally removed from real political life—that is, in essence there are two kinds of military power, usable (ground forces, tactical air, naval) and unusable (nuclear, and particularly strategic nuclear). Yet it happens to be the case that the health of the strategic nuclear balance is essential for the effectiveness of U.S. foreign and defense policies as a whole.

Alas for the views of skeptics of this argument, the logic works in both directions. First, behind American foreign policy, worldwide, is the *ultima ratio* of resort to strategic nuclear weapons: if American and allied forces face the possibility or imminent prospect of stark defeat at any point around the periphery of Eurasia when confronted by, say, locally applied Soviet military power, the existence of our strategic nuclear forces should enable us to threaten believably, or in the last resort to employ, a major measure of escalation in pursuit of an improved outcome at a higher level of violence. Second, should the Soviet Union face defeat in Europe (improbable though that must be judged to be), the eastern Mediterranean, or the Persian Gulf, it might be tempted seriously to employ strategic nuclear forces for an improved outcome—depending upon the quality of the local issues, their broader ramifications (perhaps, for Soviet reputation), *and the perceived state of the strategic nuclear balance.* This, of course, dramatizes and simplifies the likely range of choice. In particular, a Soviet Union in dire straits, in some local imbroglio involving the United States, would probably discern more alternatives than either acquiescence in a local defeat or escalation to a (superpower) homeland-to-homeland nuclear exchange. Nonetheless, the logic holds.

The foreign policy relevance of strategic nuclear forces is most easily, and credibly, demonstrated with reference to NATO. Barring some noteworthy changes in current thought and practice, the time is rapidly approaching when the NATO strategy of flexible response—or flexible escalation as Harlan Cleveland was sufficiently unkind or honest to characterize it[2]—simply should not work. Until the present day, widely acknowledged deficiencies in NATO's local stopping power have been rationalized by reference to the total panoply of Western deterrent potential. Should NATO be losing a war in Europe in a quite unambiguous way, having employed conventional and theater nuclear forces, then the United States would have to (initially, probably in a severely limited way) resort to strategic nuclear weapons in an endeavor to restore deterrence—as official jargon will have it. When NATO's basic, and still authoritative, strategy paper, MC-14/3, was negotiated in the mid-1960s, the United States enjoyed a very healthy strategic nuclear imbalance in its favor. A NATO strategy that rested, *in extremis,* upon deliberate, controlled escalation was very sensible. However, simply possessing large and reasonably diverse strategic nuclear forces does not, ipso facto, confer the needed quality of deterrence. Dramatic and apparently enduring trends in the strategic balance should matter for the integrity of NATO's strategic concept of flexible response/escalation.

By and large, participants in the current debate over strategic forces issues agree that the trend in the strategic nuclear balance is adverse: nobody, to my knowledge, is claiming that the United States is not dramatically less well situated, in strategic nuclear terms, in 1978 than it was in 1966-67. Also, after a little thought, very few people would dissent from the thesis that the critically needed backstop to NATO strategy is a United States that could, not incredibly, threaten first (very limited) employment of strategic nuclear weapons. Leaving aside contentious details over the pace of the adverse trend in the strategic nuclear balance, it is reasonably clear that strategic forces can, in principle, be relevant to the deterrence of crises, the deterrence of inimical behavior in crises, the control of the kind of military "breakout" that might be attempted in desperation from a crisis, and the character and terms of settlement of a war that emerged out of a crisis.

Back in 1974, Henry Kissinger questioned the political utility of strategic nuclear forces when he asked, "What in the name of God is strategic superiority?"[3] It was a pertinent question and it merits a direct answer. Strategic superiority translates into the ability to control a process of deliberate escalation in pursuit of acceptable terms for war termination. The United States would have a politically relevant measure of strategic superiority if it could escalate out of a gathering military disaster in Europe, reasonably confident that the Soviet Union would be unable or unwilling to match or to overmatch the American escalation. It follows that the United States has a fundamental foreign policy requirement that its strategic nuclear forces provide credible limited first-strike options.

Indeed such a requirement relates to many other potential conflict or confrontation situations and areas. Given the geopolitical asymmetries between the two superpowers (the Soviet Union having, in effect, interior lines of communication save toward the Western Hemisphere) as well as growing Soviet military outreach, it is more and more likely that it will be the United States that first feels the acute need to escalate out of a local theater for an improved outcome.[4]

This discussion could be misleading, in that it has dwelt upon the foreign policy relevance of actual strategic nuclear employment or of crises that threaten such employment. In practice, while acute confrontations arise only rarely, the strategic posture "works" day by day pervasively in diplomacy. Americans' perceptions of their country's relative standing, perceptions by others, and the American sense of what risks are involved in particular possible enterprises all rest, in part, though in ways that are incalculable, upon assessments of the state of the strategic nuclear balance. Nobody knows, with any confidence, how a World War III would terminate. Would there be a victor? Does such a concept make sense? But everybody knows which way the balance is tending, and this knowledge contributes to a constricting of American freedom of foreign policy action. Those who are skeptical of the importance of strategic nuclear forces have to explain why it is that the Strategic Arms Limitation Talks (SALT) are, by universal agreement, the centerpiece of East-West diplomatic activity, and really have become the pacer for, and symbolic of, the state of health of East-West relations as a whole. Also, skeptics have to explain why it is that the Soviet Union, which is not known for its neglect of the political meaning of military power, has been competing so vigorously, and expensively, in this region for more than ten years.

III

More than two years ago, Paul Nitze wrote:

The trends in relative military strength are such that, unless we move promptly to reverse them, the United States is moving toward a posture of

minimum deterrence in which we would be conceding to the Soviet Union
the potential for a military and political victory if deterrence failed.[5]

The situation is worse today than it was when those words were
written. The momentum of the Soviet strategic forces build-up has
continued, while the quality of Soviet weapons (and particularly the
accuracy of Soviet ICBMs) is better than was predicted then.[6] That
much is not in dispute.

In terms of the concept discussed in the preceding section—escalation
dominance, if you will—the implications are chilling. On current
trends in the strategic balance, an American president should prudently
be deterred from initiating strategic nuclear employment; should he
proceed nonetheless, the war would very likely terminate after an almost
wholly counter-military exchange (which the Soviet Union should win
unequivocally) because the United States could not possibly secure an
improved war outcome by initiating attacks against Soviet industry and
(through co-location) population. If, as seems plausible, it would likely
be the United States that was leading the escalation process—given that
some theater disaster needed to be reversed—it is very probable indeed
that the United States would be challenging the Soviet Union to a
competition in risk-running and damage acceptance that the United
States could not possibly win. *If* the Soviet Union will be able, by the
mid-1980s, to effect dramatically greater prompt counter-military
damage than could the United States, and if Soviet civil defense
programs are only half as effective as Leon Gouré and T. K. Jones
claim,[7] then it takes a very talented fiction writer to invent acute crises for
the 1980s wherein the United States either chooses to initiate nuclear
employment, or secures some political advantage from such employment.

If this argument is valid, it means that the Soviet Union would have
effectively neutralized the U.S. strategic deterrent, thereby holding the
ring square in local conflicts—would have the capability to escalate to
strategic nuclear use itself, should local events develop very adversely—
and would have a not-implausible concept for a politically meaningful
victory in a homeland-to-homeland nuclear war. Many of our more
dovish commentators like to wax lyrical on the subject of the deficiencies
of the Soviet civil defense program. What those commentators have
difficulty explaining is how the United States could rationally initiate
attacks upon Soviet urban areas in any event.

As of mid-1978, it is quite evident that the Soviet Union is determined
to pose (effectively) a total threat to the silo-housed American ICBM
force. There is no other plausible explanation for the Soviet ICBM
modernization program. Soviet fourth-generation ICBMs (the SS-16s,

-17s, -18s, and -19s) are replacing older ICBMs at the rate of 125-150 a year, while a fifth generation is nearing the stage of development when it will be flight-tested.

The SALT process has been, and promises to be, of negative value for the survivability of American silo-housed ICBMs.[8] SALT I, signed in May 1972, really was about two things in contemporary official American estimation. First, and most important, it set the seal upon, and was centrally symbolic of, superpower détente and ensured the reelection of Richard Nixon. (In syllogistic logic: if SALT means détente and if détente means "peace," how can one be against SALT?) Second, at the level of strategic reasoning, SALT I was, supposedly, an arrangement whereby the United States surrendered a greatly superior antiballistic missile technology (for the defense of ICBM silos), in return for a severe arresting of the pace of the Soviet offensive threat to American ICBM silos. Unfortunately, the arrangement did not work. In particular while SALT I effected a freeze on the construction of ICBM launchers (i.e., silos and their ancillary equipment), it did nothing to constrain qualitative improvements.[9] American ABM technology was indeed arrested abruptly, but the Soviet ICBM threat to American silos accelerated. The SALT process, at present, is irrelevant or negative in its impact upon strategic stability, essentially because the Carter Administration gives every evidence of not understanding that the central problems it faces relate not to arms control but to basic defense posture.[10]

When Paul Nitze wrote of "Assuring Strategic Stability in an Era of Détente," an unacceptably high threat to American silos seemed nearly ten years in the future, and all major strategic options were open. The situation is very different in mid-1978. An unacceptable level of threat to our ICBMs could mature as early as 1982-83 (which leaves very minimal lead time for appropriate offsetting action); the B-1 manned bomber has been canceled (which means that the Soviet Union should face far fewer problems coping with U.S. penetrating manned bombers and cruise missile carriers); the MX ICBM timetable—for an initial operating capability—has been slipped from late 1983 to early 1987 (if ever); and the strategic cruise missile program has been confined to deployment on airborne platforms and faces severe range constraints in SALT. Interacting very negatively with those facts is the prospect of a comprehensive nuclear test ban—which cannot fail to operate to the American disadvantage. If nuclear testing is prohibited, each side should be inclined to stick, for reasons of reliability, to more conservative nuclear weapon designs, which consume more volume and payload than do designs (not yet fully tested) that are pushing at the frontier of the state of the art. The Soviet Union, given the physical size of its strategic weapon systems, has all the payload necessary to accommodate such conservative designs—the United States does not.

No single indicator of relative strategic prowess can be used as *the* evidence for one, as opposed to a rival, trend in the strategic balance. But on every important indicator the Soviet Union is either ahead—as in megatons, "equivalent megatonnage" (a measure of surface blast damage potential), missile throw-weight, and numbers of strategic nuclear launch vehicles (SNLVs)—or is catching up rapidly, as in missile accuracy and numbers of warheads.[11] In dynamic as opposed to static "bean counting" terms, the prospect that we face in the 1980s is a Soviet Union that can disarm us forcibly of the land-based ICBM leg of our strategic triad, and which might possibly be able to hold down its civilian casualties to a level below that suffered in the Great Patriotic War of 1941-45—even if the United States should proceed all the way up the escalation ladder.

On current trends, the former prediction is close to certain, the latter is plausible. And SALT II, as currently designed, has no impact of merit for future stability upon these arguments. If, as reported, SALT II specifies a common SNLV ceiling of 2,250, a common MIRV (multiple independently targetable reentry vehicle) launcher ceiling of 1,200 and a common MIRVable ICBM ceiling of 820, the enormous throw-weight in the Soviet ICBM force[12]—with its clear implication for subdivision for MIRVing—provides capacity to spare for the evolution of a total threat against American hard targets (missile silos and command-and-control facilities).

IV

There are no cheap and clever solutions to the problem that Soviet theoretical silo-killing prowess poses. It is possible that the obsolescence of the American silo-housed ICBM force should be viewed not as a problem, but rather as a historic arms control opportunity. Unfortunately for the promise in this line of thought, the United States is not, at present, developing a parallel threat against Soviet ICBM silos on a scale at all likely to promote enthusiasm in Moscow for a major SALT-negotiated drawdown in strategic forces. (Indeed, the recent SALT II negotiating record illustrates unambiguously the fact that the Soviet Union is interested in effecting only the least level of reduction in offensive forces that it can secure, and in delaying the execution of such a reduction as long as possible.)

As of mid-1978, the United States cannot address the silo-vulnerability problem in SALT—because that problem is not, as yet, perceived in Moscow to be a common one. Silo vulnerability, to refer to a general point made earlier, does not become an arms control problem capable of being addressed seriously in SALT until it is first approached as an urgent defense policy problem. When the Soviet Union observes that the United States is in the process of both solving its silo-vulnerability problem and—as a consequence perhaps—developing a major potential threat to Soviet silo-housed ICBMs, then silo vulnerability (and the character of land-based missile forces more generally) should become an arms control issue relevant to SALT.

Generically, the United States has four classes of alternatives vis-á-vis the threat that Soviet fourth-generation ICBMs will pose to the 1,054 Minuteman and Titan ICBMs.[13] The United States could seek to defend its silos; threaten to launch its ICBMs on positive warning and (some) assessment of the weight and character of attack (a policy styled LOA, or launch on assessment); choose to phase out its ICBM force and rely instead upon a dyad of SLBMs and manned bombers/cruise missile carriers; or seek to preserve the strategic triad by means of land-mobile deployment of ICBMs. Three of these options have major SALT connections (defend silos; move to a dyad; and land-mobile ICBMs), but defense planners today should not presume that they will be SALT-constrained. It is prudent to assume that arms control inhibitions, as negotiated in SALT II, will apply. But it is also sensible to consider what might be done if the Senate should fail to ratify the treaty (or the Protocol), or on the expiration of a three-year Protocol that may, on present indications, ban deployment and testing but not development of a land-mobile ICBM.

At the present time, the option of defending ICBM silos is not a serious contender for the solution to the silo-vulnerability problem. Aside from the many technical issues involved, this option would involve abrogating, or fundamentally renegotiating, the ABM Treaty of 1972. Should the strategic offensive forces side of SALT be arrested by a failure of the Senate to ratify SALT II, then it is just possible that the ABM Treaty might be a casualty of the general political fallout that would ensue. However, the ballistic missile defense (BMD) option has relatively few strong advocates in 1978. This may, to be sure, be more a matter of fashions in ideas than it is of detailed analysis. Though it is widely believed that the scale and sophistication of the offensive threat has now outrun the capabilities of active defenses, this belief probably rests on untested assumptions, about resource allocations in particular. If the United States were willing to devote to ballistic missile defense (BMD) the kind of funding over many years that the MX ICBM might well require, it is conceivable that probable Soviet attack levels for the late 1980s and 1990s could be defeated, at least in the sense of limiting sharply their counter-military effect. Indeed, it is even possible that, as we approach the end of the century, the technological balance between offense and defense might be overturned in favor of the defense as a consequence of deployment of space-based laser BMD technology that could attack ICBMs in flight before they released their MIRVs.

However, for the 1980s, any ballistic missile system promises to be more a complication for the attack than a high-confidence defense.[14] Moreover, if the ABM Treaty regime were to end, the Soviet ability to deploy such systems rapidly in the 1980s is probably going to be far more impressive than the American ability to do so. Certainly even SALT I has brought no reduction in the burden of peacetime defense expenditures on the U.S.S.R.—it spent more on strategic forces in 1972-77 than it had in the period 1967-72! And, more specifically, the severe braking effect of the ABM Treaty upon American research on BMD may be contrasted with an increase in Soviet activity in that area.

The second option toward which the United States is edging, *faute de mieux,* is to adopt the ICBM firing tactic of launch on assessment (LOA). Senior Carter Administration defense officials have been uttering more and more friendly references to this tactic. For a country with a $2 trillion GNP and a defense budget of more than $120 billion—after nearly a generation's warning that the silo-vulnerability problem was coming—to be compelled even to think very seriously about LOA is little short of a disgrace.

For LOA is potentially accident-prone (what if the warning signals and even the early stages of an attack are misassessed?), vulnerable to deliberate Soviet degradation of American strategic early warning facilities, and—in effect—would represent an all-time nadir in strategic thought and planning (against what do we launch?). The Congress should discourage the slide toward acceptance of this option and instead insist upon some more intelligent and less accident-prone resolution of the problem. The most that can be said for the several variants of launch on (radar) warning is that it is healthy that Soviet leaders have, in the back of their minds, a residual fear that "the United States just might do it." Therefore, the proper place of LOA in American strategy is of the "we do not rule it out" variety. But, LAO should not be thought of as anything save a desperate, quick tactical fix and a small supportive element contributing to useful uncertainty in Soviet defense planning.

V

The last two options are the serious contenders for determination of the character of the U.S. strategic posture through the year 2000: namely, a move to a dyad—withdrawing the ICBM force from the active inventory—or a move to a *survivable* land-based missile deployment. A dyad versus triad debate is waiting just over the horizon to convulse the

American defense and arms control community. At the present time the debate is focused upon the MX follow-on ICBM, and particularly its preferred basing mode. Opponents of the triad structure may well succeed in effecting a move to a strategic dyad, by means of aborting the birth of MX—and hence may be able to sidestep fundamental strategic issues that should be addressed in a dyad-triad debate.

The case for a dyad of SLBMs and air-breathing elements (penetrating bombers and cruise missiles) is supported by arguments of greater and lesser degrees of sophistication. At its most simple-minded, the dyad case amounts to the observation that a large imbalance in silo-killing protection, in favor of the Soviets, can be neutralized—as by magic—if we remove the silos from the force posture. Great logical skill is not required in order to preceive that this argument (to stretch a term) is basically one for unilateral disarmament.

The dyadic preference is somewhat confused, in that it tends to be advanced by a scattershot of arguments. It is unclear whether the base case for a dyad rests upon the claimed irrelevance of ICBMs, per se, or the alleged deficiencies in the proposed MX ICBM program, in particular. Given that critically important elements in the MX program are, at present, undefined in detail (e.g., total size of force, number and yields of warheads, basing mode, and deployment dates), attempts at definitive and final discussion are likely to be premature at least as to specifics.[15] In any event the simmering debate on specifics should at least run alongside serious discussion of whether or not the United States needs an ICBM force: What does, or might, an ICBM force contribute to American and allied well-being that could not adequately be provided by a strategic forces dyad? This is a very serious question and it merits a more direct answer than it has received as yet.

It is usual to observe that ICBMs are the most accurate, most "ready," most reliable, most easily commanded, and generally most flexible for diverse possible employment of all U.S. strategic nuclear forces. Manned bombers and cruise missiles would be slow to reach their targets and would be subject to attention by Soviet active defenses. And current SLBMs are not always on station (40 to 50 percent of the nuclear-powered, ballistic-missile-firing submarines [SSBNs] might be destroyed in port), are less accurate than ICBMs (because of small cumulative errors in the submarine's navigation system), and cannot receive firing instructions at any depth.

Against these common arguments, advocates of accepting a dyad claim that the sea-based deterrent force can be improved to have most of the present attributes of a land-based missile force (very high accuracy, "readiness" on station—through the very long range of the Trident I and II missiles—and ease and security of communications) and that it is far from self-evident that the United States needs the particular strong attributes of an ICBM force in its military posture. For *prompt* neutralization of hardened targets, and for the execution of limited nuclear options, the ICBM clearly is superior to its SLBM and bomber/cruise missile rivals—provided it is deployed survivably. But, there are people who discern no great need for a large *prompt* hardened-target kill capability and who admit to a willingness to sacrifice an SSBN or two and probably some unfired SLBMs, as a consequence of charging the sea-based deterrent force with limited nuclear option responsibilities.

The fundamental case for retaining an ICBM force in a strategic nuclear triad does not rest upon alleged deficiencies in the sea- and air-based forces. The Trident II SSBN *will* have intercontinental range (approximately 7,500 miles), meaning that it can be "on station" to a degree dramatically better than previous SLBMs; also, if the United States proceeds sensibly to deploy an extremely low frequency (ELF) communication system for the command of SSBNs, war plan execution orders should be capable of being transmitted with a reliability very close to that pertaining to command of ICBMs. Finally, the accuracy of SLBMs can be improved to the degree desired in the 1980s by means of utilizing stellar inertial navigation to compensate for errors in the submarine's navigation instruments, "plugging in" to the satellites of the Navstar Global Positioning System, or through the employment of terminal sensing devices. In principle, at least, Navstar and terminal guidance can be degraded or "spoofed," but one would be giving the adversary a set of major technical and, above all, operational problems to solve.

Similarly, the case for retaining an ICBM force could be posed, unwisely, in terms of the uncertainties that surround the likely performance of cruise missiles. At the present time no one knows just how secure the pre-launch and penetration survivability of the air-launched cruise missile (ALCM) force will be in the late 1980s. Optimism or pessimism is, in good part, related to the preferred conflict scenario. Unlike the B-1 manned bomber, the B-52 ALCM-carrier cannot be dispersed to a very large number of airfields, does not have a very impressive runway escape speed, and is not significantly hardened against nuclear weapon effects. All of this means that a Soviet ballistic-missile barrage attack against predictable airfield escape routes is very likely to impose heavy attrition (down with every B-52 will go 20 ALCMs). How effective Soviet air defense will be against cruise missile carriers and individual ALCMs is a matter of speculation. However, it is prudent to assume that Soviet airborne warning and control systems (AWACS) directing the MiG-29 (an improved MiG-25 that can "look down" and "shoot down") will pose a non-trivial threat at (and beyond) the frontier of Soviet airspace; while the SA-10 surface-to-air missile and its successors should impose yet more attrition. Doubts concerning the survivability of cruise missiles may be well or ill founded, but they cannot be unrelated to the total strategic context, notably whether Soviet air defenses are assumed to have been suppressed effectively by precursor ICBM and SLBM strikes.

The basic case in favor of a strategic forces' triad, which includes a substantial and survivable ICBM element, is that it compels a dispersion of adversary investment, preparation, and attention. In the early 1960s, the American defense community understood, almost as an axiom, that strategic stability flowed from the existence of large and diverse forces.[16] Our current official defense and arms control community apparently has retrogressed in the quality of its strategic thought. The Carter Administration endorses, at least in principle, the idea of deep reductions in strategic nuclear forces and, in practice, has simplified the Soviet defense problem by cancelling the B-1 manned bomber and delaying (possibly aborting) the MX ICBM. It is not essential that senior officials in the defense and arms control area have credentials as strategic theorists, but it is reasonable to expect them to understand that a very large and diverse strategic posture (a triad plus) has to be inherently more stabilizing than a smaller dyad.

Behind this general proposition, two supporting arguments, in particular, need to be registered. First, if the Soviet Union faces a U.S. strategic forces dyad, as opposed to a triad, the potential payoff from research, development, and deployment in the regions of antisubmarine warfare and air defense has to rise dramatically. Also, since the Soviet Strategic Rocket Forces would be deprived of most of their hard targets in the United States—as the ICBM force is phased out—they would have warheads to spare for missions that previously, for reasons of resource limitation, had to be accorded only a low priority. Specifically, unilateral American abandonment of its ICBM force would, in the mid-1980s, free more than 5,000 megaton-range, very accurate, Soviet reentry vehicles for barrage-attack assignment against our airbreathing and sea-based strategic nuclear forces. A strategic dyad properly augmented to compensate for the loss of the ICBM force could well cost more to sustain and modernize than would a triad embracing the MX ICBM.

Second, technically trained and focused Western strategists have a tendency to forget that strategic power, latent or applied, should be developed and exercised for political ends. Even if the United States made the necessary effort to offset the absence of ICBMs, might it not— in political perceptual terms—have extreme difficulty persuading itself, and others, that a dyad was the strategic equivalent of a triad? This potential difficulty would be compounded by the fact that the move to a dyad was less than freely chosen. American ICBMs, in peacetime, would have been coerced out of their silos by the theoretical Soviet silo-neutralizing threat.

VI

The demise of the land-based leg of the U.S. strategic forces' triad, should it occur, may be traced by future historians not to the kind of arguments advanced immediately above, but rather to the fact that particular aspects of the follow-on ICBM program to the Minuteman III were intolerably vulnerable to challenge (given the context of defense debate in the United States). The dyad-triad debate now hangs in domestic political terms upon the outcome of the MX issue. If the case for the MX ICBM is lost, then—in all probability—the United States will abandon its land-based missile force.[17]

By way of basic reference, as of mid-1978 the MX ICBM concept envisages the following: a missile weighing 192,000 pounds with slightly more than 8,000 pounds payload, to be deployed in numbers ranging between 150 and 300, in a multiple aim point (MAP) basing mode. The multiple aim points may consist of buried trenches (13-20 miles in length), dispersed and hardened horizontal *or* vertical shelters, or pools of water.[18] The cost of the MX ICBM system, including ten years of operation and maintenance, could be between $25 and $40 billion. The intention is to provide, as a base case, 5,000 individual aim points— i.e., points that Soviet strategic forces would have to cover—with the possibility of economical further increases in aim point numbers should the scale of the Soviet threat expand beyond initial expectations.

The debate over MX embraces a wide range of concerns, any one of which could prove fatal to the deployment prospects of the system. These concerns include anxieties over increasing strategic instability; fears of a negative impact upon prospects for arms control; technical uncertainties over the viability of the selected MAP basing mode against plausible Soviet threats; cost considerations; environmental sensitivities; and suspicion that many, and perhaps enough, of the tasks of MX could be performed by more capable SLBMs and cruise missiles.

The paradox is that although fundamental MX program decisions, positive or negative, should be made on strategic and arms control grounds, at the present time it is the secondary issues of the basing mode and of cost that are dominating informed discussion. No honest advocate of the MX system can deny that there are indeed difficulties in both these areas which must be overcome before any clear-cut decision could be taken. The buried-trench concept, which was the leading candidate for the MAP system until the end of 1977, has fallen foul of anxieties over its potential vulnerability to ill-understood nuclear weapon effects that may have a special character in such a trench environment. And, of course, it is important to develop the most cost-effective basing mode possible, one that clearly provides a major multiplication of aim points that would force the Soviet Union, if it were to attempt to counter such a multiplication, to a scale of effort it would not readily undertake.

Yet, important as these technical issues remain, it does seem almost certain that a cost-effective and robust MAP basing mode can in fact be found, which will not be subject to easy challenge on technical grounds.

At that point, opponents of the MX are sure to raise objections on the grounds of alleged crisis and arms control instability and claimed incompatibility with the SALT process. Thus, it is important to face up now to the arguments in these areas.

To review briefly the central line of argument, the overwhelming purpose of an MX ICBM program is to support American foreign policy. To that end the United States needs a *survivable* land-based missile force. Such a force strengthens pre- and intra-war deterrence, and should improve the prospects for tolerable conditions for early war termination. Even if, in theory, a truly massive Soviet first strike could defeat MX in the late 1980s and 1990s, the existence of 150-300 MXs in 5,000-plus possible aim points cannot help but increase Soviet attack uncertainties to a very healthy degree and enforce a tremendous, and vastly disproportionate (to that destroyed), consumption of Soviet missile payload. At the least, then, early action on MX deployment would defer Soviet attainment of some facsimile of "escalation dominance" for many years.

This brings us to the question of timing. As things look from the perspective of 1978, any U.S. resort to limited nuclear options in the mid-1980s could meet with a devastating Soviet reply that would still be almost strictly counter-strategic. On this estimated timing of the increase in the Soviet threat, an MX ICBM deployed over the period 1987-91 would not, on the face of things, be a timely program. But there are no overriding technical obstacles that cannot be overcome—in the judgment of well-informed experts—so as to permit the deployment of a technically solid MX system over the period 1984-88. And such a program either defeats that Soviet advantage definitively or pushes it out into the early 1990s, thereby according us the necessary lead time to effect a basic restructuring of our strategic forces for long-term stability.

In addition, MX might restore the arms-competitive initiative to the United States. Although the expensive initial MAP basing-mode decision would have been coerced by the level and quality of the predicted Soviet threat, a sound MAP concept should pose the Soviet Union an impossible attack task—in that the United States should be able thereafter to multiply aim points at will and far more cheaply than the Soviet Union could add payload to its ICBM force. Moreover, to the degree that an American MX ICBM force poses a growing threat to the very large fraction of Soviet strategic forces capability that is housed in silos, the Soviet Union should be driven into an expensive offsetting MAP configuration. Resources that Moscow devotes to concrete-lined tunnels or dispersed shelters are resources not expended upon offensive capability (aim points, per se, are no threat!).

The instability arguments against MX reflect shallow strategic reasoning but are sufficiently popular to require answer. The most fashionable claim is that MX deployment will promote crisis instability in that it will place the Soviet Union in a condition where, in an acute crisis, it will have to use its silo-housed ICBMs or risk losing them. First, it is far from certain that U.S. MX deployment will pose a total counter-silo threat to Soviet ICBMs—an MX force *can* be designed that has only a very limited counter-force potential. Second, an MX procurement decision would be well advertised and would provide the Soviet Union with at least six-years notice for devising an offsetting survivable land-based deployment (or for a near-total move of its strategic missiles to sea-based deployment). Thus, it is implausible that the Soviet Union will ever be placed in the unstable "use them or lose them" context vis-à-vis its ICBM force that some arms control-oriented commentators have suggested.

Indeed, to the extent arms race instability does emerge, it will have been the result not of any MX ICBM deployments but of the Soviet deployments and tests that today are promoting such instability. MX is an American *response* to a potentially total Soviet threat to the silo-housed U.S. ICBM force. MX may drive the Soviet Union to an expensive MAP system that perhaps might entail some sacrifice in missile accuracy and payload—all of which would be positive developments in the American perspective. In political terms, which is the proper way to view the strategic arms competition, the ultimate point is that the United States cannot tolerate Soviet unilateral acquisition of a near-total silo-threatening capability or being coerced into a strategic forces dyad (with the attendant simplification of Soviet defensive tasks).

As I write, the status of an MX ICBM, deployed in a MAP mode, in the current SALT negotiations is uncertain. In principle, each separate aim point (particularly if dispersed vertical shelters were adopted) could be defined as a launcher—and launcher numbers were frozen in SALT I (a provision to be carried over into SALT II). Moreover, the pending three-year Protocol to SALT II prohibits the testing and deployment of land-mobile missiles. Thus, a key issue in any SALT III negotiations will be just this question of multiple aim points/launchers. Given a combination of Soviet ICBM payload, accuracy, and launcher numbers that may then be driving the United States toward possible MAP ICBM deployment, how should the United States respond if the Soviet Union claims that MAP ICBM deployment is (by multiplying missile "launchers") in violation of some agreement? A strategically sensible and appropriate reply is not difficult to identify, but the U.S. arms control community is all too likely to take such a Soviet objection seriously. The appropriate American arms control response would be to claim that each multiple aim point complex comprises *a single* ICBM launcher—a fact that may be checked through the medium of adequate verification arrangements.

Overall, MX should be thought of as a weapon program that is essential for the support of forward-placed allies, in that supportive limited first-strike options could be threatened credibly, secure in the knowledge that the United States had a residual ICBM force that could deter attack upon itself. From the standpoint of genuine progress in SALT, MX should be beneficial. Indeed, the Arms Control and Disarmament Agency should be a strong supporter of an MX program. MX is the system that should persuade very tough-minded Soviet officials that the hard-target counterforce race cannot be won. The logic of MX is fully compatible with a substantive SALT III agreement. But, for leverage in SALT, the United States cannot depend on the *idea* of the MX ICBM based survivably. The Soviet Union has to observe the evolution of a real program.

In sum, the cost, environmental, and basing mode aspects of the MX debate are all resolvable if one comes fairly to grips with the strategic and arms control issues discussed above. If MX proponents are correct or plausibly correct, then the devotion of less than three percent of the defense budget over a ten-year period to MX has to be a bargain. It is more likely than not that any of the current MAP concept contenders for MX deployment would be good enough. In looking for "the best," the United States is losing months of lead time that could be devoted to development of an adequate system.

As for the environmental arguments against MX, they too depend on perspective. The allocation of relatively small areas of the continental United States may indeed be required to provide the necessary dispersion. And such areas would then become theoretical targets of Soviet nuclear attack, just as key cities and surrounding areas already are. But the amount of actual environmental damage will surely be negligible, both absolutely and in relation to the importance of the program to an adequate defense posture for the United States and for the nations throughout the world who depend on the maintenance of a proper superpower strategic nuclear balance.

VII

One cannot be confident that the U.S. defense community will behave sensibly and preserve the triadic structure of its strategic force posture. Every major argument of merit suggests the necessity for the United States to move ahead urgently to phase out the silo-housed Minuteman-Titan ICBM force in favor of an MX ICBM deployment, housed in a multiple-aim-point system. MX should be purchased because it solves critical security issues and because every alternative suggested thus far is unambiguously inferior. The United States confronts a principal foreign adversary who addresses the problem of strategic warfare in a distressingly traditional fashion. MX should impose an impossible task upon Soviet defense planners, should provide at least the credible promise of the kind of war-waging capability that Soviet leaders respect, and should provide a major incentive for the Soviet Union to negotiate a substantive SALT III agreement.

The United States and its allies *might* be able to sustain their vital interests in the context of an American move to a strategic forces dyad of SLBMs and cruise missiles. But why should the risk be taken? The Soviet Union, irreverent of Western stability theory and defense anxieties, has chosen to develop a potentially total threat to American hardened strategic forces and facilities. The MX ICBM, deployed survivably in an appropriate MAP mode, is a modest and prospectively effective reply.

Notes

1. See Mr. Warnke's testimony in *Strategic Arms Limitation Agreements, Hearings* before the senate Committee on Foreign Relations, 92nd Cong., 2nd sess., June 28, 1972, Washington: GPO, 1972, p. 181; and his article, "Apes on a Treadmill," *Foreign Policy*, Spring 1975, pp. 12-29.

2. See *NATO: The Transatlantic Bargain*, New York: Harper and Row, 1970, p. 82.

3. In "News Conference at Moscow, July 3," *Department of State Bulletin*, July 29, 1974, p. 215.

4. A seminal discussion of this subject is in Paul H. Nitze, "Deterring Our Deterrent," *Foreign Policy*, Winter 1976-77, pp. 195-210.

5. "Assuring Strategic Stability in an Era of Détente," *Foreign Affairs*, January 1976, p. 227.

6. For example, it has been claimed that in their most recent ICBM tests the Soviet Union achieved an accuracy of close to 0.1 n.m. (or 600 feet). Clarence A. Robinson, Jr., "Soviets Boost ICBM Accuracy," *Aviation Week and Space Technology*, April 3, 1978, pp. 14-16.

7. Leon Gouré, *War Survival in Soviet Strategy: USSR Civil Defense*, Washington, D.C.: Center for Advanced International Studies (University of Miami), 1976; and T. K. Jones, testimony in *Defense Industrial Base: Industrial Preparedness and Nuclear War Survival*, Hearings before the Joint Committee on Defense Production, U.S. Congress, 94th Cong., 2nd sess., Washington: GPO, 1976, Part I.

8. Note the judgment in Harold Brown, *Department of Defense Annual Report: Fiscal Year 1979*, February 2, 1978, Washington: GPO, 1978, p. 106.

9. A different and erroneous impression was conveyed by officials before Congress in 1972. It was argued that the identification of "heavy" and "light" ICBM categories, with the latter constrained (in U.S. interpretation) to a throw-weight no larger than that of the SS-11—2,000 lbs. at most—was an important achievement in the attenuation of the threat to the silos. The worth of this SALT achievement became very evident by 1975 when the Soviet Strategic Rocket Forces began deploying "light" ICBMs (the SS-19) with a throw-weight of 7,000-7,500 lbs.

10. However, it would be unjust to level all criticism at the current administration. President Carter's negotiating leverage in SALT is hampered by a decade of American underinvestment in strategic nuclear forces.

11. See Paul H. Nitze's press conference statement, "Current SALT II Negotiating Posture," Washington, D.C.: The Committee on the Present Danger, March 28, 1978, particularly the appendix.

12. By the early 1980s, the Soviet ICBM force should enjoy roughly a 5:1 advantage in throw-weight over its American "equivalent" (ten million lbs.: two million lbs.). In strategic calculations throw-weight is not everything, but this is not a trivial advantage—particularly since Soviet ICBM accuracy is approaching that of the United States.

13. I have discussed this subject comprehensively in *The Future of Land-Based Missile Forces*, Adelphi Paper No. 140, London: The International Institute for Strategic Studies, Winter 1977.

14. This might not be true, were the United States permitted to deploy an ABM with multiple warheads.

15. For example, the most thoroughgoing critique of the MX program I have encountered rests in part on elements in an assumed program that are in fact open to change or modification. See M. Callaham et al., *The MX Missile: An Arms Control Impact Statement*, Cambridge, Mass.: Program in Science and Technology for International Security, MIT, March 1978.

16. This sound idea has been revived recently in Richard Burt, "Reducing Strategic Arms at SALT: How Difficult, How Important?", in Christoph Bertram, ed., *The Future of Arms Control: Part 1: Beyond SALT II*, Adelphi Paper No. 141, London: The International Institute for Strategic Studies, Spring 1978, pp. 4-14.

17. Logically, this need not be true. But, the B-1 analogy is a powerful one. The Carter Administration said "not the B-1," rather than "no new penetrating bomber"—however, this amounts, in practice, to a distinction without a difference.

18. See my article, "The MX Debate," *Survival,* May-June 1978 (in press).

11
Number Mysticism, Rationality, and the Strategic Balance

Thomas A. Brown

The number three is rich in symbolism. From the days of the Pythagoreans who believed the triangle had mystical significance, to the Christian church fathers who saw God as a Trinity, to Locke, Montesquieu, and the Founding Fathers who envisioned a government consisting of three branches, the human mind has seemed to fasten on the number three as particularly appropriate for great and important concerns. So when, in the early sixties, the U.S. strategic forces evolved into three major components (bombers, ICBMs, and SLBMs), it was perhaps inevitable that discussion of our strategic forces should be afflicted with a certain amount of argument which amounts to nothing more than number mysticism. The reader has undoubtedly come across such statements as, "Just as a milking stool requires all three legs to be intact or it will topple over, so too all three branches of the Triad are essential to maintain the stability of our strategic deterrent."

The actual value of the strategic triad, however, is rooted in specific, rational considerations: each form of basing has an essentially different prelaunch survival mode (thus reducing the likelihood of falling prey to tactical or technological surprise); bombers (or cruise missiles) present a different problem to the defender than do ballistic-missile reentry vehicles (RVs); command and control of land-based missiles is easier, while the inherent survivability of submarines is greater; and so on. The value of the triad, then lies in the specific qualities and complementaries of its elements; it has nothing to do with the fact that a triangle is a rigid body or that there are three dimensions to space or that a milking stool has three legs. As technology advances, we might find that two branches or four branches are preferable to three. If and when such a time comes, the required decisions will probably be impeded by our mystical attachment to the number three.

Reprinted by permission from *ORBIS*, Fall 1977. Copyright 1977 by the Foreign Policy Research Institute.

The author thanks Mr. Arthur Steiner for his many helpful comments on an early draft of this paper.

Something akin to number mysticism occurs in the use of numerical indicators to measure various elements of the strategic balance. Perhaps it reflects the general mathematization of our culture, or perhaps it is merely that, since there has never been a war in which both sides used nuclear weapons, thinking about strategic nuclear forces inevitably tends to drift toward the abstract. Whatever the reason, there has been a steady growth in the number and sophistication of the quantitative indicators used in our discussions of lang-range, nuclear-armed bombers and missiles. Almost every indicator introduced has some validity, but almost every indicator has also been misused at one time or another in debates. It is, of course, very tempting for partisans of the notion that we are ahead (or behind, or falling behind) in the strategic balance to pick and choose among the large number of strategic indices available and to emphasize those which appear to prove their case.[1] Distortions are therefore common.

I will discuss here eight indices commonly used in strategic debate: (1) number of launch vehicles; (2) explosive-energy yield, or megatonnage; (3) equivalent megatonnage; (4) throw-weight, or payload; (5) number of warheads; (6) countermilitary potential, or lethality; (7) equivalent weapons; and (8) overall military spending. As we shall see, each of these indicators has a legitimate use, but none of them is by itself a reliable measure of overall strategic strength.

II

The *number of launch vehicles* is one of the simplest strategic indicators: one merely adds up the number of strategic missiles and bombers. This provides some insight into the trend of a single nation's strategic program. For example, the fact that the Soviet Union increased its launch vehicles at a rate of more than 300 per year between 1966 and 1970—from about 400 to about 1,700—gives a fairly good picture of the dynamism of the Russian program over that period. Looking at *total* number of delivery vehicles (rather than just counting the most modern vehicles) avoids one of the most common abuses of statistics in the strategic area. One can create the illusion of a vast build-up in weaponry by citing the percentage increase of some new weapon over the early years of its deployment (since the stock is always zero in the year before the weapon is introduced, one can skew the increase considerably by choosing the years of comparison with care), while ignoring reductions in the systems it is replacing. The fallacy is obvious and has been pointed out repeatedly,[2] but writers continue to fall into it.

Although the total number of strategic-nuclear delivery vehicles avoids one pitfall, as an index it has a severe disadvantage: it says nothing about the quality of the strategic forces. For making comparisons between countries or for examining a single country over a long period of time, a simple count of launch vehicles can be very misleading, indeed. As an illustration of this, recall that on December 31, 1959, the Strategic Air Command's aircraft inventory inlcuded 2,028 strategic bombers (B-52s and B-47s). Today, the total number of operational strategic vehicles in the U.S. inventory stands at a bit under 2,000.[3] Yet, it is manifestly absurd to maintain that our absolute capability is a bit less than it was eighteen years ago, for our delivery vehicles today have greater reliability, range, and accuracy (although our degree of dominance has certainly declined due to increases in the Soviet forces).

Another problem with counting strategic-nuclear delivery vehicles is the ambiguity of the terms "strategic" and "delivery vehicle." The first ambiguity is illustrated by the dispute over whether the Soviet Backfire bomber should be considered "strategic." Since this aircraft can attack targets in the western United States on round-trip missions without refueling or anywhere in the United States with refueling, it seems reasonable for the United States to consider these bombers strategic weapons. The Soviets, however, claim they do not intend to use Backfire in this way; thus, they do not believe it should be considered a strategic vehicle. The second ambiguity is seen in the trend toward using bombers to carry cruise missiles. Which is the "delivery vehicle," the bomber that launches the cruise missile or the cruise missile itself? Since each bomber may carry many cruise missiles, the answer to this question could eventually make a difference of thousands in the number of strategic-nuclear delivery vehicles the United States is said to possess. Any indicator which depends so critically on imprecise definitions has debilitating shortcomings.

III

Another much-used quantitative index is the total *explosive-energy yield* of the strategic nuclear warheads on each side. A scientific purist would doubtless prefer to measure this energy in trillions of joules, but it has been the custom since the dawn of the atomic age to express it in terms of the energy released by detonating a given number of tons of TNT (1 kiloton equals 4.2 terajoules). In the 1940s and early 1950s, when we had a condition of what Herman Kahn has called "nuclear scarcity," total yield was perhaps a useful index for comparing the nuclear inventories of each side.

Kilotons or megatons (or, more correctly, "megatons of fission") burst on the earth's surface bear a direct relation to the amount of fallout produced. Megatons-on-alert thus bear a direct relation to the potential hazard from radioactive fallout in the event of war, just as the number of megatons detonated above ground in nuclear tests is directly related to the extent of peacetime radioactive pollution. But megatons are a misleading index in one very important respect: they do not accurately reflect the amount of direct damage from the blast (which is considered the most important effect for almost all strategic nuclear weapons). The area exposed to a given level of damage does not increase in direct proportion to the yield of a weapon, but rather in proportion to the two-thirds power of its yield. Thus, a 1-megaton H-bomb will not do as much damage as 1 million old-fashioned blockbusters each containing 1 ton of TNT—which one might suppose—but "only" the damage caused by 10,000 such blockbusters. Frightening enough, but only one-hundredth as damaging as a naive interpretation of megaton would suggest.

This distinction between energy yield and destructive potential has been exploited in polemics both by pacifists and by hawks. The pacifist distortion is based on a comparison of the energy released in conventional bombing with the much greater energy that would likely be released in a nuclear war and presumes that the damage done would be in proportion. Five million tons of conventional explosives were used in bombs during World War II, and it has often been said that one B-52 or one Titan missile could do "as much damage" as all the bombs dropped in that war. This is simply false. It would take about 500 1-megaton bombs to damage as large an area as was damaged by conventional expolsives in World War II—even under the rather extreme assumption that every bomb dropped contained a ton of high explosive. (Most contained far less, and the total area damaged per ton was therefore all the greater.) If the total megatons in the world nuclear force are divided by the population of the earth in order to come up with the equivalent of approximately 5 to 15 tons of TNT for every inhabitant, then the exaggeration of the power of nuclear weapons is magnified all the more.[4] Recall that the United States produced sufficient rifle and machinegun cartridges in World War II to kill everyone on earth five or ten times over; but no one called it overkill, and it wasn't.

The hawks' misuse of total megatonnage as a strategic index relies on the fact that the Russians tend to build bigger weapons than we do. The total megatonnage of the Soviet inventory is therefore substantially greater than ours (especially if one restricts his attention to missiles, where the Russians have the bulk of their megatons,[5] and ignores those weapons where we have the bulk of ours). Russian superiority by this index, however, does not at all correspond to superiority in destructive capacity. Technological progress in the American arsenal has normally been accompanied with a reduction in total explosive yield: when a Minuteman II is replaced by a MIRVed Minuteman III, the explosive yield is reduced by 50 per cent or more; when a Polaris A-3 is replaced by the more advanced Poseidon C-3, explosive yield is normally reduced by about 16 per cent. The total yield in the U.S. strategic inventory declined by about 60 percent between 1960 (the peak year) and the present.[6] This decline, however, reflected technological progress toward smaller but more numerous warheads, rather than a reduction in overall effectiveness. The Soviets, as they introduce more MIRVs into their missile force, will also reduce their total megatonnage.

IV

An obvious way to "fix up" total explosive-energy yield as an indicator is simply to take the two-thirds power of the yield as an index of a weapon's destructive power.[7] One may then compare *equivalent megatons,* or EMT. One EMT represents enough destructive power to expose about 60 sq. statute mi. to 5 psi of overpressure; this is sufficient to destroy unreinforced-brick and frame houses. The EMT in the U.S. missile force (ICBMs and SLBMs) is adequate to expose about 115,000 to 130,000 sq. mi. to such overpressure;[8] the Soviet missile force can expose between 222,000 and 237,000 sq. mi. to such overpressure.[9] If one adds in bombers, the Russian lead would be reduced but not eliminated. According to the U.S. Defense Department,[10] the Soviets have held the lead in equivalent megatons since about 1970.[11] However, this by itself does not mean that Soviet strategic forces are superior to those of the United States.

For one thing, one must recognize that the yield of a nuclear weapon is not easily observable (especially in this era of underground nuclear testing), so we may be overestimating the yield of the Soviet systems. Second, one can argue that many Soviet warheads, those in the 18- to 25-megaton class, are really too large for any but a very few large area-targets. By parceling out our equivalent megatons over a far greater number of targets than the Soviets do, we are better able to tailor our application of force to the target we want to destroy. (Avoiding the destruction of nontargets may be almost as important as destroying targets.) Most military targets, in strategic warfare, are point-targets and are dispersed so that no single weapon can destroy more than a few. Third, most military targets of exceptionally high value are "hardened" to resist nuclear attack. Against a hard target, accuracy is even more important than yield (or equivalent yield). But EMT tells us nothing about accuracy and, therefore, cannot fully reflect the ability of a given force to destroy hard targets.

For each of the above objections, one can find an index which meets the objection better than EMT does. For observability, we have throw-weight (or payload); for an indicator of flexibility against multiple point-targets, we have number of warheads; for an indicator of capability to kill hard targets, we have countermilitary potential (or lethality). Unfortunately, each of these indices has its own shortcomings.

V

The first public proposal to use *throw-weight* (or payload) as a key parameter in strategic-arms limitation agreements was made in 1963 by Colonel (later Lt. General) Glenn Kent.[12] In his seminal paper, the author considered three possible criteria for a limitation agreement on land-based strategic missiles: number of launch vehicles, megatonnage, and equivalent megatonnage. For reasons already noted and in order to preserve the possibility of a stable U.S.-Soviet balance (a complex matter which I will not discuss here), Kent preferred equivalent megatonnage. He recognized, however, that equivalent megatons are not directly observable. Therefore, since the EMT a missile can carry is very closely related to the total payload of the missile and since payload can be estimated from the dimensions of the missile, Colonel Kent recommended that total missile payload would be the best of the parameters considered for an arms limitation agreement. Payload has the added advantage that it limits decoys and penetration aids (a serious concern in the days before the ABM Treaty). An agreement to equal throw-weights on each side would be to the advantage of the side with the more advanced technology (presumably the United States), which would be able to extract more EMT, more warheads, and greater accuracy from the allotted payload.

This explains why the United States was willing to concur in the Interim Agreement on Strategic Offensive Forces which, while not directly cast in terms of payload, had the effect of conceding a throw-weight advantage to the Soviet Union (redressed somewhat by our superiority in bombers). Our superior technology, it is argued, is to enable us to use our limited throw-weight more effectively. But Soviet technology is not standing still (the USSR has introduced nine new ICBM types since 1970, while the United States has introduced only one),[13] and if the Soviets should overtake us technologically, our disadvantage in throw-weight would shortly be translated into a disadvantage in capability.

The U.S. strategic community is divided on the significance of throw-weight. As an example of one of the two extremes, here is Frank

Hoeber: "In the author's view, throw-weight is the most efficient measure for the limitation of strategic offensive arms. Throw-weight is definable and verifiable within fairly narrow limits. It is true that bomber payloads and missile throw-weight are not strictly commensurate; but defining them as equal, pound for pound, with freedom to change the mix of weapons, should be acceptable."[14] At the other extreme, Fred Payne:

> "The total payload of missiles and bombers was . . . proposed as a possible arms control yardstick in the early 1960's. At that time ballistic missiles carried single warheads, and the term "throw-weight" was coined to express a missile's payload in a manner comparable to a bomber's "bomb load." However, the deployment of multiple warheads aboard ballistic missiles and of stand-off missiles aboard bombers complicated the throw-weight definition and reduced its usefulness—a usefulness in any case limited by the fact that it gave no indication of the destructive capability of the weapons involved. This index has been retained primarily for historical reasons.[15]

VI

To measure each side's capability to hit "soft" point-targets, the obvious index is the *number of warheads*. Over the past decade, the United States has dedicated considerable energy to building up its warhead arsenal. During 1970-1974 the number of operational strategic-offensive warheads in our inventory was doubled (from 4,000 to 8,000),[16] thanks to the replacement of substantial numbers of Polaris and Minuteman missiles with MIRVed Poseidons and Minuteman IIIs. In 1974 we enjoyed about a four-to-one (8,000-to-2,000) advantage over the Soviet Union by this index, but the Soviets are apparently not content to let us enjoy this edge forever. Their new SS-17s, SS-18s, and SS-19s can carry 4, 8, and 6 warheads, respectively; and they are actively replacing their older missiles with these more sophisticated vehicles. By 1983, says Frank Hoeber, they could have almost 9,000 warheads in their ICBM force alone.[17] This would give the Soviet a considerable advantage in warheads-on-alert since a great many of our warheads are on SLBMs, only a small fraction of which are on patrol at any given time. So, this is one area in which we have enjoyed a substantial advantage, but it is an advantage we may lose in the immediate future.

Although the number of warheads has often been called the single most significant index of strategic power (particularly by liberals anxious to show that our strategic forces could be reduced), how significant is it really? True, it is a good indicator of the number of point-targets which could be *attacked*. But, because it takes no account of accuracy (the most critical military targets are invariably going to be either hard or mobile), it provides very little information as to the number of point-targets which could be *destroyed*.

VII

An indicator which was especially designed to reflect the capability to destroy hard targets is *countermilitary potential*, or lethality.[18] The lethality of a warhead is the two-thirds power of its yield, divided by the square of the CEP[19] of its delivery system. This formula may appear to be rather arbitrary, but actually it is a very useful index for two reasons. (1) The kill probability of a warhead against any target, regardless of hardness, is higher if its lethality is higher.[20] (2) If two independent warheads are sent against the same target, their combined kill probability will be the same as that for a single warhead whose lethality is the sum of their individual lethalities.[21] This latter property makes it attractive to add up the lethalities of all the weapons in the strategic force and use the resulting figure as an index of total force effectiveness. One might think that, by comparing this "lethality available" with the lethality required to achieve given kill probabilities against an enemy target system, one could assess the adequacy of one's force in a countermilitary role. Unfortunately, there are problems with this approach.

First of all, the total lethality depends primarily on CEP, which is one of the most difficult parameters to determine for a missile. It is hard to determine our own CEPs because of the limited amount of testing we do. It is even harder to determine Soviet CEPs: even if we are able to observe a Soviet test, we have no way of knowing for sure the intended target. Different authors have varied by a factor of 9 in their estimates of the lethality of the Soviet ICBM force in 1973-1974.[22]

The second major problem is that, even where the lethality available exceeds the lethality required to achieve desired kill probabilities against the target set, in practice it may be impossible to arrive at an assignment of weapons to targets which will achieve the damage desired. For one thing, the lethality of one big, accurate weapon can be applied only to a single target: it cannot be distributed among several targets. Nor is it possible to send more than one or two small weapons against a single hard target (the dust, debris, and radiation from the first weapon exploded will interfere with the others—an effect known as "fratricide"), unless one is willing to wait rather a long time between shots. Lethality, then, is not meaningful if one's weapons are either too big or too small, and it is difficult to calculate reliably in any case.

An alternative is to take a particular target hardness (say, 1,000 psi) and calculate the *single-shot kill probability* of each warhead in the force against it. The sum of these probabilities is the number of targets of a given hardness which the force could be expected to destroy. This index has the advantage that it does not overstate the effectiveness of a single large warhead and, I think, is easier to understand than the more abstract concept of lethality. However, the kill probability is also sensitive to errors in estimating CEP, and it, too, provides no information on the effect of multiple attacks against a single target.

The United States has enjoyed an advantage in weapons accuracy over the Soviet Union, and this gives us an advantage in hard-target kill capability. Just how great an advantage, however, is difficult to estimate since Soviet accuracies are difficult to estimate. Moreover, just as our advantage in warheads is decreasing, it is likely that our advantage in hard-target kill capability will be reduced over the years ahead.

VIII

We have seen that different indices of weapon effectiveness are appropriate for different categories of targets. For soft area-targets, EMT is the appropriate index; for soft point-targets, the number of warheads is the fitting index; and for hard point-targets, kill probability seems most appropriate. The reader may wonder if there is not some way to combine these three indices into one overall index of total effectiveness. An interesting recent attempt to do this[23] involved the use of a weighted harmonic mean to define a new indicator: *equivalent weapons*. The reasoning follows.

Suppose one has

     45 area-targets (each requiring 1 EMT to destroy),
     45 soft point-targets, and
     10 hard point-targets.

And let us say one has a stock of weapons, each having .5 EMT and a kill probability of .1 against hard targets. Then the destruction of these 100 targets will require

$$\frac{45}{.5} = 90 \text{ weapons on area-targets}$$

$$\frac{45}{1} = 45 \text{ weapons on soft point-targets}$$

$$\frac{10}{1} = 100 \text{ weapons on hard point-targets}$$

     235 TOTAL

Thus, 235 weapons are required to destroy 100 targets; so each "real" weapon is equivalent to 1/2.35 "ideal" weapons. In short, where EMT is the equivalent megatonnage of a weapon and P is its kill probability against a standard hard target, then

$$\text{EW (equivalent weapons)} = \frac{1}{.45 + \dfrac{.45}{\text{EMT}} + \dfrac{.10}{P}}$$

Summing up the EW for each weapon in a force would give us the total number of targets that force could destroy. There are several problems with this index, but perhaps the most serious is the fact that it strongly understates the effectiveness of a mixed force of moderately specialized weapons. The EW index matches each weapon against a randomly selected member of the target set, rather than matching each weapon with the kind of target against which it is most effective. This can lead to very serious distortions. To illustrate, let us suppose one had a force made up of the following weapons:

Type	No. in Force	EMT	P	EW/Weapon	Total EW
A	45	1.0	.10	.53	23.7
B	60	0.2	.67	.35	21.1
					44.8

The equivalent weapons index indicates that the above force could destroy slightly fewer than 45 targets. But if one were actually planning an attack on a target set of 45 soft area-targets, 45 soft point-targets, and 10 hard point-targets, one would assign all the Type-A weapons to soft area-targets, use 45 Type-B weapons to pick off the soft point-targets, and use the remaining 15 Type-B weapons against the hard point-targets (hitting each with a single warhead, then reattacking those that survive). It is easy to calculate that with this allocation one could expect to destroy 100 targets. In view of the general trend toward small, more accurate warheads (mixed, in the Soviet Union, with some very large warheads), this distortion might lead to extremely faulty conclusions.

IX

It appears, then, that none of the indices discussed above adequately reflects overall strategic power. Each has its legitimate use, but none is a particularly good reflection, by itself, of the "big picture." There is, however, an approach radically different from those we have examined above. One could give up the attempt to identify a single force characteristic as the key to strategic power and, instead, look at each side's *expenditures on military forces.*

This approach assumes that each side is able to gauge competently its own needs and that the side which spends more is buying more powerful forces. If the Soviet Union and the United States were hiring soldiers from a common labor pool and buying weapons from common suppliers, this approach would be valid. But this is not the case. The United States cannot hire Russian boys to serve in the U.S. Army, and the Soviets cannot buy F-15s for the Red Air Force. Quite aside from the secrecy which clouds much of the Soviet budget, it is a rather meaningless exercise to take the figure Moscow claims to be spending on arms and, with the exchange rate used by tourists, convert that figure into dollars.

How, then, should one proceed? That depends on the precise purpose for which one wishes to estimate Soviet defense expenditures.[24] If one wants to determine how great a burden defense places on the Soviet economy (information which might be of use in planning strategy for arms-control negotiations), then one must estimate costs within the context of the Soviet economy. That is, one must estimate how much the Soviets could increase their civil output if they eliminated their military output. In the United States, where military industry and civilian industry draw from common supplies and common labor pools, it is likely that a dollar's worth of defense corresponds closely to a dollar's worth of civilian output. In a command economy, however, productivity may vary widely from sector to sector. If the Soviet defense sector is considerably more efficient than the civil sector, then a rouble's reduction in defense-spending will not buy a rouble's increase in civil production.

If, on the other hand, one's purpose is to compare the gross Soviet defense effort with the gross U.S. effort, than one must proceed quite differently. Both defense efforts must be evaluated within the context of a single economy: that is, one must calculate (1) what it would cost the USSR to duplicate U.S. forces or (2) what it would cost the USA to duplicate Soviet forces. Because our knowledge of the Soviet economy is so limited and because internal Soviet prices are often set by rather arbitrary bureaucratic decisions, approach 2 is more practical. Hence, the CIA has estimated what Soviet forces would cost in the United States.[25] It is not very difficult to calculate investment costs because, over the years, we have developed "cost-estimating relationships," which give the expenditure required to achieve a given performance level in equipment of a given type. Thus, our investment-cost estimates will be accurate so long as our estimates of the amount and performance of Soviet hardware are accurate. Similarly, there is no great difficulty in estimating how much we would have to pay Soviet personnel.[26] Operating costs other than personnel are much more difficult to estimate, but fortunately these costs constitute only about 15 per cent of the total. Costs for RDT&E are also difficult to estimate with confidence.

Overall, the CIA is reasonably certain that its dollar-cost estimates fall within 15 per cent of the estimates it would make with perfect information. The "bottom line" is that the dollar equivalent of Soviet defense expenditures over the decade 1966-1976 was about equal to actual U.S. defense-spending over the same period; but, in real terms, Soviet spending steadily increased, while U.S. spending steadily declined from 1969 through 1976. In 1976 the dollar equivalent appeared to be about 40 per cent greater than actual U.S. defense-spending. If one restricts his attention to strategic forces, the dollar equivalent of Soviet expenditures was about double the United States' spending over the first half of the decade, increasing to three and a half times by 1976. Looking at these figures alone, one would conclude that the balance in strategic forces must be overwhelmingly in the Soviets' favor. But there are a number of reasons why the situation is not so bad as these numbers seem to indicate.

Expenditures do not guarantee effectiveness. First of all, Soviet strategic spending includes "peripheral attack forces," such as IRBMs and MRBMs, which do not threaten the United States. (They threaten U.S. allies, of course, but we are leaving allied forces out of account in this comparison.) Secondly, the Soviets were technologically inferior in strategic weaponry throughout most of the period (1966-1976), so their weapons are not so good as one might think. Thirdly, the Soviets began the period with a large deficit in strategic forces, and much of their big edge in expenditures went simply toward filling the gap. Finally, there is the "index number problem," which is very familiar to economists and always arises in international comparisons of this kind. The Soviets made their allocations within the context of Soviet prices, not U.S. prices. If they had to pay as much to their conscript troops as we must pay to our volunteer servicemen, they would probably reduce their manpower somewhat and spend a bit more on, say, equipment. Thus, dollar-cost figures exaggerate the size of the Soviet forces. Similarly, a rouble-equivalent cost for U.S. forces, if one could be calculated, would exaggerate the size of those forces. In short, a situation could easily arise where the dollar-equivalent cost of Soviet forces would exceed actual U.S. expenditures and, at the same time, the rouble-equivalent cost of U.S. forces would exceed actual Soviet expenditures.

One should therefore not assume that the growing difference between the dollar-equivalent cost of Soviet forces and actual U.S. defense-spending necessarily translates into a Soviet advantage in effectiveness. But how can we fail to be concerned about the general trend? How long can we watch the Soviets building up strategic forces (which would cost us three or four times as much as we are actually spending) before they eventually acquire a strategic force superior to our own in every way?

Secretary Brown, quite properly, is unwilling to translate budget differences directly into differences in military power, but the trend concerns him:

> I believe the Soviets have been spending, in constant dollars or rubles, whichever you want to measure it by, at an increasing rate; they have increased their expenditures by 3 or 4 percent a year over a period of 8 to 10 years. During much of that time, the United States was decreasing its expenditures at a rate in real dollars, constant dollars, of about 2 percent a year. Well, when that goes on for 8 or more years, it has quite an effect.[27]

The story told by a budgetary comparison is therefore similar to the story told by most other strategic indicators: it is uncertain whether we are ahead or behind, but the Soviets are clearly moving forward faster than we. Just like every other indicator we have examined, budgetary comparison is not, by itself, an adequate measure of military power.

X

The search for an all-purpose index of strategic power, one which could tell us whether we are "ahead" or "behind" and which might even itself be used in arms-control negotiations, seems to end in frustration.[28] The hang-up on numerical indicators may indeed do us more harm than good, for it distracts us from the basic question of the purpose of our strategic forces. Excessive concentration on number of warheads or throw-weight or lethality permits us to avoid facing up to a really serious lack of purpose—or perhaps I should say lack of *doctrinal development*—in regard to our own strategic forces.

The French, at the start of World War II, thought they had the edge on the Germans in tanks—in numbers, the size of their guns, and the thickness of their armor. Nonetheless, the French went under: what they lacked was a sound concept of how to use armor in combat. So, too, our concentration on indices could make us vulnerable to a foe who comes up with a sounder doctrine than our own for the actual use of nuclear forces. Nuclear weapons are so destructive that any nuclear war between the United States and Russia would undoubtedly cause horrifying damage to both sides. This damage, this horror, has been made the cornerstone of our doctrine. Washington believes war can be avoided if only we can make it prospectively painful enough.

McNamara used to talk of the destruction of 70 per cent of the industrial floor space and 30 per cent of the population of the Soviet Union as being "unacceptable damage." But can we be sure that, in the unpredictable stress and strain of world politics, there will *never* arise a situation in which such losses appear preferable to the perceived alternative? Even McNamara's standards of how much damage was unacceptable changed slightly from year to year, effectively demonstrating the arbitrariness of the specific levels chosen. Furthermore, calculations of our assured-destruction capability do not establish that we could, in a second-strike, kill 30 per cent of the population. They only establish that we could demolish the peacetime dwelling places of 30 per cent of the population.

It is not inconceivable that the Soviets would evacuate their cities during a crisis. Eugene Wigner and Joanne Gailar have estimated that if this were done, Soviet losses in all-out nuclear war could be limited to about 5 per cent.[29] More recently, T. K. Jones has estimated that ten days of evacuation could limit Soviet fatalities to fewer than 10 million people.[30] Jones's model is rather primitive and could be improved in several ways, but his basic point would seem to be valid: one Soviet source states that "evacuation of the public from major cities and industrial centers . . . in the event of nuclear strike . . . would mean a decline in losses by 8-10 times."[31] This "dangling comparative" appears to mean that, at most, 10 or 12 per cent of the urban population of the Soviet Union would be lost, which translates to 6 or 8 per cent of the general population. These are terrible losses, and it is difficult to conceive of a sequence of events which could lead the Soviets to decide that a nuclear war should be invoked. History, however, is full of surprises, and it is shortsighted to presume that the prospect of serious population losses (6 or 8 per cent, by the way, would be less than the Soviet losses in World War II) makes nuclear war an utter impossibility.

In general, the Russian military view of nuclear war seems to differ significantly from the common view in the United States that nuclear war is impossible if both sides maintain substantial forces.[32] Soviet military writers stress the importance of being able to destroy the enemy with "crushing nuclear blows."[33] They envision nuclear war continuing after the initial exchange: "Preserving the population—the basic productive force of the country—ensuring economic stability, and preserving the material and technical resources are matters of paramount importance during a war. Thus, under modern conditions, civil defense has become a factor of strategic importance. To a considerable degree, the success of civil defense measures predetermines the viability and stability of the country."[34]

Soviet military leaders do not make a sharp distinction between forces-for-deterrence and forces-for-warfighting: the best way to deter attack, the Soviets believe, is to be able to defeat the enemy, not merely to inflict some specified level of suffering upon him. However primitive these ideas might seem to Western theorists, they do make a certain amount of sense. It is not clear whether or not Soviet civilian leaders share these views: Soviet political leaders stress the horror of nuclear war and are vague, even evasive, on what Soviet goals would be should such a war actually occur.

XI

To summarize: for the Soviet military, nuclear war, while a horrifying prospect, is nevertheless a possibility. Even though the victor will suffer greatly, there will be a victor. The Soviets therefore attempt to achieve a "correlation of forces," including civil defense, which will ensure that if war comes they will be the victor; they also believe this is the best way to deter attack. Logically, this should lead the USSR to make a careful study of potential target systems, to plan on postattack production and support of military forces, to aim at protecting reserve forces during a nuclear exchange, and to carry out similar measures to ensure that, if war comes, the Soviets will ultimately enforce their will upon the enemy.

Conversely, the idea that the *sole* function of strategic forces is to deter, by threatening a potential adversary with some "unacceptable" level of damage, leads one to emphasize the appearance of the forces—their size, their index number—rather than the capability to defeat a potential enemy. Thus, a simplistic view of mutual assured destruction both reinforces and is reinforced by a tendency to overemphasize index numbers and to neglect concepts about how nuclear forces should be used if war comes, how they could deprive the enemy of victory instead of merely making his victory expensive, how they could be used to minimize the horrors which would inevitably accompany such a conflict, and how they could best be configured in order to minimize the chances of the dreaded conflict occuring in the first place.

Notes

1. Professor Paul Doty has put it, "If you are a [U.S.] hawk, you argue throw weight, and if you are a dove, you argue warheads." (*Time*, February 11, 1974, p. 17.)

2. Most recently by Albert Wohlstetter, "Racing Forward? or Ambling Back?," in *Survey*, Summer-Autumn 1976, pp. 163-217.

3. General George S. Brown, *Statement to the Congress on the Defense Posture of the United States for FY 1978*, January 20, 1977, p. 22.

4. That released energy exaggerates the destructiveness of nuclear weapons was noted by P. M. S. Blackett in *The Political and Military Consequences of Atomic Energy* (New York: McGraw-Hill, 1949), which was a fundamental

attack on American policy of the day. An interesting extreme example of exaggeration appears in G. A. Arbatov's "The Impasse of the Policy of Force," in *Problemy Mira i Sotsializma*, no. 2, February 1974 (FBIS, *Daily Report* [Soviet Union], February 20, 1974, p. B2). Arbatov wrote that at the time there existed "several thousand tons [possibly an error in translation here] of explosives in TNT equivalent for every person living on Earth." This estimate was high by a factor of from 100 to 1,000. An even more extreme example appears in Richard J. Barnet, *Roots of War* (Baltimore: Penguin Books, 1973, p. 4): "The American nuclear arsenal holds the equivalent of ten thousand tons of TNT for every man, woman, and child on earth." The fact that authors can make errors of this magnitude and not be caught immediately by editors and readers shows how feeble is the claim that the numerical treatment in their writings adds to our understanding.

5. F. P. Hoeber and William Schneider, Jr. (eds., *Arms, Men and Military Budgets: Issues for Fiscal Year 1978* [New York: Crane, Russak, 1977]) provide figures for 1975—which in turn are based on figures from the International Institute for Strategic Studies and on official statements to Congress—indicating that the U.S. ICBM force has between 1,000 and 1,720 megatons and that the Soviet ICBM force has between 7,301 and 9,942 megatons. Thus, by this limited and misleading index, the Soviet nuclear force is superior by a factor of from 4 to 10. Similarly, the U.S. SLBM force comprises 344 megatons and the Soviet force comprises 845 megatons, a ratio of Soviet superiority of about 2.5 to 1. Hoeber and Schneider provide no figures for megatons carried by bombers. In any case, the megatons carried by a given bomber will vary according to the mission to which it is assigned. Under any reasonable assumption, the inclusion of bomber-carried weapons will reduce the Soviet superiority in total megatonnage but will not eliminate it. The Soviets have probably been ahead of the United States in total megatonnage since 1969 or 1970.

6. Wohlstetter, p. 194.

7. The result—"equivalent megatonnage"—is usually defined as the two-thirds power of a weapon's yield if the yield is less than 1 megaton, and as the square root of the yield if it is greater than 1 megaton. The second formula adjusts for the fact that there are few targets so large as to justify a weapon larger than 1 megaton. Thus, a 10-kiloton weapon (.01 megatons) would have .1 equivalent megatons, and a 4-megaton weapon would have 2 equivalent megatons.

8. These calculations are based on Hoeber and Schneider's figures for 1975.

9. The twenty-six largest metropolitan areas in the United States, which have a total population of about 91 million, occupy an area of 135,000 sq. mi. One must realize, however, in contemplating these impressive figures, that in an actual war large numbers of SLBMs would not be on station and a certain fraction of ICBMs and bombers would be destroyed on the ground. Thus, the EMT delivered would be substantially less than the EMT in inventory.

10. See, for example, Donald H. Rumsfeld, *Annual Defense Department Report FY 1978*, January 17, 1977, p. 20.

11. The reader may be surprised to learn that over the past fifteen years the general trend in U.S. strategic-offensive EMT has been downward. We reached

our peak in 1959-1960 with an inventory about double that of 1972. (Wohlstetter, p. 196.) This drop corresponded, of course, to the shift from bombers to missiles. The number of *deliverable* EMT (taking into account alert rates of delivery vehicles, penetration probabilities, and so on) has probably increased, even though the total inventory has declined.

12. Glenn A. Kent, *On the Interaction of Opposing Forces Under Possible Arms Agreements* (Cambridge: Harvard University, Center for International Affairs, Occasional Paper no. 5, March 1963).

13. See Stephen J. Lukasik, "Military Research and Development," Hoeber and Schneider, pp. 190-239.

14. Hoeber and Schneider, p. 57.

15. Fred A. Payne, "The Strategic Nuclear Balance: A New Measure," *Survival*, May-June 1977, pp. 107-110.

16. Brown, *Statement to the Congress . . .* , p. 22.

17. Hoeber and Schneider, p. 36.

18. For an extensive discussion of the use of lethality as an index, see the following by Kosta Tsipis: *Offensive Missiles* (Stockholm: SIPRI, Stockholm Paper no. 5, August 1974); "Physics and Calculus of Countercity and Counterforce Nuclear Attacks," *Science*, February 1975, pp. 393-397; "The Accuracy of Strategic Missiles," *Scientific American*, July 1975, pp. 14-23; "The Calculus of Nuclear Counterforce," *Technology Review*, October-November 1974, pp. 34-47. For a skeptical analysis, see my "Missile Accuracy and Strategic Lethality," *Survival*, March-April 1976, pp. 52-59.

19. The CEP (circular error probable) in this case is the radius of a circle around the target (presumed to be a point-target) within which there is exactly a 50 per cent chance that the warhead will impact.

20. Assuming reliability is constant.

21. The lethality of a warhead is the natural logarithm (multiplied by a constant depending on hardness) of the kill probability.

22. See my "Missile Accuracy and Strategic Lethality," p. 54. Tsipis (*Offensive Missiles*, p. 20) estimated the CEPs of Soviet missiles to be 1 nm across the board. More recent estimates (e.g., John M. Collins in the *Congressional Record*, August 5, 1977, p. S14072) have indicated that the CEP of the SS-18 and SS-19 may be closer to .25 nm. Improving CEP by a factor of 4 increases lethality by a factor of 16.

23. See Payne.

24. See Andrew W. Marshall, "Estimating Soviet Defense Spending," *Survival*, March-Arpil 1976, pp. 73-79.

25. *A Dollar Cost Comparison of Soviet and U.S. Defense Activities 1966-1976*, January 1977.

26. There has been some uncertainty as to whether border guards and internal-security troops should be included or excluded from Soviet-force totals. Some have argued that these men are more like our border patrol and FBI than like our military personnel. In fact, however, they are heavily armed, have military training, and are prepared to take over military functions in an emergency. Thus, they should be included, just as the U.S. Coast Guard is now included when U.S.-Soviet naval comparisons are made. An exhaustive

reexamination of our estimate of Soviet defense manpower was completed last year, resulting in a downward revision of about 6 per cent.

27. Testimony of Harold Brown, in U.S. House, Appropriations Committee, *Department of Defense Appropriations for Fiscal Year 1978, Hearings,* February 22, 1977, 95th Congress, 1st Session, p. 4.

28. In many fields of science, there is a turning away from the search for such all-purpose indices. P. B. Medawar, in his article "Unnatural Science," in the *New York Review of Books* (February 3, 1977) writes, "We must consider first the illusion embodied in the ambition to attach a single number valuation to complex quantities—a problem that has vexed demographers in the past, and also soil physicists—as Dr. J. R. Philip, FRS, has pointed out. It bothers economists, too." Medawar goes on to discuss the fertility index in soil science, "true rate of natural increase" in demography, GNP in economics, and IQ in psychology, showing in each case that it is futile to attempt to capture complex phenomena with a single numerical index.

29. Joanne S. Gailar and Eugene P. Wigner, "Civil Defense in the Soviet Union," *Foresight,* May-June 1974, p. 10.

30. T. K. Jones, *Industrial Survival and Recovery After Nuclear Attack: A Report to the Joint Committee on Defense Production, U.S. Congress,* November 18, 1976, p. 10.

31. F. G. Krotkov, ed., *Meditsinskaya Sluzhba Grazhdanskoy Oborony* (Moscow: 1975), trans. by U.S. Joint Publications Research Service, 1976, p. 280.

32. See A. L. Horelick, "The Strategic Mind-Set of the Soviet Military," *Problems of Communism,* March-April 1977, pp. 80-85.

33. V. D. Sokolovskiy, *Soviet Military Strategy* (New York: Crane, Russak, 1975), pp. 289-291.

34. P. T. Yegorov, I. A. Shlyakhov and N. I. Alabin, *Grazhdanskaya Oborona* (Moscow: 1970), trans. by Oak Ridge National Laboratory, 1976, p. 6.

12
New Technology and Deterrence

Strategic Survey, 1977

In recent years there has been increasing concern in the West about the future stability of the global strategic balance. The counterforce capabilities of both the United States and the Soviet Union are improving significantly, threatening the survivability of fixed strategic installations, and challenging the role of the land-based components of national deterrent forces. By the mid-1980s deployment of the new technologies now being developed will seriously erode the second-strike capability of land-based missiles. Although much of the recent debate has centered on this question, it may by then no longer be relevant. Not for many years has technological change been as volatile as it is at present. With many applications of new technologies under development, others 'in the pipeline,' and still more being researched, it can no longer be assumed that the premises upon which the present strategic stability are based are assured.

Recent Developments

Of primary significance for the future of the strategic balance, at least in terms of the next ten to fifteen years, are a number of developments in strategic technologies—in engines, warheads, and guidance systems.

The greatly enhanced precision-guidance capacities which are now, or soon will be, available offer extraordinary accuracy. These guidance systems use for homing either those characteristics of a target which distinguish it from its surroundings (e.g. optical, infra-red, radio-wave, or acoustic signatures) or highly accurate navigation to strike fixed targets with known locations (or passing known locations) by such means as terrain contour matching (TERCOM), advanced inertial navigation systems, or navigation satellites. Although both the United States and the Soviet Union have made progress in this field, American ballistic-missile guidance systems are generally considered to be a generation ahead of their Soviet counterparts. Judging from the varying estimates of accuracy that have been given, the current circular error probable (CEP) of the Minuteman III ICBM seems to be as low as 600-800 ft. Software improvements in the NS-20 guidance system, now being incorporated in all Minuteman III, will reduce this margin even further. The advanced inertial reference sphere (AIRS), a 10.3-inch diameter gimbal-less inertial guidance system being developed for the US Air Force's MX ICBM, is expected to produce a CEP of around 200-300 ft, the lower figure probably being the limit attainable with purely inertial systems. Although the United States is investigating the application of various techniques of terminal homing to ICBM, it seems doubtful, given these very low CEP, that the techniques will increase accuracy enough to justify their deployment. By comparison, the CEP attributed to the latest generation of Soviet ICBM—the SS-17, SS-18, and SS-19— range from about 1,200 to 1,600 ft and are not expected to come below 1,000 ft until the early 1980s.

Increasing accuracy is also a feature of the American submarine-launched ballistic missile (SLBM) systems. The CEP of the Poseidon SLBM is currently about 1,500 ft at its maximum range of 2,500 nautical miles (nm), and the Improved Accuracy Programme (IAP) is expected to reduce this to about 1,000 ft by the early 1980s. The Trident I (C4) missile, expected to be operational before the end of this decade, will carry a full payload 4,000 nm while maintaining accuracy equivalent to that of the Poseidon missile, primarily by using a stellar sensor to take a star sight during the post-boost phase of the missile flight to correct the flight path. It is, of course, not necessary for this missile to be launched over its maximum range, and shorter flight paths produce correspondingly lower CEP: a Trident missile with a CEP of 1,200 ft at maximum range would have a CEP of under 1,000 ft if limited to the range of the existing Poseidon SLBM. These low CEP give existing and forthcoming American SLBM a substantial capability against all but the most hardened military targets; furthermore, the introduction of the Trident II (D5) missile, planned for the late 1980s, would give the American SLBM a true counterforce capability. Soviet SLBM—including the SS-N-8, which has a range of nearly 5,000 nm and uses a stellar inertial guidance system—are reported to have achieved CEP of under 1,500 ft, giving them a marginal counterforce capability.

Several important research and development (R&D) projects on propulsion are on the verge of yielding greatly improved efficiency in the use of fuel, weight, and space. They include improved solid-propellant rocket booster motors and relatively small, but highly efficient, turbo-fan and turbo-jet engines—for use in, for example, strategic and tactical cruise missiles. While developments in modern guidance systems and particularly 'area correlation' techniques such as TERCOM have excited strategic analysts and planners the most with regard to cruise missiles, they could not have been fully utilized without the development of small (100-150lb) engines capable of powering missiles over a range of 600-2,000 miles.

The technology of explosives and warheads has also changed greatly in recent years. Not only has the destructive potential of a given warhead volume and weight increased, but a variety of new warheads have been developed to meet specific requirements, particularly for theater use. The United States has developed the B-61 variable-yield ('dial-a-yield') bomb; the three-choice full-fusing option bomb with a device which, at the discretion of the bombardier, enables detonation of the free-fall bomb either in the air, on impact, or by delayed action; a series of low-yield nuclear artillery shells for the 155mm and 8-in. guns of the US Army in Western Europe; and the enhanced radiation or neutron bomb. This increased ability to control the timing, size, and type of explosion will permit greater use of these munitions where considerations of the safety of one's own troops or population centers become paramount. Although the applicability of these developments for strategic nuclear use is less clear, they have the potential to increase further the options in scenarios of counterforce and limited strategic warfare. A range of conventional explosives and warheads with potential strategic implications have also been developed recently. It is possible that non-nuclear weapons, including fuel-air explosives, improved cluster munitions for area targets, and hard structure munitions, when combined with highly accurate, long-range ballistic or cruise missiles, could be used against targets which can now be destroyed only by nuclear weapons.

Other technological developments, although outside the sphere of weapons, may also affect the strategic balance: developments in command, control, and communications (C^3) technologies (including real-time satellite observation and warning), considerable improvements in data processing, and re-targeting capabilities for both ICBM and SLBM systems. All three have greatly increased the ability of both the United States and the USSR to launch strategic nuclear strikes of a very limited and selective nature, so as to permit the fighting of an extended war involving controlled sequential exchanges. Although the United States has possessed a rather extensive capability for such controlled strategic warfare since at least 1961, Soviet developments are much more recent. It was not until July 1974 that the Soviet Union was able to launch her first geostationary satellite, and she now has at least two military communications satellites operating at geosynchronous altitude. An over-the-horizon radar system (which began test transmissions in July 1976) is being developed as an alternative long-range early-warning system. Hardened command and control installations have purportedly been constructed both in the Moscow area and within ICBM deployment fields. Interestingly, the introduction of a new technology for crisis prevention—the Moscow-Washington satellite hot-line—even provides for continuous communication between the White House and the Kremlin during a nuclear exchange, thus making a controlled nuclear war on a limited level feasible. It should be noted, however, that these supportive systems providing flexibility to existing nuclear forces are themselves vulnerable. Many of them—early-warning radars, communications links, the very-low-frequency command system of the ballistic missile submarine fleet—are large and easily attacked. Their destruction would not only rule out further controlled exchanges but would also seriously affect certain strategic capabilities. American counterforce capabilities would suffer most in this respect, since American ability to attack hard targets and the associated American strategic policy of target discrimination is much more dependent upon supportive systems than upon the large throw-weights that Soviet designers prefer. To the extent that actual war-fighting scenarios become increasingly accepted, one can expect further hardening or protection of these potential sub-systems of control against nuclear weapons effects.

Implications of Available Technology

The collective impact of more accurate, powerful, and discriminating offensive weaponry has two major implications for the maintenance of strategic stability. First, the continued viability of a basic component of contemporary strategic forces—fixed-site land-based missiles—has been called into question; second, the greater theoretical ability to fight a strategic nuclear war at controlled levels may increase pressures to launch a pre-emptive counterforce strike in a crisis.

These developments are principally a result of the very high single-shot kill probabilities (SSKP) which can be achieved by ballistic missiles with the high accuracies described above. Even against targets hardened to withstand 1,000 psi blast overpressure, the present Mk 12 re-entry vehicle of the Minuteman III (with a 170KT warhead) could achieve an SSKP estimated to be between 45 and 60 per cent with a CEP of 700ft. By comparison, the Mk 12A warhead (designed to replace the Mk 12), with its 350KT warhead and a CEP of 500ft, is expected to have an SSKP against the same target of up to 90 per cent. More significantly, an American decision to deploy a force of 300 MX ICBM would give the United States a first-strike potential of destroying well over 90 per cent of the fixed land-based Soviet missiles. Before that time—by the mid-1980s—improvements in the accuracy of Soviet ICBM will give the Soviet Union the ability to destroy a substantial proportion of the American ICBM force. However, since a greater proportion of Soviet deterrent forces consists of ICBM than is the case for the United States, ICBM vulnerability will have a greater impact on the Soviet Union than on her Western rival.

Yet at the same time that technology has increased the vulnerability of these missiles, it has also provided options which either increase their survivability or provide alternative choices for strategic forces. One possibility is to accelerate the hardening of ICBM silos so as to reduce their vulnerability to attack. About half the present American ICBM force is hardened to withstand about 1,000 psi blast overpressure, and a number of the new Soviet ICBM are reportedly being deployed in 2,000 psi silos. But silo hardening has its limits. In normal engineering practice, the maximum compressive strength of concrete is estimated to be 3,000 psi. Such hardening is very expensive (a 3,000 psi silo costs more than $15 million) and is feasible only in special geological environments. More important, if missiles with CEP as low as 600 ft are used, hardening to 2,000-3,000 psi reduces SSKP by only a few percentage points.

A second and much discussed means of reducing the vulnerability of land-based missiles is to make them mobile. The Soviet SS-16 ICBM was designed for land mobility, and the SS-20 IRBM (which comprises two stages of the SS-16) is already operational in a land-mobile mode. In the United States, the MX ICBM, if approved, will probably be deployed in some mobile form, although the specific configuration remains to be decided. Primary basing concepts now being considered for the MX consist of concealing mobile missiles in either underground trenches or multiple hardened shelters. But while the MX offers an apparently useful technical response to the threat posed by the new generation of offensive Soviet missiles, it also promises to be controversial. Not only will the cost be considerable (about $30 billion for the programme, comprising 300 MX tunnel-based mobile launchers), but the system, although less vulnerable than fixed ICBM, may still not be absolutely invulnerable to an accurate Soviet strike with high-yield warheads. Moreover, the introduction of an American mobile system might accelerate the Soviet move to mobility on a much wider scale, thus making verification of any arms-limitation agreement highly imperfect.

A third response option is to adopt a launch-on-warning (LOW) strategy, which calls for launching one's own offensive missiles as soon as radar confirms that the adversary has launched his. This would remove the need for survivable systems or redundant systems in order to ensure sufficient retaliatory, second-strike capability. However, nearly all analysts reject LOW as inherently destabilizing and lacking credibility. It is argued that a LOW posture would increase the potential for accidental war, while at the same time placing difficult, if not impossible, pressures upon decision-makers in times of crisis. More feasible might be a launch-through-attack (LTA) strategy: missiles would be launched when the full scope of the attack became clear. But the utility of an LTA posture diminishes as the synchronization and the success of the attack rise, and it remains a highly risky solution to ICBM vulnerability.

Before any of these responses is seriously considered—and none of them is either cheap or fool-proof—it will be important to put the emerging vulnerability of land-based strategic missiles in perspective. Much of the American debate on this issue has tended to draw strategic consequences from technological capabilities: because ICBM are becoming more vulnerable, it is argued, the Soviet Union could see an advantage in destroying them, thus leaving the United States in an inferior strategic position from which to respond. For both political and technical reasons, this is a scenario of questionable plausibility and thus does not provide a basis for serious assessment of the significance of ICBM vulnerability. First, it assumes that the United States will indeed recognize a massive Soviet attack on her land-based missile installations as a limited—as opposed to an all-out—nuclear strike and will be willing to respond only in kind. In his FY 1979 Defense Posture Statement, however, Secretary Brown cast doubt on this assumption: "The Soviets might—and should—fear that, in response, we would retaliate with a massive attack on Soviet cities and industry." Second, such a strike only makes sense if the attacker has complete confidence in the reliability of his counterforce systems and can be assured that a complex coordinated salvo at intercontinental range will work to perfection. Phenomena such as "fratricide" (exploding warheads creating an environment in which other incoming warheads do not function properly) must reduce confidence in any such projection. Secretary Brown also raised this question in the Posture Statement, arguing that "the Soviets would face great uncertainties" in planning a first strike, and "they must recognize the formidable task of executing a highly complex massive attack in a single cosmic throw of the dice." Most important of all, constantly deployed submarines (SSBN), bombers, cruise-missile carriers, besides surviving ICBM, would provide a retaliatory or second-strike capability for considerable counterforce, as well as for all-out, response. By the mid-1980s, the United States can expect that over 6,000 warheads will survive a surprise Soviet first strike—and perhaps as many as 10,000 if the United States were on full alert before the attack. Despite the unquestioned fact of growing ICBM vulnerability, a more sober assessment of its implications is needed before decisions can be taken on the most suitable response.

The Dimmer Future

Technologies affecting land-based missile vulnerability are not the only qualitative developments affecting strategic stability. By the time that this vulnerability becomes a reality, it may no longer be the crucial issue in determining what is an effective balance of deterrence. Potentially even more influential are technologies being researched and developed that could affect the survivability of satellites and submarines and (most fundamentally) the ability of offensive missiles to penetrate to their intended targets.

To date, greatest attention in this area has been given to satellites and the growth of anti-satellite satellites which can interfere with verification and reconnaissance, early warning, and C^3. During 1977, the Soviet Union continued her program of actively testing interceptor satellites, bringing the total number of tests to fifteen, of which eight involved maneuvering the interceptor near the target satellite, which was then destroyed by the "explosive destruction" of the interceptor. One Soviet test in 1977 involved intercepting a target satellite at an altitude of over 620 m—a capability which, if perfected, would threaten the US Navy's transit navigation link. However, the Soviet Union has yet to demonstrate a capability to intercept satellites at higher altitudes— essential if the geo-stationary satellites at 22,300 miles critical to American early-warning and C^3 functions are to be made vulnerable. The United States has responded to the Soviet effort by beginning her own anti-satellite program, based on the principle of destroying the target satellite by collision. The first tests of this American hunter-killer satellite are scheduled for 1980, and an initial operational capability is set for 1982. At the same time, the United States is improving techniques to counter Soviet advances in anti-satellite weaponry. These steps include increasing the protection of sensitive components in satellites, the development of detection and evasion capabilities, and even the use of lasers to destroy enemy interceptors. (Both countries are exploring the use of lasers and charged-particle beams to blind or destroy each other's satellites.) A third American response is political rather than technical: the proposal, first made in March, that negotiations should begin to control the development and deployment of this new category of anti-satellite weaponry, so as to nip this newest "space race" in the bud.

Less advanced, but of equal if not greater potential significance for strategic stability, are R&D efforts in anti-submarine warfare (ASW). Although no breakthroughs have occurred or seem imminent, the United States continues to make progress in its mostly acoustic ASW program. More speculative and exotic are several Soviet investigations into various "hydrodynamic signatures" (including heat, radiation, gas, magnetic, and wave) made by passing submarines and potentially detectable by satellites, surface ships, and other submarines. These efforts notwithstanding, the basic ASW problems of detection and destruction remain formidable. In addition, the increased range and reduced noise and cross-section of the new generation of American SSBN will increase the problems facing Soviet ASW experts, as will the establishment of new C³ procedures (notably the planned extremely-low-frequency Seafarer system) which will eliminate the need for submarines to reduce speed and approach the surface to communicate.

No single technological breakthrough would be as far-reaching as the development of a viable ballistic missile defense (BMD). The introduction of a comprehensive BMD system would undermine the fundamental "deterrence through mutual vulnerability" concept of contemporary strategic stability. The 1972 ABM Treaty between the Soviet Union and the United States effectively prohibits the deployment of BMD, both of then-existing and future technologies, and is of indefinite duration. But the Treaty does permit continued research and development, and there are indications that Soviet and American R&D programs continue unabated. The most interesting avenue of research involves generating streams of charged, sub-atomic particles and directing them with electromagnets at a target. While theoretically such charged-particle beams could be used to destroy incoming missiles, certain basic problems exist: the earth's atmosphere is difficult to penetrate, and its magnetic field interferes with guidance. The technology is still primitive, and the allegations of General Keegan and others that the Soviet Union has had considerable success in this field are premature. All the same, the potential development of a BMD system based on charged-particle beams or an alternative technology is a disquieting prospect.

13

Technology and the Military Balance

Richard G. Head

The United States stands at a crucial point in its relationship with the Soviet Union. George Kennan's latest prediction—widely echoed by other analysts—is that U.S. domestic reaction to the SALT II agreement will define a watershed in the U.S.-Soviet relationship. I would argue that the continuity or disruption of the détente relationship will turn on issues going far beyond arms control alone, issues involving subjective considerations and beliefs about the origins and nature of Soviet strategic objectives and the impact of technology on the military balance.

The military balance is not the only factor affecting the U.S.-Soviet political relationship. It may not even be the most important one. But it is not possible to discuss intelligently the overall relationship without due regard for the military component and the contribution that the technological element makes to national power.

The recent historical context of the U.S.-Soviet military relationship has been one of dynamic change. For at least the last 15 years the Soviet Union has invested heavily in military-related science and technology at the expense of investments in technology for all other sectors. At the same time, the Soviets have watched the United States divert its defense resources into Southeast Asia, defer service modernization programs, and cut back on military research and development. During this period the Soviet Union has made great strides in exploiting technology for military purposes, has fundamentally altered the strategic balance by the deployment of large numbers of intercontinental and submarine-launched ballistic missiles, and has dramatically improved the quality of its conventional forces. The purpose of this article is to examine some of the factors that determine where, how, and how well technology is being exploited to enhance military capabilities. Technology warrants particular consideration at this time, not only because of SALT II, but

Reprinted by permission of the author and *Foreign Affairs*, April 1978. Copyright 1978 by Council on Foreign Relations, Inc.

because there is widespread speculation that new weapons technology may be further altering both the strategic and theater aspects of the military balance.

Military technology is the set of skills and techniques that contribute to the production, operation, and maintenance of weapons and other military equipment. Technological progress, though difficult to calculate precisely, is simply the ability to accomplish objectives that were not possible to achieve or to reach presently achievable objectives more cheaply or more efficiently.

A discussion of U.S. and Soviet military technology is essentially a comparison of the total efforts of the two nations in the field of research and development (commonly called, in the military context, R&D). Comparison is made especially difficult because the two systems are the product of distinctive cultures, historical experiences, institutions, geography, external threats, and political ideologies. The complexity of the issue requires the candid admission that analysts do not even know with certainty the exact factors that drive the American R&D process, let alone that of the U.S.S.R. The best one can do is to highlight some of the most important elements and attempt to show how they may influence the process of weapons selection and development in the context of culture.

Similarly, any assessment of the military balance is partly a subjective comparison of two political-military systems. It cannot easily be reduced to a listing of intercontinental ballistic missiles (ICBMs), submarine-launched ballistic missiles (SLBMs), and nuclear warheads. Such a static, quantitative comparison omits important dynamic factors like reliability, readiness, targeting, political will, and the conditions under which such weapons would come into use. In addition, there are many semantic problems with the term "balance," implying, as it often does, a condition of equilibrium between the two superpowers. No such implication is intended in this article. Instead, the military balance will be treated as a useful shorthand for discussing the relationship between the military forces of the two superpowers. In the final analysis, the real measure of a nation's contribution to the military balance is its overall ability to perform assigned missions—the maintenance of deterrence, the preservation of stability, and the protection of human values.

The central themes of this discussion are that the impact of technology on the military balance may be revolutionary or incremental—depending on how it is exploited—and the military balance may be changed by improvement of older technology as well as by development of the new. The underlying proposition here is that the effective exploitation of technology for military purposes is dependent upon a range of essentially nontechnological factors such as military doctrine, tactics, training, resource allocation preferences, organizational processes, R&D style, budgets, and arms control. The discussion will focus on five major questions: how military doctrine can affect the kinds of weapons technology that are developed; how management of the military R&D process influences decisions on technology; how new conventional weapons technology could change the military balance; whether massive changes in the military competition are likely; and finally, a proposed framework for an American R&D "investment strategy."

II

The first set of nontechnological factors that affects weapons technology, and thus the military balance, involves the process of establishing military requirements through adherence to military doctrine. Soviet military doctrine extends from fundamentally different cultural and political roots from that in the United States. There is even great divergence in the usage of the terms doctrine, strategy, military science, military art, etc. The distinctions are not important for most Americans. Because of a unique combination of the Enlightenment, political pluralism, and continental opportunity, Americans have never put much stock in "doctrines" or doctrinaire statements of political purpose, even though we have dubbed as doctrines many broad policy statements like "containment," the "Truman Doctrine," the "Nixon Doctrine," the "Schlesinger Doctrine," etc. A high policy official in the Department of State stated that in the current Administration's view:

> There is no Carter Doctrine, or Vance Doctrine, or Brown Doctrine, because of a belief that the environment we are looking at is far too complex to be reduced to a doctrine in the tradition of post–World War II American foreign policy. Indeed, the Carter approach to foreign policy rests on a belief that not only is the world far too complex to be reduced to a doctrine, but that there is something inherently wrong with having a doctrine at all.[1]

This statement also reflects the Administration's recognition of a basic truth: that the Soviet Union is only a part of the foreign policy problem of the United States. (Soviet thinking, on the other hand, appears to be preoccupied with American developments.)

For all these reasons most Americans neglect Soviet military doctrine. Its importance, however, should be understood. Soviet military doctrine is authoritative and comprehensive, providing statements of how and with what weapons military forces are expected to fight. Military doctrine is used to define requirements for new weapons, develop operational plans and tactics, influence resource allocation for military investment, indoctrinate military members in their tasks, and mobilize popular, professional, and political support. Aside from semantic distinctions, a comparison of Soviet and U.S. military doctrines reveals differences in military thought, attitudes, and approaches to the problems of warfare.

There are at least six major areas of military doctrine that bear on the relationship between technology and the military balance, and in each of them the differences between the Soviet Union and the United States are significant. First is the way the two military establishments perceive the whole problem of warfare. U.S. writings convey a healthy appreciation of the role of uncertainty in battle and the need for flexible planning in operations and force posture. This approach leads to broad-gauged American R&D planning and general, rather than highly detailed, definitions of military missions. Hence, the United States traditionally builds weapons to be multipurpose, rather than narrowly specialized, and we expect operations to differ from plans.

In the Soviet Union an article of faith and ideology is that war is a science. To Soviet officers, military science is a unified system of knowledge about preparation for, and the waging of, war in the defense of the Soviet Union and other socialist countries against imperialist aggression. Its functions include the discovery and study of objective laws of armed conflict.[2] Soviet life is characterized by compartmentalization and secrecy. Soviet officers appear to be very intolerant of uncertainty and attempt to plan and prescribe every operational maneuver to the last detail. Soviet methods depend upon extremely centralized staffs, employ scientific methodology, examine the "objective" characteristics of warfare, and derive precise military requirements. Part of the traditional Russian emphasis on large numbers of troops and weapons ("mass") may be attributable to this fear of uncertainty. Mass can average out deficiencies caused by unforeseen circumstances, and mass lessens the responsibility to achieve optimal efficiency.

Second is a basic issue of whether doctrine or weapons is the more important factor in war. Despite all the writing about the "military-scientific revoluton," the Soviets say they reject the thesis that weapons should dictate military strategy. A "grand debate" apparently transpired in the Soviet Union in the period immediately following Stalin's death in 1953. The issue was joined in a dispute over the strategic meaning of the surprise attack in 1941, and it paralleled a struggle for power between Malenkov and Khrushchev. The military debate centered on the dilemma posed between "doctrine" and "armament norms" (weapons quantities).[3] John Erickson maintains that the debate was resolved in

1955 in favor of doctrine: that prewar doctrine had been fundamentally correct, but it could not produce victory until the requisite "armament norms" were met. Although there is a "chicken-and-egg" quality to this argument, the current implications for technology are that military doctrine is expected to produce weapons requirements to "pull" technology.

Within this perspective, the role of military professionals is amplified. Soviet officers have traditionally been preoccupied with the problems of training a mass army. Training is made more difficult if weapons are not standardized or if their designs change rapidly. Thus, the dominance of Soviet military professionals has tended to produce a conservative design philosophy that is very "user-oriented."

Doctrine can also be forward-looking and to a degree inconsistent with current military capabilities. This was a problem in the 1960s when some U.S. analysts had difficulty taking Soviet writings on land warfare seriously, particularly those parts that called for offensive break-throughs and high-speed advances. Only in recent years, with the Soviet buildup in tanks, armoured fighting vehicles, self-propelled artillery, multiple-rocket launchers, mobile bridging equipment, armed helicopters, tactical fighter aircraft, and air defense weapons, has the vision in their tactical doctrine been supported by technological capability. For the first time, the quality of these new weapons and their deployment in large numbers provide the kind of mobility and shock power so long called for in Soviet military doctrine. Although the United States also has a military requirements process, many would argue that doctrine is only one of many determinants of U.S. weapons design. Indeed, one gets the sense that military preferences for high performance and industry competition for contracts have dominated the U.S. process.

The third asymmetry in military doctrines is the striking difference in attitudes toward nuclear war. Western strategic theory has largely been conceived by academic theorists and places supreme emphasis on the use of nuclear weapons for deterrence of an attack by other nuclear weapons powers. Although the twin concepts of deterrence and defense (war-fighting) are linked, there is little doubt which is given preeminence. This emphasis extends from beliefs about the unprecedented destructiveness of nuclear weapons and the inability of technology to provide high-quality assurance of defense, validated to a degree by the Anti-ballistic Missile (ABM) Treaty of 1972.

Influenced by a different historical experience, Soviet strategic thought has largely emanated from professional military men who have never made quite the same sharp distinction between deterrence and defense. Perhaps it is the traditional search for unilateral measures of security or the deep-seated belief in "balanced forces," but both Soviet representatives in the Strategic Arms Limitation Talks (SALT) and Soviet political leaders have consistently resisted the Western concept of mutual deterrence. The Russian language has no direct equivalent to the English "deterrence," an asymmetry that may well have affected the development of Soviet strategic thought in the past three decades.

While most U.S. officials agree with their Soviet counterparts that a war-fighting capability is essential to make deterrence credible, U.S. strategic policy often draws subtle, but definite, distinction between the two concepts. Perhaps the clearest example of the difference was the emphasis of former Secretary of Defense Robert McNamara on programming forces separately for deterrence through assured destruction and defense through damage limitation. The distinction was never trivial. Whereas the weapons requirements for assured destruction are *relatively* quantifiable given certain assumptions, the requirements for security through buying a convincing war-fighting capability are much more open-ended. The arms control implications are obvious. If one side believes it has an "objective" security requirement for a well-developed war-fighting capability and high force levels, it is going to be difficult to achieve agreement that equal security can be achieved through deterrence and significant reductions in forces. Similarly, the requirements for maintaining the current U.S. policy of "essential equivalence" are much more complex and subjective than were those of assured destruction.

A related point is the contrast in the emphasis the two powers place on investment in strategic nuclear weapons. Over the ten-year period 1967-77, the level of Soviet spending on strategic forces measured in dollars has been two-and-one-half times that of the United States. While it is true that the United States made heavy investments in ICBM and SLBM forces in the previous decade (1957-67), the earlier U.S. investment only dramatizes the current divergent trends. In 1977, the Soviet investment in strategic systems exceeded that of the United States by more than three times.[4] Although one can discount some of this investment differential due to differences in efficiency, the magnitude of the disparity and the trends are disturbing.

Fourth, Soviet and American military doctrine diverge on the question of quantitative superiority. The United States has superiority in numbers of bombers, but U.S. nuclear policy has apparently abandoned the necessity, if not the desirability, of maintaining superior numbers of both ICBMs and SLBMs. Largely because of resource constraints, the NATO nations have not attempted to attain conventional numerical superiority in Europe. American R&D style has traditionally emphasized qualitative superiority, with smaller numbers; and U.S. military doctrine, while appreciating the value of mass, has adjusted accordingly. This preference for high-value, multipurpose weapons and the desire to substitute technology for manpower can be called an American "doctrine of quality." One of the results of the doctrine of quality and technological substitution has been a certain tendency for technology to drive both strategy and doctrine.

Soviet military doctrine, until recently, has had no tradition of qualitative technological excellence to draw upon, and so it has placed great emphasis on quantitative superiority. This tendency was reinforced in World War II when, faced with a qualitatively superior German force, the Soviet Union found quantity sufficient to its needs. Although most Westerners think of Russian military men as being preoccupied with "mass" in both manpower and matériel, a close reading of their doctrine indicates they are not talking simply about "mass," but about "armament norms." These are designed in the conventional case as planning guides to provide distinctive relative superiority sufficient to seize the initiative, overwhelm an expected Western superiority in quality, and strike at the opponent's central nervous system.

In the case of strategic forces, the effect of "armament norms" is much less clear. While the Soviet Union has achieved an evident level of quantitative superiority in ICBMs, SLBMs, and air defense forces, its leaders are apparently committed to the principle of equal aggregates as a result of the 1974 Vladivostok agreement. Whether SALT has had a significant impact on Soviet military doctrine and the tendency to acquire "safe margins" is still open to question.

Fifth, Soviet and American views diverge on the question of the first battle in the case of a possible NATO–Warsaw Pact confrontation. Despite certain weapons design characteristics like long range in tactical fighter aircraft, NATO declaratory policy, doctrine, force posture, and deployment all signal an intention to fight the first battle on the defensive. Soviet doctrine, on the other hand, reflects a clear belief in the primacy of the offensive.[5] Though their precise policy may be obscure, their written doctrine, professional debates, forward deployment, readiness, and ground force weapons all indicate a formidable offensive posture. Further, the preoccupation with concealment, deception, and surprise attack places a premium on preemption as the core value of Soviet military doctrine. Many Soviet officials frankly admit to having a "June 22 syndrome," which increases the credibility of Malcolm Mackintosh's dictum to "strike first in the last resort." Thus, Senator Sam Nunn can state with some assurance:

What confronts NATO across the inter-German border today is not 935,000 Pact troops, but 935,000 Pact troops organized, deployed, trained

and equipped for *blitzkrieg*, and governed by a doctrine based on surprise
and a postulated rate of advance of 70 miles per day.[6]

Finally, a related, but not precisely doctrinal, precept is that of "troop
control." Here the United States really has no equivalent: we emphasize
command, control, and communications, but that is not exactly what
the Soviets mean by the term. What the Soviets apparently fear is the
disorientation that comes when precise plans do not work out smoothly.
They have an inordinate fear of the unknown and the unexpected,
reflected in writings about "loss of bearing" by commanders. Soviet
leaders attempt to deal with this in three ways: by placing a tremendous
emphasis on troop indoctrination and officer education, by increased
efforts at obtaining detailed intelligence for more precise planning, and
by attempts to develop the "science of military management." This
"science," Soviet military authors maintain, is the most recent of the
military-scientific revolutions and is centered in the concept of military
cybernetics. The characteristics of the "scientific" management of
"troop control" are ever-increasing centralization, computerization,
automation of control processes, "scientific" selection of engineer-
commanders, repetitive training to routinize and automate human
reactions, and development of mathematical models for prediction.

Troop control as a doctrinal precept appears to Western observers to
be a pessimistic prediction of human behavior and an attempt at the
manipulation of personality, but it is also derived by Soviet military
tradition from a basic organizational evaluation of the educational
quality and cultural heritage of Soviet recruits. For at least the last
century the Russian Army has been conscripted from unskilled and
uneducated manpower. With the dramatic decline in the birthrate
among Russian nationalities, the Soviet Army is projected in the next 10
years to include a high percentage of non-Russian recruits. The
tremendous Soviet efforts at education have had remarkable results, but
compared to Western armies, Soviet manpower is clearly less technically
skilled and less oriented toward individual initiative.

The question of troop control is related to technology. Both the Soviet
Union and the United States are investing heavily in command, control,
communications, and intelligence systems to obtain better capabilities
in the areas of warning and battle management. But the investment
patterns differ. The United States is attempting to *centralize* intelligence
and communications, based on the development of high-data-rate
computer systems, but to *decentralize* execution of plans and operations.
In contrast, the Soviets are investing heavily in systems that will
centralize *both* intelligence and command, relying on highly redundant
communications channels to pass orders to tactical units.

Examples of the contrasting approaches to mission areas include air defense, where the Soviet Union has traditionally chosen to centralize its technology in ground-based missile systems and in ground radar stations, while the United States allocates a greater percentage of its air defense/air superiority electronics to the individual aircraft. Soviet anti-submarine warfare doctrine stresses team tactics with many ships; American R&D design has placed more technology and more faith in the hands of the individual ship captain. U.S. enlisted men handle command and management responsibilities that are only entrusted to officers in the Soviet Union.

III

The second set of nontechnological factors that affects weapons technology is a nation's R&D process, or style. It is popular in some circles to deride Soviet military capability and research and development by comparing the quality of selected Soviet weapons with supposed U.S. equivalents. It should be kept in mind when analyzing individual weapons, however, that such comparisons have limited utility. Differences in capabilities are exaggerated by individual comparisons, and we tend to forget that weapons are rarely used singly. Weapons are designed, developed, produced, and deployed as part of a larger cultural and military matrix, involving support systems, logistics trains, maintenance facilities, allies, terrain, manpower, doctrine, training and plans about how wars are to be fought. At best, static comparisons of present technology can provide useful guidelines in contrasting approaches; at worst, they hide trends and specifically, as far as U.S. policymakers are concerned, can delude them into thinking that "technological superiority" guarantees peace. Superior arms provide real advantages, but at some point greater quantity in deployed lower-quality weapons confers the capability to overwhelm the highest quality defense.

The main difference between U.S. and Soviet R&D systems is grounded in the contrasts between a competitive market economy and an ideologically constrained, centrally planned economy. In the United States, industrial producers draw from a superior technology base, tend to conduct civil and military research and development simultaneously, and satisfy a high civil demand for advanced technology products. In the Soviet Union, government ministries are sharply divided between civil and military R&D, and the civil market is controlled to restrict the supply of high-quality technological goods.

The Soviets have developed a distinctive national style for weapons development and acquisition that produces large numbers of weapons of increasing quality to meet the requirements of Soviet military doctrine. The R&D decision process for weapons designs includes the Politburo, the Council of Ministers, the State Planning Commission, the Ministry of Defense, the General Staff, the Armed Services, and the nine defense-industrial ministries. Research and development decisions are made in a closed subsystem of the Soviet government, with the military and Party leadership composed of narrow, technically oriented professionals. The political leaders have extensive technical expertise, but are poorly equipped to review professional military advice on doctrine, weapons, or training against broadly based cost-effectiveness, foreign policy, or arms control advice. The compartmentalized, secrecy-dominated political system, operating largely on the principle of consensus, reinforces the tendency toward conservatism noted in the development of military doctrine. The compartmentalization reduces the flow of information and makes comparisons of effectiveness between force components (e.g., ground-attack aircraft and tanks) very difficult. Compartmentalization and continued high defense budgets also tend to reduce interservice rivalry.

Despite the bureaucratic nature of most Soviet decision-making, the lack of pluralism makes the R&D decision process perhaps less elaborate and certainly more hierarchical than that in the United States. The Soviet process is characterized by fewer reviews of major projects, less overlap of organizational responsibilities, fewer checks and balances, and more stable budgets.

The American R&D process includes a large number of industrial contractors, university research laboratories, the military departments, the office of the Under Secretary of Defense for Research and Engineering, the Executive Office of the President (including the National Security Council and the Office of Management and Budget), and the Congress. Comparatively, this American R&D process is more fragmented, more open to citizen and external influences, more concerned with "due process," and more responsive to arguments over arms-control implications, environmental impact, and a fair allocation of government contracts. Responsibility is diffused, and weapons programs are subjected to multiple reviews and yearly budget cycles. The constant exposure to external influences and the intense competition for annual budget funds give the U.S. policy process a program orientation that is probably not felt to the same degree in the Soviet Union. Despite the structural deficiencies, the U.S. system operates amazingly well because of the skill, flexibility, and ingenuity of its smaller number of scientists, engineers, and technicians.

The major Soviet institutions that actually control weapons design are the defense-industrial ministries, which are vertically integrated, each one having under its jurisdiction research institutes, design bureaus, and manufacturing plants. Although nominally controlled centrally, the organizations are usually both geographically and functionally distinct. Theoretically, research and testing is done by the research institutes, weapons design and prototype construction are done in the design bureaus, and production is accomplished by the manufacturing plants. In reality, a complex network of inter-ministry communications, agreements, and bargaining exists.

For the more mature technologies, research institutes constrain weapons design from the very beginning by publishing handbooks for designers that specify not only research results, but an approved list of structures, design forms, components, materials, and manufacturing techniques. Designers, for their part, have a great deal of internal autonomy, but they are restrained by the research institutes, the lack of sophistication in production technology, the technical level of Soviet troops, and incentives to produce new prototypes frequently. Design bureaus exercise technical restraint, not so much because they do not have the materials or training to develop more advanced designs, but because of the influence of the doctrine that military capabilities are enhanced more by large numbers of deployed weapons with modest individual capabilities than by smaller numbers of higher quality weapons.

Soviet weapons produced from this traditional approach tend to have three main characteristics: design simplicity, interchangeable parts, and evolutionary growth.[7] Design simplicity is exemplified in the T-62 tank, which has a manual transmission, a manual, lever-type steering mechanism, and a 40-year-old engine design.

Common parts on weapons of the same type, with standardization across different weapons systems of the same vintage, is the second major Soviet characteristic. For example, many types of warships use the same auxiliary equipment and propulsion plants. In aircraft, the same turboprop engine was used in the An-22 transport as in the old Tu-20 bomber. Common parts are also used in the West, but not to the same degree. Soviet equipment is also produced by East European allies with the result that Warsaw Pact weapons—though not completely standardized—are more standardized than those of NATO.

The third traditional feature of Soviet weapons is incremental growth or cumulative product improvement as opposed to the U.S. tendency to favor whole new weapons systems. An outstanding example is the MiG-21 aircraft. The MiG-21 was first developed in the mid-1950s as a lightweight, clear-weather fighter. It has evolved with steady improvements in engine thrust, aerodynamics, fire control systems, electronics, and airborne weapons, and in the late 1970s performs the mission of all-weather interceptor of enemy aircraft, while other versions of the same basic aircraft have a considerable ground attack capability. This evolutionary improvement of subsystems, with extensive prototype testing, has increased Soviet military capabilities, while minimizing the large expenditures on research and development and retraining that are required with wholly new systems.

U.S. weapons development, on the other hand, is primarily oriented toward high performance. Complex computer models permit the calculation of kill probabilities and weapons lethality for different systems, and technology is then applied to maximize these numbers. Given the U.S. military requirements for high performance and low attrition rates, U.S. industrial contractors tend to respond with proposals for revolutionary developments, new subsystems, and sophisticated design. All too often, however, the resultant weapons have been overly complex, less reliable than past models, and increasingly expensive. The cost per unit of these new weapons has increased an average of four-and-one-half times per decade in constant dollars since 1950. In addition, while substituting technology for manpower at the operational end of the spectrum, the sophistication of U.S. weapons has tended to generate higher support costs and increased maintenance manpower requirements.

Occasionally U.S. weapons have made good use of incremental product improvement—most notably the Boeing B-52 and McDonnel Doublas F-4, whose longevity extends from early 1950s designs to present-day operation. In addition to lowering training costs and providing a high return on investment, such improvements in existing designs have only increased cost by a factor of two per decade. But such evolutionary developments do not have many advocates in the U.S. acquisition process.

The nature of the American R&D process has produced two other problems that are increasingly being recognized. One is the trend for the large number of decision centers to introduce procedures that lengthen the time between the beginning of a weapons program and the deployment of the system (12 years in some cases). The second is the tendency for the budget to provide less than planned funding of the number of systems placed into full-scale development and production. This discrepancy between planning and implementation often reduces production rates to well below what is considered efficient. The effect of both of these process characteristics is to stretch out the American R&D cycle and to greatly increase the cost of weapons development and acquisition.

Having described the central features of the American R&D system and characteristics of what some call the "traditional" Soviet style, an important question remains: To what degree are Soviet weapons development trends departing from the traditional pattern and adopting a more innovative style? The answer to this question is uncertain, but some data are becoming available on Soviet weapons innovations. Examples of totally new systems are not numerous, but those that exist have all appeared in the last 10 years. Many of the innovations are on systems that are better than similar U.S. systems or for which the West has no comparable items. Three examples are the BMP armored fighting vehicle; the ZSU-23/4 radar-directed, antiaircraft gun system; and the *Krivak* guided missile destroyer. The BMP contains a unique combination of innovative capabilities. It is a lightweight, armored personnel carrier with complete chemical and nuclear shielding and a low-velocity gun, firing rocket-assisted projectiles and antitank guided missiles. In service in large numbers in 1978, it is the primary vehicle (along with T-62 and T-72 tanks) that makes the doctrine of surprise attack, high-speed advance, and deep envelopment a credible threat to NATO.

Even more important, the general rule that the Soviet Union uses a conservative, traditional, incremental R&D style while the United States develops revolutionary new technology may be reversed in the ICBM case. Since 1967 when the U.S. ICBM force leveled off at 1,054 missiles, only one new strategic land-based missile has been introduced—the Minuteman III, deployed in 1970. In the intervening 11 years, the Soviet Union has deployed six major new ICBMs and several variations. In fact, it is the United States that has switched to an incremental style of development, while the Soviets, with the SS-17, SS-18, and SS-19, have made dramatic increases in ICBM capability. Incrementalism has many advantages, but most analysts agree that further improvement of the Minuteman will not solve the basic problem caused by Soviet ICBM developments—i.e., drastically increased silo vulnerability.

An estimate of the contribution of better technology to Soviet ICBM capability can be obtained by examining the SS-19's improvements over the SS-11. According to one congressional analyst, the SS-19 represents a 15 percent increase in length and diameter, which produces a 32 percent increase in hard-target kill capability, or lethality. A series of technological improvements provide the SS-19 with multiple independently targetable warhead capability, increased payload efficiency, and increased accuracy. Taken together, the technological improvements of the SS-19 over the SS-11 increase the new missile's counter-silo capability by something over 40 times.[8] These improvements in technology threaten to alter the balance of military power much more than the Soviet achievement of quantitative superiority in ICBM/SLBM force levels.

Thus, the tentative answer to our question is that the Soviets are apparently demonstrating some signs of more, if not much, innovation in conventional weapons design and have shown a surprisingly rapid evolution in ICBM/SLBM performance.

The next question concerns the relationship of the characteristics of the two R&D systems to implications for the military balance. What is the relationship between inputs to the systems and tangible military outputs? On the input side, the Soviet investment in research and development when measured in dollars was about one-half that of the United States in 1964-68, equal by 1970, and in excess of American R&D outlays by 50 percent in 1976.[9] In the category of weapons procurement and military construction, the Soviet Union by 1976 was investing *twice* as much as the United States. This large investment in procurement activity has currently given the Soviets a six-to-one advantage in tank production; three-to-one in infantry fighting vehicles; eight-to-one in artillery; two-to-one in tactical aircraft; and slight advantages in helicopters and antitank missiles.[10] The resultant defense-industrial capacity provides the Soviets a considerable technological base, with production potential that is usually not thought of in comparisons of technology.

The combination of what may be increasing innovation with the continuity, steady quality growth, and high production rates of new and improved military systems indicates a technological trend in the balance of deployed military capability that is adverse for the United States.

IV

This review of U.S. and Soviet doctrine and R&D style has stressed how these essentially nontechnological factors influence the two nations' development of military technology. A third nontechnological factor that affects weapons is arms control. Many observers feel that the failure to incorporate sufficient consideration of technical factors into the SALT negotiations is a serious flaw. With the brief discussion of the SS-19 it can be seen that qualitative technical factors far outweigh numerical ceilings and physical size constraints in determining the military effectiveness of intercontinental missiles. At the same time, the adoption of the principle of equal aggregates and the continued Soviet deployment of mass would seem to make it all the more imperative that the United States not constrain itself in the area where it has traditionally demonstrated a capacity for excellence.

Military doctrine and R&D style affect other areas of military preparedness, influencing both strategic and tactical programs. In the strategic area, for reasons that we do not fully understand, the Soviets are pushing hard on scientific research in antiballistic missile defense, high-energy lasers, charged-particle beams, and anti-satellite interceptors. Some analysts see in these intensive efforts (and associated reports of civil defense activity) an attempt to fulfill a Soviet doctrinal prescription to develop a complete war-fighting capability. The development of an operational capability in any one of these areas could seriously alter the military balance.

Military doctrine and acquisition style also interact with dramatic developments in new conventional weapons technology. Advances in solid-state electronics, propulsion, and computer-related fields appear to offer tactical weapons capabilities in the mid-1980s that could cause major changes in warfare. First demonstrated in combat during the 1973 Middle East War, the new technologies are clustered in the areas of tactical intelligence, precision-guided weapons, and improved conventional munitions.

While it is too early to tell whether the impact of the new conventional weapons technologies will be revolutionary or incremental, the role of military doctrines and R&D styles is going to be a key factor. While many predict that the general influence of the new weapons will be to increase the vulnerability of large ships, aircraft, tanks, and armored fighting vehicles, it is not at all clear whether such changes will ultimately benefit NATO or the Warsaw Pact. The potential firepower of a "new technology" NATO defense would tend to shatter the Soviet doctrine of the offensive, but the capability of the Soviet R&D process to produce great numbers of heavily armed vehicles tends to offset high loss rates. In addition, the Warsaw Pact has begun deploying large numbers of antitank guided missiles and making other weapons and organizational changes to exploit the new technologies. Changes to date, however, have been in the direction of increasing the tactical efficiency of combined arms operations and have not indicated a revision of the basic doctrinal concepts discussed above.

In the Western alliance, there is excitement at the possibility that the new technologies may for the first time make possible a conventional defense of Europe. But such enthusiasm should be tempered by acknowledgment that NATO is not currently structured for the dispersed and decentralized warfare that seems to favor the new weapons. Changes will have to take place before the potential of the new technology can be fully explored. No area of defense policy in the next decade will require a more concerted effort to sort out the intermingled threads of military doctrine, organization, training, tactics, weapons design, and acquisition.

V

The context of the U.S.-Soviet relationship has been characterized by massive investments in military-related science and technology and a gradual improvement of the Soviet position from strategic inferiority 15 years ago to one of essential equivalence today. Looking into the future, there are some indications the Soviet Union in the next decade will be facing a period of economic and political crisis. Will arms limitation agreements and the scope of these emerging problems engender any change in policy priorities toward a redistribution of investment away from military programs into the civil sector?

Much as we would like to see a slackening of the Soviet military effort, there has been none to date, and there are reasons to doubt any massive changes in the future. Although strategic arms limitation agreements are desirable, they are more likely to redirect than to diminish defense efforts. In the area of conventional arms, where the Soviet Union has already achieved well-defined advantages, arms control has moved very slowly and has had no discernible impact on Soviet armament levels. After centuries of lagging behind the West militarily, Russia has only recently achieved a position of parity. The confidence and self-assurance that this status breeds are only slowly becoming apparent. While militarily equivalent, the Soviets apparently still perceive themselves to be technologically and economically inferior and show every indication of continuing to strive energetically for further military gains. The major development decisions that will affect Soviet force posture in the next five to eight years have already been made—in a period of striking Soviet increases. Finally, Soviet leaders may find it difficult to renounce, or even modify, cultural beliefs that base domestic political stability on the acquisition of military power.

This discussion has stressed that U.S. and Soviet technology are driven by unique military doctrines, resource allocation preferences, and R&D styles. Soviet weapons appear to be remarkably well designed and consistent with Soviet military requirements, industrial capability, level of troop training, and employment doctrine. Furthermore, massive investments and a disciplined R&D strategy have permitted the technology in deployed Soviet weapons to approach that of the United States in enough specific military mission areas so that the future stability of the military balance is in question. SALT and conventional arms control may provide new boundaries and incentives for technological development, but to date there have been no signs of slackening in the long-term military competitive relationship.

In a military balance where many quantitative measures accrue to the other side, most U.S. policymakers place a high value on retaining technological superiority. Yet recent trends indicate this superiority will be increasingly difficult to maintain without an appropriate investment strategy and the associated organizational and doctrinal changes. While many agencies of the U.S. government invest heavily in research and development, it is not clear that such a strategy now exists.

VI

There are four general areas in which a U.S. strategy needs to respond to the Soviet buildup. The first is perhaps the most difficult—the need to recognize that the United States is in a long-term competition with the Soviet Union and political leadership will have to be directed to obtain popular support for a responsible and measured position. As a corollary the United States should respond in a way that strengthens the political cohesion of the Western alliance and does not overly distort U.S. global and domestic priorities.

The second area is in the coordination and integration of several macro-elements of an investment strategy. These are government-wide policies that can only be developed and implemented in an inter-agency forum, supervised by the National Security Council and the Executive Office of the president. They include U.S. policy in the difficult areas of arms control, arms transfer, technology exports, international cooperative research and development, and the technology base. Arms control policy is critical because, more than most other areas, it influences Soviet expectations about the overall political relationship. The United States should continue to strive for reasonable, verifiable agreements, not expecting arms control to solve the entire security problem.

Arms transfer policies should be included in this framework because the volume of sales and the technological component of U.S. weapons are a vital aspect of our global influence. Similarly, civilian technology like high-speed computers and microcircuitry is eagerly sought by the Soviet Union and Eastern bloc countries, and unchecked exports could have an adverse effect on U.S. security. The international development of cooperative R&D policies and programs is an essential ingredient in our relationship with NATO allies. The growing cost of research and development makes it apparent that the Alliance cannot afford highly redundant and wasteful national efforts. Economies of scale, an expanded fighting capability, and increased political cohesion are only some of the reasons why NATO standardization and interoperability are essential to a U.S. strategy.

A macro-approach to a U.S. investment strategy should also include a reinvigoration of the technology base. This is essential because of growing signs of slackening in the growth of U.S. industrial productivity, a decline in private investment in basic research, and a steady reduction in the number of U.S. scientists. Scarce capital and continued high inflation have caused U.S. industry to cut back on investments in the technology base for at least the last seven years. Increases in defense and government-wide budgets for basic research should be supported as an investment in our "technological future."

The third major area of a U.S. investment strategy is where technology, military strategy, and military doctrine intersect—military mission areas. Pressed by the Soviet buildup and the altered military balance on one side and the opportunities presented by the new technologies on the other, there is a critical need to review U.S. strategic and doctrinal concepts. This has already been started with detailed mission-area analyses now being conducted in the Defense Department. When completed, these studies should provide the essential core for the development of individual investment portfolios tailored to the mission areas.

Only a few military mission areas will be mentioned here. In the strategic area, there is a growing acknowledgment that the United States will need to make a major decision to meet impending threats to the land-based missile force either by modernizing or by other means. In space, the United States has a general technological lead that should be exploited by accelerated development of both manned and unmanned systems.[11] But it is now apparent that these systems will have to be hardened and provided with essential defensive capabilities to reduce their vulnerability to interference. In general purpose forces, the Soviet buildup requires an immediate U.S./NATO response to field more antitank, artillery, and air defense weapons. Over the longer term, the challenge of the new weapons technologies requires an especially searching review of organizational and doctrinal concepts.

The fourth major area of the framework consists of the micro-elements of a U.S. investment strategy. These elements deal with R&D management and style. The overwhelming need here is to devise new methods to accelerate the flow of affordable technology into the field forces. The number of formal steps in the acquisition process should be reduced, and those that remain should be viewed as flexible. Programs should be tailored to match need and technical risk. Innovative organizational styles should be attempted. Procedures should be streamlined to reduce the length of the R&D cycle in an attempt to reduce the effect of inflation and reduce overall costs. The number of systems in full-scale development and production at any one time should be controlled so that the selected systems can be fully funded at efficient production rates.

The military services should examine more closely the opportunities for meeting military requirements through the improvement of existing systems. New systems development should be reserved for those cases where evolutionary growth will not provide the capacity to meet the military challenge or where technological opportunity is unusually promising. Experimental prototyping can be a valuable guide in determining the feasibility and cost of shifting from an incremental improvement to a revolutionary jump. Even in completely new systems, the United States should expand the development of the so-called high-low mix. First attempted in tactical fighter aircraft, the concept should be applied vigorously to surface ships, tanks, and other major programs. By developing a combination of high-quality/high-cost systems with larger numbers of adequate-quality/lower-cost weapons, the American R&D process should be able to fully exploit the potential of the new technologies and provide sufficient quantities of deployed systems to compete over the longer term.

Finally, an investment strategy should serve as the focal point to bring together the technical and tactical communities and to clarify the interaction of technology, the R&D process, military doctrine, and organizational changes. Only with broad public support and effective implementation of an investment strategy can American defense policy relate advancing technology to the military balance.

Notes

1. Leslie Gelb, "National Security and New Foreign Policy," address given at the U.S. Army War College, June 8, 1977, printed in *Parameters* (Army War College), November 1977.

2. General-Major S. N. Kozlov, *The Officer's Handbook (A Soviet View)*, trans. U.S. Air Force, Moscow: Voyenizdat, 1971, pp. 47-48.

3. John Erickson, "Soviet Theatre-Warfare Capability: Doctrines, Deployments, and Capabilities," in *The Future of Soviet Military Power*, Lawrence L. Whetten, ed., New York: Crane, Russak, 1976, p. 144.

4. Central Intelligence Agency, *A Dollar Cost Comparison of Soviet and US Defense Activities, 1967-1977*, January 1978.

5. A. A. Sidorenko, *The Offensive (A Soviet View)*, trans. U.S. Air Force, 1974, Moscow: Voyenizdat, 1970; and S. N. Kozlov, op. cit., p. 65.

6. *New York Times*, November 14, 1977, p. 17. The "June 22 syndrome," in the text, refers to the date of the all-too-successful German attack on Russia in 1941.

7. Arthur J. Alexander, *Armor Development in the Soviet Union and the United States*, R-1860-NA, Santa Monica: The Rand Corporation, September 1976, p. 48.

8. Robert Sherman, "A Manual of Missile Capability," *Air Force Magazine*, February 1977, p. 39.

9. Central Intelligence Agency, supra, footnote 4, p. 6.

10. U.S. Department of Defense, *Annual Report FY1978*, January 17, 1977, p. 114.

11. Two programs that could have revolutionary effects on military operations are the Space Transportation System (shuttle) and the NAVSTAR Global Positioning System, a set of 24 satellites that will permit three-dimensional positioning with accuracies of ten feet.

14
NATO Defenses and Tactical Nuclear Weapons

Manfred Wörner

In the continuing discussion of security issues within the Atlantic Alliance, tactical nuclear weapons (TNW) remain the stepchildren of NATO strategy.

The existence of these weapons is well known: indeed, it would be difficult to ignore the stockpile of some 7,000 tactical nuclear warheads that have been emplaced in Western Europe over two decades. Yet, serious consideration of the actual use of these weapons—and of its possible consequences—tends to be smothered under a psychological blanket. If questions about their employment are nevertheless raised, the vague responses more often than not reflect a blend of confidence and fatalism. There is the belief, on the one hand, that TNW contribute to the securing of the peace—but the fear, on the other hand, that a future conflict in Europe would mean inexorably the nuclear extinction of the Federal Republic of Germany and many other important parts of Western Europe. Tactical nuclear weapons are central to the general numbing effect that the sheer magnitude of the problems of nuclear deterrence and defense in the European context has exerted on public opinion.

Contrasting Concepts of Deterrence

If Europeans thus shy away from an honest look at the deterrent threat and actual use of tactical nuclear weapons, this tendency has been encouraged by the reticence of the American alliance partner. In 1967, the United States persuaded NATO to adopt "flexible response" as the official strategy of the Alliance, but it was left essentially to the member states to implement the new strategy. The score sheet of implementation, after some ten years, is hardly encouraging. Although lip service was paid to "flexible response," the NATO countries neither adequately

Reprinted by permission from *Strategic Review*, Fall 1977. Copyright 1977 by United States Strategic Institute.

increased their efforts toward a viable conventional defense of Western Europe nor adapted their concepts of deterrence to the new realities of the strategic environment. Now, as before, strategic thinking in the Federal Republic, and in Western Europe more generally, is handcuffed to a conception of deterrence that dates back to the era of U.S. nuclear monopoly—the conception that the *mere existence* of nuclear weapons is enough to deter a potential adversary from military adventures. In contrast, the United States, in the context of its own translation of "flexible response," long ago shifted to a conception of deterrence which ties deterrent credibility to the "implementable threat."

European strategists have thus basically remained mired in the notion of deterrence through nuclear retaliation ("deterrence by punishment"), whereas strategists in the United States, pondering the implications of the advent of strategic nuclear parity between the superpowers, have gravitated toward a conception of deterrence that is based on the idea of denying the enemy the ability to attain his objectives ("deterrence by denial").[1] For European security policies the consequences of entwining a realistic defense doctrine with an unrealistic concept of deterrence are all too ominously clear: defense and deterrence will drift further and further apart until they lose all relationship with each other. Illustrating the logical dilemma is the following sentence in one of the most-discussed recent West German books on security policies: "In the case where the capability for successful defense is lacking, in that case deterrence in its narrower sense sets in."[2] This raises the obvious question: If deterrence in Europe—that is, prevention of conflict—is possible without effective defense capabilities, why render any kinds of financial sacrifices for defense at all?

The conflict between conceptions of deterrence is particularly germane to the issues of tactical nuclear weapons in Europe. For years, Europeans have clamored for the presence of these weapons on European soil but have evaded discussion of a rational doctrine for their employment. The luxury of debating simply the "if" of TNW—but not the concrete "when," "how," and "where" of deployment—is drawing to a close.

Several developments support this prognosis. First of all, recent months have witnessed an intensified discussion of tactical nuclear weapons in the United States—not only among strategic analysts, but in the political arena as well. The discussion has featured proposals for modernizing TNW, improvements in their command and control, and reductions in their vulnerability. But arguments have also emerged for reductions in, and even the complete removal of, the stockpile of U.S. tactical nuclear weapons in Europe.

Second, the NATO proposal at the MBFR negotiations in Vienna for a *quid pro quo* involving Western tactical nuclear weapons and Soviet armored divisions has pushed TNW more prominently into European opinion currents. This trend has been reinforced by Warsaw Pact proposals for a "no-first-use" agreement with respect to nuclear weapons.

Finally, Western Europe has experienced recently a veritable flood of publications containing critical analyses of the current state of West European security and proposals for new directions. One example is the book by Belgian General Robert Close, *Europe Without Defense*, in which he avers that a concerted conventional attack, launched beneath the nuclear threshold, could put Warsaw Pact armies on the Rhine within forty-eight hours of the start of battle. Other authors have proposed a defense of Western Europe without either nuclear weapons or classical conventional forces, adducing the vision of a "defense without self-destruction."[3]

In any event, NATO Europe can no longer turn its back conveniently upon problems related to the deterrent value and employment doctrine governing tactical nuclear weapons. One qualifying comment is immediately in order. It is incontrovertible that a difference of interests divides the transatlantic partners in NATO. The United States is obviously interested, in the event of a breakdown of the deterrent in Europe, in containing the military conflict to the Continent as long as possible—in keeping it from escalating and prevailing on the battlefield without endangering American territory. By contrast, it is in the European interest that the risk for the aggressor be heightened by the prospect of a relatively quick escalation of the battle and its consequent endowment with new qualitative and geographical dimensions. This conflict of interests is probably irreconcilable; NATO must live with it and reflect it in its military doctrine. This is the case today. Deliberately or not, "flexible response" is formulated as vaguely as it is because the interests of all NATO countries must be straddled. In this light, Colin Gray is perhaps correct in suggesting: "In such a situation, the best doctrine tends to be the least doctrine."[4] This does not mean, however, that a curtain of silence should be drawn over tactical nuclear weapons. To the contrary, everything that can be resolved in the Alliance, politically and conceptually, must be resolved. Beyond that, a margin of uncertainty must be accepted as a given. It is small consolation, but consolation nevertheless: that which has not been defined by the West remains an incalculable risk for the East.

Nevertheless, it is essential that publicity be given—through declaratory policies as well as visible deployments—to the roles that NATO has assigned to tactical nuclear weapons, namely:

1. To deter the Warsaw Pact from conventional aggression against Western Europe and, if necessary, to blunt such aggression.

2. To deter the Warsaw Pact from the use of tactical nuclear weapons and, if necessary, to respond at the same level.

3. To signal to the Warsaw Pact that the United States is willing to accept the risk of escalation in the defense of Europe and is prepared even to resort to strategic nuclear weapons in that defense.

Tactical nuclear weapons thus contribute substantially to the uncertainties in the risk calculations of the Soviet planner. For this reason alone, no margin of doubt can be conveyed with respect to NATO's willingness to resort to the weapons if the battlefield situation so dictates. By the same token, it would be imprudent—and potentially damaging—to signal to the enemy in advance when and where the weapons would be invoked.

But the tactical nuclear weapons in Europe serve a function that transcends pure military rationale—one that tends to be overlooked in the American strategic debate. Tactical nuclear weapons represent, in more than simply symbolic dimensions, the community of fate that links the United States and Western Europe. In European eyes the weapons connote the tangible guarantee that the United States is engaged in the defense of Europe with all the consequences that might be entailed. This visible guarantee is important particularly for the Federal Republic of Germany, which has renounced any nuclear weapons development of its own and has consciously made the security of its national existence a dependency of the Alliance.

It needs to be pointed out that this linkage function of tactical nuclear weapons should not simply be interpreted as U.S. altruism toward allies in need of protection: American interests are clearly at stake as well. The risk to the United States of becoming embroiled in a conflict in Europe is lowered in direct proportion to the clarity, persuasiveness, and comprehensiveness of America's recognized intent to invoke all required weapons, conventional or nuclear, within and on behalf of Western Europe.

Imbalance in Conventional Capabilities

NATO has traveled a long road from the Lisbon meeting of 1952, when the Alliance set a force goal of ninety-six divisions to counter the might of the Red Army and satellite divisions in Eastern Europe. This goal was quickly abandoned as impractical in light of the financial and manpower resources of the Alliance. Nevertheless, the NATO member nations continued their efforts toward building a conventional option. The advent of nuclear parity between the superpowers triggered a profound shift in the strategic context relevant to Western Europe. Yet, recognition of this shift did not modify the basic conviction among the West European members that a conventional balance in Central Europe lay beyond the reach of the Alliance. There was a sense of acquiescence in a "calculable conventional inferiority." In the meantime, the imbalance in conventional capabilities in Europe widened. This imbalance can perhaps be described best in dynamic terms, assuming three basic modes of possible Warsaw Pact conventional aggression in accordance with the following scenarios.

Scenario A: If the leadership of the Warsaw Pact decided to launch an attack against Western Europe from a "standing start," this would probably unfold as an extension of a Pact military maneuver—at the very least under the prior guise of preparations for a military exercise. One could even project that the Warsaw Pact would meet its obligation under the Helsinki Declaration by dutifully giving prior notice of such a maneuver, thus offering no ostensible cause for NATO preparations for an attack.

In order to provide combat-readiness to the first-echelon Category A forces of the Warsaw Pact (which are at 85 per cent of full strength and fully equipped), the Soviet Union would presumably have to give the attack order some seventy-two hours before the start of battle. This could give NATO a maximum warning period of between twenty-four and thirty-six hours.

Under these assumptions—and postulating an unhampered NATO mobilization—the hour of attack would witness hardly more than eighteen combat-ready NATO divisions confronting thirty-nine divisions of the Warsaw Pact. The latter would be augmented by parts, and possibly the total, of the six Warsaw Pact airborne divisions. Moreover, it cannot be taken for granted that the Soviet divisions now stationed in Hungary would not be pitted into the offensive.

Scenario B: If the Warsaw Pact decided to stage an attack from a "moving start"—that is, after rapid forward deployment of its forces— some ten days would be required. This option would permit the mobilization, beyond the first-echelon Category A divisions, of Category B forces (which are somewhat over half-strength and fully equipped, even though their equipment is qualitatively inferior to that of the forces in Category A). The ten-day period would also allow the Warsaw pact to bring its Category A divisions of the second echelon close to their staging areas by D-Day.

In this scenario the West could look toward a warning period of approximately three days. Under the above assumptions—and again accepting the premise of an undelayed NATO mobilization—seventy-seven Warsaw Pact divisions would face some twenty-five NATO divisions on the day of battle. And again these figures do not include the possible use of five Soviet airborne divisions, which are not part of the second echelon, or of the Soviet divisions encamped in Hungary.

Scenario C: If the Warsaw Pact decided to launch an attack against NATO after a comprehensive mobilization and without concern for strategic surprise, the preparations would span three weeks. This period would allow for the movement of both Category A and B forces in the first and second echelons to their launch points along the Central Front. Moreover, the forces of the Soviet strategic reserve (totaling some twenty-two divisions) would by then have reached their assembly areas in the western part of the Soviet Union and in Poland.

In this scenario, the West could receive warning of between ten and twelve days. Reiterating the assumption about the unhampered mobilization of NATO—but including among the attacking forces the Soviet divisions in Hungary and all Soviet airborne divisions—at the start of battle some 32 NATO divisions would confront approximately 110 divisions of the Warsaw Pact.

The above dynamic comparisons suggest that under realistic assumptions—and even with the optimistic premise that the NATO leadership would translate intelligence data into the requisite political and military decisions—the conventional superiority of the Warsaw Pact forces over their NATO counterparts ranges consistently between two-to-one and three-to-one. A more detailed analysis of possible scenarios, which cannot be attempted in the short space of this article, would show time phases in which the situation would be in some cases marginally worse. In general, however, it can be adduced that in the first months of a conventional conflict in Europe the military relationships would turn ever more starkly to the disadvantage of the West.

The penalties to NATO in a protracted conflict in Europe derive first of all from the geostrategic ramifications of the battlefield—the fact that the Soviet Union can bring reinforcements and reserve forces to bear over comparatively short land routes, whereas the United States would have to muster such reinforcements over the Atlantic Ocean. To this must be added that Soviet reserve and reinforcement units destined for the Central Front already exist—even if those Category C forces are presently at 20 to 30 per cent manpower strength and 75 per cent equipment strength—and could be deployed within approximately five weeks. By contrast, comparable Western reserves and reinforcements would have to be contrived virtually "from scratch," and much of their weapons and equipment would emerge from factory assembly lines only after the start of conflict. From the NATO vantage point, the tide of battle could be stabilized and improved only after the arrival in Europe of substantial forces from the United States—an operation that would require at least three months.

Under present and foreseeable circumstances, it would be impossible for NATO to wage such a protracted conflict without giving up significant parts of Western territory. The stark fact is that, in view of the political imperative of "forward defense," the limited depth of NATO territory, as well as the vulnerability of the Alliance's arms supplies, NATO could not resist a concerted Soviet conventional offensive for more than several days. Taking into account the enemy's advantages of tactical surprise, about all the conventional forces of NATO could aspire to would be to engage successfully the first-echelon forces of the Warsaw Pact. This would mean that they could probably buy time for the NATO leadership to enter into negotiations with the adversary and/or to make the decision to escalate the conflict. With the arrival of second-echelon Warsaw Pact forces, however, NATO conventional forces would have to resign themselves to a retreat and substantial loss of territory.

It is impossible, therefore, under present circumstances to come up with a realistic scenario of *conventional* conflict in Central Europe that holds any prospect of a successful outcome for NATO—that is, the restoration of the territorial *status quo ante*. Achievement of this potential through a genuine conventional balance in Europe is effectively foreclosed. No NATO country is today prepared, or in a position, to pay the financial—and, in the final analysis, political—costs that are entailed.

Preconditions for a Viable NATO Defense

Let there be no misunderstanding: The West European members of NATO must do more in the way of building up their conventional capabilities. Even if a genuinely viable conventional option is beyond reach, every measure that strengthens the conventional components of the Alliance means a gain in operational time and flexibility, as well as in the credibility of the defensive posture. Yet, if NATO wants to be in a position to repel *(and thus deter)* a large-scale Soviet conventional aggression, it must not only deploy adequately strong, fully manned and equipped forces with high initial striking power and cover their rear with quickly mobilizable reserve forces; it must also take the following measures:

1. Exploit optimally all technological posibilities that loom beyond the classical spectrum of conventional weapons (e.g., area munitions designed to disperse and disrupt, precision-guided munitions, and cruise missiles).

2. Assure that the conceptual, institutional, and material preconditions are created for a possible use of tactical nuclear weapons.
3. Render it clear, through the placement of tactical nuclear
   weapons and corresponding declaratory policies, that escalation
   in the event of a conflict does not have strict limits but instead
   extends to the possible use of U.S. strategic nuclear systems.

Only through such measures can the Alliance muster the wherewithal
for a successful conventional defense until the decision point of
changing the terms of battle or triggering escalation—and waging the
defense over a period of time that would not be too debilitatingly short in
terms of the effective harnessing of NATO capabilities. And, applying
the principles of deterrence by denial, only through such measures can
the risk element in the Soviet utility-versus-costs-versus-risk calculus be
made prohibitively high. The *a priori* concept of a conflict that will
remain limited to Europe, no matter what, not only will degrade the risk
variable in the calculations of a Soviet planner—and thus heighten the
likelihood of conflict—but it will also promote the notion among
Europeans that they have been left in the lurch by their transatlantic
partner. There is no more potent explosive potential in the Atlantic
Alliance than such a loss of confidence.

It also follows from the above that the territory of the USSR cannot be
allowed, in theory or in practice, to become a sanctuary in the nuclear
phase of a conflict in Europe. The Soviet Union cannot be invited to
contemplate a war limited exclusively to Western Europe, or even to
German territory. Moscow must at all times be forced to reckon with the
full ladder of escalation. The prevention of conflict in Europe can be
assured in the final analysis only through the palpability of this risk.

There is thus no question that without the threatened, and if necessary
implemented, use of tactical nuclear weapons, neither can Western
Europe be defended against a large-scale Soviet aggression nor can
deterrence—as the outgrowth of a realistic defense concept—take its
effective toll. To be sure, tactical nuclear weapons cannot replace
conventional capabilities, but they necessarily augment those capabilities.

From this relationship between conventional and nuclear weapons
emerge the imperatives for tactical nuclear capabilities—imperatives
that represent at the same time cogent replies to the arguments of those
who have urged reductions in, or total withdrawal of, tactical nuclear
weapons in Europe. TNW must be deployed optimally in such a way
that their use is rendered both practicable and credible. If the enemy can
assume confidently that a weapons system is not likely to be invoked in a
rational response to a battlefield requirement because it cannot be

invoked, then the threat steeped in the given system is not apt to frighten anyone—anyone, that is, beyond the population which it is designed to protect. In light of what is known about the existing TNW stockpile in Europe,[5] it is clear that it is in urgent need of modernization. To be sure, the large-caliber and stationary weapons should not disappear entirely from the inventory; nevertheless, the proportion of smaller and more mobile systems needs to be increased. Moreover, a task for the medium-term future is to replace the manned delivery systems—especially those assigned to nuclear interdiction and strike missions—with unmanned vehicles like cruise missiles. Finally, technology must be exploited to produce the kinds of weapons that can minimize unintended casualities and damage to civilian populations and the civilian economy: enhanced radiation weapons, or so-called neutron bombs, clearly fall into this category.

The effectiveness of the TNW stockpile, however, is a function not only of quality, but also of quantity—a requirement that tends to be disregarded in sweeping proposals for numerical reductions in the current inventory of some 7,000 weapons. If NATO wants to retain the capability of appropriate responses to a wide variety of possible tactical situations, then every NATO unit must have recourse to a commensurately broad spectrum of tactical nuclear weapons. Reductions on the order of 5,000, as proposed by Jeffrey Record;[6] of 6,000, called for by Alain Enthoven,[7] or even more than 6,000, as suggested in the 1974 testimony of Paul Warnke,[8] who has since become chief U.S. arms control negotiator, simply cannot be justified on military grounds.

Nor can tactical nuclear deployments be determined within a strictly military framework: some salient political and psychological considerations are at stake. For example, it has been suggested that the missions of current land-based tactical nuclear systems in Europe could well be assumed by more remote and less vulnerable sea-based systems in European waters or even by the flexible and selective targeting of long-range U.S. strategic weapons. Even if there were military merit to these notions—and effective substitutability is highly debatable—such a displacement of TNW from the Central Region would seriously weaken their credibility value. For one thing, a Soviet planner must in all prudence assign a higher probability of potential use to weapons systems emplaced in the path of an invasion than to platforms remote from the battlefield. To that extent, it could be argued that the very vulnerability of land-based systems enhances the credibility of their use and thus their deterrent value.

Perhaps even more important, aside from the American forces encamped in Europe, tactical nuclear weapons on European soil represent the most tangible tokens of the security linkage between the two sides of the Atlantic. Formal security guarantees are one thing; visible presence is quite another.

Soviet First-Use of Tactical Nuclear Weapons

Warsaw Pact maneuvers in the last ten years, as well as changes in the structure and weapons of Pact forces have traced a relatively clear-cut Soviet concept of the offensive land battle in Europe.

In September 1967, the Soviet Union conducted in southwest Russia a large-scale exercise under the code-name *Dnieper*, which has since established its significance as a model for Soviet conceptions of the strategic offensive in Europe. Operation *Dnieper* featured one of the most massive exercises of armor, artillery, and air in the repulsion of a "Western" attack reaching eastward as far as the Dnieper. In the exercise, the Soviets followed up this successful defense by an armored breakthrough and deep penetration into "Western" territory.

The Soviet strategic concept for the land battle thus anticipates the overwhelming of enemy forces and their destruction through the sudden deployment, striking power, and speedy advance of substantially superior and tightly coordinated forces—and the overwhelming of the enemy before he can mount an orderly defense. If possible, the enemy lines should be overrun. If large-scale resistance should nevertheless be encountered, the offensive must be sustained through the sheer weight and momentum of superior force, even at the cost of substantial casualties to the attacking divisions. Depending on the severity of battle, the Soviets prescribe a daily rate of advance of between forty and eighty kilometers.

It is a moot question whether the Soviets would fire nuclear weapons in support of such an offensive. The current Soviet military doctrine is not unequivocal in that respect, notwithstanding the fact that traditionally Soviet strategists have not been enticed by the notion of a "firebreak" between conventional and nuclear conflict—a concept that has preoccupied Western planners and analysts. The trend of improvements in Warsaw Pact conventional capabilities along with occasional statements by Soviet military analysts could be interpreted to mean that a higher probability is being attached to a conventional conflict without escalation. Nevertheless, the equipment and training of Warsaw Pact forces, as well as prevailing Soviet military doctrine, continue to emphasize the concept of a fully integrated conventional and nuclear offensive.[9]

In light of this fact, the answer to the question whether tactical nuclear weapons are needed in Western Europe becomes all the clearer. A nuclear-armed opponent cannot be countervailed with purely conventional capabilities—not militarily or politically or psychologically. To that extent Alain Enthoven is correct at least in the latter part of the following statement: "While two-sided tactical nuclear war makes no sense at all, one-sided nuclear war is even worse for the side that doesn't have nuclear weapons."[10]

Defense or Self-Destruction?

There is still one other question to be answered with respect to tactical nuclear weapons and their escalatory effect, and this has to do with allegations about their futility—with the notion that their use will mean the destruction of everything that they are supposed to defend. Many European analysts tend to side-step this question by blinking their eyes and contending that tactical nuclear weapons are useful only for deterrence but not for the potential battlefield. This notion is not only inadequate but self-contradicting. Anyone who weighs the deterrent effect of tactical nuclear weapons in Europe cannot do so in isolation of a realistic—if not thoroughly defined—doctrine regarding their actual use in a conflict. There is no question that this imperative is a painful one; nevertheless, it must be faced.

Deterrence in Europe is inescapably tied to the willingness of the NATO nations to suffer significant human and material losses in the event of a conflict. This willingness relates not only to the decision whether to use tactical nuclear weapons, but to the prior decision of whether to defend at all. The nations of Western Europe have determined—and are determined—to defend their territorial integrity and political values with all available means, including military ones. Anyone who believes that effective deterrence is predicated on a realistic concept of conventional defense, as well as the credible threat of escalation, must face up to the use of both conventional and nuclear weapons. No one in Western Europe—least of all in the Federal Republic—looks forward to a conflict, conventional and/or nuclear. The goal of NATO endeavors continues to be the prevention of war through deterrence. Yet the essence of deterrence is that he who wants to deter a conflict must be prepared to wage it.

Notes

1. See R. H. Sinnriech, "NATO's Doctrinal Dilemma," *ORBIS*, Summer 1975, p. 461 ff.

2. See H. Afheldt, C. Ptoyka, U. P. Reich, P. Sonntag, C. F. von Weizsacker, *Durch Kriegsverhütung zum Krieg?*, Munich: 1972, p. 10.

3. See E. Spannocchi, G. Brossollet, *Verteidigung ohne Schlacht*, Munich:

1976; H. Afheldt, *Verteidigung und Frieden*, Munich: 1976; C. F. von Weizsacker, *Wege in die Gefahr*, Munich: 1976.

4. Colin S. Gray, "Theater Nuclear Weapons, Doctrines and Postures," *World Politics*, January 1976, p. 302.

5. Jeffrey Record, *U.S. Nuclear Weapons in Europe: Issues and Alternatives*, Washington, D.C.: The Brookings Institution, 1974.

6. Ibid., p. 69.

7. Statement of A. C. Enthoven to the Subcommittee on U.S. Security Agreements and Commitments Abroad and the Subcommittee on Arms Control, International Law and Organization of the Committee on Foreign Relations, U.S. Senate, 93rd Congress, 2nd Session, on U.S. Nuclear Weapons in Europe and U.S.-USSR Strategic Doctrines and Policies, March 7, 14, and April 4, 1974, p. 74.

8. Statement of Paul C. Warnke in ibid., p. 57.

9. James R. Schlesinger, "The Theater Nuclear Force Posture in Europe," A Report to the United States Congress in compliance with Public Law 93-365, p. 9; S. T. Cohen and William R. Van Cleave, "Tactical Nuclear Weapons: Doctrine, Capabilities and Strategy," in *Toward a New Defense for NATO, The Case for Tactical Nuclear Weapons*, New York: Crane, Russak & Co., 1976; Leon Gouré, Foy D. Kohler, Mose L. Harvey, *The Role of Nuclear Forces in Current Soviet Strategy*, Coral Gables, Florida: Center for Advanced International Studies, University of Miami, 1974.

10. Enthoven, op. cit., p. 73.

15

Negotiations on Force Reductions in Central Europe

Lothar Ruehl

We now stand on the threshold of the fourth year of the Vienna Conference on mutual force reductions between countries of the Warsaw Pact and NATO[1] in Central Europe, and we find that the proposals made by the two sides are unbalanced. On 16 December 1975, NATO introduced an offer aimed at getting the negotiations moving again after they had bogged down because of the diametrically opposed positions of the two sides.[2] The Warsaw Pact's reaction to this new proposal was basically negative, although the Eastern negotiators did not reject it out of hand but tried to exploit it as a point of departure for discussion. In the discussion about individual aspects of this offer they seem to be looking for an opening which would enable them to place their own objectives into the center of the negotiations with greater prospects of success.

The course of the Conference since 30 October 1973 has been determined by the tactics of both sides, which have negotiated only on the basis of their own proposals while refusing to accept the other side's proposals as a basis for discussion.

Until last June the Warsaw Pact countries did not make available any numerical data on the strength of their forces but limited themselves to rejecting NATO's figures as being wrong—without supplying any evidence for this contention. For this reason, the Warsaw Pact's proposals—as far as their reduction element is concerned—could, up to now, be calculated and assessed only on the basis of agreed NATO figures.

The figures for the Warsaw Pact which the Soviet delegation provided last June—for the first time since the beginning of the negotiations in October 1973—do not, in principle, alter this state of affairs in any way, because these figures are too general and too incomplete to allow any valid conclusions.

They are more than 100,000 men below the NATO figure for the

Reprinted by permission from *NATO Review*, No. 5, October 1976.

strength of the Warsaw Pact's ground forces in Central Europe. Since 1973, there has been no change in the NATO assessment that the Warsaw Pact maintains 925,000 ground force personnel in Poland, Czechoslovakia, and the GDR compared with 777,000 men in NATO's ground forces in the Federal Republic, the Netherlands, Belgium, and Luxembourg. This has led to the conclusion that the East has a numerical superiority of about 150,000 men.

Nevertheless, these first Eastern figures provide a point of departure for a discussion on both force levels and on bases for calculations. After two and a half years of negotiations, the possibility is now emerging that the Conference will be able to compare figures and to arrive at agreed data and a common yardstick for force reductions.

The Problems of Mutual Force Reductions

The position of the two alliances facing each other in Europe is characterized by a fundamental geostrategic and structural asymmetry which manifests and perpetuates itself in numerous disparities. The military force relationship between NATO and the Warsaw Pact forms part of this asymmetry, and any changes in this relationship can only reduce or increase the asymmetry but cannot eliminate it. The regional situation in Central Europe and the force relationship existing there cannot be separated from the overall strategic power relationship in Europe and be determined in isolation. To include neither Hungary nor parts of the Soviet Union in the reductions area is questionable from a military and geographical point of view, but it may be politically necessary if agreement is to be achieved with the Soviet Union.

NATO's negotiating position and the course of the negotiations up to now have clearly outlined these discrepancies between the geostrategic/military unity of the entire area and the political need to define the reductions area within narrower limits. Whatever the result of the Vienna Conference may be, it can only marginally change the strategic situation on the Continent; it cannot solve the fundamental problem of security in Europe, because this problem is the imbalance between the Soviet Union and the rest of Europe.

The Soviet Union is the only European power which has the means to wage a war of aggression on the Continent and to win it—under favorable circumstances—against any possible coalition of other European countries. The Soviet Union would still exercise military control over her zone of influence in Central Europe even if she withdrew some of her forces from that region. Even if she evacuated all her forces to garrisons within her own frontiers, this would not diminish—let alone eliminate—the military imbalance in Europe and the military superiority of the Soviet Union. What would be changed would merely be the point of departure for a military conflict. While this would represent a considerable security gain for Western Europe, it would not be a decisive change, especially in view of the offensive IRBM/MRBM capabilities of the Soviet Union in Europe.

As far as the negotiations on mutual force reductions in Central Europe are concerned, this goestrategic asymmetry has been narrowed down by the NATO countries to two aspects:

1. the distance between the Soviet Union and the demarcation line in Central Europe compared with the distance of the United States from this line: 650 kms as opposed to 6,000 kms;
2. the frontier situation of the Soviet Union vis-à-vis two of the three Eastern countries in the reductions area (Poland and Czechoslovakia), which gives Soviet forces direct access to this area.

Three further aspects should be added: Hungary—where four Soviet category-one divisions are stationed with about 1,100 tanks and 55,000 to 60,000 men—borders on this Central European reductions area in the south. Geographically, Hungary forms just as much a part of Central Europe as does Poland. The Soviet Union borders on Hungary in the east and can exert a military infuence on Central Europe via Hungary. Moreover, Hungary can serve as a pivotal point for military operations directed against the west, south, and north, as was the case during the invasion of Czechoslovakia in 1968 in which Hungarian forces took part. In 1973, Hungarian airfields and depots served as a staging area for the support of Egypt and Syria in their war against Israel. Hungary herself has about 105,000 men in her forces, of whom 90,000 are Army personnel in six divisions with about 1,500 tanks.

Secondly, the geographical proximity of the Soviet Union to Central Europe means: a) that she can effect the rapid return via ground and air of any units and weapon systems withdrawn; b) that she can rapidly reinforce all Warsaw Pact forces across her western frontiers by means of units garrisoned in the three western military districts of the Soviet Union. Their number is estimated by NATO at about 30 divisions of the first and second categories. Some of them took part in the major build-up of the Warsaw Pact in the GDR in 1961 during the summer maneuvers preceding the Berlin crisis, as well as in the occupation of Czechoslovakia in August 1968.

Moreover, another 32 divisions—most of them of category two—are stationed in the other western military districts of Kiev, Leningrad, Moscow, and Odessa. In 1973, 7 airborne divisions were concentrated in the Kiev and Odessa districts with a total of 50,000 men for operations in the Middle East—an indication of the possible forward deployment of Soviet forces in times of crisis.

Thirdly, the Soviet Union maintains a uniform military organization in north and central Europe within which the redeployment of forces, especially by air, and of tactical air forces from north to west is easily possible at great speed.

Within this overall geostrategic asymmetry there are other disparities in the political structure and military organization of the two alliances which have an influence on mutual force reductions in Central Europe. They concern, particularly, the stationing of American forces on the European continent. This stationing is based on the concept of bringing in additional American forces in case of need. Four and one-third US Army divisions and further support units are permanently stationed on German territory. Two additional brigades are in the process of being redeployed there. This will leave a total of almost three US Army divisions in the United States for NATO use in Central Europe. Heavy equipment for these units when redeployed is stored in the Federal Republic. Regular air lifts with subsequent Reforger exercises are designed to maintain cohesion and to ensure a smooth redeployment. This NATO arrangement raises the question of whether an agreement with the Warsaw Pact on mutual force reductions in Central Europe will permit, restrict, or forbid the temporary return of the units of this American dual-based contingent to Germany. If the agreement should extend to air forces as well, the same question would apply regarding their dual-based components in the reductions area. Quite apart from the issue of the return of the nine brigades and their support units kept in readiness in the United States for this purpose, the question must be asked whether the heavy equipment for over two divisions stored in the Federal Republic will be allowed to remain there under such an agreement.

For the defense of the central sector in the NORTHAG region in northwest Germany there are, in addition to a German and a British Army Corps, a Belgian and a Dutch Army Corps—the bulk of which are stationed on their national territories. In case of war, they would have to be moved across the German frontier in order to occupy the defensive sectors allocated to them. The same would apply in the case of maneuvers, with these border crossings taking place inside the Western reductions area. Since the Belgian and the Netherlands units would be stationed in the treaty area even while on their national territories, their transfer across national frontiers within this area should remain permissible. Moreover, these national contingents would have to retain their full freedom of movement within the Federal Republic of Germany even after a force reduction agreement. They should not be regarded as foreign forces "stationed" on the territory of the Federal Republic of Germany.

As far as ground forces are concerned, the military disparity in the Central Region mainly consists of the Warsaw Pact's numerical superiority of approximately 150,000 men—based on the NATO figures of 925,000 versus 777,000 men—and of the much higher number of Warsaw Pact main battle tanks. According to NATO figures, the Warsaw Pact has at least 8,000 more tanks in the reductions area than NATO and, according to the German Defence White Paper for 1975/76, as many as 13,000 more. (The total figure given by the White paper was 19,000 Warsaw Pact tanks, of which 11,000 are deployed with Soviet units.) However this difference may be explained and assessed, there can be no doubt that the tank ratio between East and West in Central Europe, without including Hungary, amounts to between 2.5 to 1 and 3 to 1. As the NATO spokesman at the Vienna Conference pointed out once again on 21 July 1976, it is in this tank ratio that NATO sees the main element of the Warsaw Pact's offensive structure in this area.

Of course, this mere numerical relationship between a calculated figure of 15,500 tanks on the Eastern side and 6,000 on the Western side with a numerical superiority of, at first, 9,500 in 1973 and then of 13,000 in 1976 is, as such, insufficient to explain the real military power relationship. Apart from the fact that an offensive posture and an aggressive capability against an organized defense depend on a certain quantitative superiority, one should also introduce into the calculation the relationship between tanks and anti-tank weapons, i.e., the number and effectiveness of anti-tank weapons. The Warsaw Pact's quantitative superiority in tanks and armoured infantry fighting vehicles will be counterbalanced at least to some extent by NATO's strong anti-tank defense, which is being further improved, and the lethal effect of the modern anti-tank precision weapons with target-seeking projectiles, some of which have been introduced and some of which are being tested or developed and will become available in the next few years. In addition, other weapon systems such as close-support aircraft with armor-piercing air-to-ground weapons of great precision, as well as tactical nuclear weapons, should be included in the mathematical equations on operational capabilities on the battlefield.

In order to avoid the need to enter into a complex negotiation regarding all equipment and the organization of forces, NATO has emphasized only the manpower levels and the number of tanks as subjects for the negotiations. It remains an open question whether the Vienna negotiations can in fact be limited to these two sets of figures. If the negotiations were expanded, the air force systems would be bound to become a subject of negotiation sooner or later, and with them the nuclear weapons. The Warsaw Pact countries demanded this from the very beginning and have unremittingly sought to find an opening to extend the negotiations to cover the whole field of armaments including air forces.

A disparity between the political structures in East and West reveals itself in the differing effects which a reduction agreement would have on the two sides if it imposed national armaments limitations and international controls on national territories within a reductions area. While the socialist countries of Eastern Europe are not working towards a political union to which some of their national sovereignty would be transferred, the countries of Western Europe are planning to create a confederation of states or even a federal state. In order to be able to do so, they must retain their territorial sovereignty as well as the unrestricted freedom to arrange their forces and armaments as they see fit. They cannot allow any international control zone to exist on the future territory of their political union, causing differences in the international status of its members. This would restrict their freedom of action in the field of common defense in favor of the rights of outside countries.

Proposals of the Two Sides in Vienna

Warsaw Pact Draft Agreement, 1973

After a negotiating program had been agreed between the participants of both alliances during the exploratory talks in Vienna, which underlined "undiminished security" but did not mention the word "balanced," the Warsaw Pact countries opened the negotiations on substantive points on 8 November 1973 by introducing a draft agreement of ten articles. It aimed at reductions in equal proportions, i.e., the maintenance of the existing relationship of forces, and the inclusion of nuclear weapons and air forces in addition to ground forces.

They suggested a three-stage plan which was to begin in 1975 with a first reduction of 20,000 men on each side. Later, it was said that this figure could be broken down into 10,000 Russians, 5,000 East Germans, and 5,000 other Eastern Europeans, i.e., Poles and/or Czechoslovaks, on the Eastern side; and 10,000 Americans, 5,000 West Germans, and 5,000 other Western Europeans on the Western side. The remaining personnel strengths were to be reduced by a further 5 percent in 1976 and another 10 percent in 1977.

Altogether this proposal, which the East is, in principle, maintaining, would entail a reduction of about 15.5 percent of the total personnel strengths of both ground and air forces of the two alliances in the reductions area. The equality of these reductions is to be ensured by the "approximate similarity in weapons and types of units." A supplementary protocol in the form of an integral part of the agreement would list the units to be reduced along with their equipment. The reductions would be put into effect by the withdrawal of whole units which would have to take all their equipment with them. The draft refers to "foreign" and "national" forces. The reduction units of the former would have to be withdrawn to their countries of origin, while those of the latter would have to be disbanded, their personnel demobilized and their equipment decommissioned. They could not be replaced by other units. On this basis, the size, structure, armament, and equipment of all remaining national and foreign forces in the reductions area would be exactly defined and listed in the supplementary protocol. Within this framework, exchanges of personnel and equipment would remain free. National and foreign forces would be covered at the same time.

Assessment

According to NATO figures, this plan would reduce NATO ground forces by about 133,000 to approximately 644,000 men and those of the Warsaw Pact by about 155,000 to 775,000 men. The difference between the force strengths of the two sides in terms of ground force figures would only be reduced by approximately 22,000. On the other hand, about 78,000 Soviet soldiers would leave the reductions area compared with only about 33,000 American soldiers.

After this mutual reduction, the forces of both sides would be frozen at the new level by an international agreement. The calculation is imprecise because the Warsaw Pact countries did not communicate any strength figures with their plan and because their proposal extends to ground and air forces while NATO's proposal only covers ground forces. NATO assumes that the manpower levels of the air forces in the reductions area amount to 200,000 men on each side so that they could be eliminated on both sides of the equation. The percentage reductions would vary, of course, depending on the absolute figures. Including air forces, a reduction of 15.5 percent would lead to a withdrawal of about 174,000 to 175,000 men for the Warsaw Pact and 149,000 men for NATO, i.e., a difference of between 25,000 and 26,000 men.

These reductions would not bring the two alliances essentially closer to the originally declared objective of the Reykjavik signal of 1968, i.e., to reduce the military confrontation of somewhat more than two million men on both sides.

Although it does not provide for any great reduction in force strengths, the Eastern plan foresees far-reaching armaments limitations which would freeze the military and military-political status quo in

Central Europe and would, according to the NATO calculation, also lay down a numerical superiority for the Warsaw Pact forces over those of NATO as a characteristic of common security and as a yardstick for the contractually agreed balance of power between the two alliance systems. It is true that the countries of the Warsaw Pact have never claimed or admitted that their forces are stronger in Central Europe than those of NATO. However, they assert that the maintenance—at a lower level—of the existing balance of power—which, by their interpretation, has "grown historically"—must be the object of the negotiations and the condition for "undiminished security."

The Eastern plan, if accepted by NATO, would have the following consequences:

1. a unilateral partial disarmament of the European countries concerned, since they would have to submit to national ceilings for their forces and armaments;
2. the countries which station forces in the reductions area would be banned from providing equipment, in excess of that remaining after the withdrawal of the reduction units, in order to provide for these forces should they return to the area;
3. as a result of the mutual reductions the alliances could no longer change—except downward—their national ceilings once they have been reached in the reductions area;
4. the air forces would be included, although they are not suitable for reductions in such a narrowly limited area in view of their mobility; furthermore, effective controls could only be carried out through on-site inspection, i.e., on airfields or by aerial observation;
5. nuclear armaments would be reduced in the same percentages as the reduction units, although the draft does not specify which standards would be adopted.

While this draft goes into many details to be covered by an agreement, it has many gaps and interesting discrepancies. This applies especially to the freezing of national force ceilings and equipment compared with the practical possibilities of verifying such commitments through international channels. As a matter of principle, verification controls within the reductions area should be of equal effect. Detailed controls in the West, in order to be acceptable, should be accompanied by equivalent controls in the East.

It is obvious that the objective of this plan cannot be a major reduction of the American forces in Central Europe, because it would have, rather, a stabilizing effect. At any rate, it is not designed to roll back the American military presence and differs considerably from the program contained in the Bucharest Declaration of July 1966. Nevertheless, its acceptance would hamper any attempt to organize the defense of Western Europe. It would not allow an American force reduction to be counterbalanced by increases in European troops. The redeployment of European nuclear weapons into the reductions area would be ruled out. It is not clear whether the reductions within the alliances would be carried out on a percentage basis between the various national contingents, but the draft permits the conclusion that this is what the East has in mind. The arguments used by the East since 1973 also point in this direction. The main aim appears to be a reduction in the strength and armaments of the Bundeswehr, which is being presented as the main element facing the Soviet forces. In its logical conclusion, this argument means that the reduction of German forces would have to correspond approximately to that of the Soviet forces in the reductions area. However, there is an important difference: while the Soviet units would only have to be withdrawn, those of the Bundeswehr would have to be disbanded. In 1976, the Soviet Union made it clear that the foreign stationed forces which are to be withdrawn should also be disbanded, although their personnel could be used for other units outside the reductions area, so that the Soviet forces in the Soviet Union would not suffer any reduction.

Western Proposals of 1973 and 1974

The Western proposal of 22 November 1973 provides for an asymmetrical reduction of ground forces in two phases to a common ceiling of 700,000 men on either side. Only American and Soviet forces would be withdrawn in the first phase. The withdrawal of 29,000 Americans is offered in exchange for the withdrawal of 68,000 Russians, and the Western proposal also specifies that the Soviet reduction is to comprise a tank army with all its equipment. The number of Soviet main battle tanks to be withdrawn has now been stated by NATO as amounting to 1,700.

In the second phase, non-US and non-Soviet forces would be reduced. The aim of the second phase would be to reach a common ceiling of 700,000 men on either side without any national ceilings and armaments limitations. The reduction would not extend to nuclear weapons.

Assessment

Compared with the NATO offers of Reykjavik (1968) and Rome (1970), which did not specify which type of forces were to be reduced, this plan only covers ground forces, only extends to personnel strengths and the number of main battle tanks, and does not affect nuclear weapons. Its breakdown into two different phases which are to succeed each other is also a new element compared with the Reykjavik and Rome proposals. In addition to this two-phase approach, the concept of the common collective ceiling (no national sub-ceilings) is essential. Before non-US and non-Soviet forces are reduced within the reductions area, those of the two major powers are to be reduced. A concrete arrangement on the reduction of non-US and non-Soviet forces is to be made after the American-Soviet reduction.

Under the additional Western proposal of 12 December 1974, the overall level of active-duty military personnel of both sides in the reductions area would not be increased between the two phases and this would include the air force personnel within the treaty area. (Naval and amphibious forces are not covered by the negotiations.) This constitutes a conditional and partial expansion of the Western offer in order to meet the Eastern concern that the NATO countries would reserve the possibility of increasing their non-US forces between phases in order to compensate for the reduction of American forces.

Western Offer of 1975

The special Western offer of 16 December 1975 introduced a version of the so-called "Option III" under which nuclear weapons would be brought into the negotiations, an offer which had been held back since 1973. In the form in which it has now been presented it offers a one-time special withdrawal of 1,000 American nuclear warheads with their related means of delivery, especially 54 nuclear-capable F-4 combat aircraft and 36 Pershing weapon systems.

This offer is conditional and limited. It is based on three prerequisites:

1. that the Warsaw Pact countries accept asymmetrical reductions to a common collective ceiling of 700,000 ground force personnel on each side within the treaty area;
2. that the Warsaw Pact countries agree to the two-phase concept;
3. that the Soviet Union withdraw a complete Soviet tank army with all its equipment, especially 1,700 main battle tanks, in exchange for the withdrawal of 29,000 US Army soldiers.

The offer is also linked to another proviso, i.e., that a 900,000-man combined common collective ceiling be accepted for all ground and air force personnel, which would include the 700,000-man ceiling for ground force personnel on each side. This means that both sides would be free to increase their air force personnel in the treaty area, but only at the expense of a reduction in their ground force personnel to less than 700,000 men.

Assessment

This conditional one-time offer is designed to make it easier for the Soviet Union to accept the NATO plan. It represents a broadening in the negotiating position which the NATO countries have maintained since 1973, because it includes US air force elements as well as nuclear weapon systems in the reduction but rules out any negotiation about their selection or on the air forces and nuclear forces in the reductions area in general. Non-US air force units and nuclear weapons are not offered for reduction.

A time limit for the acceptance of the offer was not given. It involves the risk of an expansion of the negotiations, but this danger is to be met by the conditions and limitations which the proposal contains. However, this possibility may still be seized upon by the Warsaw Pact. Although there is no formal and direct link with a review of the nuclear weapons available to the NATO forces and the types and numbers of the American nuclear weapons in Europe, an indirect, substantive context cannot be denied.

Eastern Supplementary Proposal 1976

On 19 February 1976, the Soviet delegation in Vienna, acting on behalf of all the Warsaw Pact delegations, made a supplementary proposal to its draft agreement of 8 November 1973. It provides that between 2 and 3 percent of the overall personnel strengths of both alliances in the reductions area should be withdrawn in 1976 in the form of American and Soviet reductions. Both reductions are also to comprise 300 tanks, one Army Corps headquarters, 54 nuclear-capable F-4 combat aircraft or SU 17/20 A and C, 36 Pershing and Scud-B missile systems, as well as the customary conventional and nuclear armament including ground-to-air defense systems, in particular an unspecified number of Nike-Hercules and SAM-2 air defense systems on either side. In 1977, the alliance forces on both sides would not be increased, while in 1978 the European forces would also be reduced by 2 or 3 percent. The reduction would be carried out according to the rules of the 1973 draft treaty, i.e., by complete units including their entire equipment.

Assessment

This proposal contains the basic elements of the old Soviet concept of 1973, i.e.:

- reductions in equal percentages,
- inclusion of air forces,
- inclusion of nuclear weapons,

- reductions by units with all weapons and equipment,
- introduction of national ceilings for all countries in the reductions area,
- commitments by all countries from the beginning.

The new elements are:

- implementation in two reduction stages, beginning with an exclusively Soviet-American reduction,
- the units withdrawn from the forces of the two major powers are also to be disbanded outside the reductions area, although their personnel can be added to existing units there,
- withdrawal of one Army Corps headquarters on each side,
- inclusion of ground-to-air systems.

This form of reduction would more profoundly affect the nuclear potential and the tank forces of NATO than those of the Warsaw Pact. On a comparative basis of 15,500 Warsaw Pact tanks to 6,000 NATO tanks, the withdrawal of 300 tanks each would reduce the already much lower NATO tank figure by a percentage more than double that for the Warsaw Pact: 5 percent as opposed to a little more than 2 percent.

According to official Western estimates, the Soviet air forces possess between 270 and 280 combat aircraft of the SU 17/20 Fitter type. Of these, about 90 are of the latest "C" version. In addition, there are about 320 Soviet nuclear-capable tactical aircraft in the reductions area. If 54 of them were to be reduced, this would amount to only 17 percent of this figure. The US forces have 114 nuclear-capable F-4s in the reductions area. A reduction by 54 would correspond to 47 percent. In the case of missiles, the relative figures are less unbalanced because the American forces have 108 Pershing systems in the reductions area and the Soviet forces 120 Scud launchers. However, the reduction proposed would still be qualitatively unequal in view of the great difference in the ranges of these weapon systems, which are not comparable, since the F-4 has a much longer range and more than double the combat weight and thus about double the carrying capacity and throw-weight.

The Soviet proposal bears the signs of an ad hoc draft which reflects NATO's proposals of the December offer in order to extend even further what the East sees as an opening in the negotiations and achieve the Eastern negotiating aim of including air forces and nuclear weapons in the talks.

The proposal for a two-stage approach to reductions in the Eastern counter-proposal does not correspond to the Western concept and was thus described as inadequate by the spokesman of the NATO group in

Vienna on 21 July 1976. Nevertheless, it can be regarded as a step towards a possible compromise. Seen as a whole, the counter-proposal does not meet essential Western security interests. It merely seeks to expand the opening introduced into the NATO negotiating position in December 1975 in order to serve Eastern objectives and ensure the inclusion of the whole nuclear arsenal and air forces in the negotiations. It does not deal with the basic Western stipulation for asymmetrical reductions to an identical ceiling, i.e., the principle of balanced reductions to achieve parity, or with the need to reduce the numerical superiority in tanks on the Eastern side. Accordingly, the NATO spokesman said that the East had introduced "no change whatever in its basic reduction approach."

Two Aspects of Interest

In this context, two aspects are of interest:

1. NATO seeks approximate parity for the ground forces of both sides in the reductions area. On 10 June 1976, the Warsaw Pact provided data in Vienna on the strength of its ground forces in this area. The Eastern figures create the impression that a new argument is to be built up suggesting that "approximate parity" already exists in this area, so that asymmetrical reductions, as demanded by NATO, would be unnecessary. No figures for tanks were given.

2. By making its December proposal, NATO unilaterally offered to include nuclear weapon systems having a long range and a high yield, for which no adequate compensation can be found in the Soviet tactical nuclear weapon arsenal in Central Europe. The Soviet Union has taken up this offer and has tried to turn it to its own advantage. Under the NATO offer, the Soviet Union would not have to withdraw a single nuclear weapon system or aircraft in return for the 54 F-4s and the 36 Pershings but would simply have to agree to approximate parity for ground force personnel and to the withdrawal to the Soviet Union in the first phase of the First Guard Tank Army (the only Soviet tank army presently in the reductions area).

Both aspects point to the new situation which has arisen in the negotiations—although a possibility for agreement has not yet emerged. However one may judge that NATO offer and its timing or NATO's overall negotiating strategy, it must be said that a reduction of the Western nuclear warhead figure in exchange for a reduction in the number of Eastern tanks is by no means an unsuitable method of compensation. On the other hand, the existing asymmetries in armaments and deployment place narrow limits on any such barter deal. It is a different question whether, in view of the Eastern rejection of both numerical parity and the concept of limiting the reductions to ground forces, the attempt to sign a binding agreement should not be abandoned in favor of a voluntary mutual force reduction by reciprocal notification without specific figures, without controls, and without other restrictions.

Notes

1. The participants are: USSR, Poland, Czechoslovakia, and GDR; Belgium, FRG, Canada, Luxembourg, Netherlands, UK, and USA as direct participants which have either forces or territories in the reductions area, plus Romania, Bulgaria, and Hungary; Italy, Turkey, Greece, Denmark, and Norway as participants having a "special status," since they are not represented in the reductions area.

2. See *NATO Review* No. 3, 1976, p. 30.

16
Security and Arms Control:
A View from NATO

Wiegand Pabsch

Visitors and students of NATO often show surprise when they are told that NATO, an institution created mainly for the organization of an effective defense, takes an active interest in matters of disarmament and arms control. They are astonished to learn that the Allied negotiating position for the negotiations in Vienna on Mutual and Balanced Force Reductions (MBFR) is coordinated by the NATO Council; that the Political Committee at Senior Level regularly meets twice a week to assist the Council in this task; that the Political Committee, at its regular weekly meetings as well as semi-annually with disarmament experts from capitals, consults on disarmament matters; and that the International Secretariat of NATO has, in its Political Division, a Disarmament and Arms Control Section.

The reactions of visitors to these facts vary. To some, it is worrying that NATO devotes so much attention and effort to disarmament at a time when the Warsaw Pact is building up its military potential in almost every field. Others, particularly among the young, seem pleased; they consider the rising defense expenditure in most Allied countries a costly waste and often profess the view that, in this period of détente, all one really needs to do is seriously press for progress in disarmament in order actually to achieve it. To them, the spiraling cost of armaments in both East and West is a challenge to *pure* reason; but if they were ready to apply *practical* reason to the problem (to borrow a famous distinction from Kant), they would have to admit that things are not all that simple. External security, the fundamental condition for any society to exist and develop in accordance with its own basic political choices, is first and foremost the function of an adequate military capability to deter a potential aggressor and, if deterrence fails, to thwart attempts at aggression by an adequate military response. This point need not be stressed here; NATO's primary role, as everyone knows, is indeed to provide the military capability for effective deterrence and defense, a role

Reprinted by permission from *NATO Review*, No. 1, February 1976.

it has fulfilled successfully in the past and will doubtless continue to fulfill in the future.

Fundamental Assumptions

Nevertheless, the military planner will readily agree with the protagonist of realistic disarmament policies that the adequacy of the capability to deter and defend cannot be defined in absolute terms, but only as a function of the military capability of any potential aggressor. Ideally, therefore, once parity with the military forces of the other side in a potential military conflict was reached and stabilized, the defense effort could also be stabilized at that level. Similarly, a reduction in the military strength of a potential aggressor would allow for a commensurate reduction in defense effort, resulting in savings in defense expenditure. It is on this rationale that all disarmament and arms control endeavors are based and from which they derive their justification. If it were possible to limit and progressively reduce the threat represented by the military capabilities of the potential adversary, a limitation and even progressive reduction of the defense effort could reasonably be undertaken without unacceptable risks for security.

Moreover, a more sophisticated analysis would not overlook that the dimensions of security go beyond considerations of the relative military strength of the two sides in a conflict; psychological and political elements are also at play. Thus whether and to what extent a country's military posture is considered a security threat by its neighbors will depend to a great extent on such factors as the general political behavior of that country towards its neighbors. Progress in arms control could therefore reduce the feeling of threat, create confidence, and thereby enhance security in a real sense.

In fairness, one must admit that this, in principle, applies to both sides in the East/West contest; it would be too simplistic to dismiss the security needs so often invoked by the Soviet Union and her Allies as mere propaganda incantations. The subjective security concerns of the Soviet people must be taken as real; whether they are objectively justified, given the enormous military capabilities of the Soviet Union, is a different matter. It would, however, be beside the point here to judge the respective record of either side with regard to its behavior towards neighbors or the objective justification of its security concern and the ensuing military effort; any impartial observer, though, would not have difficulties in reaching a definite conclusion for himself. All that needs stressing here is that arms control touches on the most sensitive nerves of the collective consciousness of peoples in both East and West. It is obvious that meaningful arms control measures are therefore possible only if they take these concerns fully into account. But it is equally obvious that any progress achieved in this field would probably have even greater significance through its psychological impact than through the immediate changes in the military situation which would result from it. It is for these reasons that the Alliance has repeatedly stated that if political détente is to mean anything, it would have to be complemented by measures designed to reduce the military confrontation, and that most Allied countries have urged the East to enter into negotiations on MBFR and SALT.

Unilateral Disarmament

It follows from the above that any disarmament and arms control measure to be undertaken has to respond fully to the security needs of both sides. Not only must disarmament not diminish security in the objective sense; it should also increase security in its psychological ramifications. This excludes, for all practical purposes, unilateral disarmament steps since they would create, or accentuate, a military imbalance and consequently undermine the confidence of people in the adequacy and credibility of existing security arrangements. Only if corresponding steps were taken by the potential adversary, would security be unimpaired. However, such corresponding steps rarely or never occur spontaneously; they can only be achieved in a coordinated process on which both sides must have reached prior understanding through negotiations.

Some proponents of unilateral disarmament measures often assert that such measures taken by one side would not only allow, but almost compel, the other side to follow suit. To the realist, this would seem to be a rather dangerous proposition. Firstly, it is highly doubtful whether the Soviet Union—to be concrete for once—which in recent years has built up her forces everywhere without much correlation to the military strength of the West, would see any incentive in such a measure to forego this added chance to surpass the West in military strength. Secondly, such proposals overestimate the responsiveness of states to moral persuasion. Thirdly, if corresponding disarmament steps were not to follow, there would hardly be a political possibility of undoing the unilateral step later; this would almost certainly be interpreted by the other side as a hostile act, would create additional tensions, or even trigger further escalation in armaments by the other side.

Principle of Equality

It also follows from the above that meaningful arms control measures have to be firmly anchored on the principle of equality. The definition of such equality, however, is a very difficult thing, given the complexities of the military arsenals of both sides. In the abstract, it can be defined as equivalence in military power or, in a more restricted sense, as parity of the forces of both sides. Most of the disarmament negotiations between East and West center around this problem; SALT I and II and MBFR are cases in point.

Some protagonists of disarmament recommend total and comprehensive world-wide disarmament as the safest and surest way to the utopian world without arms. The Soviet Union continues to take this line; her long-standing proposal for a World Disarmament Conference may have attraction for the impatient or the thinker in absolutes. Again, the constructive realist in arms control would warn against such an all-out approach, not only because there is simply no short cut to total disarmament, but because it would soon be bogged down in a mess of complicated problems and thus lead to frustration and resignation or simply serve as an excuse to do nothing in the meantime until the glamorous goal is reached in one stroke. In the interest of concrete achievements, limited though they may be, the realist would prefer to approach the problem step-by-step, carefully analyzing the chances for meaningful arms control measures in the given strategic situation and in the various fields of armaments, and pressing for coordinated action wherever a chance arises. This may seem tedious and uninspiring, but it offers the only realistic chance for genuine progress in at least some fields.

If disarmament is to lead to enhanced security, there must be full confidence in the implementation of any agreed measure. Therefore, procedures have to be created to assure each side that agreed measures are faithfully executed. In the deadly consequential business of arms control, there can be no room for blind confidence in the good will of the other party in an agreement. Trust may be good, but controls are better. Without adequate verification, any arms control agreement could well turn out to be suicidal for a country which carries out its obligations faithfully but finds out later that the other party has cheated.

Important Developments

The requirements just outlined may seem to many as hampering rather than encouraging progress in arms control. But they have nevertheless allowed for some important developments in recent years[1] in which Allies have played their part. Of course, arms control measures are usually more easily agreed upon when they involve weapons which are not yet conceived or are even imaginary or which are not fully developed in all countries taking part in such a measure. This was demonstrated by the signing of a Convention on the Prohibition of the Development, Production and Stockpiling of Biological Weapons in 1972 and the draft proposal for a convention banning hostile uses of environmental modification techniques tabled jointly by the United States and the Soviet Union at the Conference of the Committee on Disarmament (CCD) and introduced at the present United Nations General Assembly. Similar efforts to reach agreement on a convention to prohibit the development, production and stockpiling of chemical weapons, however, have not led to similar success. Any such agreement would have to provide for efficient verification measures, which the Soviet Union is not prepared to accept. Discussions in the CCD in Geneva have for years wrestled with this problem, but a solution is not yet in sight.

A more important field is nuclear disarmament. Here, some achievements can be registered after the first US/Soviet interim agreement on "certain measures with respect to the limitation of strategic offensive arms" (SALT I) and the antiballistic missile (ABM) treaty, both of 1972. In the meeting between President Ford and General Secretary Brezhnev at Vladivostok on 24 November 1974, the Soviet and US governments agreed on the basic principles on which SALT negotiations should be pursued, setting a ceiling of 2,400 for strategic delivery vehicles of which 1,320 could be fitted with multiple independently targetable re-entry vehicles (MIRVs). Although no final SALT II agreement has yet been reached, the prospects still seem good; if concluded, such an agreement would provide the basis for further efforts in this field, leading perhaps to actual reductions of strategic nuclear arms. In any event, the agreement of Vladivostok will remain noteworthy since, for the first time, the Soviet Union accepted the principle of parity as the basis for an important arms control measure.

In the same context of nuclear arms control, two earlier Soviet/US agreements signed during President Nixon's visit to Moscow on 3 July 1974 have to be mentioned, one providing for the reduction of the ABM deployment areas permitted under the 1972 ABM Treaty from two to one, and the other imposing a threshold of 150 kilotons on underground military test explosions ("Threshold Test Ban Treaty"—TTBT). Since the latter treaty would allow the continuation of peaceful nuclear explosions regardless of yield, the entry into force of this treaty depends on agreement on verification measures which would enable both sides adequately to monitor whether a nuclear explosion alleged to be for peaceful applications is not misused to obtain new experience for the development of new nuclear weapons. It remains to be seen whether the Soviet Union is willing to accept additional verification measures for this purpose; if it does, this would encourage other efforts in arms control in areas where progress depends only on mutually acceptable verification procedures.

The Non-Proliferation Treaty (NPT) of 1968, which entered into force in 1970, is still the major international agreement to prevent the acquisition of nuclear arms by non-nuclear weapon states. The Review Conference held in May 1975 confirmed the treaty in this function and alerted the world community to the dangers of nuclear proliferation; on a number of points this Conference suggested measures to strengthen the non-proliferation regime. Its effectiveness, however, will greatly depend on the adoption of stricter safeguards and a coordinated export policy by the states supplying nuclear industrial technology and equipments to non-nuclear weapon states, whether parties to the NPT or not.[2]

The NPT Review Conference also highlighted the danger of vertical proliferation in nuclear weapon states. A number of participants deplored the lack of progress towards a reduction of nuclear weapons in the possession of nuclear weapon states and pressed for additional measures by these states to halt the nuclear arms race. A comprehensive test ban treaty would be a constructive step in this direction; but the project has not advanced in spite of the pressure applied by non-nuclear states in the United Nations and other fora, mainly because of the unresolved problem of peaceful nuclear explosions and the difficulty of agreeing on verification procedures to assure that such explosions are not used to develop further military nuclear capabilities. However, entry into force of the TTB of 1974 on 31 March 1976, as foreseen in the Treaty, could be the harbinger of progress in this field, since it would indicate at least some degree of Soviet willingness to accept verification by other than national means.

Nuclear Free Zones

Another important step reducing the dangers of nuclear proliferation could be the creation of nuclear weapon free zones (NWFZ) in certain regions of the world; many specific proposals were introduced in past UN General Assemblies, and some of them have been endorsed by UN resolutions. So far, only one such zone was created, in Latin America, by the Treaty of Tlatelolco of 1967. Even though most states support the idea of establishing such zones in principle, there are a number of important difficulties hindering an easy solution. Firstly, any such proposal would have to arise from a regional initiative and could not be imposed by an outside power or a UN majority. It is difficult to imagine that, with the heightened sensitivity against outside interference prevailing everywhere in the world, the states concerned would go along with an initiative coming from outside their region. Secondly, it would have to be accepted by all important states located in the area since the notion of a zone in which one or several important powers retained the option to hold or develop nuclear weapons would not be very reassuring to the other states in the area. Thirdly, the creation of the zone would have to safeguard the security interests and arrangements of *all* participants, granting equality of advantage and "misery" among them; a privileged status for one or several members of a zone would create instability rather than enhance the area. And lastly, any nuclear weapon free zone agreement would have to provide for adequate verification.

All these requirements can be derived from the general considerations set out earlier; in fact, all of the existing proposals with the single exception of the Latin American NWFZ were rejected by one or several states in the area concerned on account of one or other of these considerations. In the Northern Hemisphere, the issue is further complicated by the fact that most non-nuclear weapon states are linked by alliances with nuclear weapon states. These alliances are part of the overall strategic balance; in any case, the security of Western Europe vitally depends on the nuclear deterrence provided by the United States. It is impossible to envisage states located in Central Europe or in an adjacent region, be it Scandinavia, the Balkans, or the Mediterranean, being prepared to agree to a NWFZ proposal which would eliminate the very weapons on which their security depends.

Similar security apprehensions have to be voiced with regard to pressures by non-nuclear states interested in NWFZ to obtain security guarantees from the nuclear powers. Positive assurances to use nuclear weapons in case of an attack by one state in the region upon another, such as Pakistan would prefer to obtain from the nuclear powers as a condition for the establishment of a NWFZ in South Asia, would, if given, immediately involve the nuclear powers in any conflict arising in that strife-torn region; it is more than questionable whether this would really enhance security in South Asia, or not rather increase the risk of an escalation of any such conflict into a world conflagration.

Negative assurance by the nuclear powers *not* to use nuclear weapons against states in a NWFZ, for which Mexico and other Third World countries have constantly pleaded, face similar objections. They may be acceptable to the nuclear powers in the areas where their major interests do not directly clash, as in the case of Latin America or Africa. It is worth noting that, while the United States, the United Kingdom, France, and China signed the additional Protocol II of the Treaty of Tlatelolco which contains a non-use assurance clause, the Soviet Union has chosen not to do so. In areas closer to the interests of the nuclear powers, the same considerations apply to non-use assurances as to the establishment of NWFZs in general; it is clear that the effect of nuclear deterrence as the foundation of security would be greatly diminished by the elimination of a whole range of strategic options which a non-use commitment would entail.

MBFR

In the field of conventional armaments, the most important arms control effort concerns the negotiations in Vienna on Mutual and Balanced Force Reductions, which are a NATO initiative, proposed by Allies[3] for the first time in 1968. It took the Soviet Union and her Allies until 1973 to accept the proposal. The main objective of these negotiations is the achievement of undiminished security at a lower level of forces which, in the Western view, should be brought about by the reduction of ground forces of both sides to a level of approximately 700,000 men on each side in a area encompassing Poland, the GDR, and Czechoslovakia in the East, and the Federal Republic of Germany, Belgium, the Netherlands, and Luxembourg in the West. Up to now, these negotiations have not made any progress since the East constantly refuses to accept the basic Western demand of approximate parity of ground forces as a result of reductions.

This brings us back to the beginning of this reflection. If measures in arms control are not to affect detrimentally the security of the countries participating, parity of forces must be accepted as the key principle. It is an untenable proposition to expect that a party in an arms control negotiation would formally endorse an agreement that allows its potential adversary to retain greater military strength in the area in question. The Eastern superiority in ground forces of some 150,000 men and about 9,500 tanks is the main destabilizing factor in this area; if disarmament is to achieve undiminished security and lead to greater stability, it must take account of such striking disparities if it is not to constitute surrender in stages.

These negotiations, as well as the US/Soviet talks on Strategic Arms Limitations, are decisive for the future of arms control. They constitute limited, but so far the most meaningful, steps undertaken in a key area of the military confrontation. There is still hope that the patient and detailed discussions going on in an unpolemical way between East and West on these issues, drawing into their orbit the military establishments on both sides, will help the military planners in the East to redefine their security requirements in a more realistic, less inflated sense and thus eventually produce the flexibility required.

This should not be impossible at a time when the overall military strength of the Soviet Union and her Allies is about equal and in some areas has surpassed that of the NATO Allies. The percentage of GNP the Soviet Union devotes to her tremendous military build-up is estimated to be within a range of 10-15 percent whereas it is a meagre 4.5 percent or less in most Allied countries; this means that over 5-10 percent of her GNP is withheld from her people with no other justification than the big power aspirations of her leaders. If there is a moral case for disarmament as a precondition for more social progress, as many of its protagonists in the West assert, its claims would certainly weigh more heavily against the Soviet Union than against the West. But even if one sticks to common sense as a less presumptuous guide for political action, the Soviet Union would do well not to overlook that a breakdown of the present arms control negotiations would constitute a severe setback in détente from which she and her people have derived significant economic advantage.

Notes

1. This article restricts itself to reviewing developments since about 1972. Therefore earlier disarmament or arms control measures are not discussed.

2. See the Author's article "The NPT—Success or Failure?" on the NPT Review Conference in number 4, volume 23/1975 of *NATO Review*, pp.24-27.

3. France does not participate.

17
Nuclear Spread and World Order

Lincoln P. Bloomfield

Until a year or two ago we were entitled to believe that the Nuclear Nonproliferation Treaty (NPT) could successfully hold the line at five nuclear weapons powers, if only a few holdout countries would sign or ratify it. Two events have thrown into serious doubt the ability of present policies to stem the further proliferation of nuclear weapon capabilities among additional nations.

The first event was the Indian "peaceful" nuclear explosion in May 1974, which jumped the firebreak between the five permanent members of the U.N. Security Council—who are also the nuclear weapons powers—and all other nations. That barrier had held for ten years since the first Chinese detonation in 1964.

What seemed to undermine the earlier mild optimism that the NPT could do the job was not that "nuclear-weapons-capable" countries such as Sweden, Canada, Switzerland, Australia, Netherlands, Italy, Poland, Argentina, Brazil, Japan, and West Germany, or even nations in conflict like Pakistan, Taiwan, South Africa, South Korea, Israel, or Egypt were on the verge of exploding their own nuclear devices (though many think Israel is in fact the "seventh" nuclear weapons power). It was rather that the general climate of expectation about what was likely to take place had changed significantly. Many now believe that there *will* be nuclear weapons powers numbers seven, eight, nine, ad infinitum. Members of the international professional strategic community have already been discounting the future and shifting their planning to ways of living in a world of many nuclear weapons powers. The crucial new reality is thus not merely the existence of a sixth (or seventh) such power; it is above all the altered predictions that influential people around the world are making as a consequence.[1]

Having one more "nuclear-capable" power does not change the world. But what could change it would be a snowballing, fatalistic belief that becomes a self-fulfilling prophecy unless it is countered by a

Reprinted by permission of the author and *Foreign Affairs*, July 1975. Copyright 1975 by Council on Foreign Relations, Inc.

different belief that is equally potent.

The second event was the worldwide energy crisis. Predictions of numbers of future nuclear power plants now far exceed the figure planners had been using prior to the Arab oil embargo of 1973-74. The amount of plutonium to be produced over the next decade will be enough to put a major dent in the energy shortage—*and* to make thousands of atomic bombs.

These two portentous shifts in perception and planning came at a time when 55 of the 90 or so countries that have signed the 1970 Nuclear Nonproliferation Treaty were attending its May 1975 five-year Review Conference in Geneva. Just prior to the conference, and doubtless in anticipation of it, ratification had been completed by five West European states and South Korea.

The conference concentrated on tightening up technical controls and safeguards over the rapidly growing worldwide nuclear power-generating industry as well as the flow of nuclear fuels, uranium and plutonium, that go in and out of peaceful atomic reactors. The hair-raising specter of nuclear blackmail by hijacking and sabotage sharpened the delegates' concern for better means of guarding against capture of nuclear materials by terrorist groups.

The International Atomic Energy Agency (IAEA) is even now doing a competent, though limited, job of inspecting peaceful reactors to catch (or at least discourage) clandestine diversion of plutonium or enriched uranium. Most of the countries that are able to supply nuclear fuels and reactor technology, notably the United States and the Soviet Union, have agreed among themselves to export only to recipient countries that adopt IAEA safeguards (though last year's U.S. offer to Israel and Egypt showed Washington still unwilling to require inspection of older facilities as the price for new help).

All in all, many laudable efforts are going into strengthening the NPT "regime," which is clearly the best answer so far to limiting the further spread of nuclear weaponry. The great majority of nations, and certainly of human beings, clearly support its goal. A few people may remain comfortable with the scenario of dozens of countries, some at war with one another, newly enabled to destroy humankind by the millions, or even able to trigger the apocalypse of superpower strategic war. But overwhelmingly the rest of us cling to the conviction that, as someone put it, "when you have five, or even six, idiot children, it's time to practice birth control." Certainly no one can quarrel with this concentration on the contingent problem of clandestine nuclear activities, aimed at preventing cheating as well as making peaceful nuclear technology more readily available under safeguards.

But now that the Review Conference is out of the way, it is time to raise the sobering possibility that all this activity, while essential, will not be enough. For what has never been adequately dealt with, probably because it seemed politically insuperable, is the inherently discriminatory nature of the present system.

II

In our epoch, the evidence is everywhere of the dominant role of national status-seeking and the drive to "feel equal." An entire philosophy of resentful Third World economics bears the telltale name "dependency theory." Third World proposals for a "New Economic and Social Order" reflect a veritable obsession with eradicating the stigmata of inferiority. The walls of every international conference room, from OPEC to the U.N. General Assembly, resound with strident demands for equal status. At the symbolic level (which Harold Isaacs reminds us is anything but trivial[2]) there are few nations, however poor or tiny, that cannot boast of a flag airline, diplomatic limousines (usually longer than that of the U.S. Ambassador), international hotels, supersonic jets—and nuclear power reactors.

Even at the superpower level, no serious negotiation with the Soviets on strategic nuclear arms was possible until Moscow felt it had acquired "parity." And if final proof were needed, even those Indians most critical of their government for other deeds or misdeeds unanimously express pride over its achievement in exploding a "peaceful" nuclear device.

It is against this backdrop that the NPT regime has to be assessed. The cold fact is that, without exception, every single aspect of the nuclear nonproliferation system is discriminatory. Indeed, the more successful the NPT system, the more absolute the distinction between those who have nuclear weapons and those who do not.

The most obvious distinction is of course that between 5 (or 6) nations possessing the means of mass nuclear destruction and the remaining 140 or so which do not and, according to the proposed rules of the game, never will.

This distinction carries the further division between openness to verification by the Vienna agency's inspectors (for all nonweapons' countries) and secrecy for all the great powers' reactors, even their peaceful ones. The exception is the United States, which has offered to open its peaceful reactors, though of course not its military ones, to IAEA inspection. Conversations in Moscow in the spring of 1975 confirm the insistence of the other nuclear superpower on increased controls for everyone *but* the great powers.

Article VI of the Nonproliferation Treaty commits the superpowers to good-faith efforts toward nuclear disarmament, but few outside Moscow and Washington believe the process was seriously begun with the 2,400-launcher agreement of Vladivostok in 1974.

Brazil for one (and India before it) apparently believes that some of its economic development projects could benefit from peaceful nuclear explosions (PNEs). The United States now argues that peaceful nuclear explosions are bad for others since we don't find them cost-effective for us. If other countries still want PNEs they are free to come, hat in hand, to Washington, Moscow, London, Paris, or presumably Peking, as supplicants for Big Brother's technical fix.

Security guarantees were offered in 1968, but they are subject to the veto, and moreover it seems absurd to guarantee only against nuclear attack when countries can be devasted by nuclear powers using conventional weapons.

As for the spent fuel rods coming out of nuclear reactors and requiring reprocessing in expensive plants to recover the residual plutonium, the position Washington has taken is that we will do the reprocessing for our clients. But of course India, once deciding to acquire a nuclear explosion capability, built her own chemical separation plant and thus bypassed the controls the doner—Canada—had put on the power reactor that produced the used fuel rods.

In all of these ways the system provides that the "first-class" nuclear states not only have a monopoly on the weapons but also on the international decision-making about peaceful uses.

In the same vein, it is a fact that all current anti-proliferation policies, however worthy, are in the realm of denial. More than that, except for the inspection performed by IAEA inspectors, these policies are overwhelmingly on a nation-to-nation rather than a multilateral basis. Both of these features—denial and nation-based action—may actually reinforce the possible trend toward proliferation to the extent that the trend arises from a sense of inequality, resentment against what is perceived as discrimination, and a desire for equivalent rights and status.

The irony is that, while we live, *pace* Marx, in an age of international class struggle, the international "ruling class" of nuclear weapons states (led, *pace* Lenin, by the U.S.S.R.) demands its right to exclusive status unto perpetuity. In an era dominated by demands for identity, respect, equity, and participation, it seems reasonable to ask whether, with the best will in the world, the present NPT system of discrimination, denial, and second-class citizenship will in fact achieve its aim of preventing the further spread of nuclear weapons. For if my reasoning is correct, it is considerations of prestige and nondiscrimination that in an age of rampant nationalism stand as the chief obstacles to universal agreement on nonproliferation.

III

It follows that the chief danger in the years ahead is not that any given country will secretly cheat in its nuclear bookkeeping—which is what the present international system seeks to inhibit. It is that a country will *openly* decide to acquire a nuclear weapons capability, for reasons which since time immemorial, and today as never before, drive nations to seek prestige, influence, and above all equality.[3]

Of course, if all countries were to sign and ratify the Nonproliferation Treaty, and the Treaty regime were greatly strengthened, the problem would presumably be solved. But this is a tautology: in fact, a dozen key "threshold countries" have *not* fully joined, countries such as Brazil, Argentina, Israel, Japan, Pakistan, Egypt, Spain, and South Africa, whose importance to international peace and stability is obvious. India may not actually fabricate a bomb; but neither is she likely to take a "morning-after" pill that will return her to pre-1974 nuclear innocence. Each new nuclear weapons country tends to stay that way. Even the present safeguard procedures may become inadequate as new technical options, such as the breeder reactor and high-temperature gas reactor, call for much more intrusive inspection.

Yet if the conclusion is correct that the problem of proliferation is as much psychological as it is technical, political, or military, current incentives to take the pledge are insufficient. No matter what the rhetoric, a world in which five or six nations control the weapons technology is by definition discriminatory; a system which leaves all the decision-making in their hands is by definition paternalistic. Clearly there is an unfilled need for a more attractive option than either accepting the monopolistic position of the "nuclear OPEC" or going it alone.

It follows that to provide not just negative but also positive incentives to the principal holdouts, additional measures need to be developed that go beyond technical safeguards, important as these are. In the classic language of criminology, efforts at nonproliferation need to aim not only at means and opportunity—means which are universally increasing while opportunity for open violation of the spirit of the treaty remains unhindered—but also at the motives for going nuclear as a political act.

Such measures would have to confront directly the political and psychological foundations of the potential drive toward further nuclear spread. Perhaps no steps even in this direction would deflect leaders determined to acquire the weaponry they believe will give them an edge, even if strategic analysis proves them overwhelmingly wrong. But to the extent the drive is primarily motivated—as I believe it to be—by nonstrategic and to that extent non-"rational" feelings and perceptions, the countries that presently hold the power and the institutional leadership will now have to open their minds to some hitherto "unrealistic" answers to the central question: What policies by those who favor the Nonproliferation Treaty are most likely to change the climate surrounding nuclear spread back to one in which the normal expectation is continued nonproliferation?

A comprehensive answer to this question must be two-tracked. On the first track it is still essential to pursue the goals of effective controls and safeguards—"disincentives" to going nuclear.

But the second track, to which little attention has been given, is to reduce the political and psychological incentive to become a nuclear weapons power.

How is this to be done?

IV

The logic of the situation requires that an expanded nonproliferation strategy focus on tangible ways to give the outsiders a far more genuine sense of participation in the system. It is obviously not enough to say to them, with the late President Kennedy, "Life is unfair." Deep-rooted feelings of political alienation and resentment can be overcome only by greater true equality. There must be shared opportunities to gain prestige through participation in decision-making, which in turn requires that responsibilities be much more broadly allocated than under the present two-class system. The operative hypothesis is that a seat at the top table of nuclear institutional diplomacy is the price the "monopolists" must pay to others who agree to forgo a seat at the top table of nuclear weaponry.

When we speak of "participation," we are no longer dealing in symbols but in the hard currency of political power. And if the number of those becoming involved in decision-making about international nuclear activities is to grow to include at least the "near-nuclear" countries, here too we come to the end of abstractions and into the creation, design, and operation of political forms and structures appropriate to the problem.

Are we then talking about a new Baruch Plan? Nuclear disarmament? World government?

The Baruch Plan of 1946 (based on the so-called Acheson-Lilienthan Report) called for "managerial control or ownership of all atomic energy activities potentially dangerous to world security," along with "power to control, inspect, and license all other atomic activities." That program entailed internationalization of the whole vertical structure starting with uranium ore, through isotope-separation plants, processing of fuel, and *a fortiori*, the making of nuclear weapons, which were to be totally banned without national veto.

Soviet antagonism to supranational schemes in a U.S.-led world, the weakness of the United Nations in a era of cold war, and despair at the prospects of nuclear disarmament all made a dead letter of the Baruch Plan approach. Even apart from political unreality, international ownership of the entire vertical industrial nuclear structure, from mine to power generator, is inconceivable today given the enormity and complexity of that structure compared with 1946. Uranium is everywhere in the ground, and soon nuclear reactors will be in virtually every country in the world. In addition, to link progress toward nonproliferation to effective nuclear disarmament (as the Baruch Plan did) would ensure the former's automatic failure. It was hard enough to negotiate SALT I and II over a five-year period, and these leave enough weapons in superpower hands to destroy the planet many times over. Our puzzle is how to change the system enough to get a better political-psychological base under nonproliferation *without* having to work a total transformation in man or in the basic geometry of his political world.

What *can* be done is to turn the 1946 Plan on its head, so to speak, and, while candidly admitting the possibility of indefinite possession of nuclear weapons in national hands, to concentrate on internationalizing, to the extent necessary, the nonweapons aspects of the fuel cycle that represent key avenues to further weapons proliferation. The text could well be Henry Kissinger's comments that a "new international structure" has to be built "not on the sense of preeminence of two power centers, but on the sense of participation of those who are part of the global environment."[4] It is a mark of our recent loss of confidence in international institution-building that neither Secretary Kissinger nor many of those concerned with nuclear spread have seriously tried to implement such insights with the kind of thinking that made the mid-1940s a relatively Golden Age on international political inventiveness and institution-building.

Even in this age of limited vision, the NATO Nuclear Planning Group, for instance, went a good distance toward draining tension from the two-class Atlantic Alliance structure by the device of sharing in planning on a matter vital to all. Similarly, a partial approach to nonproliferation would seek to create a changed political environment in which some key elements of peaceful nuclear activities were actually regulated by the international community and in which important nonweapons countries were full participants in international decision-making. If this were achieved, the political motive to go nuclear arising from resentment at discrimination would be significantly diminished. And so also would the technical means to do so.

V

Four things can be done within the framework of a partial approach. None of them requires nuclear disarmament, a working collective security system, or total international ownership à la Baruch—all of which seem far-fetched in the present world of nationalism. But the partial approach would call for some degree of change in the operating international political and economic ground rules. Starting with the least threatening or "revolutionary" steps, candidates for significantly greater international control are: (1) the reprocessing of plutonium from reactors; (2) peaceful nuclear explosions; (3) nuclear fuels, notably those based on plutonium and highly enriched uranium; and (4) more distantly, the uranium enrichment processes. Success with the first steps would generate momentum toward next steps. But each step taken, beginning with the first, would have enormous significance for nonproliferation.

First, plutonium which is sufficiently pure to be used in a light-water reactor—or a bomb—requires in most cases processing in a chemical separation plant that separates it from unspent uranium and other materials contained in fuel rods which have been irradiated in a reactor. For most of the reactors being built, where the spent fuel rods are reprocessed is where weapons-grade plutonium could also be produced.

The number of spent fuel rods that will be moving about in the years to come is staggering. The Stockholm International Peace Research Institute (SIPRI) estimates there will soon be between 7,000 and 12,000 shipments annually between reactors and reprocessing plants. By the early 1980s this will mean that the present nonweapons countries will have available to them annually 26,000 or so kilograms of Plutonium 239—enough to make 50 atomic bombs a week if they choose to. Thus plutonium need only be extracted from the spent fuel rods through reprocessing techniques which, as India has shown, can be readily built at least on a small scale.

This seems an excellent candidate for immediate internationalization. Not many reprocessing plants have yet been built, thanks to the expense, which runs to the hundreds of millions of dollars. The United States has arranged to have recipients of U.S. nuclear fuels send their spent fuel rods for reprocessing to the United States (or in some cases a third country). Little of this is actually being done yet, and the present is thus a good time to rethink the system. For current arrangements simply perpetuate the politically pernicious system of patronage and multiclass citizenship.

A series of internationally controlled facilities, along with internationally regulated and protected transport of this lethal material to and from plants, would represent "community" control of a process that is crucial to all but is currently held by the "nuclear monopolists." It would upgrade vital safety and ecological considerations by standardizing the process. And it would ensure economies of scale by means of consolidated facilities, located on economically rational rather than political-nationalistic grounds. This is clearly a case where a planned regional approach makes sense (as on a regional scale Eurochemique, an agency of the OECD, today reprocesses the spent fuel rods of OECD members in Europe). Regionalization also reduces the danger of domination or capture and, more positively, spreads control facilities and thus participation.

A second candidate for genuine international management is peaceful nuclear explosions (PNEs). As I suggested earlier, the value of PNEs for engineering purposes is highly controversial. Various groups of U.S. scientists have tried hard in recent months to persuade their Soviet counterparts that on the basis of the American "Plowshare" experiments, PNEs are uneconomic, dangerous—and a spur to proliferation. Moscow today seems as divided as Washington was a decade ago between skeptics and enthusiasts and may still want to use PNEs to reroute rivers, dredge canals, and move mountains.

Both India and Brazil have talked of the need to retain the "PNE option," given that their only choice was between asking for great-power help or going nuclear themselves. Recognizing this incentive, some modest efforts have been made to implement the NPT's promise of international procedures to ensure the benefits of peaceful nuclear explosions. The current U.S. position calls for "internationally approved facilities," national in nature although sprinkled lightly with U.N. or IAEA holy water. In fact the Mexican government—a pioneer in innovative NPT thinking—seven years ago proposed internationalization of the PNE program. Officials of the Agency for the Prohibition of Nuclear Weapons in Latin America (OPANAL) justifiably point out that both Argentina and Brazil—two current NPT holdouts—supported that 1968 initiative; perhaps even India would have found it hard to justify her unilateral explosion if the Mexican initiative had been followed up.

Proposals to internationalize PNEs have usually foundered on military security grounds reflected by the question, "Would you want to give an atomic bomb to Waldheim?" There are, as always, pros and cons to this question, including the danger that creation of a new facility for peaceful nuclear explosions might persuade countries to believe it to be a good idea and thus encourage them to acquire the capability nationally. Against this is the more likely contingency of other countries doing what India did: acquiring a nuclear capability on the pretext—or genuine belief—that peaceful nuclear explosions may contribute to their economic development.

Given the great importance of creating a new political-psychological climate for nuclear power, it would seem more important to move to internationalize these peaceful capabilities than to temporize further on debatable technical and engineering grounds. Even if such explosions prove to be uneconomic, the purpose of designing a truly international facility will have been served if, through its symbolism, it contributes to the belief on the part of nations that there is a real promise of a new and fairer international order involving nuclear power, in which all will be assured of receiving benefits.

But a changed approach would also have to be for real. An "international PNE facility" would not affect the stockpiles of nuclear weapons in the hands of the big powers. But it must give to countries that hold back from the NPT on grounds of status and autonomy a greater sense of participation in a far less discriminatory system.

The technical and security issues in a joint international PNE service are complex but not insurmountable. The challenge would be to find a political-technical mix between the extremes of "giving a bomb to Waldheim" and continuing to require proud nations to come to Washington or Moscow to appeal for the technology for peaceful explosions. As a first approximation, the technology for a reasonably clean and efficient nuclear device could be set at the lowest level of common technical knowledge between the United States and the Soviet Union, a level that is probably fairly sophisticated. To reach that point, a joint research project could be undertaken to define and engineer such a "state of the art" device.

Security precautions would of course be required to ensure against risks of theft or sabotage. Some of the means already in existence include making explosive devices unwieldy, utilizing multiple electronic "keys," and applying such proven measures as the warhead security procedures of the U.S. Air Force.

By keeping the technology simple, it seems plausible that the facility could operate at the threshold of common technical knowledge and still be genuinely multinational in composition, security, and decision-making. This is the chief point—that the essentially political decisions about rendering PNE services, including policy questions of cost, personnel, priorities, timing, and the like would be made by an international board consisting of all the nuclear weapons powers plus the principal near-nuclear powers.

Already some countries such as Australia and Canada have endorsed proposals for international arrangements for peaceful explosions. This is a case where leadership could best come from those states most affected by the problem rather than from Washington. But what needs to come from Washington (and Moscow and London and Paris and Peking) is a willingness to implement their words about equality and world order.

This brings us to the third point. Looking ahead to a climate in which steps have been taken to share at least some important peaceful nuclear responsibilities and privileges, it may become possible to consider the means by which the international community could get a handle on the basic element of the process—the uranium itself.

Given the widespread existence of uranium in natural local formations in many parts of the world, it is out of the question to transfer title of uranium ore, even of high (say one percent to two percent) concentration, to the international community. But a partial plan might in its later stage provide for international title over all processed uranium-based nuclear fuels, which would include all enriched uranium and all plutonium. All such fuels would be defined as "public goods." Compensation to present owners for fuels now in process would be made through a bond issue to be amortized over a period of years from the proceeds of future sales to power and research plants. Licenses would be issued for extraction and primary processing and shipping, and efficient surveillance and record-keeping would be maintained to ensure that shipments went to their intended destinations. The control process would be supported by fees from licensing.

The legal principle for plutonium, and for high-grade uranium, would be that these "goods" have the same international legal standing as the seabed beyond the likely 200-mile economic resources zone. Under international rules the seabed and the seas above it represent "the common heritage of mankind" whose exploration will, with any luck, be licensed and regulated by an international authority. Similarly, an international authority would license and regulate national or private production of enriched uranium. The international community would also prescribe standards for the handling of enriched uranium and its insertion into the power reactor network. IAEA inspection would be performed at *all* nuclear power reactors using both U-238 and U-235.

One reason for deferring this step is that historically some weapons-grade fissionable material is produced by power reactors and some by military reactors. This kind of complication would be bypassed by taking the larger arms-control step of ending production of all fissionable material for military purposes. We should return to the 1966 U.S. proposal for a cut-off in the production of all weapons-grade material and the transfer of substantial military stocks of U-235 and plutonium to peaceful uses.

The final element of the scheme is to bring under international control the means of enriching uranium. The expensive and complex isotope-separation method of gasious diffusion may in time be replaced by much less expensive and less complex techniques such as gas centrifuge technology, lasers, and the South African nozzle process. The last stages of an agreed partial plan would require that all means for generating enriched uranium be regarded as a public utility. Private or national ownership under licensed international supervision would continue in the first stage, but by the final stages such plants would be publicly owned and operated either directly or under international license. Compensation would be as above.

VI

Each step in the suggested plan entails empowering an international authority to do an increasingly complex job. Where to start?

One approach would be to start with the principal nations willing to proceed now rather than to await universal agreement. For instance, China and France might not join at the outset, but agreement might be reached among a substantial number of nations to designate international reprocessing facilities and outline a workable system of control and management under the IAEA—or as a separate agency.

If a "coalition of the willing" could be formed by the United States, the Soviet Union, Britain, and India, plus most of the key "threshold powers," a partial community with embryonic common institutes could be set up among them, creating a standard to which the unwise could be encouraged to repair. Whether the new authority is a specialized agency of the U.N. family or a new agency or attached to the IAEA is far less important than that the membership in the first instance include most of the present nuclear supplier powers and, above all, most of the crucial *potential* nuclear powers.

Alternatively, the proposal could be put to the United Nations and to the IAEA to be adopted and implemented by the existing organizations. The IAEA, the U.N., or the parties to the Treaty could decide to create blue-ribbon panels of experts to study and report, by a specified deadline, recommendations which a reconvened NPT Review Conference might consider.

In proceeding to increase the power of the international community, a step-by-step process is essential, with a final stage that does not put the entire plan in jeopardy because of its obvious absurdity or its failure to take into account persistent characteristics of the human condition. Such a phased plan could specify one function on which work should begin without delay, e.g., international reprocessing facilities; the urgency of this step is underlined by the proposal of Iran—a full party to the Treaty—to build its own separation plant. Stage Two could create an international facility for PNEs; Stage Three, control over refined fuels of a specified type; and Stage Four, international control or ownership of uranium enrichment facilities. Or steps could be taken on each of these fronts in each stage, with modest steps in Stage One and completion across the board in Stages Three or Four.

To begin with, however, in the spirit of the proposal, consultations should begin with others so the plan can become theirs as much as it would be ours. Those others must include the present nuclear weapons powers. But above all it must involve those whose decisions, both on capabilities and intentions, will be the fateful ones. For all parties, even the partial approach calls for a leap of imagination. But so does living in a world of proliferated nuclear weapons where every minor international quarrel could become genocidal.

Notes

1. An informal poll of leading U.S. nonproliferation experts meeting privately in March 1975 showed 14 our of 21 anticipating the existence of one to four additional nuclear weapons powers in the next decade. Four experts expected seven to ten more "bomb powers," and none predicted that the line would be held at six.

2. Harold Isaacs, "Nationality: End of the Road?" *Foreign Affairs*, April 1975.

3. On April 1, 1975, in introducing a bill calling on the Argentine government to build a nuclear bomb, one legislator declared: "Recent events have demonstrated that nations gain increasing recognition in the international area in accordance with their power." The example he cited was China, deliberately ignored by the great powers until she went nuclear.

4. See the *New York Times*, October 13, 1974.

18
The Proliferation of Conventional Arms

Helga Haftendorn

The issue of conventional arms proliferation has become a central concern of the arms-control community owing to a number of facts: (a) the enormous increase in quantity and quality of weaponry deployed all over the world, (b) the changed pattern of arms transfers and arms-acquisition processes, and (c) the disturbing consequences of these developments to international stability and crisis management.

In the last ten years military expenditures have increased by some 30 per cent, from $222 billion in 1965 to about $286 billion in 1974.[1] While the rate of growth appears to have been slowing in the industrialized world since 1969, it has been accelerating in quantity and quality in the less-developed countries. At the same time arms-acquisition processes have become much more complex, as arms transfers have changed from surplus equipment given away to alliance partners and political clients to front-line technology being sold worldwide on a cash-and-carry basis. Though government control on all arms deals is tighter than ever before, in many cases its influence is geared not towards restraint but promotion. International conflicts or civil wars are almost exclusively fought, and no longer controlled, by imported weapons, and the existing instruments of arms control have so far proved wholly inadequate for effective restraints.

This paper will focus on the transfer of conventional armaments, military know-how, and arms-production facilities from technologically advanced industrial states to less-developed countries. One of its central hypotheses is that this process has now acquired a dynamic of its own. This does not facilitate the task of shedding light on the motives of supplier countries for exporting armaments and of recipients for acquiring more, more expensive, and more sophisticated weapons. Neither the security-related action-reaction model standard in the strategic community, nor the market-place argument common among liberal economists, nor the military-industrial complex phenomena or

Reprinted by permission from *Adelphi Papers*, No. 133, Spring 1977. Copyright 1977 by The International Institute for Strategic Studies.

dependency theorem—favorites of neomarxist critics—will provide adequate explanations (nor, incidentally, did they do so for the "classical" East-West arms race). Instead, we have to look at a cluster of politico-military *and* economic motives, varying from country to country. In some cases political goals may parallel economic incentives, with the interests of suppliers matching those of recipients, while in others there may be conflicting priorities, or ends and means may not be discernible at all. Still more difficult will be the evaluation of the implications of continued arms proliferation for international security and the chances for restraint and control.

Dimensions of Conventional Arms Proliferation

The actual value of the global traffic in weapons, equipment, and related services can only be estimated. According to American sources it has increased from $5.3 billion in 1965, via $6.7 billion in 1970, to $8.4 billion in 1974 and is estimated to reach $11.2 billion in 1977 (in 1973 dollars). Some 90 per cent of the global arms business is handled by four countries: the United States, the Soviet Union, France, and Britain (see Figure 1). Other industrialized countries, like West Germany, Italy, Canada, Belgium, Sweden, and Switzerland, are still relatively minor suppliers but show striking increases between 1973 and 1974. Among the arms-exporting countries of the third world, China, and Israel occupy important positions because of their domestic arms industry. Collectively, the third-world arms-exporting countries were the fifth-ranking source of major weapons supplied to less-developed countries in 1974.

In 1974 three-quarters of global arms exports were transferred to less-developed countries (56 per cent in 1965), of which the Middle East received the lion's share—according to ACDA 45 per cent, according to SIPRI as much as 56 per cent. This is a significant change compared with the early postwar years when the major recipients of arms transfers were the NATO allies and the Warsaw Pact members, and the 1960s, in the wake of the Vietnam war, when the largest share of armaments went to Southeast Asia (see Figure 2). Today six Middle East countries— Israel, Iran, Egypt, Syria, Iraq, and Saudi Arabia—account for 96 per cent of all imports.

The forms of transaction and the methods of payment have also changed. At the height of the cold war most arms transfers were gifts or grants. In the 1960s and early 1970s all major supplier countries reduced their military assistance programs drastically and switched to foreign military sales. Their political motiviation was underlined by favorable credit terms and sometimes discount prices. Today, with the appearance of the affluent oil-exporting countries on the arms market, the majority

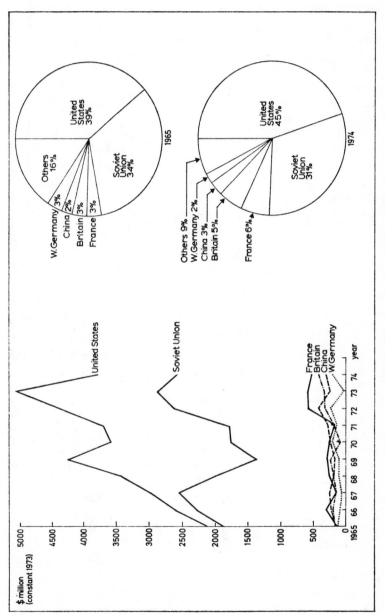

Figure 1: Major Suppliers of Conventional Armaments

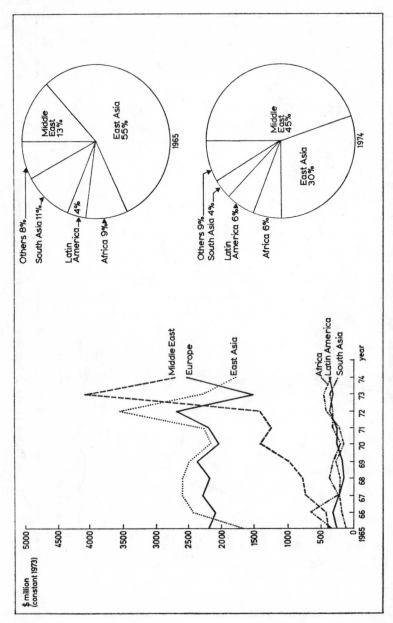

Figure 2: Regional Distribution of Conventional Arms Imports

of sales are transacted on a cash basis, thus avoiding some of the restraints inherent in budgeting processes but not those of government control. On the contrary the role of the state has increased as some governments have set up special agencies for the promotion of arms exports (like International Sales Negotiations in the Pentagon) or have nationalized key industries (Britain) or subsidized them (France, Germany). At the same time, some parliaments, like the US Congress, are in the process of assuming a larger degree of responsibility for supervising and controlling national arms-transfer policies.

Of even greater significance than the rapid increase in the total value of transfers and the size of the arms market is the steady progression in the sophistication of weaponry. A number of less-developed countries are demanding and receiving the very latest technology across almost the entire spectrum of conventional weapons systems, including Mach-2.5 supersonic fighters, various kinds of surface-to-air and surface-to-surface missiles, and anti-tank weapons, including precision-guided munitions and systems of dual capability. Many of the arms contracts signed go far beyond the mere transfer of weapons to include training, technical support, maintenance and repair facilities, and even construction projects. (Only 40 per cent of the budgeted 1976-1977 American arms exports account for weapons and ammunition; the rest is spent on supporting equipment, spare parts, training, and construction.) The export demands are, however, not confined entirely to orders for existing weapons systems; a number of development contracts have also been negotiated. Regional conflicts at the same time serve as testing grounds for newly developed weapons systems of the major powers.

Another feature of the present proliferation pattern is the spread of defense industries in the less-developed countries. The first step is usually the assembly of imported components, followed by the production of foreign systems under license. Argentina, China, India, and Israel have indigenous aircraft programs under way, while Brazil, India, Israel, South Africa, and Taiwan are developing or producing various types of missiles. An important new development along this line of greater self-realiance in weapons production is the establishment of an Arab defense industry in Egypt, the Arab Military Industrialization Organization, funded mainly by Saudi Arabia and Kuwait. A serious problem in most less-developed countries, however, is the shortage of capital funds and skilled labor. Thus, for most of them, with the exception of China and Israel, building up an indigenous weapon-design and development capability still has far to go.

The Dynamics of Arms Races in the Third World

Our understanding of the political, strategic, and economic dynamics and consequences of conventional arms proliferation is very primitive, despite a growing literature on the statistics and mechanisms of the international arms transfer. Is the increasing demand for conventional arms by less-developed countries based above all upon genuine security requirements, caused by an external threat to foreign policy objectives, or is it caused by internal challenges to the central power of the government and the ruling elites? Or is the primary stimulus for arms races in the third-world countries to be seen in the easy accessibility of a lavish arms market? Are the major supplier nations the primary promoters, engaging in competitive policies to mark political interest and influence, to support sympathetic regimes, and to exercise control in areas of potential conflict? Or is the unprecedented growth of armament rates to be attributed to the forces of market economies in the industrialized countries? A closer look at the military build-up in the Middle East might shed some light on the different threads of the present arms-proliferation fabric.[2]

At the core of the Middle Eastern arms race is the Arab-Israeli conflict, which is historically a struggle between Israeli and Arab (Palestinian) nationalism over the same territory. The depletion of weapons inventories in the 1973 October war between Israel, Egypt, and Syria and the ensuing arms race only highlighted the volatilities and instabilities inherent in this region. But in its present configuration the Middle East is also central to the global balance of power between the United States and the Soviet Union. In this context the military accumulation does have ambivalent implications. On the one hand, it aggravates the existing potential for conflict and will most certainly increase the scope and intensity of any future war. On the other hand, given the dependence of Israel and Jordan, Egypt and Syria on the United States and the Soviet Union respectively for arms supplies and replacements, it constitutes an element of super-power control and may thus enhance regional stability.

While the Arab–Israeli conflict is essentially clear-cut, the Persian Gulf is characterized by a much more complex pattern of varied and partly overlapping tensions. In recent years Iran has achieved a dominant position based on her growing economic as well as military power. Her main concern has been to secure her vital trade routes and to prevent the establishment of revolutionary regimes on the western shore of the Gulf which might endanger not only Iranian security but also the regime itself. Iraq has in the past challenged the Iranian bid for dominance and has entered into a competitive military build-up which has, in its turn, triggered a massive armament program in Kuwait. Saudi Arabia, like Iran, has a vested interest in preserving the present situation in the Gulf area and the Arabian peninsula, and she is using the flow of petro-dollars and the assembly of very modern weaponry partly as a security investment and partly as a bargaining card in OPEC and Arab affairs.

The steep increase in the price of crude oil and the OPEC policy of scarcity contributed to rising production costs, spiralling inflation, and worldwide recession. The heavy interdependence of the major western industrialized societies spread the effects of the recession fairly evenly between the United States, Western Europe, and Japan and made these countries search for alternative export markets in the face of worsening balance-of-payments difficulties and rising unemployment at home. True, balance-of-payments problems have been with most industrialized states, like the United States and Britain, for some time, and the smaller weapons-producing countries have always been concerned to extend production runs in order to lower unit costs. But in this case perceived economic necessities and market opportunities did coincide and caused a steep increase in arms exports. The high oil revenues not only gave the oil-producing countries tremendous buying power, but the depletion of stocks in the 1973 war also created a strong demand for new, sophisticated weapons systems.

The arms-export market does, however, have different economic justifications for the various supplier countries. The American market is in itself large enough to sustain a sophisticated arms industry, but longer production runs tend to reduce unit costs and thus give it a significant export advantage. A sizeable foreign demand allows France and Britain to maintain otherwise highly uneconomic domestic arms industries, but it has never been sufficient to offset the cost explosion inherent in the increasing technological sophistication of modern weapons systems. In order to stay in the arms business the smaller producer countries either have to specialize in one or a few advanced weapons systems (like the French and British supersonic aircraft and various missile systems), enter into co-production with other countries and attract foreign capital investment in national enterprises (the German-British-Italian Tornado multi-role combat aircraft, or the Lockheed shareholding in Messerschmidt-Bölkow-Blohm), or diversify their defense manufacturers into a variety of defense and civilian products (examples are Krauss-Maffei, makers of the Leopard tank, in Germany and Saab, makers of the Viggen aircraft, in Sweden).

Weighing the economic benefits that sizeable foreign sales bring to a national economy, it should be kept in mind that there are limits to the financial resources of the oil-rich buyer countries and also to their capacity to absorb and effectively operate sophisticated technology. Before long the less-developed countries will have to make a decision as to whether and in what proportion they plan to spread their capital and manpower resources among armaments and investment goods. In canceling some naval orders Iran does seem to be reconsidering her development priorities. At the same time the arms-producing countries, which are also the biggest suppliers of investment goods, might find it in their long-term economic interests to encourage the industrialization rather than the armament of third-world countries. Food for thought might be provided by the fact that during the last recession Germany and Japan, which are leading exporters of capital goods but are of secondary importance in the arms market, have increased their overall exports to less-developed countries by a sizeable percentage, while most of the other countries, like Britain and France, suffered substantial losses in spite of increased arms exports.[3]

In analyzing the Middle East proliferation pattern and some of its incentives it should be remembered that it is linked with arms races in neighboring regions—for example, India and Pakistan, or Egypt, Libya, and Sudan—and that there are other independent armament processes in other parts of the world. One arms race is taking place in the highly volatile region of Southern Africa, reflecting escalating tensions between the black states (notably Angola, Mozambique, Tanzania, Zaire, and Zambia) and the white minority governments of South Africa and Rhodesia, with a wide range of industrialized and less-developed countries serving as arms suppliers (apart from some indigenous production in South Africa). Another area of high arms purchases is Latin America, the largest purchasers being Chile and oil-rich Venezuela, followed by Peru, Brazil, and Argentina. In an attempt to counteract the 1960s United States policy of limiting the proliferation of advanced weapons systems in the western hemisphere outside North America, Latin American countries have often turned to France and Britain. However, this trend is being reversed with the ready availability of sophisticated weaponry from the United States herself.

The dangers inherent in conventional arms proliferation are multiplied with the growing availability of nuclear fuel to countries of the Middle East, South Asia, Latin America, and Southern Africa. The Indian case has recently shown how relatively easy it is to pass over the threshold from peaceful to military uses of nuclear energy. A number of easily adaptable delivery systems—such as the F-4, the F-14, the Mirage, the Tu-16, and MiG-23—or dual-capability short-range ballistic-missiles—like the American Lance or the Soviet Scud—are already operational in less-developed countries. Though considered 'tactical' when deployed in Europe, these systems have strategic implications when transferred to areas such as the Middle East. Moreover, they may have highly de-stabilizing effects when sent to geographical areas replete with sources for military conflict.

Restraints on Arms Transfers

First, it should be borne in mind that arms proliferation is inherently neither good nor bad and that arms competition does not cause wars, though it does exacerbate tension and encourage perceptions that make war more likely. War in and between third-world countries, as in other parts of the world, is bad because it not only upsets social, political, and economic development processes but may also endanger international stability if other powers, notably the super-powers, feel compelled to intervene.[4]

Second, no comprehensive national or international regulation of the transfer of arms and weapons technology would serve the interests of all the states concerned. Which purpose should restraints primarily serve? One purpose might be to reduce the danger of military conflicts, made more likely be regional arms build-ups and the distrust they would generate, and—should war break out—to keep it limited and collateral damage low. A second might be to control manifest or latent conflicts by strengthening the available mechanisms for crisis management and political mediation. A third might be to channel resources into economic development which would otherwise be spent on weaponry. (It might be argued, however, that any one of these purposes, or all three, could also be served by arms transfers.)

Third, it would be wrong to assume that there are no restraints currently in existence regarding arms-proliferation and arms-acquisition processes. Restrictions may be unilateral or multilateral, quantitative or qualitative, specific or general, tacit or formal, and may be applied by the supplier or the recipient. Their effectiveness might be circumscribed by a number of factors, but their application does nevertheless indicate that there exist corresponding interests among states.

One element of control has to be seen in the fact that strict governmental monitoring and licensing of all arms transfers has replaced the discreet military programs and *laissez-faire* commercial sales of the 1950s and early 1960s. In the first place, it is the national executive that lays down specific arms-transfer rules or policies—both the promotional *and* the restrictive ones! Examples of the latter have been Germany's decision to limit the export of weapons to NATO allies, Britain's determination not to sell arms to Chile and South Africa, and the United States' endeavor in the 1960s not to transfer advanced aircraft to Latin America. Such restraints were motivated by foreign policy considerations, to avoid international embarrassment (as was the case when Germany's military assistance to Israel was made public in 1965) or to respond to domestic pressure (most spectacularly, the cessation of supplies to Turkey in the aftermath of the Cyprus crisis, or the Humphrey Bill as debated currently in the US Congress).

Restrictions may apply to:

- certain types of weapons like "significant military equipment" (Canada to Middle Eastern countries), or "lethal equipment" (United States to Pakistan);
- certain volatile regions, like "areas of tension" (West Germany), or "areas of direct conflict" (Britain);
- certain domestic conditions such as "no oppressive regime" (Sweden), or "respect of internationally recognized human rights" (United States);
- quantity of arms to be transferred by annual and regional ceilings (US Congress), or to be replaced (1973 Paris agreement on Vietnam);
- the use, deployment, or combat role of weapons, such as "NATO treaty area" (West Germany to Portugal) or "non-use for external defense" (Britain and France in 1963 to South Africa);
- prior consent to reselling weapons to third countries, a so-called "end-use clause" (United States, West Germany, Italy).

The effectiveness of such national restraints depends above all on the continuing determination of a country to adhere to them in spite of temptations. There are numerous loopholes in the enforcement of any restrictions, beginning with the definition of "significant military equipment," "area of tension" or "oppressive regime" and the strictness of application—for example, whether to include goods "in the pipeline" or spare parts. From a foreign-policy point of view, those restraints seem to serve their purpose best which are limited to very broad declarations of principles, permitting flexible adjustment to changing circumstances; from an arms-control perspective, on the other hand, very specific regulations, applicable to a certain region or situation and of fixed duration will be most successful.

Adherence to any national policy of restraint will also depend on domestic factors. Confronted with a negative balance of payments and high unemployment figures in Britain, a member of the traditionally arms-control-conscious Labour government refused to accept a parliamentary motion calling on the government to deny arms supplies to countries where human rights were abused, and did so unchallenged by public opinion. The Social-Liberal coalition in West Germany, caught between increased lobbying by both industry and trade unions to relax its restrictions and admonitions by its left-wing party base to curb the national arms industry, maintained its policy of restraint but at the same time increased its exports of non-sensitive equipment and arranged for compensatory economic benefits from items jointly produced and exported by partner countries. In the United States, Congress has been extending its legislative surveillance over all foreign military grants and sales and is trying both to impose an overall ceiling on all sales and to establish expanded reporting procedures on all arms transfers. Though national ceilings have a tendency to be taken for floors, and limits tend to stimulate the search for circumventions, national restraints have so far proved to be fairly flexible and effective in restricting the flow of armaments, but they still need to be improved.

Broad national policies of restraint have often facilitated rather than limited arms transfers and have exploited the ambiguities inherent in any formal doctrine. The Italian government, for example, could declare that it was scrupulously adhering to the UN embargo and at the same time sell light reconnaissance and strike planes as well as production licenses to South Africa, for neither planes nor know-how were treated as 'weapons' by the Italian arms-export legislation. Increasingly, the supply of hardware is being replaced by the transfer of licenses, technological know-how, and production facilities—quite often without any clear-cut military designation—and is thus very difficult to monitor and restrain. National measures, varying from one supplier country to another, are furthermore inadequate if applied to weapons systems produced on a joint basis by two or more countries. Thus a less-developed country may buy the German–French Alpha Jet from France, while Germany will withhold export licenses to non-NATO countries. Besides its inherent military and economic benefits, this recent trend in international arms production provides governments with any amount of camouflage on the arms market.

Multilateral restraints, likewise, have so far been of limited effectiveness. The Tripartite Declaration signed by the United States, France, and Britain in 1950, in which they pledged to maintain a military balance between Israel and the Arab states, was successful only as long as it served the interests of the major parties concerned. It became worthless when Egypt turned to the Soviet Union for arms supplies and, after the nationalization of the Suez Canal, France and Britain sided with Israel to attack Egypt. The Johnson-Kosygin understanding of 1967 to restrict arms imports into the Middle East likewise collapsed during the Yom Kippur war. UN embargoes, like that against South Africa, have shown some success when directed against a politically unpopular state, but even in these cases comprehensive bans have often been circumvented. Moreover, the embargoes against South Africa and Israel have had a catalytic effect in encouraging the development of indigenous arms-production capabilities. To curtail these will be extremely difficult, as the line of demarcation between defense and civilian production is heavily blurred, and even the most self-righteous paternalist may not deny a country the means of social and economic development.

Recipient states have generally opposed measures to control the conventional arms trade, contending that restrictions imposed by supplier nations were encroachments on their sovereign right of self-defense and arrogant manifestations of inherently discriminatory character. This position has contributed much to the fruitless negotiations at the Geneva Conference of the Committee on Disarmament on this topic. In the light of the manifest distrust on the part of less-developed countries, regional initiatives taken by recipient states may have a better chance of success than those imposed by outside powers. In December 1974, in the Declaration of Ayacucho, eight Latin American countries expressed their desire to create "conditions which will make possible the effective limitation of armaments and put an end to their acquisition for purposes of war" (Brazil did not sign this declaration). However, this promising approach fell short of expectations held in the arms-control community, since in the meantime all major signatories have not only purchased supersonic aircraft and other advanced weaponry but also have accelerated their indigenous arms production. Its effectiveness was further weakened by the fact that it was not complemented by a similar undertaking from the major supplier nations.

It has recently been suggested that the London nuclear "Suppliers Club" might be a useful model for restricting by quantity or quality the flow of armaments to less-developed countries. This group of major exporters of nuclear technology has agreed on a set of regulations and standards to govern their exports. However, its effectiveness is limited because no enforcement capabilities exist and common ground shrinks with the increasing number of members. Nonetheless, because a club of conventional arms suppliers might be one possible measure to control the uninhibited proliferation of conventional armaments, this model should be further explored. Most realistic would be a rather pragmatic and limited approach. The major producers of advanced weapons sytems, like supersonic fighters or ballistic missiles of a certain range (say, 600 miles), might work out specific transfer policies that all members of the cartel would adhere to. Or a group of nations (like the United States and the EEC members) might agree on quantitative or qualitative restraints for joint implementation that would contribute to some shrinkage of the international arms market. The other, more ambitious, approach would be to work for a more general and complete, highly efficient solution. The club would then need to include the major supplier countries, including the Soviet Union, and encompass weaponry, defense-related equipment *and* technological know-how. It would need to be complemented, first, by an undertaking from the major recipient countries not to procure armaments exceeding a specified quantitative or qualitative ceiling, and, second, by an undertaking from the major military powers similarly to reduce their defense spending.

Another approach might be to negotiate regional arms-control arrangements or zones of limited armaments. The initiative to restrict weapons procurement might come from within the region, as with the Ayacucho declaration, and then be complemented by a similar policy of regional restraint on behalf of the major supplier nations; alternatively, national ceilings might be agreed among the major suppliers and then negotiated with those countries concerned. However, any agreement will be a dead letter from the beginning if it does not take into account the variety of interests of the member states or if it is not complemented by non-military forms of regional conflict management. It might be further supplemented by the establishment of a development fund financed jointly by the richer countries in the region and major outside trade partners.

A third option might be the further promotion of national restraints, which, in spite of all difficulties, have proved the most flexible instrument of control so far. Their effectiveness might be increased if the economic incentives for arms sales could be reduced. Stable rates of growth in industrialized countries and a restructuring of exports to stress capital goods might be one step in this direction. National policies are not, however, formulated in a vacuum but are responsive to domestic and international challenges, and in a time of growing international interdependence a country will thus have to take into consideration the actions of others. Among the Nine or within NATO, for example, it might be quite difficult to maintain unharmonized arms-transfer policies without undermining the internal cohesion of the bloc, though a joint policy of restraint will imply some kind of compensation for those countries currently most heavily dependent on arms sales.

Impact on the International System

In the long-term international perspective, industrialized and less-developed countries might be well-advised to consider further the implications of uninhibited conventional arms proliferation—its effects not only on international stability and the conditions of peaceful change but also on the social and economic development of the Third World, and thus on the relations between the haves and the have-nots of this earth. This is perhaps the most important question, since it concerns the effect of today's actions on the quality of tomorrow's international system. What kind of options does the transfer of arms give—or withhold from—suppliers and recipients? Will the dispersal of advanced weapons create new centers of power in the world which defy the East-West pattern and limit the control of major outside powers? Will it increase the likelihood of regional conflict, and if so can the suppliers of weapons avoid becoming entangled in conflicts they can no longer control? And how will their relations towards each other be affected by the result? How will power relations, hostilities, and conflict in the Third World influence those between East and West in the years to come?

Notes

1. Unless otherwise noted, all figures are given in constant 1973 US dollars and are derived from the United States Arms Control and Disarmament Agency, *World Military Expenditures and Arms Transfers 1965-1974* (Washington DC: ACDA 90, 1976). The term 'arms' generally includes not only combat equipment but also supporting equipment and spare parts but excludes training and technical services. Owing to different methods of data collection and computation procedures, the ACDA data are not comparable to those of the Stockholm International Peace Research Institute (SIPRI). See SIPRI, *World Armaments and Disarmament, SIPRI Yearbook 1976* (Stockholm: Almqvist & Wiksell; Cambridge, Mass. and London: MIT Press, 1976) and *Arms Trade Registers: The Arms Trade with the Third World* (Stockholm: Almqvist & Wiksell; Cambridge, Mass. and London: MIT Press, 1971). SIPRI arms-transfer figures tend to be lower than those of ACDA, since they include only major weapons and concentrate on deliveries to third-world countries. Its arms-trade registers cover items on order or delivered or believed to be ordered, while ACDA reports only effected exports· or imports.

2. For an analysis of proliferation processes in the Middle East, see Geoffrey Kemp, "The Military Build-up: Arms Control or Arms Trade?" in *The Middle East and the International System: Part I: The Impact of the 1973 War*, Adelphi Paper No. 114 (London: IISS; 1975), pp. 31-37; Wolfgang Mallmann, *Die israelisch-arabische Aufrüstung 1967-1974* (dissertation, Bonn 1976); Hanns Maull, "The Arms Trade with the Middle East and North Africa," *The Middle East and North Africa 1975-76* (London: Europa, 1976), pp. 102-109; Roger F. Pajak, "Soviet Arms and Egypt," *Survival*, July/August 1975, pp. 165-173.

3. There have been few knowledgeable analyses of the multi-faceted economic aspects of international arms transfers. For one, see Peter Lock and Herbert Wulf, "Rüstungsexporte und ihre volkswirtschaftlichen Auswirkungen für die Bundersrepublik" (unpublished paper, 1976).

4. Colin S. Gray, "Traffic Control for the Arms Trade?" *Foreign Policy No. 6*, Spring 1972, pp. 153-169. See also Anne H. Cahn, "Arms Transfer Constraints: Who, What, When, How and Why?" (unpublished Paper, May

1976); Geoffrey Kemp, "The International Arms Trade: Suppliers, Recipients and Arms Control Perspectives," *Political Quarterly,* October–December 1971; Jean Klein, "Vent d'armes et d'équipements nucléares: les politiques des Etats Unis et des pays d'Europe occidentale depuis la guerre d'octobre 1973," *Politique Etrangére* No. 6, 1975, pp. 603-620.

19
Arms Sales
Leslie H. Gelb

No one has a good answer to what to do about world arms orders that in 1976 exceeded $20 billion, including almost $10 billion from the United States. The fact is that the solutions are not very satisfactory.

In the last several years, Congress or some of its committees have successively called for a phasing out of grant military aid and credit arms sales and a phasing in of cash sales, then a phasing out of government-to-government cash sales and a phasing in of commercial sales, then a move back to government-to-government sales, then a desire to cut back on all kinds of sales. Congress also passed a law giving itself the power to veto individual sales of $25 million or more then never exercised this veto. Congress also mandated a reduction in U.S. military advisory groups and training missions only to later discover that the military men were being replaced by even greater hordes of civilian advisers who were even more difficult to control.

This record of well-intentioned confusion has been a response to the administration's apparent policy of selling virtually anything to virtually anybody. In fact, however, the administration has nothing that could be called an agreed interagency policy on arms sales at all. Efforts have been made on several occasions over several years to draft such a document. These efforts have been variously described by some of the participants as "unsatisfactory" and "unfinished."

Jimmy Carter interjected the arms sales issue into the presidential campaign. He said that we cannot be "both the world's leading champion of peace and the world's leading supplier of weapons of war."

To many liberal legislators, arms sales are an unmitigated disaster that must be sharply curtailed. From their perspective, to sell arms is to be an accomplice in their use, to be a partner in aggression and killing. But from an equally legitimate perspective, to withhold arms is to deny the right to legitimate self-defense.

To Secretary of State Henry Kissinger, arms sales are an unprece-

Reprinted by permission from *Foreign Policy*, Winter 1976-77. Copyright 1976 by National Affairs, Inc.

dented opportunity to win friends and influence events. But it is one thing to sell arms to buttress foreign policy goals and quite another to use them as a tactical device with little attention to their aftereffects on those goals.

To most political moderates, arms sales are a serious problem that must be better controlled. True, but then what? Their proposals for mutual restraint, making distinctions about the lethality and sophistication of weapons, and for human rights tests are easier to advocate than apply. They tend to exaggerate the extent to which the United States can, in the long run, influence the devolution of arms in the world. Their handwringing also seems to ignore that they themselves only very recently were urging the United States to promote more military self-reliance for friendly countries.

This essay may in the end have to confess to similar errors, but until then, it will advance three propositions.

First, the volume of arms being transferred in the world today is not much larger than it was 10 years ago, except for sales to the Middle East, and, even when it doubles in the next few years, U.S. sales will be about the same as U.S. grant military aid 25 years ago. What is different is the method of transferring arms, the kinds of arms being transferred, the recipients, and the relationship between supplier and recipient. Nations are increasingly demanding and receiving arms for their own purposes as well as those of the suppliers. Thus, the opportunities to control the flow of arms will get worse before they get better, if they get better at all.

Second, the United States should approach arms sales as a foreign policy problem, not as an arms control problem. Sales are so intertwined with other matters that they have to be treated on a country-by-country basis with decisions based on pragmatic tradeoffs. Kissinger's general criteria for making arms sales seem to be reasonable, but some of his specific decisions are highly questionable. He has been too preoccupied with his purposes in selling rather than with their purposes in buying.

Third, the overall policy dilemma for the United States is how to use arms sales to foster measures of self-reliance in those purchasing the weapons for both our purposes and common purposes without these sales entangling us in enterprises that do not suit our ends. The answers lie not in new policy schemes or institutional reforms, but in simple prudence. At the same time, the United States should undertake long-range diplomacy aimed at mitigating conventional arms transfers and their effects on others and on ourselves.

The Trends

It is not at all clear that the total amount of arms being transferred (by grants, government-to-government cash and credit sales, and commercial sales) in the world today is appreciably greater than it was 10 years ago—except for imports by Iran, Saudi Arabia, and Israel. Measured in constant 1973 dollars, all transfers in 1965 totaled $5.315 billion as compared to $8.365 billion in 1974.[1] The difference is accounted for almost entirely by the Middle East and Persian Gulf states, where arms sales rose from $397 million in 1965 to $2.712 billion in 1974. Over the same period, deliveries to Africa rose from $253 million to $386 million and to Latin America from $104 million to $370 million. Given the real increases in gross national product in these areas in the last 10 years, the increases do not appear out of line.

The overall pattern holds true for the United States, the biggest supplier of all. Except for commercial sales (which were less than half a billion dollars in 1974), all U.S. transfers as measured in constant 1974 dollars went from $3.523 billion in fiscal year 1964 to $5.176 billion in fiscal year 1974. In that same period, all transfers to the Near East leaped from $17.5 million in 1964 to $1.732 billion in 1974.[2] For both worldwide and U.S. transfers, the real jumps began in 1972 with the onset of rising oil prices and the Arab-Israeli war.

Nor is there much evidence to show that arms imports are more of a burden to non-oil-producing developing nations than they were years ago. Of all the recipients of all forms of American aid, the State Department has identified only 14 states where the ratio of military expenditures to GNP exceeded the average for less-developed countries. In 1975, they were: the Middle East rivals (Egypt, Israel, Syria); African states facing internal difficulties (Ethiopia, Tanzania, Zaire, Zambia); Latin-American states finally modernizing their defense establishments (Bolvia, Ecuador, Nicaragua, Peru, Uruguay); and Cambodia and Thailand.[3] Put another way, military expenditures as a percentage of GNP in all developing nations rose from 4.3 per cent in 1963 to 5.3 per cent in 1974.

None of this is cited as an excuse for arms transfers. The data has been noted simply to establish that if there has been a real change in the arms picture or a special problem resulting from U.S. and worldwide exports of arms through 1974, it was not a problem of quantity except for the Middle East area. The recitation is also a way of getting at the real changes: the terms of transfer, the kinds of weapons being exported, the shift in recipients, and the new buyer-seller relationship.

The major change in the terms of transfer has been from aid (grants, excess stocks, and service-funded equipment) to trade (government-to-government foreign military sales for cash and credit and commercial sales). Military aid fell from a high of $5.7 billion in 1952 to under $600 million in recent years. Further, Congress has now mandated the end of the Military Assistance Program in two years.

As aid declined, sales rose. Sales deliveries reached the $1 billion mark for the first time in 1966, then averaged about $1.8 billion in the early 1970s, then hit $3.4 billion in 1974 and $4 billion in the following fiscal year. The offsetting increase in sales was not surprising as more states became economically able to pay cash and with the oil-producing states rolling in petrodollars.

The kinds of arms being paid for were of a much higher quality than the arms previously given away. Grant aid consisted mostly of weapons and equipment no longer used by U.S. armed forces, except for those given to NATO allies. The new buyers, with the money now coming out of their own pockets, began demanding and receiving weapons and equipment being currently used by American forces (including various kinds of missiles, tanks, bombs, aircraft, radar, and communications equipment).

This, in turn, created two serious problems for the U.S. military. First, by selling some of its most sophisticated weaponry, the United States was losing technological superiority over other forces and running the risk of the technology falling into hostile hands. Second, buyers such as Israel and Iran were demanding early delivery of these items thereby compelling U.S. forces to share current production lines. The result has been a loss in U.S. superiority and readiness. The Soviet Union, to be sure, was running into similar problems.

The shift from aid to trade and from obsolete to sophisticated items was attended by a shift in recipients. U.S. priorities went from NATO in the 1950s to Asia in the 1960s to the Middle East in the 1970s. There has been a comparable shift in Soviet sales, with Syria, Iraq, and Libya becoming principal buyers.

What all of this adds up to is an incipient revolution in supplier-recipient relationships. For instead of the United States dictating to others what they need to meet the common external Communist threat, others are telling us what they feel they need for their own purposes. It is the beginning of a move from giving aid to maintain the Soviet-American strategic balance as seen from Washington and Moscow, to selling in order to deal with regional balances and internal situations as perceived by other capitals.

Kissinger has acted almost invariably as if there were a dovetailing of his purposes and theirs. He thus opened up the floodgates of policy to all manner of sales to support his short-term diplomatic objectives and to maintain a general political influence with the buyers. But this is another power curve that Kissinger will not be able to stay in front of. For while he is using arms sales to patch together ad hoc anti-Soviet alliances, most of the buyers (some African states doing quite the contrary are discussed later) are treating the sales as a chance to establish their independence from the United States. It seems safe to assume that the new buyers, when it comes to dealing with their own rivalries and power struggles, do not count upon American military intervention in their behalf.

An increasing number of states want to buy more arms, an increasing list of suppliers want to sell more, and constraints on sales are weakening all the time. The reasons for this need not be belabored. About two-thirds of the world arms exports are to countries classified as developing. Most of these countries have little or no indigenous arms industries and so import all or most of their weapons. As they adjust to greater American reluctance to use force, they will buy more for their own ends. Some of these buyers (like India, Brazil, Israel, Taiwan, and Argentina) are even carrying efforts at self-reliance to the highly uneconomical point of building their own military industries.

Suppliers have a growing economic incentive to sell. From 1965 to 1974, the world market was dominated by the United States (49 per cent) and the Soviet Union (29.2 per cent). These two will continue to be the most competitive suppliers, since their industries have the largest internal markets and the most vigorous research programs. The averages for other sellers were: France, 4.4 per cent; China, 3.3 per cent; United Kingdom, 3.2 per cent; Czechoslovakia, 1.9 per cent; Poland, 1.9 per cent; West Germany, 1.9 per cent; and Canada, 1.8 per cent, leaving only 3.3 per cent for all other suppliers. Nations like France and England must export; their internal markets are too small to support their arms industries otherwise.

Real economic dependence on arms exports is a difficult thing to assess, but even for a nation like the United States, it is growing in terms of jobs and percentage of total exports. Estimates are that jobs related to arms exports will increase from about 200,000 at present to about 400,000 when U.S. arms exports reach the $10 billion level next year. And, at that level, arms exports will be about 8 per cent of total U.S. exports, up from the earlier average of about 5 per cent.

U.S. government-to-government sales orders (as distinguished from exports or actual deliveries) reached $10.8 billion in FY 1974, $9.5 billion in FY 1975, were estimated to be $8.2 billion in FY 1976, and were projected at $9 billion for the following 14 months. Commercial deliveries also began to exceed the half-billion mark after FY 1974. This is all part of a worldwide backlog of sales estimated to be about $24 billion. This can be translated into a world arms trade of about $20 billion annually for the rest of this decade—or twice the high of the previous decade. For the United States alone, however, the $10 billion total will be about the same in value as American grant military aid of $5.7 billion in 1952.

Some of this increase over the previous decade can be attributed to inflation and to the higher cost of more sophisticated weaponry. Most of the increase remains tied to the Middle East area. But a part also represents a real increase in sales to other areas of the world.

The full impact of this is yet to be felt. The question now arises as to how to make sense of what is happening, at least with respect to U.S. foreign policy.

Foreign Policy Considerations

Over the next three to five years, it is difficult to see how to apply a classic arms control approach to this situation. Such an approach requires two elements: the likelihood of mutual restraint and the feasibility of making tight distinctions among weapons systems. Significant mutual restraint among regional buyers and world suppliers is extremely unlikely for reasons already discussed. To be sure, the United States could exercise unilateral restraint, and, to some degree, the present administration has. But even its few limits on sales of strategic delivery vehicles and hand-held surface-to-air missiles have been eroding. It is not easy for the administration to make distinctions stick between offensive and defensive weapons or between too sophisticated and acceptable weapons—except in specific cases. Deciding whether or not to sell in specific cases is in the realm of foreign policy more than arms control.

The Senate Foreign Relations Committee issued a report on the Foreign Assistance Act of 1974 stating that its intent was "to insure that government officials, when weighing proposed arms sales to foreign countries, have uppermost in their thinking the foreign policy interests of the United States and not that of selling more United States military equipment." The committee was right in excoriating the hard sell but wrong in suggesting that Kissinger did not have foreign policy considerations uppermost in his mind when approving sales.

Considerations for arms sales can be cast into nine identifiable categories. Kissinger's actions can be analyzed in terms of these considerations.[4] The considerations seem to be reasonable ones. What follows is a discussion of how and why his decisions based on these considerations could have been made otherwise. The discussion is meant to be suggestive, not inclusive or conclusive.

1. *Preventing Nuclear Proliferation.* There have been three recent instances of Kissinger's using arms sales to retard or prevent the spread of nuclear weapons: South Korea, Pakistan, and Iran. In each instance, France had contracted to sell nuclear reprocessing plants. These plants, which reprocess the spent fuel from nuclear power reactors, can be used to make weapons-grade plutonium. As a result of Kissinger's efforts,

South Korea and Iran have opted for multinationally owned and run reprocessing plants rather than plants located in their own territory.

By law and by administration policy, it is now virtually established that if a country takes steps to acquire the capability to build nuclear weapons, the United States will cut off all forms of aid, except food. What is not wholly clear is whether the administration has been prepared to sell conventional weapons that otherwise would not have been sold as an inducement for a country to refrain from developing nuclear arms. The trade-off is this: the likelihood of setting off regional conventional arms races and imbalances now weighed against the possibility of a world filled with nuclear weapons in the future.

With respect to South Korea, it appears that the administration used the cutoff of more arms as a threat rather than the prospect of more arms as a sweetener. Seoul was simply told that if it bought the plant, credit sales would be stopped. With regard to Iran, one gets the impression that the shah's restraint on the reprocessing plant was tied to a Kissinger commitment to continue open-ended arms sales. In the case of Pakistan, it seems as if Kissinger is prepared to sell A-7 attack bombers as a bribe. If the sale of some 100 A-7s were to be judged on its own merits independent of the proliferation issue, most experts would be strongly opposed to it. Unlike the F-5e, the A-7 is more of an attack aircraft, and thus its sale to Pakistan would run counter to the sensible and long-standing policy of selling only clearly defensive weapons to nations on the Asian subcontinent.

Officials have naturally been reluctant to acknowledge the link. They do not want to put the United States in a blackmail position where countries can get undesirable arms by threatening to buy a reprocessing plant. But that is precisely the precedent Kissinger seems likely to set in the Pakistan case and perhaps in the others as well. He seems ready to bribe in order to avoid blackmail, and that is an unwise course.

2. *Self-sufficiency.* Providing aid and sales to make a country strong enough to defend itself without direct American intervention has long been a rhetorical, but not a real, goal of policy. It was not and is not possible to attain that capability against the Soviet Union, but it is possible against regional adversaries. The administration has managed some of the most prominent self-sufficiency cases in a manner that has aroused little criticism.

The stated goal of U.S. sales to Taiwan is to bring about self-sufficiency. To this end, the administration recently approved sales in excess of $200 million for an advanced radar defense system, a doubling of Taiwan's holding of Hawk ground-to-air missiles, and an increase of co-produced F-5es from 120 to 180. If a future administration were to decide to abrogate the defense treaty with Taiwan, this capability would make it easier to do so. But in the short run, the sales and their goal could lead Peking to conclude that Washington was acting in bad faith by trying to promote the permanent separation of Taiwan from the mainland. The present administration's gamble, however, seems a reasonable one.

The United States and Israel share a strong desire to avoid direct American involvement in future Middle East wars. This can be accomplished, in addition to continuing diplomatic efforts, only by providing Israel with first class armaments. A few weapons sytems, however, should be excluded even here. Kissinger's promised sale of Pershing long-range ground-to-ground missiles carriers a nuclear connotation. The Pershings also would likely cause the Russians to provide a comparable capability for the Arabs, thus laying open Israeli cities to easy destruction. The administration has not sought self-sufficiency for South Korea, and this, too, seems wise. There may be almost as much danger of war being started by Seoul as by Pyongyang. As long as U.S. troops remain in South Korea, Seoul should not be sold sufficient aircraft to permit it to take independent military action without U.S. support.

3. *Internal Security and Human Rights.* For most of the years of the military aid program, a good deal of aid was justified on the ground that the United States had an interest in the internal stability of certain regimes. In almost all cases, this meant supporting repressive and dictatorial leaders. The character of the regime was overlooked in view of the overriding importance of stopping communism. As of now, however, Congress has mandated an aid cutoff to regimes that demonstrate a consistent pattern of gross violations of human rights.

Unless there are overriding considerations, sales should not be made to such regimes. In most instances (the Philippines and South Korea, for example), there are bound to be overriding considerations, and only nations of lesser importance (like Chile and Ethiopia) will be denied. Still, while human rights concerns often cannot be applied, they should not be ignored. Where sales are made, the relationship should be correct, not friendly.

4. *Alliance Relationship with Industrialized States.* The policy toward NATO allies and Japan is and should be virtually open-ended. The need is for standardization of arms and equipment. Many different brand and country names in NATO make for wasted billions of dollars and combat inefficiency. The administration has made some hesitant steps in this direction, and the steps cannot be much more than hesitant so long as the allies do not share a common world view and a common economy. Since neither is likely to eventuate, no major NATO ally is likely to entrust the whole or a part of a major weapons system to another.

For the time being, the administration has agreed to purchase parts of a new Main Battle Tank from Germany, a French-German-made Roland missile, and heavy machine guns from Belgium. The $2 billion sale of F-16s to four NATO countries provides a good model to go further. Belgium, the Netherlands, Denmark, and Norway will produce 40 per cent of the 348 F-16s they ordered for themselves, plus 10 per cent of the 650 ordered by the United States Air Force, and 15 per cent of all F-16s made for export. At the same time, however, each component produced in the four will also be made in the United States.

5. *The Strategic Balance of Power.* Some of the trickiest questions relate to making arms close to countries whose fates directly impact on the Soviet-American world balance. Most sales do not fit into this category. Those that do—like China, Yugoslavia, and, to listen to administration officials, some parts of Africa as well—are of the utmost importance.

Given the state of Soviet-American relations, any arms relationship with China would entangle the United States in explosive and complicated struggles between Peking and Moscow.[5] While there were some indications within the last two years of Chinese interest in American arms, Peking now emphatically states that it does not want to buy American. Nevertheless, Peking did show interest in buying sophisticated computers that could be used for military and civilian ends. The administration first denied the sales, principally because it would have led either to pressures to sell the same computers to Moscow or to being accused of choosing sides in the Sino-Soviet conflict. Finally, Kissinger agreed, in October 1976, to sell Peking two Cyber 172 computers as a gesture of support toward the post-Mao leadership.

There are legitimate grounds for concern that after President Tito dies, Yugoslavia will become an inviting target to Moscow. Soviet success in bringing Yugoslavia under control would have profound implications for all Europe. Because of Belgrade's anti-American role in the Third World, the administration has not dealt seriously with a pending Yugoslavian request for hundreds of millions of dollars of arms. Some of this equipment may be too sophisticated, but in general the United States should be more forthcoming in providing significant military support for Yugoslavia.   ·

The strategic rationale for the administration's new arms sales to Kenya and Zaire is laden with flypaper. The arms these nations need against local adversaries supplied by Moscow can be purchased from traditional suppliers in Western Europe. Kenya and Zaire have a short-term interest in dramatizing the Soviet threat to Africa in order to make new bonds with the United States. But the United States can safely rest its interests in Africa on the strength of its economic relationships. These arms sales would only have the effect of putting the United States in a position of having to make decisions about the future of these countries that it did not have to make before.

6. *Regional Balances of Power.* While the administration continues to justify sales to so-called potential regional superpowers on anti-Soviet grounds, the Soviet threat to most of these states is thin. The real reasons are to ensure access to resources, particularly oil, and to have general political influence. Sales levels to Brazil, Indonesia, and Nigeria have been modest. Iran and Saudi Arabia, however, raise special problems.

Sales to these two countries could turn into the functional equivalent of a treaty, not simply because of the volume of sales, but because of the secondary effects of the sales. The items sold have become so extensive and so sophisticated that in many cases they cannot be operated by the buyers. A recent staff report by the Senate Foreign Relations Committee concluded that Iran is now so heavily dependent on American personnel that it could not go to war "without U.S. support on a day-to-day basis." The report estimates that almost 20,000 Americans are now in Iran in a training capacity and projects 50,000 to 60,000 by 1980.

This might be called the white-collar mercenary phenomenon. After the weapons are delivered, American civilians arrive en masse to do the administering and training for up to 10 years. Under pressure from Congress to reduce military training missions abroad, the Pentagon has increasingly turned these tasks over to civilian contractors who are relatively immune from government control. These civilians could become willing comrades-in-arms or hostages as well as trainers. If Washington were to choose not to support the shah in a conflict of his choice, it would risk placing these Americans in jeopardy and risk rupturing relations with Teheran. If the shah found that his men could not use the weapons he bought, he is not likely to blame himself.

There is another problem attendant on the size of the sales. These nations could become storehouses for other nations. The administration tried to persuade Congress that the Saudis needed 2,000 Sidewinder air-to-air missiles and literally thousands of smart bombs, Maverick air-to-surface missiles, and TOW antitank missiles. The justification was Saudi Arabia's need to defend itself against a simultaneous attack by Iraq and Southern Yemen. The projected sales went far beyond the Saudis' needs, and thus raised the specter of massive transfers to other Arab states. And even though sales contracts stipulate that transfers to third parties require American approval, they are not so easily stopped.

Related to this are increasing pressures to grant licensing and co-production arrangements. Some such arrangements are inevitable with large volume sales and demands for greater self-sufficiency. But to license Iran to produce missiles like TOW and Maverick is surely beyond the pale.

7. *Conflict Resolution.* The idea of arming to parley has time-honored support in historical legend and scholarly articles but has to remain suspect nonetheless. There are few instances in this century where the acquisition of arms has produced fruitful negotiations. There are two recent examples of the link between the sale or denial of arms and peace.

On one side of the ledger is Turkey. In 1974, Congress banned further military aid to Turkey after that country used American arms illegally in intervening in Cyprus. The cutoff did not induce Ankara to settle the Cyprus problem. After pleas from the administration, the aid and sales were restored without any apparent change in Turkey's attitude. In this instance, there were factors that mattered more to Ankara than U.S. arms.

On the somewhat positive side of the ledger, the massive amount of arms Kissinger arranged to sell Israel and the security supporting assistance he provided for Egypt and Syria after the Yom Kippur war seem to have contributed to the first Arab-Israeli troop separation agreement and to the subsequent Egyptian-Israeli troop withdrawal agreement. For Israel, the added military capability constituted a trade-off for relinquishing territory. The arms also helped to make it politically palatable for Israeli leaders to negotiate and compromise.

8. *Base and Transit Rights.* Obtaining these rights used to be a major rationale for past grant military aid; but it may no longer be a compelling reason for special sales arrangements. The principal base-rights countries now place so many restrictions on American use that the whole policy of bases for aid requires review.

Greece and Turkey have progressively narrowed their views of acceptable American use of bases in their countries. U.S. aircraft could not use these bases, for example, in Middle East contingencies. The same was true for Spain. And in the new agreement with Spain, the United States is denied the use of Rota for nuclear submarines. There seems to be little quarrel with sales to Morocco in return for operating certain intelligence and command facilities. The terms of the ongoing base renewal negotiations with the Philippines are more complicated. President Marcos is said to be demanding somewhere in the neighborhood of $1 billion in grants and credit arms sales which he will employ against internal dissidents in return for continued use of Subic Bay and Clark Air Base. Subic Bay is still an important facility, and Marcos will get some support, but the question is how much and with what political costs for the United States.

9. *General Political Influence.* A good many sales are justified simply because they maintain political good will with foreign leaders and, in particular, good relations between foreign military establishments and the American military. As long as the proposed sales are not harmful for

other reasons, it is hard to argue against them. Sales to Latin-American nations rest on this rationale, and, with a few exceptions, the policy seems sensible.

A few brief observations can now be made about these nine considerations for arms sales and about the administration's recent experience with the arms sales program.

First, most of the sales were made for legitimate reasons. Even most of the sales of sophisticated equipment to Saudi Arabia and Iran seem justifiable. The Saudis needed a modern air force and bought F-5es, and Sidewinders go along with F-5es. The issue there was not whether, but how much. It probably is excusable to agree to sell Iran the new F-16, even though it made little sense to sell the F-14. The F-14 requires extensive use of American personnel for training and maintenance; the F-16 is relatively simple to maintain. It is difficult to take any one of these arguments against sales and turn it into a useful generalization because there are too many exceptions.

Second, Kissinger, following the policy of sell now and worry about the future later, has been quite careless about making those few but important exceptions that ought to have been made. He has made virtually open-ended arms commitments to states like Iran and Saudi Arabia. He has even made commitments to sell specific armaments—like Pershings to Israel and F-14s to Iran—without first subjecting these to any expert analysis. He seems to have consistently over-estimated the diplomatic leverage accruing to the United States from arms sales.

Third, arms sales gave the United States some, but not much, leverage on buyers. Again, while generalizations are tricky, the United States seems to have gotten better leverage from denials or threats to deny sales than by completing sales. Threats to deny sales appear to have convinced South Korea not to buy a reprocessing plant, to have persuaded Turkey not to invade Cyprus in 1964 and 1968, and perhaps made Israel more amenable to negotiations with Egypt. But most cases suggest only limited leverage. Just as the United States makes sales for its own reasons—and sometimes for shared purposes—countries buy and behave according to their own drummers.

Some Very Modest Proposals

The overall policy problem for the United States is how to make arms sales for its own good reasons and goals shared with those purchasing the weapons, without becoming entangled in the separate "good reasons" of the buyers. A short-run guide to preventing arms sales from degenerating into the functional equivalent of a treaty might look something like this:

Be Willing to Say No Sale. Future presidents and secretaries of state should not be enticed by the mindless argument that "if we don't sell, others will." If the sale is wrong, stop it, and there is even some chance that the buyer may not shop elsewhere. It is not by accident that the United States has cornered 50 per cent of the arms trade market. Nations may threaten to shop elsewhere, but they usually end up buying American. U.S. weapons, where they are not superior to their foreign competitors, have the added value of being backed by the U.S. government (most sales by other Western states are commercial) with reliable training missions and dependable spare parts. If countries buy from someone else nonetheless, they should be made to realize that they thereby jeopardize future sales relations with us. Congress has been more clear-sighted about this than the administration. Despite its failure to veto any sale, occasional threats by legislators to oppose certain sales have caused the administration to rethink and lower some of its requests. For example, the threat of a veto succeeded in getting the administration to reduce the number of Sidewinder missiles for Saudi Arabia from 2,000 to under 1,000.

Make the Purposes of the Sale Crystal Clear—to Buyers, to Congress, to the American people, and within the National Security Bureaucracy. Most administration rationales have been careless and catchall (to create self-sufficiency or to modernize forces) and misleading (to help protect Kenya against Uganda). Most of all, they make little effort to specify uses.

Be Prepared to Cut Off Supplies. If arms are used for purposes other than those specified, further shipments must be stopped. This is now required by law, but, since the purposes stated in the law are so vague and general and since Kissinger likes total flexibility, the law has not been effective. Kissinger's attack against Congress for applying the law to Turkey served only to further erode buyers' belief that we were serious. Both the United States and its customers must be clear about the penalties for violating trust and agreement.

Try to Avoid Becoming the Sole or Dominant Supplier. There are some instances, like Israel, where this is impossible, but in most cases, the United States should seek to multilateralize sales. Rather than seeking to drive out competitors (as in Saudi Arabia and Iran) or supplant them (as in Kenya and Zaire), we should actively encourage others to share in each buyer's market. This accomplishes several things. It diffuses American responsibility and American identification with a particular regime. It also makes it easier for an administration to cut the supply line if the purposes of the sale are ignored. We can then say that if France and Great Britain won't provide spare parts and ammunition for their tanks and artillery, we won't for our aircraft. Multilateralizing sales also fits with the desire of many buyers to diversify their sources of

supply—to reduce their dependency on and identification with the
United States—even as they continue to seek to buy most of their
weapons from the United States for the reasons previously stated.

Over the long run, the United States should do more than occasionally
exercise self-restraint. The arms trade market is virgin territory for
diplomacy. Administration officials have made only perfunctory efforts
at mitigating the future effects of arms sales for others and for us. They
have scoffed at proposals for suppliers' conferences and regional buyers'
conferences for multilateral restraint and have thereby condemned these
efforts to failure before trying them. The prospects for multilateral
restraint are not good; the desires to buy and the pressures to sell are
great. But future administrations should undertake sustained diplomacy to begin the dialogues, including continuing dialogues within
NATO on standardization.

Of equal importance, future administrations should begin talking to
the Russians about their arms sales objectives, and ours. It is shocking
that no such conversations have taken place about Soviet and American
sales to Africa and the Middle East. That many nations around the world
will engage in battle over local and regional disputes seems tragically
inevitable. That the United States and the Soviet Union persist in tying
their futures to these disputes through military aid and sales—without
even a hint of bilateral diplomacy—seems the height of foolishness.

As stated in the beginning of this article, arms sales is not a subject that
lends itself to broad-gauged solutions, or indeed even to satisfactory
solutions. Arms sales are an integral part of what the United States feels
it has to do and what it wants to achieve in different parts of the world.
Decisions to sell or not to sell will be no better than the policies that
embrace them. These policies should look to long-term effects and
should not be at the service of momentary tactical "needs."

Notes

1. Except where cited otherwise, all data is from U.S. Arms Control and
Disarmament Agency, *World Military Expenditures and Arms Trade 1963-73*
(Washington, D.C.: Government Printing Office, 1974); and U.S. Arms Control
and Disarmament Agency, *World Military Expenditures and Arms Trade
1965-74* (Washington, D.C.: Government Printing Office, 1976).

2. U.S., Congress, Senate, Committee on Appropriations, *Department of
Defense Appropriations, Fiscal Year 1976: Hearings*, Part 5, p. 198.

3. U.S., Congress, Senate, Committee on Appropriations, op. cit., pp. 222-
223.

4. Some conceptual liberties have been taken in compiling this list from the
one provided by Kissinger. For a list of considerations as stated by Kissinger and

the State Department, see U.S., Congress, House, Committee on International Relations, *International Security Assistance Act of 1976: Hearings,* p. 7 and p. 212.

5. For a different view, see Michael Pillsbury, "U.S.-Chinese Military Ties?" *Foreign Policy* 20.

Glossary

Absolute weapon: A weapons system of theoretically total and final effect likely to prevent any type of war.

Alliance or regionally oriented (related) systems: Nuclear systems, other than central systems, deployed by the United States and USSR to carry out responsibilities to their respective allies and to help maintain regional power balances. Used by the United States in preference to the Soviet term "forward-based systems (FBS)" to convey more accurately the notion that both the United States and USSR have deployed tactical nuclear-capable forces in support of their respective allies.

Antiballistic missile defense: All measures to intercept and destroy hostile ballistic missiles or otherwise neutralize them. Equipment includes weapons, target acquisition, tracking and guidance radars, plus ancillary installations.

Antiballistic missile (ABM)/interceptor missile: A defensive missile designed to intercept and destroy a strategic offensive ballistic missile or its payload. This term is used interchangeably with "ballistic missile defense interceptor missile." ABM interceptor missiles are generally divided into three classes: (1) those which attempt to destroy attacking missiles very early in their flight and before the attacking missiles deploy penetration aids, (2) those which attempt to destroy attacking ballistic missiles at relatively long range outside the atmosphere, and (3) those which attempt to destroy attacking missiles at relatively short range in the atmosphere (terminal interceptors). All Soviet ABM (Galosh) interceptor missiles employ nuclear warheads.

The deactivated Safeguard ABM system utilized two types of interceptor missiles: Spartan and Sprint. Spartan was a 55-foot, three-stage missile launched from an underground silo, with a long range, intended to destroy or disable attacking missiles beyond the atmosphere. Sprint was a 27-foot, two-stage missile launched from an underground silo, with a shorter range, intended for terminal defense against reentry vehicles in the atmosphere.

Antiballistic missile system: A system to counter strategic ballistic missiles or their elements in flight trajectory, currently consisting of three components: (1) ABM interceptor missiles, which are interceptor missiles constructed and deployed for an ABM role, or of a type tested in an ABM mode; (2) ABM launchers, which are launchers constructed for launching ABM interceptor missiles; and (3) ABM radars, which are radars constructed and deployed for an ABM role, or of a type tested in an ABM mode.

The Soviet Galosh site deployment around Moscow is the only ABM system currently activated. The U.S. Safeguard site at Grand Forks, North Dakota for the protection of ICBM silos has been deactivated. As a result of the ABM Treaty (1972), both the United States and the Soviet Union are limited to 100 ABM launchers and interceptors at one site. The treaty contains additional provisions which prohibit (1) establishment of a base for nationwide ABM defense and (2) giving non-ABM systems (missiles, launchers, or radars) the capability to counter strategic ballistic missiles. Prior to the deactivation of the Grand Forks site, the two major types of radars in the U.S. Safeguard system were perimeter acquisition radar (PARs) for long-range detection and missile site radars (MSRs) for precise, close-in target data. Both were electronically steerable, phased-array radars rather than the older mechanically steered type.

Arms control: Explicit or implicit international agreements that govern the numbers, types, characteristics, deployment, and use of armed forces and armaments.

Arms limitation: An agreement to restrict quantitative holdings of or qualitative improvements in specific armaments or weapons systems.

Arms race: A competitive relationship between two or more nations that results in weapons proliferation, an increase in the virulence of weapon-systems, and a quantitative and qualitative growth in the armed forces of those nations.

Arms stability: A strategic force relationship in which neither side perceives the necessity for undertaking major new arms programs in order to avoid being placed at a disadvantage.

Assured destruction: A highly reliable ability to inflict unacceptable damage on any aggressor or combination of aggressors at any time during the course of a nuclear exchange, even after absorbing a surprise first strike.

Atomic demolition munition: A nuclear device designed to be detonated on or below the ground surface or under water as a demolition munition.

Atoms for Peace plan: The Eisenhower proposal of 1957 calling for cooperation among the nuclear states and other nations to develop peaceful uses of atomic energy. The Atoms for Peace plan called for the establishment of an international agency to promote atomic cooperation and called on nuclear states to contribute to peaceful nuclear research by diverting fissionable material from their weapons stockpiles.

Balanced collective forces: The requirement for "balance" in any military forces stems from the consideration that all elements of a force should be complementary to each other. A force should function as a combined arms team, and the term "balance" implies that the ratio of the various elements of this team is such that the force is best constituted to execute its assigned mission effectively and efficiently. Applied multinationally, the term "balanced collective force" may be defined as a force comprised of one or more armed services furnished by more than one nation, the total strength and composition of which is such as best to fulfill the specific mission for which it is designed.

Balance of terror: A state of mutual deterrence between the superpowers based on their possession of weapons which permit either side to deliver a devastating blow to the other.

Ballistic missile defense: All measures to intercept and destroy hostile ballistic missiles or otherwise neutralize them. Equipment includes weapons, target acquisition, tracking and guidance radars, and ancillary installations.

Blitzkrieg: A fast-moving war waged for the purpose of gaining victory over the enemy in the shortest possible time, measured in days and weeks.

Containment: Measures to discourage or prevent the expansion of enemy territorial holdings and/or influence. Specifically, a U.S. policy directed against Communist expansion.

Controlled counterforce war: War in which one or both sides concentrate on reducing enemy strategic retaliatory forces in a bargaining situation and take special precautions to minimize collateral casualties and damage.

Controlled response: Response to a military attack by military action that is deliberately kept within certain definable limits for the purpose of avoiding all-out nuclear war.

Conventional pause: In the defense of Western Europe, a time period following an attack during which NATO would respond with conventional forces, rather than nuclear weapons, in order to assess the attacker's intentions and to consult among the Western allies. See also **Flexible response.**

Countercity strategy: Strategy of nuclear warfare implying that the attacker will strike at the enemy's population and industrial centers.

Counterforce: The employment of strategic air and missile forces to destroy or render impotent military capabilities of an enemy force. Bombers and their bases, ballistic missile submarines, ICBM silos, ABM and air defense installations, command and control centers, and nuclear stockpiles are typical counterforce targets.

Counterforce strike: Attack, thermonuclear or other, of a strategic nature, conducted with the aim of destroying an enemy's strategic means of attack and any other military installation pertaining to his offensive capabilities.

Counterforce strategy: Strategy specifying the targeting of enemy forces, particularly those which it could use in retaliation. At Ann Arbor in 1962, Secretary of Defense McNamara stated that, in the event of a nuclear war, the principal military objective should be the destruction of enemy military forces, not his civilian population.

Countervalue: The concepts, plans, weapons, and actions used to destroy or neutralize selected enemy population centers, industries, resources, and/or institutions. See also **Counterforce**.

Cruise missile: A pilotless aircraft, propelled by an air-breathing engine, that operates entirely within the earth's atmosphere. Thrust continues throughout its flight. In-flight guidance and control can be accomplished remotely or by onboard equipment. Conventional and nuclear warheads are available.

Although both the United States and the Soviet Union deploy cruise missiles, technological asymmetries separate the cruise missile systems of the two powers. In contrast to the American system, the Soviet SS-N-3 Shaddock (deployed on cruise missile carriers and Echo-class submarines) is a relatively inaccurate missile, propelled by an inefficient turbojet engine over a range not exceeding 550 nautical miles. The SS-N-12, the follow-on system to the Shaddock, measures, like the Shaddock, 40 feet in length and 6 feet in diameter. It is reportedly capable of ranges approaching 2000 nautical miles. See also **Tomahawk.**

CSCE (Conference on Security and Cooperation in Europe): The 1975 Conference on Security and Cooperation in Europe (held at Helsinki, Finland), in which 35 nations participated, produced agreements in three areas.

Basket I embodied a ten-point "Declaration of Principles" governing relations between participating states and from the Eastern perspective embodied the primary concern of the conference, security. While the Western participating states placed no particular emphasis on any of the "baskets," this section of the agreement did codify the postwar European status quo (in the absence of a postwar peace treaty) through the following principles: the inviolability of frontiers, territorial integrity, non-intervention [in participating states'] internal affairs, and the sovereign equality of states. The inclusion of Confidence-Building Measures (CBMs) in Basket I represents a significant contribution towards the lessening of politico-military tension in Central Europe.

Basket II provides for cooperation in the field of economics, science, technology, and the environment and should bring material benefits to both East and West through increased trade and commercial exchanges.

The provisions of *Basket III* represent the extension of improved East-West governmental relations into the following areas of interstate activity: human contracts, free information flows, increased cultural exchange, and educational cooperation.

Damage limitation: Active and/or passive efforts to restrict the level and/or geographic extent of devastation during war. Includes counterforce actions of all kinds as well as civil defense measures.

Détente: Lessening of tensions in international relations. May be achieved formally or informally.

Deterrence: Steps taken to prevent opponents from initiating armed actions and to inhibit escalation if combat occurs. Threats of force predominate.

Type I Deterrence. Deterrent power inhibiting a direct attack against the United States.

Type II Deterrence. Deterrent power inhibiting serious infractions short of attacks against the United States, i.e., aggression against friends and allies.

Type III Deterrence. Deterrent power inhibiting aggression by making limited provocations unprofitable.

Deterrence by denial: The Soviet conceptualization of deterrence is conceived on a denial basis. The Soviet Union deters another power (by developing a disarming and damage-limiting capability) from a first strike by convincing the opponent that no military gain could accrue by striking first. Essentially a counterforce posture.

Deterrence by punishment: The American conception of nuclear deterrence, based on a capacity to survive a nuclear first strike and to inflict unacceptable damage on the aggressor in a retaliatory (second) strike. Although military advantages accrue to the nation which strikes first, it is deterred from such action by the knowledge of the unacceptable damage it would suffer in a retaliatory blow.

Deterrent: The sum total of those policies and capabilities which, because of the threat of unacceptable damage, deter the opponent from military aggression.

Equivalent megatonnage (EMT): A measure used to compare the destructive potential of differing combinations of nuclear warhead yields against relatively soft countervalue targets. EMT is a computed function of yield (given in megatons) which compensates approximately for the fact that blast damage resulting from a nuclear detonation does not increase linearly with an increase in yield. EMT calculations are useful in estimating the effects of small numbers of smaller-yield warheads against the same targets.

EMT is computed from the expression: $EMT = N\ Y^x$, where $N =$ number of actual warheads of yield Y; $Y =$ yield of the actual warheads, in megatons; and $x =$ scaling factor. Scaling factors vary with the size and characteristics of the target base and the number of targets attacked.

Firebreak: A psychological barrier that inhibits escalation from one type of warfare to another, as from conventional to nuclear combat.

First strike: The launching of an initial strategic nuclear attack before the opponent has used any strategic weapons himself.

First-Strike strategy: Strategy based on the notion that only by striking first can a nuclear power gain the advantage and prevent defeat.

Flexible response: A strategy predicated on capabilities to act effectively across the entire spectrum of war at times, at places, and in manners of the user's choosing.

Foreign policy: Foreign policy comprises the totality of purposes and international commitments by which a nation through its constitutional or otherwise designated authority seeks by means of influence, power, and sometimes violence to deal with foreign states and problems in the international environment.

Forward-based systems (FBS): A term introduced by the USSR to refer to those U.S. nuclear systems based in third countries or on aircraft carriers and capable of delivering a nuclear strike against the territory of the USSR. The Soviet Union took the position in both SALT I and early in SALT II that U.S. tactical forces capable of delivering nuclear strikes against the territory of the USSR had to be included in any permanent agreements on strategic arms; however, it was agreed at Vladivostok (1974) that FBS would not be a SALT issue.

Forward defense: Protective measures taken to contain and/or repulse military aggression as close to the original line of contact as possible.

Hard target: A point or area protected to some significant degree against the blast, heat, and radiation effects of nuclear explosions of particular yields.

Heavy bomber: A multi-engine aircraft with intercontinental range, designed specifically to engage targets whose destruction would reduce an enemy's capacity and/or will to wage war.

Heavy ICBM: The 1972 SALT I Interim Agreement on the limitation of selected strategic offensive offensive systems identified heavy ICBMs as those having a volume significantly greater than that of the largest light ICBM. The U.S. Titan II and the Soviet SS-7, SS-8, SS-9, SS-18, and SS-19 are heavy ICBMs.

Intercontinental ballistic missile (ICBM): A land-based, rocket-propelled vehicle capable of delivering a warhead to intercontinental ranges (ranges in excess of about 3000 nautical miles). Agreed interpretations of the SALT I agreement define ICBM as strategic ballistic missiles capable of ranges in excess of the shortest distance between the northeastern border of the continental United States and the northwestern border of the continental USSR (about 3000 nm).

ICBMs fly to a target on an eliptical trajectory outside the atmosphere. The missile is guided during the initial powered phase of the trajectory with the altitude, bearing, and velocity setting the missile on a programmed course to an apogee and then descending to target. Terminal guidance can be provided for the reentry system.

An ICBM consists of a booster stage, one or more sustainer propulsion stages, a reentry vehicle(s), possibly penetration aids, and, in the case of a MIRVed missile, a post-boost vehicle. The U.S. Minuteman III and the Soviet SS-11 are examples of ICBMs.

Intermediate-range bomber aircraft: A bomber designed for a tactical operating radius of between 1,000 to 2,500 nautical miles at design gross weight and design bomb load.

Maneuvering reentry vehicle (MARV): A ballistic missile reentry vehicle equipped with its own navigation and control systems capable of adjusting its trajectory during reentry into the atmosphere. The advantages of MARV are two-fold. First, the onboard guidance and control systems give some types of MARVs a greater ultimate potential for accuracy due to corrections in the terminal reentry phase. Such accuracy may be essential if the intent is to strike key targets while avoiding or minimizing collateral damage. Second, one type of MARV has high maneuverability and thus the inherent ability to evade terminal ABM defense interceptor missiles.

Manhattan Project: The War Department program during World War II that produced the first atomic bombs. The term originated in the code-name, "Manhattan Engineer District," which was used to conceal the nature of the secret work underway. The Atomic Energy Commission, a civilian agency, succeeded the military unit January 1, 1947.

Massive retaliation: The act of countering aggression of any type with tremendous destructive power, particularly, a crushing nuclear response to any provocation deemed serious enough to warrant military action. The doctrine was first set forth by Secretary of State John Foster Dulles in an address delivered on January 12, 1954. This doctrine, essentially seen by many as a cost-cutting measure, was part of the Eisenhower Administration's "New Look" approach to defense.

Means: Money, manpower, material, and other resources converted into capabilities that contribute to the accomplishment of national securities aims.

Medium-range ballistic missile: This term usually refers to a ballistic missile with a range capability from about 600 to 1500 nautical miles. The United States has no MRBMs. The Soviet SS-4 is an example of an MRBM.

Megaton weapon: A nuclear weapon the yield of which is measured in terms of millions of tons of TNT equivalents. (One million tons of TNT=1,000 kilotons.)

Military cybernetics: In Soviet usage a military-technical science which is a branch of cybernetics. Military cybernetics deals with the structure and laws of operation of systems for the control of troops and weapons, and also defines the tactical technical requirements which the technological equipment of such systems must meet.

Minimum deterrence: Deterrent strategy based on the possession of a small and limited strategic nuclear capability yet sufficient to deter any nuclear power from rational attack since the penalty for aggression would be unacceptable.

Mini-nukes: Small tactical nuclear weapons of yields as low as .01 kilotons. These weapon systems are fitted with precision guidance systems and target deliverable with a CEP of almost zero.

Minuteman: A three-stage solid-propellant second-generation intercontinental ballistic missile equipped with a nuclear warhead, designed for deployment in a hardened and dispersed configuration and in a mobile mode on railroad trains. It is a simpler, smaller, lighter missile than earlier **intercontinental ballistic missiles** and is designed for highly automated remote operation. Designated as LGM-30. See also **Hard target, Intercontinental ballistic missile (ICBM), Mobile missile.**

Missile: A non-manned delivery vehicle which can be guided after having left the launching base, during part or the whole of its trajectory. Strategic missiles are classified as follows: intercontinental ballistic missile (ICBM); intermediate range ballistic missile (IRBM); medium-range ballistic missile (MRBM); submarine-launched ballistic missile (SLBM); and modern large ballistic missile (MLBM).

MK-12A: A higher yield, more accurate warhead designed to replace the MK-12 warhead presently deployed on Minutemen III missiles. MK-12A warheads may also be deployed on M-X ICBMs and Trident II SLBMs.

Mobile Missile: Any ballistic or *cruise missile* mounted on and/or fired from a movable platform, such as a truck, train, ground effects machine, ship, or aircraft.

Modern large ballistic missile: An intercontinental ballistic missile (ICBM) of a type deployed since 1964 and having a volume significantly greater than the largest light ICBM operational in 1972 (the Soviet SS-11). The United States has no MLBMs. The Soviet SS-9 (deployed) and the SS-18 (under development) are MLBMs.

Multiple independently targetable reentry vehicle (MIRV): Two or more reentry vehicles carried by a single missile and capable of being independently targeted. A MIRVed missile employs a "bus" or other warhead dispensing mechanism. The dispensing mechanism maneuvers to achieve successive desired positions and velocities to dispense each RV on a trajectory to attack the desired targets. Thus the reentry vehicles are aimed at separate targets over a large geographical area called the MIRVed missile's footprint. The exact size of the footprint depends on a number of detailed factors including the amount of propellant in the dispenser (bus) and the time period over which individual RVs are dispensed. U.S. MIRV missiles currently deployed are the Minuteman III ICBM and the Poseidon (C-3) SLBM. The Soviet Union is known to be testing several types of MIRV ICBMs.

Mutual and Balanced Force Reductions: The Mutual and Balanced Force Reductions (MBFR) negotiations have been in progress in Vienna since November 1973. These negotiations are considering proposals for exchanges of information and real reductions and limitations of forces.

The NATO nations directly participating in these talks are Belgium, Canada, the Federal Republic of Germany, Luxembourg, the Netherlands, the United Kingdom, and the United States. Warsaw Pact direct participants are Czechoslovakia, the German Democratic Republic, Poland, and the Soviet Union. Direct participants are

those states which have forces in the geographic area to be covered—
the so-called "reductions area." This includes the territory of the
Federal Republic of Germany, the German Democratic Republic,
the Benelux countries, Poland, and Czechoslovakia.

Eight other nations are also participating—Denmark, Greece,
Italy, Norway, and Turkey on the Western side; and Bulgaria, Romania, and Hungary on the Eastern side. However, forces in the territory
of these nations would not be reduced although the Western side
has reserved its right to address the status of forces in Hungary
further.

At the outset of the negotiations, the Western side provided its
estimate of major disparities favoring the Warsaw Pact in geography,
manpower, and the structure and equipment of opposing forces.

Accordingly, the NATO Allies have proposed to the East that the
final outcome of the reduction process be approximate parity in the
form of a common collective ceiling on the overall ground and air
manpower of each side and that the major imbalance in tanks be
diminished at the outset. The common ceiling, according to the
Western proposal, would be reached through two phases of reductions. The first phase would result in reduction of a Soviet tank
army of 68,000 men and 1,700 tanks and reduction of 29,000
U.S. ground force personnel. The 1,000 U.S. nuclear warheads,
54 F-4 Phantom nuclear-capable aircraft, and 36 Pershing surface-to-
surface missile launchers would also be reduced as part of the first
phase of reductions.

All the direct participants would join in a second phase of
reductions to achieve the common collective ceiling on forces in the
reductions area. The West has indicated that this ceiling might,
illustratively, be set at about 700,000 men in ground forces and
900,000 in air and ground forces combined.

To maintain undiminished security while increasing stability,
other measures associated with the reductions would be needed.
These include measures to verify compliance and safeguards to
assure that forces withdrawn from the central region are not used
to increase the threat to nations on the northern and southern
flanks.

In addition, the West has proposed other measures such as
prior notification of troop movements. These proposed measures are
intended to diminish the risk of miscalculation and to reduce
ambiguities about the activities of forces remaining after reductions
have been completed.

The initial Eastern approach in the MBFR talks was essentially to propose equal percentage reductions—a reduction of about 17 percent in ground and air forces and their armaments, including nuclear weapons, of all direct participants. The reductions would be carried out in three stages of about 2 percent, 5 percent, and finally 10 percent.

The Western nations opposed this Eastern approach to reductions, since it would have implicitly codified in an international agreement the major source of concern to NATO in Central Europe—the disparity in ground forces, particularly in tanks. And the Eastern proposal would have even tended to aggravate that imbalance if accepted.

In February 1976, the Eastern negotiators presented a new proposal. This proposal provided for reduction of U.S. and Soviet troops in a first stage, with the other participants freezing their forces until they are reduced in a second stage. This new proposal appears to retain many of the basic deficiencies of the original Eastern approach. In particular, the proposed manpower and equipment reductions do not eliminate, or even reduce, the disparities in ground force personnel and in tanks. Major differences remain between the Eastern and Western positions, but the discussions are being continued.

Mutual assured destruction: A condition in which an assured destruction capability is possessed by opposing sides.

Mutual deterrence: A stable situation in which two or more countries or coalitions of countries are inhibited from attacking each other because the casualties and/or damage resulting from retaliation would be unacceptable.

M-X: The M-X is being developed as the next generation of U.S. ICBMs. It would provide enhanced survivability and increased capability. The M-X is currently planned to have approximately four times greater throw-weight, significantly greater accuracy, and more numerous, higher-yield warheads than Minuteman III. These characteristics are expected to give each M-X warhead a very high probability of destroying very hard targets. The M-X is also being designed to permit deceptive mobile basing, sometimes called the "shell game." This involves the random movement of missiles and launch control facilities among hardened above-ground shelters or in hardened covered trenches. The ultimate deployment scheme has not yet been selected, but the trench concept appears to be the preferred candidate. Mobile basing for the M-X is expected to improve the survivability of the system significanlty over fixed-based ICBMs. It would require the Soviets to attack all shelters or trench areas in which the M-X could possibly be. To conduct such an attack, the Soviets would have to expend more ICBMs than the number of M-X they would destroy. This reduces the Soviet incentive to attack the system.

Parity: A condition in which opposing forces possess capabilities of certain kinds that are approximately equal in over-all effectiveness.

PGM (Precision Guidance Munitions): These weapon systems are successors to older surface-to-air missiles such as the Navy's radar-guided Terrier and the Soviet infra-red homing SA-2. The acronym PGM refers to bombs, missiles, and artillery projectiles with single-shot kill probabilities from ten to one hundred times greater than unguided munitions. This increase in accuracy is made possible by new guidance technologies which reduce the Circular Error Probable of delivery vehicles to 20 meters or less.

Plowshare: The Atomic Energy Commission program of research and development on peaceful uses of nuclear explosives.

Polaris: U.S. submarines that carry the first generation of submarine-launched Polaris missiles. Each submarine can carry 16 missiles. Expected to be phased out in the early 1980's.

Reentry vehicle: That portion of a ballistic missile designed to carry a nuclear warhead and to reenter the earth's atmosphere in the terminal portion of the missile trajectory.

Sea control: The employment of naval forces, supplemented by land and aerospace forces as appropriate, to destroy enemy naval forces, suppress enemy oceangoing commerce, protect vital shipping lanes, and establish local superiority in areas of naval operations.

Sea-launched cruise missile (SLCM): A cruise missile capable of being launched from a submerged or surfaced submarine or from a surface ship. The U.S. SLCM under development is sized for launch from standard submarine torpedo tubes, and thus could be carried by SSBNs or SSNs. The SLCM is to be developed in both strategic and tactical variants, the former being able to carry a nuclear warhead about 1500 nm. The latter will be designed to be launched from surface ships as well as submarines, primarily as a non-nuclear anti-ship missile with a range of up to several hundred miles. The SLCM will have a low cruise altitude flight profile and will have a high accuracy. The Soviet Union currently has SLCMs of a shorter range deployed on both nuclear- and diesel-powered submarines and surface ships.

Second strike: A term usually used to refer to a retaliatory attack in response to a first strike. A high-confidence second-strike (retaliatory) capability is the primary basis for nuclear deterrence. To provide this capability U.S. forces have been structured on the basis of well-hedged assumptions regarding force survivability following an enemy first strike and the level of retaliatory destruction needed.

Options for second strike include attacks on cities, industrial facilities, and military installations.

Second-strike strategy: The employment of strategic nuclear weapons only in reprisal for a nuclear first strike by the enemy. This strategy implies a capability sufficiently large and invulnerable to sustain an enemy first strike with residual forces available to inflict unacceptable levels of destruction.

Silo: Underground facility for a hard-site ballistic missile and/or crew, designed to provide prelaunch protection against nuclear effects.

Single Integrated Operational Plan (SIOP): The strategic nuclear war plan of the United States.

Soft target: A target not protected against the blast, heat, and radiation produced by nuclear explosions. There are many degrees of softness. Some missiles and aircraft, for example, are built in ways that ward off certain effects, but they are "soft" in comparison with shelters and silos.

Strategic Arms Limitation Talks:

SALT I: The first SALT agreements were signed in May 1972, following two and a half years of negotiations. The ABM Treaty and the supplementary Protocol of 1974 limit ABM systems to one site on each side, with low limits on the number of permitted ABM interceptor missiles and radars. This Treaty is of unlimited duration, and every five years is subjected to review by the two sides. The first such review took place in 1977.

The ABM Treaty reflected a decision on the part of both the United States and the Soviet Union to avoid a massive arms race in ballistic missile defenses that in the end could not prevent destruction of both societies in a nuclear attack. Had the United States and the Soviet Union gone ahead with plans to deploy ABM systems, both nations would also have built more numerous weapons to insure penetration of these defenses, with consequent reduced stability, heightened political and military tensions, and substantially greater costs.

The Interim Agreement on offensive weapons froze for five years the numbers of ICBM and SLBM launchers to the number operational or under construction at the time of signature of the agreement. The five-year duration of the Interim Agreement expired on October 3, 1977. Given the substantial progress toward a SALT II agreement and in order to maintain the status quo while the negotiations are being completed, the United States issued a statement indicating its intention not to take any action inconsistent with the provisions of the Interim Agreement or with the goals of the ongoing negotiations. The Soviet Union issued a similar statement expressing the same intentions.

SALT II: The SALT II negotiations began in November 1972. The primary goal of SALT II was the achievement of a comprehensive agreement limiting strategic offensive arms to replace the Interim Agreement. Early discussion between the sides covered a variety of issues, including the systems to be addressed, the means of establishing equality in strategic nuclear forces, as well as specific quantitative and qualitative limits. The positions of the sides differed widely on many of these questions, however, and only limited progress was made.

A major breakthrough occurred at the Vladivostok meeting in November 1974 between President Ford and General Secretary Brezhnev when they agreed on basic guidelines for a SALT II agreement. The key elements were: (1) the duration of the new agreement would be through 1985; (2) the sides would be limited to equal aggregate totals of 2,400 strategic nuclear delivery vehicles; (3) the sides would be limited to 1,320 MIRVed (multiple independently targetable reentry vehicles) systems; (4) forward-based systems (i.e., nuclear-capable U.S. systems based in Europe such as fighter-bombers) would not be included. The principle of equal aggregate totals was a major U.S. objective for SALT II and a particularly significant achievement of the Vladivostok accord.

The delegations in Geneva resumed negotiations working toward an agreement based on this general framework. During these negotiations, however, it became clear that there were serious disagreements between the two sides on two major issues: the limits on cruise missiles, and whether a new Soviet bomber known as Backfire was to be considered a strategic heavy bomber and therefore counted in the 2,400 aggregate. While progress was made in other, less contentious areas, the negotiations reached a stalemate on these issues. Discussion continued on other issues, including MIRV verification provisions, bans on new strategic weapons, definitions, and missile throw-weight limitations.

Early in 1977, the Carter administration, in its desire to reach significant strategic arms limitations, undertook a detailed interagency review of unresolved SALT issues. On the basis of this review, it was decided to build on the elements agreed to at Vladivostok by adding significant reductions in strategic arms and by emphasizing limits on those elements in strategic arsenals which are most destabilizing.

These basic considerations were embodied in the comprehensive proposal which was presented to the Soviets by Secretary of State Vance and Ambassador Warnke in Moscow last March. This proposal called for major cuts in the Vladivostok ceilings, as well as limits on the number of land-based ICBMs equipped with MIRVs and the number of very large, or "heavy," ICBMs. The proposal also called for restrictive limits on the testing and deployment of new types of ICBMs.

At this Moscow meeting, the United States also offered an alternative deferral proposal under which the SALT II agreement would be based upon the Vladivostok numbers, with resolution of the Backfire bomber and cruise missile issues to be deferred until SALT III. Both proposals were rejected by the Soviets on the grounds that they were inconsistent with their understanding of what was agreed to at Vladivostok.

SALT II agreement framework: In further negotiations in May, Secretary of State Vance and Ambassador Warnke reached agreement with Foreign Minister Andrei Gromyko on a general framework for SALT II which accommodated both the Soviet desire for retaining the Vladivostok guidelines and the U.S. desire for more comprehensive limitations. The agreed SALT II framework has three principal elements: (1) a treaty lasting until 1985, based on the Vladivostok guidelines; (2) a protocol which would on an interim basis deal with remaining contentious issues not ready for long-term resolution; and (3) a statement of principles for SALT III.

The SALT II treaty will establish equal limits for the Soviet Union and the United States on each side's aggregate number of strategic nuclear delivery vehicles—ICBMs, SLBMs, and heavy bombers. The numerical level specified in the treaty will be the same as the level agreed to at Vladivostok, with provision for reduction to a lower level.

Specifically, the treaty includes the following major provisions: (1) an initial aggregate level of 2,400 strategic systems, to be reduced to an agreed number between 2,160 and 2,250 during the term of the treaty; (2) a 1,320 sublimit on MIRVed ICBM and SLBM launchers and aircraft equipped with long-range cruise missiles; (3) a sublimit of an agreed number between 1,200 and 1,250 on MIRVed ballistic missiles; (4) a sublimit of 820 of MIRVed ICBM launchers.

Within the numerical limits set by the Treaty, each side may determine its own force structure. In other words, the sides would have "freedom to mix" among these strategic systems. This combination of equal numerical limits, with the freedom to choose the force mix within overall ceilings, resolves the otherwise difficult problem of providing for equivalence given differences in the composition of U.S. and Soviet strategic forces.

The treaty's subceilings on MIRVed ballistic missiles and on ICBMs equipped with MIRVs will place an upper limit on the deployment of the most threatening of the Soviet strategic weapons.

In addition, the treaty will include detailed definitions, restrictions on certain new strategic systems, and provisions designed to improve verification.

Certain issues not ready for longer term resolution, such as restrictions on new types of ICBMs, cruise missiles, and mobile ICBMs, will be included in the protocol. These issues will be topics for discussion in SALT III.

Specifically, the proposed protocol includes the following provisions: (1) a ban on deployment of mobile ICBM launchers and on the flight testing of ICBMs from such launchers; (2) limitations on the flight testing and deployment of new types of ballistic missiles; (3) a ban on the flight testing and deployment of cruise missiles capable of a range in excess of 2,500 km, and on the deployment of cruise missiles capable of a range in excess of 600 km on sea- or land-based launchers.

The third element of the SALT II package will be a Joint Statement of Principles for SALT III. These agreed upon principles will serve as a general guidance for the next stage of SALT. The principles will include commitments to further reductions, more comprehensive qualitative constraints on new systems, and provisions to improve verification.

Strategic nuclear sufficiency: A term used by U.S. strategic planners to denote a posture in which the United States possesses a nuclear capability able to: (1) maintain an adequate second-strike capability, (2) provide no incentive for the Soviet Union to strike the United States first in a crisis, and (3) prevent the Soviet Union from gaining the ability to cause considerably greater urban/industrial destruction than the United States could inflict on the USSR in a nuclear war.

Strategic nuclear weapons systems: Offensive nuclear weapons systems designed to be employed against enemy targets with the purpose of effecting the destruction of the enemy's political/economic/military capacity and defensive nuclear weapons systems designed to counteract these systems.

Strategic sufficiency: A force structure standard that demands capabilities adequate to attain desired ends without undue waste. Superiority thus is essential in some circumstances; parity/essential equivalence suffices under less demanding conditions; and inferiority, qualitative as well as quantitative, is sometimes acceptable.

Strategy of minimum deterrence: Essentially a countercity strategy that targets a limited number of countervalue targets with a limited number of invulnerable strategic nuclear weapons on the belief that such a threat will be sufficient to deter aggression.

Surface-to-surface missile (SSM): A surface-launched missile designed to attack targets on the surface. Pershing and Lance are examples of U.S. tactical, land-based nuclear SSMs. Their Soviet counter-

counterparts are SCUD and FROG. Naval SSMs include the U.S. Harpoon (non-nuclear) and the Soviet Styx and Shaddock missiles.

Tactical airlift: Transport aircraft (military only in the United States) used to move armed forces, equipment, and supplies expeditiously within theaters of operation.

Tactical nuclear delivery vehicles: Nuclear delivery vehicles designed to be employed against enemy targets in a limited conflict. Usually relating to vehicles of shorter range than those which are necessary for the conduct of strategic operations.

Tactical nuclear weapon forces or operations: Nuclear combat power expressly designed for deterrent, offensive, and defensive purposes that contributes to the accomplishments of localized military missions; the threatened or actual application of such power. U.S. tactical nuclear delivery systems are concentrated in general-purpose land- and carrier-based figher-attack aircraft and tube artillery. The Soviets deploy cruise and ballistic missiles, the Backfire bomber being their latest generation tactical aircraft.

Threshold: An intangible and adjustable line between levels and types of conflicts, such as the separation between nuclear and non-nuclear warfare. The greater the reluctance to use nuclear weapons, the higher the threshold.

Throw-weight: Ballistic missile throw-weight is the maximum useful weight that has been flight tested on the boost stages of the missile. The useful weight includes weight of the reentry vehicles, penetration aids, dispensing and releasing mechanisms, reentry shrouds, covers, buses, and propulsion devices with their propellants (but not the final boost stages) which are present at the end of the boost phase.

Titan: A liquid-propellant, two-stage, rocket-powered intercontinental ballistic missile equipped with a nuclear warhead. Designated as HGM-25, it is guided by radio-inertial guidance. The LCN-25C, an improved version of the HGM-25, is guided by all-inertial guidance and equipped with a higher-yield warhead. The system is for deployment in a hardened and dispersed configuration.

TNT equivalent: A measure of the energy released from the detonation of a nuclear weapon, or from the explosion of a given quantity of fissionable or fusionable material, in terms of the amount of trinitrotoluene (TNT) that would release the same amount of energy when exploded.

Tomahawk cruise missile: There are two versions of the Tomahawk missile: a shorter-range, conventionally-armed, anti-shipping missile and a longer-range, nuclear-armed missile to attack land targets. Both versions use the same cylindrical airframe to permit launching from a torpedo tube. This design is also readily adaptable to launching from surface ships, ground platforms, or aircraft. The nuclear-armed Tomahawk is not currently planned to have a strategic nuclear role, except insofar as it would constitute an ultimate strategic nuclear reserve. Rather, it is apparently conceived as a theater nuclear weapon intended by the United States for use against targets outside the Soviet Union, such as in Eastern Europe. This mission would not require the launching ships to be continuously available to deliver nuclear strikes and so would not impair their conventional operations.

The only strategic nuclear application for Tomahawk that is currently contemplated is the possibility of an air-launched version (Tomahawk air-launched cruise missile or TALCM). While the TALCM is the only version of the Tomahawk currently envisaged for a strategic role, sea- or land-launched versions of this weapon could always be adapted to strategic nuclear missions if desired. The sea-launched nuclear capable Tomahawk is 20 feet long and 21 inches in diameter and fits into standard submarine torpedo tubes. See also **Cruise missile**.

Triad: The term used in referring to the basic structure of the U.S. strategic deterrent force. It is comprised of land-based ICBMs, the strategic bomber force, and the Polaris/Poseidon submarine fleet. The U.S. Triad of forces evolved from an allocation of national resources and priorities in order to meet certain strategic objectives, the most important of which was the capability to deter nuclear conflict.

Each element of the Triad relies on somewhat different means for survival; hence, an enemy's potential for a successful first-strike attack is severely complicated. Bombers rely on warning, fast reaction, and ground or air-borne dispersal for survival; ICBMs are placed in individual hardened silos for survivability; SLBMs depend on the uncertainty of location of the submarine to enhance survivability.

Truman Doctrine: The provision of American military and economic aid to those nations (initially Greece) resisting Soviet aggression and expansion. The foundation for American containment policy.

Verification: The process of determining the degree to which parties to an agreement are complying with provisions of the agreement. The verification of arms control may be said to have three distinct purposes.

First, verification serves to detect violations of an agreement (or to provide evidence that violations may have occurred) and hence to furnish, as far as is possible, timely warning of any threat to the nation's security arising under a treaty regime.

Second, by increasing the risk of detection and complicating any scheme of evasion, verification helps to deter violations of an agreement. The deterrent value of verification depends to a considerable extent on a potential violator being ignorant of the exact capability of the intelligence techniques used to monitor his compliance with an agreement—a fact which helps to explain the importance of secrecy regarding many of these techniques.

Third, verification serves to build domestic and international confidence in the viability of an arms control agreement. By providing evidence that the parties to an agreement are in fact fulfilling the obligations they have assumed, verification contributes to mutual trust among the parties and helps to create a political environment necessary for further progress in arms control. At the same time, it provides an important safeguard against wishful illusions and against possible manipulation of an atmosphere of trust in the pursuit of unilateral advantage.

War-fighting strategy: A strategy designed primarily to fight any kind of war at any level in the conflict spectrum (as opposed to deterrence strategies, which are designed to prevent wars).

Warhead: That part of a missile, projectile, torpedo, rocket, or other munition which contains either the nuclear or thermonuclear system, high-explosive system, chemical or biological agents, or inert materials intended to inflict damage.

Appendixes

Appendix A:
Chronology of Arms Control and
Disarmament Agreements

Geneva Protocol
Protocols for the Prohibition of the Use in War of Asphyxiating, Poisonous or Other Gases, and of Bacteriological Methods of Warfare. Signed in 1925: entered into force, 1928.

The Antarctic Treaty
Prohibits Any Military Use of the Region. Signed, December 1959; ratified by United States, August 18, 1960; entered into force, June 1961.

"HOTLINE" Agreement
Established a direct communications link between the United States and the U.S.S.R. Signed and entered into force, June 1963.

Limited Test Ban Treaty
Bans nuclear weapons tests in the atmosphere, in outer space, and under water. Entered into force, October 1963.

Outer Space Treaty
Governs the activities of states in the exploration and use of outer space, including the moon and other celestial bodies. Signed, January 1967; entered into force, October 1967.

Treaty For the Prohibition of Nuclear Weapons in Latin America
Signed at Tlatelolco, Mexico February 1967; entered into force, April 1968. Additions to the Tlatelolco Treaty were signed by the United States in April 1968; ratified with understandings and declarations by the United States, May 1971.

Non-Proliferation Treaty
Treaty on the non-proliferation of nuclear weapons. Signed, July, 1968; entered into force through U.S. ratification, March 1970.

Seabed Arms Control Treaty
Treaty on the prohibition of the emplacement of nuclear weapons and other weapons of mass destruction on the seabed and the ocean floor and its subsoil. Signed, February 1971; entered into force through U.S. ratification, May 1972.

"Accidents Measures" Agreement
Agreement to reduce the risk of outbreak of nuclear war between the United States and the Soviet Union. Entered into force, September 30, 1971.

"Hotline" Modernization Agreement
Agreement between the United States and the Soviet Union on measures to improve the U.S.A.-U.S.S.R. direct communications link. Entered into force, September 30, 1971.

Biological Weapons Convention
Convention prohibiting the development, production, and stockpiling of bacteriological (biological) and toxin weapons. Signed at Washington, London, Moscow, April 10, 1972.

ABM Treaty
Treaty between the United States and the Soviet Union on the limitation of antiballistic missile systems. Signed at Moscow, May 16, 1972. Entered into force through U.S. ratification, October 3, 1972.

Interim Agreement (SALT I)
Interim Agreement between the United States and the Soviet Union on limitation of strategic offensive arms. Signed at Moscow, May 26, 1972. Entered into force through U.S. ratification, October 3, 1972.

ABM Protocol
Protocol to the treaty between the United States and the Soviet Union on the limitation of antiballistic missile systems. Signed at Moscow, July 3, 1974. Entered into force, May 24, 1976.

Prevention of Nuclear War
Agreement between the United States and the Soviet Union relating to cooperative relations. Entered into force, June 22, 1973.

Threshold Test Ban and Protocol
Treaty between the United States and the Soviet Union and Protocol to the Treaty on Underground Nuclear Explosions for Peaceful Purposes. Signed at Moscow, July 3, 1974.

Underground PNE Ban and Protocol
Treaty between the United States and the Soviet Union and Protocol to
the Treaty on Underground Nuclear Explosions for Peaceful Purposes.
Signed in Washington, Moscow on May 28, 1976.

Environmental Modification Ban
Convention prohibiting hostile use of environmental modification
techniques. Signed in Geneva, May 18. 1977.

Appendix B:
U.S.-Soviet Strategic
Nuclear Balance

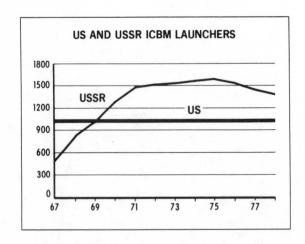

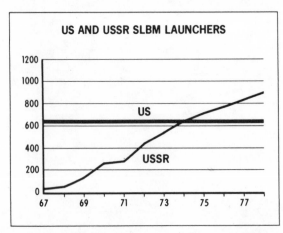

Source: U.S. Arms Control and Disarmament Agency. *Army Control 1977,* ACDA Publication 96, May 1978.

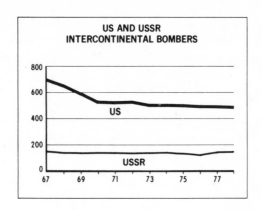

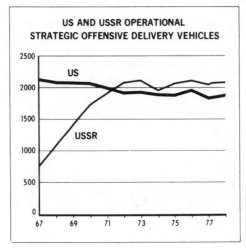

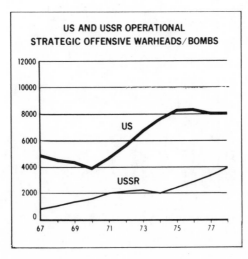

TABLE 1

U.S. STRATEGIC NUCLEAR FORCES: PRESENT FORCE

Launcher	Number	Warheads per Launcher	Total Warheads	Yield in Megatons	Total Megatons	Equivalent Megatons	Reliability	Circular Error Probable
Minuteman II	450	1	450	1.0	450.0	450	0.80	1,800 ft.
Minuteman III	550	3	1,650	0.17	280.5	512	0.80	700 ft.
Titan II	54	1	54	9.0	486.0	232	0.75	3,000 ft.
Total ICBMs	1,054		2,154		1,216.5	1,194		
Polaris	160	1	160	0.6	96	163	0.80	3,000 ft.
Poseidon	496	10	4,960	0.04	198	595	0.80	1,500 ft.
Total SLBMs	656		5,120		294	758		
B-52 G/H	255	4 SRAM	1,020	0.2	204	347		
		4 Bombs	1,020	1.0	1,020	1,020		
B-52D	75	4 Bombs	300	1.0	300	300		
		2 SRAM	120	0.2	24	41		
FB-111	60	2 Bombs	120	1.0	120	120		
Total Bombers	390		2,580		1,668	1,828		
Grand Total	2,100		9,854		3,178.5	3,780		

Source: Congress of the United States, Congressional Budget Office. Counterforce Issues for the U.S. Strategic Nuclear Forces. Background Paper, January 1978, pp. 16-19.

TABLE 2

U.S. STRATEGIC NUCLEAR FORCES: MID-1980s PROJECTIONS

Launcher	Number	Warheads per Launcher	Total Warheads	Yield in Megatons	Total Megatons	Equivalent Megatons	Reliability	Circular Error Probable
Minuteman II	450	1	450	1.0	450.0	450	0.80	1,800 ft.
Minuteman III	550	3	1,650	0.17	280.5	512	0.80	700 ft.
(with MK-12A)	(550)	(3)	(1,650)	(0.35)	(572.5)	(825)	(0.80)	(600 ft.)
Titan II	54	1	54	9.0	486.0	232	0.75	3,000 ft.
Total ICBMs	1,054		2,154		1,216.5 (1,508.5)	1,194 (1,507)		
Poseidon	336	10	3,360	0.04	134	403	0.80	1,500 ft.
Poseidon C-4	160	8	1,280	0.10	128	282	0.80	1,500 ft.
Trident I	240	8	1,920	0.10	192	422	0.80	1,500 ft.
Total SLBMs	736		6,560		454	1,107		
B-52 G/H	165	6 SRAM	990	0.2	198	337		
B-52CM	165	4 Bombs / 20 ALCM / 2 SRAM	660 / 3,300 / 120	1.0 / 0.2 / 0.2	660 / 660 / 24	660 / 1,122 / 41		300 ft.
FB-111	60	2 Bombs	120	1.0	120	120		
Total Bombers	390		5,190		1,662	2,280		
Grand Total	2,180		13,904		3,332.5 (3,629.5)	4,581 (4,894)		

Source: Congress of the United States, Congressional Budget Office, Counterforce Issues for the U.S. Strategic Nuclear Forces. Background Paper, January 1978, pp. 16-19.

TABLE 3

ESTIMATED SOVIET STRATEGIC NUCLEAR FORCES, 1985

Launcher	Number	Warheads per Launcher	Total Warheads	Yield in Megatons	Total Megatons	Equivalent Megatons	Reliability	Circular Error Probable
SS-11	330	1	330	1.5	495	432	0.70	3,000 ft.
SS-17	200	4	800	0.6	480	560	0.75	1,500 ft.
SS-18	308	8	2,464	1.5	3,696	3,228	0.75	to
SS-19	500	6	3,000	0.8	2,400	2,580	0.75	1,200 ft.
SS-16	60	1	60	1.0	60	60	0.75	
Total ICBMs	1,398		6,654		7,131	6,860		
SS-N-6	600	1	600	1.0	600	600	0.70	6,000 ft.
SS-N-8								
SS-N-17	300	3	900	0.2	180	306	0.70	3,000 ft.
SS-N-18								
Total SLBMs	900		1,500		780	906		
Bear	100	1	100	20	2,000	740		
Bison	40	1	40	5	200	116		
(Backfire)	(250)	(2)	(500)	(0.2)	(100)	(170)		
Total Bombers	140 (390)		140 (640)		2,200 (2,300)	856 (1,026)		
Grand Total	2,438 (2,688)		8,294 (8,794)		10,111 (10,211)	8,622 (8,792)		

Source: Congress of the United States, Congressional Budget Office. Counterforce Issues for the U.S. Strategic Nuclear Forces. Background Paper, January 1978, pp. 16-19.

Appendix C:
NATO–Warsaw Pact Military Balance: How To Make the Balance Look Good/Bad

This book has shown some of the differences various assumptions can make in portraying the military balance. This section combines many of these assumptions into two separate groupings which result, on the one hand, in a pessimistic view of the balance and, on the other, in a more optimistic view. Each construct in internally consistent, and while few of the many balance assessments may conform fully to one or the other of these frameworks, we believe each is fairly typical of one of the two general classes of balance assessments.

Pessimistic Assessments

Pessimistic assessments of the NATO/Pact balance tend to see the Warsaw Pact as efficient because its command structure is hierarchical and dominated by a single nation, the USSR. This view stresses the relative unity of the Warsaw Pact, arguing that the decision-making process in the Warsaw Pact—less subject to outside scrutiny, delay, compromise, and the influence of domestic or nationalistic concerns— can make decisions on strategy faster. And once they are made, it is believed the hierarchical rigidity of the communist system allows the decisions to be carried out with speed, facility, and vigor. In this view, the Pact has an advantage over the NATO system where decisions are made by committee and are implemented through a process of negotiation, compromise, and consensus. Thus, relative unity and speed characterize the Pact's military behavior; delay and disarray are typical of NATO's behavior.

Another characteristic of pessimistic assessments is the belief that it is better to err by giving the Pact the benefit of the doubt in the absence of information than to underestimate Pact strength. A primary focus on wartime fighting rather than deterrence also tends to support such a conservative bias regarding uncertain Pact capabilities.

Pessimistic assessments tend toward symmetrical counting, but not toward symmetrical assumptions regarding the military behavior of the Pact and NATO. That is, they tend to compare totals of like things— manpower strengths, units, weapons systems—rather than evaluate how well each side can pursue its differing strategies. As a result, the categories of comparison are relatively limited; these assessments tend to exclude elements of strength on both sides which are not easily comparable. And when such unlike elements are included in pessimistic assessments, the analyst chooses those techniques for comparison which give greater weight to the relative strengths of the Pact.

Pessimistic assessments also tend to include more elements of Pact strength in their calculations of the balance than do optimistic assessments. They will often include forces from the Soviet strategic reserve and from Soviet deployments outside the Central Front area in discussions of the Central Front balance, count authorized rather than actual strengths, and sometimes include paramilitary forces—border and security troops—in Pact totals.

In contrast, pessimistic assessments normally disregard French forces in their tallies of NATO strength, or include only those based in Germany. Danish forces are usually included only in terms of the NATO/Pact balance on the Northern Front, not the Central Front. And non-NATO members of Western Europe are generally ignored in these assessments. More importantly, forces such as the German Territorial Army may be disregarded.

Pessimistic assessments are often tied to a short-warning scenario. This is due in part to the commitment to see the balance in terms of NATO's problems in fighting a war and a consequent fascination with those points in a scenario where the disparity in forces is greatest. It is also a function in part of the tendency to give the Pact the benefit of the doubt in areas where, one way or the other, evidence is lacking. These assessments tend to disregard command and control difficulties in moving large ground force units and to assume relatively high levels of readiness on the part of Pact forces.

It is important to note how some of the characteristics of pessimistic assessments reinforce each other. The assumption that the Pact political system facilitates military decisions and their efficient implementation, for example, supports the assumption of a short-warning attack. Efficiency, in this view, can be translated into a greater capability to carry out a well disciplined and concealed movement of large forces, a necessary condition of the short-warning attack assumption. The assumption of a short-warning attack, in turn, reinforces the assumptions that French forces would not be involved on the NATO side and that German territorial forces would not play a significant role. (The shorter the warning, the more difficult it would be to reintegrate the French back into a NATO command structure and to turn the German territorial forces into an integral part of NATO's defense.) It would also make it more difficult for NATO to adjust its forces along the Front to bolster any local areas of weakness. This, in turn, could mean that the Pact could build a local force edge of up to 12:1 in areas like the North German Plain, where NATO's forces are relatively weak. Thus, the assumption of Pact efficiency, because it supports the assumption of a short-warning attack, tends to reinforce the assumptions that French forces and German territorial forces should not be counted. In short, pessimistic analysts develop an internally consistent chain of logic, rooted in judgments on the military effectiveness of the Pact political system.

Optimistic Assessments

Optimistic assessments judge the Pact political system very different-ly. They tend to view its hierarchical rigidity not as a source of military efficiency, but as inhibiting individual and lower-level initiatives, incapable of rectifying errors in data or judgment, and because of internal secrecy and distrust, more cumbersome than the negotiation and consensus associated with NATO. Optimistic analysts do not equate Soviet domination of the Warsaw Pact with effective use of its military resources. Instead, the Soviet-Pact relationship is seen as fundamentally insecure. Soviet forces are seen not as partners in a military alliance, but in part as occupation troops, repressing nationalistic tendencies of the rest of the Pact.

One implication is a reluctance to grant the Pact the benefit of the doubt in areas of uncertainty. Where pessimistic assessments note the dangers of NATO's need for consensus and envy the military simplicity of the Pact's unified political system, optimistic ones tend to see the command problems as the same in both alliances—but dealt with less efficiently by the Pact. That difference in judgment is a major reason why the calculations of the military balance in optimistic assessments do not usually grant the Pact the benefit of the doubt in areas of uncertainty.

In contrast to pessimistic assessments, optimistic assessments typically tend toward asymmetrical counting. That is, they tend to avoid one-to-one comparisons of like entities and attempt instead to assess the capability of NATO to carry out its strategy of defense against the capability of the Pact to carry out a strategy of aggression. This tendency introduces more complexity to the comparative effort. It is in optimistic assessments that greater efforts are found to introduce the contribution of air and naval forces to the ground force balance, and comparisons move away from numbers of entities toward numerical expressions of capability.

Optimistic assessments generally include forces on the NATO side of the equation which are left out by pessimistic assessments. Thus, French forces are added to NATO's totals; West German territorial forces are included, as are small, but incrementally important contributions from non-NATO West Europeans; and Danish forces are seen in terms of their contribution to the critical Central Front balance, not in terms of being limited to the flanks.

Optimistic assessments also tend to discount large drawdowns from Soviet strategic reserve forces or from the forces deployed along the flanks or the Sino-Soviet border in their calculations of the Central Front balance. They also tend to discount contributions by Polish and Czech forces. Some assessments degrade the level of Soviet forces in these countries on the grounds that some of them would be oriented toward rear security. Nearly all optimistic assessments disregard potential contributions made by Pact paramilitary forces—border and security troops—in their calculations.

Optimistic analysts tend to discount surprise or short-warning Pact attacks. If the Pact launched an attack without warning, they believe, the strength of the attack would necessarily be limited. The Pact could not build to a clearly predominant level of force, in this view, in a short time, and the effort could not be done without alerting NATO. This tradeoff is premised on a series of assumptions which stress the command and control difficulties associated with moving Pact forces and preparing them for an attack. Optimistic analysts do not question the physical capacity of the road and rail networks to accommodate the movements required. They do discount the human capabilities to manage the movement and establish the necessary command and control structures.

As in the case of pessimistic assessments, optimistic ones have their internal logic and consistency. The view that the Pact is limited by distrust and repression, for example, supports arguments against including non-Soviet Pact forces in strength tallies, justifies not counting border or security troops as part of an attacking force, and suggests that even some regular Soviet forces might be charged with rear security missions in the event of conflict. Given the kind of conservative biases these assessments associate with Soviet decisionmakers, the probability that the Soviets would risk redeployments from the flanks logically declines. Thus, judgments regarding the Pact's political system support the view that it would take the Pact relatively long to assemble and prepare a large attack. And given the deductions that a Pact build-up would be obvious and long, it becomes logically more consistent to assume a reintegration of French forces to the NATO command structure and to count them on the NATO side of the balance. It also makes it logical to assume that NATO would have more opportunity to adjust its forces along the Front to correct any weaknesses in its current posture.

Illustrative Underlying Assumptions in NATO/Warsaw Pact Balance Assessment

Pessimistic	*Optimistic*
Major aim is to defeat Pact forces in event of war. Valid therefore to hedge against not having enough military resources.	Major problem is to deter Pact attack. Implies level of capacity that may not be as high as necessary to defeat Pact forces.
Authoritarian/hierarchical system allows Pact nations to carry out military plans effectively and quickly.	Pact concern with control and secrecy degrades efficiency. Inhibits lower unit initiatives. Leads to internal distrust.
Better to err on the side of over-estimates of Pact military strength.	Not advisable to give Pact forces benefit of the doubt in absence of data. Pact forces likely to have at least as much difficulty in command and control as NATO's.

**Illustrative NATO/Warsaw Pact Balance Comparisons:
Central Front Ground Forces**

A.   Pessimistic Views

Military Personnel		*Rationale*
NATO	Pact	Includes active U.S./NATO divisions only; Soviet Category III divisions at full strength on assumption that these could be filled rapidly; excludes German territorial and French Forces on the assumption that these forces would not be involved directly in conflict with Pact.
1.045 million	1.216 million	

Tanks		Tanks viewed as a valid measure because of Soviet doctrine; data include prepositioned stocks for two U.S. divisions; estimated stocks in storage for USSR.
NATO	Pact	
6,615.	16,000	

Divisions		Includes all active divisions in NATO center region less French, which are not under NATO control; Category I divisions in East Germany, Czechoslovakia, and Poland; excludes separate brigades and regiments.
NATO	Pact	
24	51	

Size of Pact Threat After 30 Days Mobilization	*Pact/NATO Force Ratio at:*			Assumes rapid reinforcement of Central Front by Soviet forces elsewhere; delayed entrance of French forces. Does not count West German territorial forces.
	M-Day	*M+14*	*M+30*	
85 Divisions	1.5	2.1	1.6	
128 Divisions	1.5	2.4	2.4	

B. *Optimistic Views*

Military Personnel		*Rationale*
NATO	Pact	Includes active duty German territorial forces and forward deployed French and Danish forces on assumption they would be involved; includes Category II and III divisions at less than authorized strength.
1.096 million	1.124 million	

Numbers of tanks not included because one-on-one comparisons considered misleading.

Divisions		
NATO	Pact	Includes separate brigades and regiments aggregated as division equivalents; includes five French divisions on assumption that French would be involved in event of conflict.
32	51	

Size of Pact Threat After 30 Days Mobilization	*Pact/NATO Force Ratio at:*			
	M-Day	*M+14*	*M+30*	Assumes delays in Soviet reinforcements; early entrance by French forces; counts West German territorial forces.
85 Divisions	1.4	1.6	1.4	

**Illustrative NATO/Warsaw Pact Balance Comparisons:
Central Front Air Forces**

A. *Pessimistic Views*

Combat Aircraft		Rationale
NATO	Pact	Data refer to aircraft in Central Europe on argument that this is best comparative basis; excludes French, U.S. carrier-based and U.S. dual-based aircraft.
1,810	2,500	
		Generally does not seek additional comparative measures.

B. *Optimistic Views*

Combat Aircraft		Rationale
NATO	Pact	Data refer to resources that can supplement aircraft already in place. Includes U.S. dual-based and French aircraft and naval air from two carrier wings, plus some rapid deploying reserves.
3,462	3,680	
NATO/Pact Ratio of Bomb Tonnage Drop Capability at Equi-distances		Accounts for variation in aircraft capabilities and missions and allows easier integration to ground force balance.
100 nm.	200 nm.	
3:1	7:1	

DATE DUE

MAR. 16.1981	MAY 1 4 1987		
APR ~ 1913	APR 2 0 1989		
APR. 14.1983	NOV 28 '01 DEC 2 5 2002	2002	
APR. 28.1983			
NOV. 10.1983			
NOV. 24.1983			
5/C 5/1/84			
MAY 10.1984			
OCT. 25.1984			
MAR. 14.1985			
MAR. 14.1985			
MAR 28.1985			
MAY -2.1985			
APR 1 6 1987			
APR 1 6 1987			
APR 3 3 1987			

GAYLORD NOV 0 1 '02

PRINTED IN U.S.A